Globalization Matters

At the turn of the twenty-first century, globalization—both the process and the idea—bestrode the world like a colossus. Widely acclaimed by political and economic pundits as the most important phenomenon of our time, it took the world by storm. Two decades later, it has come under sustained attack from the reinvigorated forces of the extreme right and radical left. Does globalization still matter in our unsettled world? Responding in the affirmative, this study develops and applies a new framework of an engaged theory of globalization to analyse some of today's most pressing global challenges: the rise of national populism; ecological degradation; rapid urbanization; new sources of insecurity; and the changing landscape of higher education. Offering a comprehensive appraisal of globalization in our unsettled times, this study addresses why and how trans-planetary interrelations continue to matter in a world that is wavering between globalist expansion and nationalist retrenchment.

Manfred B. Steger is Professor of Sociology at the University of Hawai'i at Mānoa and Global Professorial Fellow of the Institute of Culture and Society at Western Sydney University. He has served as an academic consultant on globalization for the US State Department and is an author or editor of 27 books on globalization, social and political theory, and nonviolence, including *The Rise of the Global Imaginary: Political Ideologies from the French Revolution to the Global War on Terror* (2008), *Justice Globalism: Ideology, Crises, Policy* (2013), and *Globalization: A Very Short Introduction* (2017).

Paul James is Professor of Globalization and Cultural Diversity at Western Sydney University, where he is Director of the Institute for Culture and Society. He is a scientific advisor to the Mayor of Berlin and a Metropolis ambassador. He is an editor of *Arena Journal* and an author or editor of 35 books, including *Globalism, Nationalism, Tribalism: Bringing Theory Back in* (2006). He has been an advisor to a number of agencies and governments, including the Helsinki Process, the Canadian Prime Minister's G20 Forum, and the Papua New Guinea Minister for Community Development.

Globalization Matters

Engaging the Global in Unsettled Times

Manfred B. Steger

University of Hawai'i at Mānoa and Western Sydney University

Paul James

Western Sydney University

CAMBRIDGE
UNIVERSITY PRESS

CAMBRIDGE
UNIVERSITY PRESS

University Printing House, Cambridge CB2 8BS, United Kingdom

One Liberty Plaza, 20th Floor, New York, NY 10006, USA

477 Williamstown Road, Port Melbourne, VIC 3207, Australia

314–321, 3rd Floor, Plot 3, Splendor Forum, Jasola District Centre, New Delhi – 110025, India

79 Anson Road, #06–04/06, Singapore 079906

Cambridge University Press is part of the University of Cambridge.

It furthers the University's mission by disseminating knowledge in the pursuit of education, learning, and research at the highest international levels of excellence.

www.cambridge.org
Information on this title: www.cambridge.org/9781108470797
DOI: 10.1017/9781108557078

First published 2019

Printed and bound in Great Britain by Clays Ltd, Elcograf S.p.A.

A catalogue record for this publication is available from the British Library.

ISBN 978-1-108-47079-7 Hardback
ISBN 978-1-108-45667-8 Paperback

Cambridge University Press has no responsibility for the persistence or accuracy of URLs for external or third-party internet websites referred to in this publication and does not guarantee that any content on such websites is, or will remain, accurate or appropriate.

Contents

Figures

Acknowledgements

In late 2013, Barry Gills, editor of the journal *Globalizations*, asked us to guest-edit a special issue on the topic 'Globalization: The Career of a Concept'. At the time, we had already engaged in scholarly collaborations for more than a decade and had worked closely together as colleagues at RMIT University from 2005 to 2012. This welcome opportunity to join forces again on the special issue became the unexpected incubator of the idea behind this study. As with our past collaborations, we have enjoyed our shared writing experience on this book and suspect that this project might not be the last time we embark on the arduous but rewarding journey of co-producing a substantive study on a topic situated at the very core of our engaged interest: globalization. So please stay tuned.

Some of the writing here draws upon previous work, but all of it is much further developed and revised. Chapter 2 incorporates some materials that appear in our co-authored article, 'A Genealogy of Globalization: The Career of a Concept', *Globalizations* (2014). Some paragraphs in Chapter 4 have been adapted from our co-authored article, 'Levels of Subjective Globalization: Ideologies, Imaginaries, Ontologies', *Perspectives on Global Development and Technology* (2013). Chapter 7 draws on some parts of Manfred's article, 'Reflections on "Critical Thinking" in Global Studies', *Protosociology* (2017b).

We have numerous debts of gratitude. First, we want to thank our colleagues, students, and friends at both the University of Hawai'i at Manoa and Western Sydney University. Manfred wants to extend his special thanks to faculty members, students, and administrative staff in the Department of Sociology for welcoming him so warmly to the department three years ago and for their subsequent support. Paul is deeply indebted to his colleagues at the Institute for Culture and Society for providing an intellectual home, and to fellow travellers associated with *Arena Journal* for sharing a critical grounding. Nothing is more important in academic life than stimulating engagement with colleagues and students.

viii   Acknowledgements

In particular, we wish to thank those colleagues who profoundly influenced our thinking in this book: Ien Ang, Arjun Appadurai, Barrie Axford, Ursula Baatz, Benjamin Barber, Clyde Barrow, Paul Battersby, Roland Benedikter, Roland Bleiker, Steve Bronner, Franz Broswimmer, Alison Caddick, Terrell Carver, Manuel Castells, Nayan Chanda, Peter Christoff, Nadège Clitandre, Simon Cooper, Louise Crabtree, Lane Crothers, Eve Darian-Smith, Mike Douglass, Tommaso Durante, Robyn Eckersley, Cynthia Enloe, Victor Faessel, Michael Freeden, Jonathan Friedman, Kathy Gibson, Anthony Giddens, Barry Gills, James Goodman, Damian Grenfell, Brien Hallett, Mary Hawkesworth, David Held, John Hinkson, Chris Hudson, Mark Juergensmeyer, Isaac Kamola, Paul Komesaroff, Hagen Koo, Tim Luke, Liam Magee, Brad Macdonald, Phil McCarty, Jim Mittelman, George Modelski, Colin Moore, Yaso Nadarajah, Tom Nairn, Jamal Nassar, Brett Neilson, Deane Neubauer, Heikki Patomäki, Roland Robertson, William Robinson, James Rosenau, Steve Rosow, Ned Rossiter, Ravi Roy, Juan Salazar, Saskia Sassen, Hans Schattle, Jan Aart Scholte, Joseph Stiglitz, Timothy Ström, Charles Taylor, Amentahru Wahlrab, Heloise and Martin Weber, and Erin Wilson.

We also want to express our appreciation of the anonymous reviewers of the present study and the numerous readers, reviewers, and audiences around the world who, for more than two decades, have made insightful comments in response to our public lectures and publications on the subject of globalization. We salute John Haslam and his colleagues at Cambridge University Press as shining examples of professionalism. Finally, we want to thank our families for their love and support—especially our partners, Perle Besserman and Stephanie Trigg. Many people have contributed to improving the quality of this book; its remaining flaws are ours.

1 Introduction
What Is Happening to Globalization?

At the turn of the twenty-first century, globalization—both the process and the idea—bestrode the world like a colossus. Widely acclaimed by political and economic pundits as 'the most important phenomenon of our time', it became one of those rare concepts that took the world by storm (Friedman, 1999; Giddens, 1999; Micklethwait and Woolridge, 2000: xii). In his 1998 speech at Harvard University's Weatherhead Center for International Affairs, United Nations Secretary Kofi Annan offered a definition that captured the positive popular meaning of the new buzzword: 'Globalization is commonly understood to describe the advances in technology and communications that have made possible an unprecedented degree of financial and economic interdependence and growth. As markets are integrated, investments flow more easily, competition is enhanced, prices are lowered and the living standards everywhere are improved' (Annan, 1998).

Indeed, corporate and political elites welcomed the swelling transnational flows of goods, services, capital, and ideas as the new engines of social progress. Global media conglomerates saturated the world with powerful images of an interconnecting world economy powered by the information and communications technology (ICT) revolution. The jet-setting power elites gathering at the annual World Economic Forum meeting in Switzerland championed business deregulation, privatization of public assets, and liberalization of trade and finance while squeezing out redistributive visions of globality. Billions of ordinary people around the world succumbed to their neoliberal temptation, confident that they, too, would reap the material benefits of market globalization in the not-too-distant future.

By the end of the 1990s, popular and academic discourses on globalization had converged, thanks to the efforts of attentive scholars who had seized upon the concept in their efforts to explain the massive social transformation in the waning years of the old century. Their intellectual labours assisted in the birth of 'global studies'—a hybrid field of enquiry into globalization and its impacts. Crucially,

1

this new scholarship recognized that realizing the rich potential of its subject depended on two profound academic transformations: the retooling of conventional disciplinary modes of social analysis and the transcending of the dominant 'international relations' framework (Darian-Smith and McCarty, 2017; Steger and Wahlrab, 2017). In particular, global studies pioneers sought to break the long-standing dominance of 'methodological nationalism' in the social sciences by criticizing the reification of the nation-state as the basic unit of social analysis. While squabbling over the precise features and impacts of globalization, most researchers found common ground in their conviction that a new era of globality was dawning. The buzzword 'globalization' had generated widely shared associations of inevitability and irreversibility that seemed to make the nature and direction of social change a foregone conclusion.

Only two decades later, 'globalization' is rapidly losing its lustre. In fact, it has become a political punching bag for the resurgent national populist forces of the right and left around the world (King, 2017; Bremmer, 2018; Galston, 2018; Judis, 2018; Castells, 2019; Crouch, 2019; Eatwell and Goodwin, 2019; Norris and Inglehart, 2019). The 'irrational exuberance' of market globalists has given way to widespread fears that their great experiment of transcending the nation-state has spiralled out of control and needs to be curbed. Numerous commentators have been feeding the growing public perception that the integration of markets and societies has failed to deliver on its promises. This intensifying 'globophobia' has been reflected in popular culture in numerous ways such as the record amazon.com sales enjoyed by 'Stop Being a Globalist' and 'Not a Globalist' T-shirts.

But the current crisis of globalization goes deeper, for it has shaken the very pillars of liberal democracy. This troubling dynamic is perhaps most visible in the loss of political legitimacy by conventional representative governments. There is a growing gap between what is pledged by conventional politicians and what is delivered to ordinary citizens who still expect their national governments to protect them against a seemingly hostile 'outside' associated with multiculturalism and immigration. Hence, added to this democratic crisis is an identity crisis born of an aversion to the global that makes rural people, in particular, take refuge in their nation, locality, and god (Castells, 2019: 14–15). No wonder, then, that authoritarian populists resort to accusing footloose 'cosmopolitan elites' of cheating the toiling masses. Promising a return to national control, the emotional promises of populists to 'the forgotten people' are finding more resonance than the rational assurances of neoliberal globalists that, in the long run, trade liberalization and the worldwide integration of markets are bound to benefit everyone.[1]

Such nation-first attitudes also fuel today's intensifying immigration restrictions, as well as the decline of transnational approaches to crucial social and ecological problems such as social inequality and climate change.[2] As Human Rights Watch Director Kenneth Roth observes, 'Populists tend to respond less by proposing genuine solutions than by scapegoating vulnerable minorities and disfavored segment of society. The result has been a frontal assault on the values of inclusivity, tolerance, and respect that lie at the heart of human rights' (2017: 2). Moreover, the internationalist promise of multilateral cooperation has been hit on multiple fronts, but perhaps hardest by a brash American president in search of new outlets for his profoundly illiberal instincts. And, to make things worse, the unpredictable Trump administration has been flirting with a global trade war that has the potential to bring down the world economy. Fearing the dismantling of the post-war order and a return to the destructive great power politics of past centuries, leading foreign policy experts have sounded the alarm, wondering whether liberal democracy can survive the dawning age of 'deglobalization' (Ferguson and Zakaria, 2017; Castells, 2019; Eatwell and Goodwin, 2019).[3]

As the world appears to waver between globalist expansion and nationalist retrenchment, it is hardly surprising that two questions related to the perceived 'globalization backlash' have taken centre stage in relevant popular and academic discourses. *What is happening to globalization? Does it still matter in our unsettled times?* These fundamental questions traverse the chapters of this book. Our answer is affirmative. Globalization still matters a lot, we contend, just not in the same ways it

[1] We agree with Heikki Patomäki's assessment that Karl Polanyi's influential theory of 'double movement' only partially explains the appeal of the populist 'countermovement' to neoliberal globalization. As Patomäki (2018: 71) rightly notes, if the core purpose of the countermovement is to protect society against 'self-regulating markets', why should 'Trump's voters then approve his selective but sweeping pro-market reforms, such as major public spending cuts, financial deregulation and tax concessions to corporations and very wealthy individuals?'

[2] François Bourguignon (2015) and Branko Milanović (2016) assert that globalization dynamics fuel contradictory dynamics that make it increasingly hard to separate out the factors leading to domestic and international inequality. They argue that while inequality has declined across the world as a whole, it has increased within most countries. This trend also holds for China, where the Gini coefficient rose from 0.30 in the 1970s to 0.55 in the 2010s—more unequal than the United States at 0.42 (Crouch, 2019: 24–5). Challenging this widespread assumption of globalization as the primary cause of rising inequality, Helpman (2018) has recently put forward an alternative explanation.

[3] It should be immediately noted that we do not share this alarmist—and rather monolithic —assessment of imminent and inevitable 'deglobalization'. Our position will become clearer as our narrative unfolds.

did 25 years or even a decade ago. The main task of the present study is to demonstrate, describe, and analyse this reconfigured significance of globalization in both theory and practice. We begin our engagement with the global in our time of crisis by recounting the highlights of the most recent chapter in the story of globalization: why and how it rose to superstardom only to fall into infamy in the short span of three decades.

Why Globalization Mattered in the Popular Discourse of the Roaring Nineties

Soon after the collapse of the Soviet empire, the named process of 'globalization' became the linchpin in the American-led project of constructing a 'new world order'. It was built on the expansion of US influence around the world as the sole remaining superpower. The concept drew much of its popularity from a teleological master narrative claiming that the passing of the Cold War order proved not only the social and moral superiority of democratic capitalism over authoritarian communism, but marked the end of history as such. Francis Fukuyama, then a young US State Department official and rising political theorist, gave this triumphalist vision its most influential articulation. The 'unabashed victory of economic and political liberalism', he proclaimed, portended nothing less than the 'universalization of Western liberal democracy as the final form of human government' (Fukuyama, 1989: 1). For Eurocentric thinkers of Fukuyama's ilk, the apparent victory of Anglo-American liberalism over both communism and fascism in less than half a century amounted to an irreversible epochal shift in human evolution. It vindicated not merely the philosophical triumph of reason, progress, secularism, and individualism, but also demonstrated the political efficacy of these Enlightenment ideals. Hegel's dream of the unity of the Real and the Ideal seemed to have been realized in the Liberal Idea.

With the Iron Curtain permanently ripped asunder, serious ideological or geographical barriers no longer blocked the fulfilment of liberalism's grand promise. Beneath the surface, economic, political, and cultural life was being profoundly unsettled. But, for the new liberalism, humanity's abiding purpose would finally burn bright at the end of the long tunnel of history. Ordinary people everywhere would finally be free to pursue happiness within the universal framework of limited government devoted to human rights, the rule of law, fair elections, and, crucially, a free-market economic system that came to be known as 'neoliberalism' (Peck, 2010; Steger and Roy, 2010; Slobodian, 2018). The globalization of these laissez-faire principles was likened to an unstoppable train barrelling towards a destination preconceived by its liberal makers: the *good life* consisting of more freedom, yet greater equality; more choices, yet fewer risks; greater prosperity, yet deeper spirituality; expanded cultural pluralism, yet greater toleration; reinvigorated civic virtue, yet enlightened self-interest; the universalization of democratic principles, yet firmer political leadership. So, what could conceivably matter more than getting the 'rest' of the world to board the globalization train as quickly as possible?

As the dizzying decade of the Roaring Nineties drew to a close, a growing number of influential free-market advocates were making great strides in their efforts to sell liberalism's promise of the good life. Thomas Friedman, Martin Wolf, Jagdish Bhagwati, Paul Krugman, and Joseph Stiglitz, together with powerful international corporate and political elites who gathered annually at the World Economic Forum in Davos, Switzerland, had perfected their sales pitch. It boiled down to the endless intonation of the mantra 'the globalization of markets', popularized a decade earlier by Theodore Levitt (1983), then dean of the Harvard Business School. Building on the familiar theme of unstoppable modernization in the image of the West, this shibboleth was meant to evoke a providential dynamism destined to reach the farthest corners of the Earth. Amplified in the corporate media, the steady stream of hegemonic 'globalization talk' provided the discursive glue that held together the applied neoliberal policy project of deregulating economies, opening up trade, privatizing public enterprises, cutting marginal tax rates, emasculating labour unions, and creating 'flexible' labour markets—both offshore and at home. Soon, the new social structure of neoliberal capitalist accumulation acquired the stability and authority required to promote corporate profitability and stable expansion during the 1990s and beyond (Rupert, 2000; Kotz, 2015).

The 'globalization of markets' also served as the central metaphor for a refurbished version of the old liberal utopia of social harmony—the notion of a society in automatic balance thanks to the autonomous forces of the 'magic market' (Mills, 1956: 336). Economically, this claim of general agreement was presented as a peerless New Economy powered by new technologies such as the Internet and operating according to the neoliberal rules of the Washington Consensus, which were to be exported wholesale to the 'developing world'. Its associated culture of consumerism was celebrated as a homogenizing global force that enabled people everywhere to experience the exhilarating freedom of increased buying choices. As Pulitzer Prize-winning journalist Daniel Yergin asserted, the neoliberal success of decamping the state from the commanding heights of the economy marked the great divide between the twentieth and twenty-first centuries (Yergin and Stanislaw, 1998).

Politically, this liberal myth of the neoliberal consensus was promoted as a global *pax mercatus*—an American-led market peace that drastically reduced the likelihood of large-scale conflicts between states. The global integration of markets was portrayed as *the* democratic medium of social harmony because it was said to express the popular will more accurately and more meaningfully than the messy political process controlled by privileged elites who were detached from ordinary people and their everyday concerns (Frank, 2000).

Ideologically, neoliberal consensus received a catchy expression in Margaret Thatcher's famous TINA slogan: 'There Is No Alternative'. Embraced and swiftly spread across the globe by the global corporate media, Thatcher's rhetorical one-way street was a potent weapon in the larger neoliberal effort to delegitimize dissenting worldviews while reinforcing ongoing efforts to depoliticize the public sphere and foster new forms of rationality that reached ever more deeply into the microstructures of self and identity (Foucault, 2010; Brown, 2017). Hailed as creative 'entrepreneurs', working people were encouraged to shed their old class-based self-image of being passive industrial cogs in the exploitative capitalist machine and imagine themselves instead as proactive 'human capital'. Reinvented as a 'flexible workforce', they could be more easily motivated to invest their labour power in the perfection of their own personal 'brand'. The headline of a leading 1998 *Newsweek* story perfectly captured the tremendous ideological punch behind the creation of neoliberal subjectivity: 'The Market "R" Us'.

Technologically, the neoliberal myth of benign social convergence appeared in quasi-religious public invocations of the countless blessings of the ICT revolution, especially the Internet's delivery of worldwide simultaneity and instantaneity. The daily glorification of digital technology served to legitimize and naturalize the economic imperatives of what later commentators would call 'cybercapitalism' or 'platform capitalism' (Srnicek, 2017; Ström, 2017). Combining the language of technological determinism with established neoliberal practices of profit extraction, cybercapitalism fed on the growing influence of giant oligopolistic corporations such as Microsoft, Sony, Intel, and Apple. Joined some years later by Google, Amazon, Verizon, Facebook, and Twitter, these transnational media conglomerates incessantly promoted free-market policies as the only way to realize their techno-utopian vision of an automated, carefree future that promised receptive consumers. By the second decade of the new century, such 'exciting' novelties as self-driving cars, machine-precise haircuts, and algorithmic suit selections were within reach (Ström, 2017: 306).

In spite of its deeply depoliticizing and dehumanizing effects, cybercapitalism relied heavily on democratic rhetoric to justify neoliberalism's equation of democracy and free markets: the unleashing of market forces would usher in a democratic global age. Technological innovations like the World Wide Web and mobile phones, it was asserted, would put free markets, not governments, in charge of democratization. Turbocharged by the microchip, ceaseless global flows of goods and information would empower ordinary people to improve their lives by plugging into multiplying networks capable of connecting the global to the local in both physical space and cyberspace. Leading acolytes of cybercapitalism like Thomas Friedman lionized the new digital technologies as cutting-edge democratic models of communication that played a crucial role in imparting 'digital literacy' on a global citizenry. As the world was becoming flatter, the *New York Times* columnist asserted, the democratic ideals of accountability and transparency could be more easily achieved (Friedman, 2005).

At the turn of the twenty-first century, such neoliberal globalization talk had become canonical, solidifying into the hegemonic ideology of market globalism (Steger, 2009). At the same time, however, the market-fundamentalist alliance of advanced economies headed by the United States habitually turned a blind eye to hard empirical data suggesting that the results of neoliberal capitalism had been highly uneven, both socially and geographically. Its institutional forms and sociopolitical consequences varied significantly across spatial scales and among major different zones of the world economy (Brenner, 2017: 43). East and South Asia, for example, enjoyed impressive growth rates and rising living standards, while vast regions in Africa and other parts of the Global South stagnated or declined. Moreover, the dominant phalanx of market-globalist forces routinely ignored mounting evidence that corporate-led globalization was producing social inequalities at an alarming rate—both within and among nations (Milanović, 1999). They also paid little attention to the troubling ecological 'externalities' of neoliberal capitalism, which were most spectacularly reflected in escalating global climate change and rapid loss of biodiversity. These ominous developments at the end of the twentieth century received only scant scrutiny from the global corporate media that celebrated—to use the title of Microsoft CEO Bill Gates' bestselling book—the wonders of *Business @ the Speed of Thought* (1999).

Overall, then, market globalists in the Roaring Nineties experienced little pushback to their overarching ideological vision of the economy, society, democracy, and history. For them, globalization mattered a great deal because it would secure, once and for all, the universal rule of freedom, rights, property, and mobility enshrined in the American-led neoliberal world order. Furthermore, globalization mattered because it opened up countless new economic opportunities for ordinary people, rhetorically invoked in the dominant discourse as the 'hundreds of millions lifted out of poverty', rather than the top 0.1 per cent of elites whose wealth had been exploding during the 1990s. Social actors critical of global capitalism were denigrated as 'globalization losers'—a catch-all category meant to shame those bold enough to dissent, thus disparaging any form of political resistance to a historically ordained neoliberal project deemed too big to fail. Finally, globalization mattered because it propelled humanity towards a harmonious 'Future Perfect' where rational individuals pursued their material interests largely free from government intervention, enjoyed instant access to unlimited digitalized information, and overcame the age-old tyranny of distance through new technologies of interconnectivity and hypermobility operating in both geographical space and cyberspace (Micklethwait and Woolridge, 2000).

Why Globalization Mattered in the Academic Discourse of the 1990s

Facing few challenges to its neoliberal meaning structure in popular discourse, globalization encountered a more contested terrain in the academic environment. Since the early 1990s, there had been a slow turn of the social science and humanities disciplines to engage with contemporary and historical processes of globalization and their related 'global issues'. As the debate on the subject heated up over the course of the decade, it reflected a fundamental shift in analytical and spatial perspectives towards an engagement of global contexts and the development of new global theories and perspectives that were previously understood as either universal, national, or local. This 'global turn' also entailed suggestions to adopt explicitly transdisciplinary frameworks critical of methodological nationalism (Darian-Smith and McCarty, 2017; Steger and Wahlrab, 2017).

Innovative social thinkers stimulated scholarly investigations into the global that covered not only its techno-economic aspects, but also explored its much-neglected sociocultural and political dimensions. In spite of their sincere efforts to overcome parochial modes of knowledge production confined to the Euro-American academy, the principal participants in these intensifying academic debates on globalization resided in the Global North. Such a limited geographical framework of globalization scholarship reflected not only existing power relations in the world, but also highlighted the hegemony of Western universities that also served as potent economic job magnets for scholars hailing from the Global South (Keucheyan, 2013).

As might be expected in any academic context, scholarly consensus proved to be elusive in the 1990s. In spite of the steady growth of globalization studies, researchers remained divided on definitional matters; the utility of various methodological approaches; the value of available empirical evidence for gauging the extent, impact, and direction of globalization; and, of course, its normative implications. Still, their failure to arrive at a broad agreement on the subject should not detract from significant intellectual breakthroughs achieved by a relatively small number of global studies pioneers. In particular, the contributions of three scholars—Roland Robertson, Arjun Appadurai, and Saskia Sassen—stand out for their tremendous impact on the academic globalization debate of the 1990s and thus deserve to be considered here in some detail.

It is perhaps most fitting to start with the British sociologist Roland Robertson, who played a leading role in putting 'globalization' on the agenda of the social sciences for good (Steger and Wahlrab, 2017). Criticizing the economistic understanding of globalization as a material process of marketization that dominated the popular discourse, Robertson emphasized the equal importance of the cultural and subjective aspects of the phenomenon. His influential definition of globalization contained two dimensions: increasing transnational social connectivity and growing reflexive global consciousness: 'Globalization as a concept refers both to the compression of the world and intensification of consciousness of the world as a whole' (Robertson, 1992: 8). In the first introduction to the subject published in 1995, the Australian sociologist Malcolm Waters (1995: 3) affirmed Robertson's status as 'the key figure in the formalization and specification of the concept of globalization ... His [Robertson's] own biography might itself be seen as an instance of a link between what might be called transnationalization and global consciousness'.

Robertson's second seminal contribution to the globalization debate of the 1990s concerns his popularization of the term 'glocalization'. He argued that in the 'real world' of lived social relations, the macroscopic level of the global always intersected with microscopic aspects of the local. Thus, globalization did not occur on an isolated spatial scale hovering above the national and local, but only became concrete and empirically observable in the local. Robertson (1994: 33–52) derived his notion of glocalization from the Japanese *dochakuka* ('global localization'), which had achieved special salience in the 1980s in Japanese marketing circles concerned with their country's success in the global economy. Rent from such specialized business language, 'glocalization' extended its meaning into the general cultural sphere by positing the interdependence of local and global processes in the formation of collective identities and symbolic interactions.[4] Moreover, Robertson used the term to combat influential views offered by prominent sociologists like George Ritzer (1993), who asserted that cultural globalization inevitably led to homogenized formations labelled 'Americanization' or 'McDonaldization'. Conversely, Robertson argued that homogenization tendencies coexisted with equally strong social dynamics favouring expressions of cultural diversification and hybridization.

The second major contribution to the study of globalization discussed here flowed from the pen of Arjun Appadurai. Foregrounding the role of imagination in contemporary social practices that shape new global subjectivities, the Mumbai-born cultural anthropologist followed in Robertson's footsteps by favouring a more balanced approach that gave equal attention to cultural and economic meanings of globalization. For example, Appadurai argued that 'globalization'—reflected in transnational investment flows as well as in material culture such as clothing styles—constituted a pivotal concept that provided innovative resources for new identities and subjectivities that were no longer exclusively anchored in the modern nation or the traditional tribe.

Most importantly, Appadurai (1996) introduced a five-dimensional conceptual model by which to analyse the complex disjunctures between economic, cultural, and political flows. He argued that the conditions under which current global flows occur could be classified in terms of five distinct 'landscapes'—'ethnoscapes', 'mediascapes', 'technoscapes', 'finanscapes', and 'ideoscapes' (Appadurai, 1996: 33). These combined into collective perspectives or 'imaginaries' that allowed individuals and groups to make sense of the shrinking world. Noting that human history had always been characterized by 'disjunctures' in the flows of people, machinery, money, images, and ideas, Appadurai nonetheless argued that the sheer speed, scale, and volume of each of these flows had become so strong in the late twentieth century that these contemporary 'disjunctures' had moved to the centre of a 'politics of global culture'. Moreover, these disjunctures in the global flows of goods, services, information, and ideas encouraged the formation of 'multiple worlds' constituted by the historically and politically situated interactions of persons and groups spread around the globe. These 'worlds' included transnational corporations, nation-states, diasporic communities, non-governmental organizations, and subnational groupings and movements. Appadurai's work

---

[4] For a comprehensive study of the evolution of the term 'glocalization', see Roudometof (2016).

generated tremendous interest in global cultural dynamics and stimulated established cultural theorists to comment on these new 'globalization matters'.

Finally, let us consider the academic contribution to the 1990s' globalization debate made by Saskia Sassen. The multicultural social and urban theorist developed of path-breaking 'global city model' that offered new ways of analysing the strategic roles of global cities like New York, London, Tokyo, Shanghai, Seoul, and Paris. Although most of these 'global cities' had long served as international economic and cultural centres, Sassen (2001: 3–4) argued that recent globalization processes had produced 'massive and parallel changes in their economic base, spatial organization and social structure'. Thus, global cities had assumed great significance as pivotal places of spatial dispersal and global integration located at the intersection of multiple global circuits and transnational flows involving migrants, ideas, commodities, and money.

Sassen insisted that global cities should no longer be conceptualized as bounded units but as complex structures capable of coordinating a variety of cross-boundary processes and reconstituting them as urban activities. Functioning as highly specific places encased in national territory and as a transnational network linked to hinterlands and other urban centres, cities like New York or Tokyo owed their growing stature to accelerating processes of deterritorialization while at the same time serving as crucial catalysts for the formation of new transboundary spatialities epitomized in the global economic system. Countering influential 'hyperglobalist' claims that the globalizing economy would soon spell the 'end of the nation-state' (Ohmae, 1990; 1995), Sassen, too, embraced Robertson's logic of 'glocalization', which emphasized the partial embeddedness of the global in national and local contexts. In fact, she took the concept a step further by suggesting that denationalizing dynamics operated alongside the more familiar localizing trends.

Their remaining differences notwithstanding, these three pivotal globalization scholars of the 1990s agreed on one fundamental proposition: globalization mattered a great deal. Like it or not, the concept had captured the popular imagination and thus had acquired significant social currency worthy of scholarly scrutiny. Even inveterate sceptics, who sneered at globalization as an exaggerated fad based on little empirical evidence, could not wish away the fact that globalization—both the idea and the process—was shaping the world in significant ways. Globalist discourses were yielding significant material effects, and material processes of time–space compression resulted in new ideas. In other words, academic attempts to understand globalization required paying as much attention to its 'subjective' ideational factors as to its 'objective' material dynamics.

Globalization also mattered in the academic discourse of the 1990s because, thanks to the efforts of scholars such as Sassen and Appadurai, the concept was quickly acquiring considerable academic cachet. Inspiring the formation of new research frameworks centred on processes of worldwide interconnectivity, the new transdisciplinary field of global studies became an 'ascending paradigm' in universities around the world (Mittelman, 2004). Leading global studies researchers like the 1990s pioneers profiled above served the crucial academic function of 'para-makers'. They engaged in theoretical stocktaking, located incipient problem areas, pointed to exciting new avenues of global enquiry, and offered a fresh way of thinking about the world. Conversely, conservative 'para-keepers' located in the established disciplines continued to cling to the prevailing social science frameworks of methodological nationalism—even in the face of the explosion of academic publications and pro-grammes dedicated to transdisciplinary investigations of the global. As we elaborate in Chapter 7, scholars on both sides of this academic battle locked horns on a conceptual terrain indelibly shaped by the dynamics of globalization.

Why Globalization Mattered Less (*and* More) in the 2000s

In the first years of the new century, globalization encountered unex-pected turbulence at both its material and ideational levels. As the overly optimistic and simplistic claims of market globalism began to diverge ever more noticeably from the social reality of runaway levels of inequality, a growing number of popular commentators and academic observers began to wonder whether the globalization project was getting into ser-ious trouble (Saul, 2005). As the shine came off the concept, it suddenly seemed to matter much less than it did only a decade earlier.

Four major social crises in particular undermined the centrality of the globalization paradigm in business and political circles while also chip-ping away at its stature in the ivory tower: the worldwide trade clashes of the early 2000s; the September 11 attacks and the ensuing so-called Global War on Terror; the 2008 Global Financial Crisis (GFC) and its lingering effects as reflected in the prolonged Great Recession and Eurozone Sovereign Debt Crisis; and the political success of a specifically anti-globalist strain of national populism on both sides of the Atlantic.

This period of unsettlement intensified throughout the 1990s with the increasingly common perception that globalization was failing ordinary people, and especially the white working class in cybercapitalist countries. This drop in public confidence began to undercut the political legitimacy of mainstream neoliberal governments, which, in turn, led to the construction and dissemination of alternative globalization discourses. On the political left, progressive activists increasingly banded together in transnational 'networks of networks' that converged in the formation of a heterogeneous 'global justice movement' that focused on issues of distributive justice, participatory democracy, solidarity with the Global South, and environmental sustainability. As we discuss in Chapter 4, such 'justice globalism'—the political belief system associated with the movement—emerged as a serious challenge to the dominant model of corporate globalization (Steger, Goodman, and Wilson, 2013). This new, alternative ideology of globalization found its social manifestation in successive waves of worldwide protests against sweeping new free-trade agreements, powerful international economic and political organizations, and other visible social formations of what social activists criticized as 'globalization from above'. From the spectacular 1999 anti-World Trade Organization demonstrations in Seattle to the deadly street protests at the 2001 G8 Summit in Genoa, massive displays of popular dissent provoked not only a more polarized globalization debate among business and political elites, but also created an upsurge of critical academic literature examining the anti-systemic effects of these transnational social movements (Della Porta and Tarrow, 2004; Tarrow, 2005).

For many commentators on both sides of the political left–right divide, the wide scope and remarkable durability of these progressive alterglobalization movements suggested that the momentum of neoliberal market integration could be slowed down, halted, and perhaps even reversed. A number of prominent market globalists responded to these global justice demonstrations with public admissions that some of these popular 'discontents' with the dominant model were, indeed, based on legitimate grievances. Former architects of neoliberal globalization such as George Soros (2002), Joseph Stiglitz (2002), Paul Krugman (2003), and Jeffrey Sachs (2005) now publicly criticized the 'excesses of market fundamentalism' that had thrived under their watch during the Roaring Nineties. Converting to a moderate reformism, they conceded that self-interested politicians and greedy corporate executives had oversold the alleged virtues of globalization. They also acknowledged the growing global and domestic divide between the haves and the have-nots, which demonstrated that the benefits of global capitalism had bypassed much of the developing world. Over the next years, this vocal group of market globalists-turned-reformists steadily moved to the political left, in the process producing a stream of critical publications that called for 'better management' of the global system and its associated international economic institutions. Insisting that is necessary to put a 'human face' on globalization, reformists began to offer constructive proposals of how to make globalization 'work for ordinary people' (Stiglitz, 2006).

Still, these reformers never fully disavowed the neoliberal credo in the global integration of markets by means of trade liberalization and deregulation. Rather, they shifted the blame for the alleged mismanagement of globalization from the domain of economics—portrayed as the neutral 'driver' of the process—to the political domain, where globalization was said to have been perverted by policymakers in advanced industrial countries who had set 'biased rules of the game' (Stiglitz, 2006: 4). Less conciliatory market globalists, however, remained unrepentant and instead recommended hard-power police tactics to crack down on justice-globalist mass demonstrations. To justify their unexpected philosophical willingness to support coercive state powers against democratic and largely non-violent protesters, these neoliberal hardliners used sympathetic corporate media outlets to disseminate the stereotype of black-clad, cobblestone-throwing, 'anti-globalization' anarchists whose violent actions endangered the neoliberal promise of the good life (Friedman, 1999).

Then came the spectacular al-Qa'ida attacks of 11 September 2001. Fanning the flames of a growing global climate of fear and insecurity, transnational terrorism exposed what many public commentators now began to call the 'dark side of globalization'. These new anxieties raised the spectre of a return to a deglobalized world of fortified borders and protectionist barriers stemming the global flow of goods, services, ideas, and people. Proliferating news stories of the coming end of the globalization paradigm dovetailed with equally pessimistic academic accounts touting the impending 'collapse of globalism'. Globalization sceptic John Ralston Saul asserted, 'At the most basic level of societal knowledge, we do know that Globalization—as announced, promised, and asserted to be inevitable in the 1970s, '80s and much of the '90s—has now petered out' (2005: 270).

A number of neo-Marxist thinkers agreed with the gloomy assessment of their liberal counterparts. Justin Rosenberg (2005), for example, offered a lengthy 'post mortem to globalization theory', which concluded that the phenomenon had ceased to matter in the new post-September 11 world. He even went so far as to allege the intellectual bankruptcy of the entire globalization model, adding that the much-touted 'worldwide compression of space and time' probably never existed in the first place. And even if it did, Rosenberg quipped, there was no doubt in his mind that, 'The "age of globalization" is over . . . Globalization will become just another word for interdependence' (Rosenberg, 2005: 3, 66). Other critical voices on the left, however, argued that globalization was not collapsing, but swiftly morphing into a US-led imperial globalism, which, in their view, provided clear evidence for the seriousness of the mounting backlash against the neoliberal phase of global capitalism (Harvey, 2003; Pieterse, 2004; Robinson, 2014).

As Western liberal democracies recovered from their terror-induced shock and pursued their so-called Global War on Terror under American leadership, the world slowly returned to its pre-September 11 globalizing gestalt. By the mid-2000s, it seemed that the obituaries for globalization had been written far too hastily. Enter the 2008 GFC that morphed into the Eurozone Sovereign Debt Crisis. The unexpected economic melt-down of global proportions shattered the market globalists' newly found confidence in the inexorable integration of finance, trade, and political structures. It affected a profound shift in the public mood away from the neoliberal vision of a globally integrated world.[5] Indeed, with the benefit of hindsight, the GFC and the ensuing Eurozone crisis marked a watershed in the development of disintegrative tendencies in the global system (Patomäki, 2018: 122). Caught in the immediacy of an unfolding catastrophe, journalists and academics alike proclaiming the 'end of the globalization era' once more, speculating that the Great Recession might turn into a chronic condition, ushering in a long period of economic stagnation, political instability, and social fragmentation. To add insult to injury, when neoliberal governments bailed out the corporate financial sector at the expense of ordinary taxpayers, even avowed market globalists no longer disparaged a possible retreat to the golden age of regulated capitalism as the unrealistic knee-jerk reaction of 'globalization losers'. Respected mainstream economists like Dani Rodrik (2012) sought to impress upon their readers the enduring importance of national regula-tion of the global economy. They argued forcefully that when the social arrangements of democracy clashed with the demands of neoliberal glo-balization, there was only one rational solution: national priorities should take precedence over global concerns.

Such centrist defenders of national and local socioeconomic arrange-ments were soon joined by more progressive globalists like World Bank economist Branko Milanović (2013) and University of California Berkeley economist Thomas Piketty (2014), who suggested a global tax on wealth administered by new global institutions as the antidote to runaway levels of social inequality within and across nations. In

---

[5] For a fascinating sociological investigation of the power of mood as related to the GFC and other structural crises, see Bude (2018).

a political arena fundamentally altered by the economic crisis, new transnational social justice movements like *Los Indignados* and Occupy Wall Street absorbed into their ranks scores of experienced justice globalists who had been denouncing corporate globalization since the 1999 Seattle protests. The influential public intellectual and Filipino politician Walden Bello (2013), for example, argued that the GFC and its aftermath had terminally discredited the much-heralded process of financial and trade interdependence, thus pounding 'the last nail into the coffin of globalization'. The time had come, he announced confidently, for political leaders in the Global South to reverse globalization and instead embrace the virtues of deglobalization and reinvigorated localism.

But once again, the globalization project rebounded. The gradual return to economic stability and thus globalist normalcy in the early to mid-2010s emboldened neoliberal business circles while boosting the sagging fortunes of globalization theory in the academy. The zombie-like ability of the globalization paradigm to continue defying its predicted demise puzzled scores of discerning social scientists like Colin Crouch (2011), who struggled to make sense of this 'strange non-death of neoliberalism'. Paradoxically, globalization seemed to matter less *and* more.

Then arrived the watershed year of 2016, which dealt the fourth and perhaps hardest blow to the globalization model. Although public discontent with globalization had been spilling over from the Global South to the privileged developed countries for several years, many commentators found themselves entirely unprepared for the remarkable speed and vigour with which right-wing nationalists in Western democracies exploited this new discontent with those 'globalist elites' widely held responsible for the disappearance of 'good jobs' in manufacturing and the service sector. As national populists succeeded at the ballot box beyond their wildest dreams, mainstream journalists and academics went into crisis mode, utterly confounded by the mass appeal of such unabashed anti-globalism. Indeed, the core message of the new nationalism was perhaps most potently sloganized in 'Americanism, not globalism, will be our credo'—the centrepiece of presidential nominee Donald Trump's 2016 Republican National Convention speech in the Midwestern rust-belt city of Cleveland, Ohio.

Less surprised pundits reminded their readers that this populist explosion had been in the making for a long time. The result of a long-term tendency towards economic inequality, it had shifted into hyperdrive during the Great Recession and its aftermath (Judis, 2016). Others argued that the economic revolt against globalization and its main beneficiaries was only one aspect of the populist phenomenon. Cultural factors such as hate-mongering against immigrants, racial minorities, women, and the LGBTQ community had been equally important in producing this fiery mixture of right-wing *ressentiment*. Amplified by instant news streams and widely shared on social media, anti-globalist vitriol had moved from the social fringe into the political mainstream (Mishra, 2017: 9–10). Such thoughtful assessments seemed to be borne out by a massive wave of anti-globalist literature, often distributed online as self-published tirades that denounced globalism as a 'vicious, violent, and murdering ideology' hatched by cosmopolitan political and cultural elites (Weston, 2017). While rejecting the extremism of such vengeful denouncements, many mainstream commentators nonetheless accepted the underlying claim that the gospel of neoliberal globalization had failed ordinary citizens around the globe. Market globalist elites, in particular, were chastised for refusing to listen to the real concerns of white working-class voters in the Global North, arrogantly brushing off the complaints of these 'little people' as 'ignorant', 'parochial', and 'racist' (Hochschild, 2017; Williams, 2017; Bremmer, 2018).

Unsurprisingly, a new avalanche of globalization obituaries did not lag far behind the stunning outcome of the 2016 Brexit referendum and Donald Trump's presidential election victory a few months later. As we describe in Chapter 8, the populist wave swept the globe—a phenomenon reflected in the 2018 presidential election victories of Mexican left-wing populist Andrés Manuel López Obrador and Brazilian right-wing populist Jair Bolsonaro. Once again, scores of journalists and academics interpreted the populist explosion as portending the 'end of globalization' and a 'nationalist revival' (Judis, 2016; 2018; King, 2017). Entire issues of leading political periodicals like *Foreign Affairs* (2016, 2017) served as influential echo chambers for some of the most prominent international relations experts who marvelled at the power of rekindled nationalism, pondering what suddenly appeared as a real possibility: the collapse of the post-war liberal international system. Had we reached a defining moment in modern history, they wondered—a moment that marked the birth of a new nationalist and protectionist era? Ironically, it was left to the nationalist Chinese President Xi Jinping to defend the teetering neoliberal globalization agenda before a dwindling crowd of deflated market globalists at the 2017 World Economic Forum meeting in Davos.

For the fourth time in fewer than two decades, the globalization paradigm had been profoundly unsettled, and it has remained in that destabilized state ever since. The once hegemonic market-globalist discourse has struggled to contain a rising national populist narrative that unleashed its fury on the grand liberal vision of the good life in open and interconnected societies. As the outcomes of recent elections in Europe and Latin America make clear, frustrated voters across different national and cultural environments continue to vent their anger at 'elitist globalists'. Populist demagogues who capitalized on the backlash against globalization are riding high, demonstrating the resilience of the national imaginary. 'Globalization' remains the paradigm to beat, but it is increasingly becoming a pejorative term in an unsettled world increasingly enthralled with an alternative vision of 'deglobalization'.

Purpose and Objectives of the Book

To a significant degree, then, contemporary globalization is characterized by the intensifying contradiction between enduring economic and digital interdependence at the global level and serious political fragmentation at the national level (Martinelli, 2018: 65). Former United Nations Secretary General Kofi Annan (2001) addressed this tension as early as 1999: 'The problem is this. The spread of markets outpaces the ability of societies and their political systems to adjust to them, let alone to guide the course they take'.[6] In the ensuing chapters of this book, we contend that global studies scholars in particular are called upon to assess the relevance of globalization in our time of crisis characterized by what we call the *Great Unsettling*—shorthand for the profound dynamics of volatility and destabilization manifested in economic dislocation, automation, precarious work, inequality, migration, technological transformation, cultural shifts, and climate change.

What is the current status of globalization—both the process and the idea? How can we theorize on globalization to arrive at better explanations—and justifications—for the continued relevance of conceptual frameworks that treat global inter-relationality as the basic unit of social analysis? Can we generate generalizable knowledge about the global in systematic ways that cut across entrenched academic disciplines without falling prey to either runaway abstractions or empiricist reductionism? What conceptual frameworks have been associated with globalization over the past decades and how do they stack up in light of recent developments? Is it possible to identify significant historical patterns of globalization that might shed light on today's developments? What sort of

---

[6] Commenting on this contradiction through a more culturalist lens, Manuel Castells (2019) speaks of an 'opposing tension between globalization and identity' that has become more acute across the whole world. As he puts it, 'The nation-state constructed within the modern era finds itself caught between these two tendencies, thanks to its internal tension between acting as a node within the global networks where the fate of its citizens is decided, and in representing citizens who refuse to give up on their historical, geographical and cultural roots, or to lose control over their work' (Castells, 2019: 85).

intellectual initiatives and disciplinary reconfigurations are required to generate new insights into shifting globalization dynamics? How can scholarship on the global respond to today's practical challenges to globalization in innovative ways?

It is the central purpose of this book to engage these crucial questions. The intensifying dynamics of the Great Unsettling offer a suitable moment to take stock of globalization matters. Hence, we struck upon the title of the present study, *Globalization Matters*. It reflects its contents in three distinct but related ways. Firstly, it responds to current deglobalization challenges by providing explanations for why and how globalization—including the *study of globalization*—continues to *matter* in a world that has come to doubt its purpose and relevance. Secondly, the book is methodologically crafted in ways designed to overcome the unhelpful divide between *material* and *ideational* analysis that has haunted the modern social sciences since the days of Karl Marx and Max Weber. We consider both matter and ideas as indispensable ingredients in the formation of theories aiming to yield a better understanding of the constitution of our lives on this planet. Thirdly, we present our views on a variety of pressing theoretical and practical *matters of globalization* that continue to be debated passionately in both scholarly and non-academic circles.

Some of the extant globalization literature deals exclusively with theories, concepts, and domains, while other studies focus on concrete global issues. In contrast, this book intertwines matters of theory and practice, thus offering a more comprehensive reappraisal of globalization. Chapters 2–6 tackle crucial theoretical and historical matters. Our discussion culminates in our outline of a new conceptual and methodological framework of studying the global that we call an *engaged theory of globalization*. Chapters 7–10 apply our theoretical approach to some of today's most pressing practical challenges: the rise of national populism, ecological degradation, rapid urbanization, deepening insecurity, and the increasing pressures on conventional infrastructures of higher education.

2   Mapping a New Genealogy of 'Globalization'

How did the concept of 'globalization' come to matter so much as to utterly dominate the popular and academic discourse of the 1990s and beyond? How did such a new and relatively technical term enter so quickly into common usage while its origins and conceptual evolution remained so obscure, scattered, and uncontested, at least during the incipient period of its emergence? How and why did a concept that accumulated different and sometimes incommensurable meanings become associated with certain understandings, whereas others dropped out or were relegated to a secondary status? Who were some of the principal codifiers and shapers of these meanings in the twentieth century and what are their contributions to the emerging scholarship on the global? Responding to the genealogical challenge implied in these guiding questions, this chapter opens our assessment of the relevance of globalization in our unsettled time with a critical mapping exercise of the keyword in the English language.

As we will discuss in much detail in Chapter 7, objective processes of globalization began centuries—indeed, millennia—before the concept was named as such and acquired its subjective stature as a keyword of our time. Still, the focus of this chapter is on the few decades before globalization underwent those unprecedented quantitative and qualitative changes that called for a single term or phrase naming these dramatic social transformations. Refining the story of globalization told in Chapter 1, we suggest that any systematic attempt to understand today's dynamics of space–time compression requires a careful genealogical investigation of the concept's relatively recent meaning formation. As the intellectual historian Reinhart Koselleck (2002; 2004) notes, concepts do not simply depict 'objective reality', but underpin and inform a distinct manner of being and acting in the world. As ideational and material planes continuously interact with each other, key concepts like *globalization* act upon the world into which they are inscribed and thus shape concrete socio-political practices.

We commence our genealogical enquiry nearly a century ago when 'globalization' was used rather sparingly and episodically along largely isolated branches of knowledge. We end it in the immediate post–Cold War era of the early 1990s when, as we described in Chapter 1, the convergence of popular and academic discourses on the subject contributed to a sudden 'explosion' of use of the term. Given the high intellectual stakes connected to any archaeology of key concepts, it is surprising that the pertinent globalization literature has largely remained silent on such important genealogical matters.[1] Seeking to fill this scholarly gap, we fashion the present chapter as both an expanded narrative enquiry and a critique of this scholarly neglect that has contributed to an inadequate and often distorted understanding of the phenomenon itself.

The Significance and Methodology of Critical Genealogy

Let us consider an instructive example that illustrates the negative consequences of such genealogical sloppiness. Some years ago, *The New York Times* featured an article headed, 'Theodore Levitt, 81, who coined the term "globalization", is dead' (6 July 2006). Unsurprisingly, the generous obituary that followed was organized around this singular origin claim. As we demonstrate in this chapter, several 'globalization' concepts had been in use in the English language in various senses at least as early as the 1920s and possibly for even longer. Admitting to their error a few days later, *The New York Times* (11 July 2006) was obliged to run the following correction:

An obituary and headline on Friday about Theodore Levitt, a marketing scholar at the Harvard Business School, referred incorrectly to the origin of the word 'globalization'. While Mr Levitt's work was closely associated with the idea of globalization in economics, and while he published a respected paper in 1983 popularizing the term, he did not coin the word. (It was in use at least as early as 1944 in other senses and was used by others in discussing economics at least as early as 1981.)

Conventional genealogies built on linear narratives of single origins are also troubling because they tend to reinforce personality cults. Naming

---

[1] The only substantive genealogical treatment of the subject in English that also includes interviews with academic globalization pioneers remains Steger and James (2015). Nearly two decades ago, Jens Bartelson (2000) offered an insightful, but limited, enquiry into the meanings and functions of the concept of globalization within the social sciences in the 1990s. Osterhammel and Petersson's (2005) short history of various globalization processes includes a general opening chapter on the conceptual history of the term that also focuses mostly on the 1990s. For a sustained treatment in German, see Olaf Bach's untranslated study of the historical formation and transformation of the concept (2013). This chapter has greatly benefited from the research findings presented in Bach's excellent book.

the person who first conceived of a significant word or thing has been a crucial feature in the evolution of the modern Western public consciousness. At least since the European Industrial Revolution, intellectual and technological inventors have been singled out and showered with praise for their Promethean efforts. Over the last century, in fact, this practice has become even more individualized—as if something as complex as electricity or the computer was the sudden and single-handed invention of a lone genius. Hence, it should not surprise us that this potent individualizing drive has been busily at work in recent times with regard to the emergence of new keywords such as 'globalization'. It has become a widespread phenomenon that the French sociologist Stéphane Dufoix (2012: 30–1) aptly refers to as 'the religion of the first occurrence'.

Our attempts to understand how the concept of 'globalization' developed—and what sorts of meanings initially emerged—are predicated upon our renunciation of this faith of the first occurrence. Such metanarratives of fixed starting points tend to harness the real-world dynamism of untidy conceptual developments and meaning-making practices to the singularity of frozen positions in space and time. As we discuss below, Levitt played an important role in the 1980s by acting as a chief codifier who imbued globalization with economistic meanings centred on the 'free market' signifier. Our critical genealogical investigation, however, will show that he neither invented the term ex nihilo, nor did it originate in a single meaning cluster associated with economics and business.

Dispelling this influential yet utterly spurious *New York Times* story debunks the efforts of neoliberal power to produce truth claims that serve clear political purposes by naturalizing the origins of 'globalization' in free market relations. Challenging such claims requires us to advance genealogical enquiries as 'critical analyses of our own condition' (Foucault, 1998: 263). Hence, Michel Foucault aptly described genealogy as a 'method of critique' bearing a strong affinity with histories of knowledge that aim to uncover how the 'truth' of a present idea or situation has become established through a series of contingencies and accidents. Rather than framing the realities of the present in a post hoc fashion by means of those normalizing categories we know as 'logics' and 'chronologies', our critical genealogical approach to the meaning-making practices of globalization de-emphasizes stability in favour of highlighting the accumulated contingencies *and* structural continuities that shaped the globalizing world we perceive ourselves to inhabit today.

In this manner, the chapter tracks the twists and turns in the early discourses on globalization to underscore how the 'global now' actually represents a rather unstable victory won over several decades at the expense of other possible 'global nows' (Shapiro, 2012: 59). Resisting the utopian impulse to provide a comprehensive description of the past, we settle for the more modest goal of assembling selected 'snapshots' into an episodic configuration of the main branches of the concept's genealogical tree. Thus, our critical approach eschews the construction of linear narratives that connect fixed points on a single timeline and instead opts for a more episodic sketch of crucial junctures, notable tipping points, instructive examples, and multiple pathways of the past.

The Methodological Framework

The methodological framework guiding our critical genealogy involves a number of conceptual elements and levels of analysis that we will explore in more detail in the following three chapters. As we elaborate in Chapter 4, our approach allows us to analyse the overlay of different *ideas* with *ideologies* as they articulated evolving social *imaginaries*, both national and global. These three analytical layers—ideas, ideologies, and imaginaries—are set within a fourth level of ontological analysis that seeks to understand how the dominant formation of modernity comes into tension with other ways of being and knowing. We proceed by heeding some careful genealogical precepts. Firstly, we do not ask which person invented the concept, but provide a more accurate picture of multiple entry points. Secondly, we construct an archive populated by relevant early texts featuring 'globalization' and related terms. Thirdly, we record some significant sequences and patterns of usage, conceptualized as four major branches of the 'globalization tree'. Fourthly, we scan these texts for principal meanings and probe the extent to which their authors show a reflexive understanding of globalization and related concepts.[2] Fifthly, we draw on interviews with key academic figures to find out how they have chosen to narrate 'globalization' and what meanings they have left out. Finally, we pay close attention to the shifting social contexts of the twentieth century in which a concept such as 'globalization' emerged as a keyword because the tangibility and visibility of increasing global inter-relationality called for a single word or phrase naming this interdependence.

While sharing Michel Foucault's appreciation of genealogy as a method of critique, our methodological approach draws much inspiration from Raymond Williams's (1958) seminal contributions to social theory, while recognizing its very different lineage from Foucault's. Williams's analysis of the concept of culture, for example, helped elaborate better understandings

---

[2] In both the academic and public discourse over the last quarter of a century, such generic meanings of globalization are usually imbued with economic–technical signifiers. Cultural meanings tend to play a subordinate role.

in the field of literary studies and, later, cultural studies. His ambitious investigation surveys a two-century period; our examination of globalization covers a much shorter time span from the 1920s to the early 1990s. In Chapter 3 of this study, we extend this discussion by delineating and analysing some key approaches to globalization from the 1990s to the present. Our methodological framework is also indebted to Williams's (1983: 22) particularly insightful articulation of what he calls 'keywords'—pivotal terms that show 'how integral the problems of meanings and relationships really are'. Although keywords serve as potent catalysts for the evolution of the entire vocabulary of any given era, the history of their meaning construction often remains underdeveloped and thus obscure. 'Globalization' is no exception. While the meanings of other keywords such as 'economics', 'culture', or 'modernity' developed rather slowly and in a relatively continuous fashion, 'globalization' has had a rather short and discontinuous history. After a few tentative, episodic, and disparate uses across the mid-twentieth century, it remerged at the fin de siècle in energized discourses that sought to make sense of what was then widely perceived as a period of dramatic 'time–space compression' (Harvey, 1989).

Finally, our methodological framework recognizes the importance of Pierre Bourdieu's (1990) notion of 'social fields'. As the evidence assembled in this chapter shows, the concept of globalization emerged from the intersection of a number of interrelated 'communities of practice' populated by academics, journalists, publishers/editors, and librarians (Wenger, 1998). This notion of 'communities of practice' intersects with both Stanley Fish's (1980) 'communities of interpretation' and Bourdieu's (1990) work on 'fields of practice'. Unlike the French sociologist, however, we find that individuals working closely with the concept of 'globalization' as it rose to prominence were not always associated with a clear taxonomy of status. But this last point is only one of emphasis. As we elaborate below, this does not mean that the career of the concept and the professional careers of individuals were unrelated. In fact, their engagement with globalization often proved to be an important factor in the making of their professional careers.

Assembling a clearer picture of the complex career of globalization is bound to both mediate and frame how we envision our increasingly interconnected world. And yet, there still exists no comprehensive genealogy or critical history of its meaning formation in the English language.[3] This glaring omission reveals the poverty of our history of

---

[3] Over recent decades, the term has spread to major world languages and beyond. But, as we discuss below, only the French term *mondialisation*—though not quite a semantic equivalent of 'globalization'—appears to have similarly early roots. The German equivalent *Globalisierung* did not appear until the 1950s and 1960s (Bach, 2013: 72, 87).

globalization as one of the most important ideas for visualizing the passage of human society into the third millennium. Although there have been intense academic efforts to define and delineate the concept and its main thematic domains from a variety of theoretical perspectives, the very quality of such projects depends on the careful construction of a proper genealogical framework.

Why, then, has there been such a dearth of genealogical research on globalization? After all, the concept's meteoric rise at the end of the twentieth century represents an extraordinary phenomenon, especially since the term did not enter general dictionaries until the 1961 *Merriam-Webster's Third New International Dictionary*.[4] Half a century later, most major books on the subject begin with a seemingly mandatory paragraph or two defining globalization, locating it historically, and telling us that it is now used ubiquitously (Robertson, 1992; Scholte, 2005; Bisley, 2007; Held and McGrew, 2007). Substantial dictionaries and encyclopaedias of globalization as well as multivolume anthologies of globalization, including by the present authors (James et al., 2006–14; Steger, 2011; Steger, Battersby, and Siracusa, 2014; Juergensmeyer, Steger, and Sassen, 2019), have been published that explore the phenomenon in all its complexity. Moreover, since the early 2000s, there has been a proliferation of projects seeking to measure globalization with a composite index such as the A.T. Kearney Foreign Policy Globalization Index or the KOF Index of Globalization (Martens et al., 2015).

Thousands of works on the subject have been written to cover primarily the objective aspects of globalization such as transnational economic flows or pertinent technological innovations. Today, we can now track these works through such 'big data' mechanisms as the search engine *Ngram*, Google's mammoth database collated from over 5 million digitized books available free to the public for online searches (Michel et al., 2011). The exceptionally rich *Factiva* database lists 355,838 publications referencing the term 'globalization'. The *Expanded Academic ASAP* database produced 7,737 results with 'globalization' in their titles, including 5,976 journal articles going back to 1986, 1,404 magazine articles going back to 1984, and 355 news items going back to 1987. The *ISI Web of Knowledge* shows a total of 8,970 references with 'globalization' in their titles going back to 1968. The *EBSCO Host Database* yields 17,188 results reaching back to 1975. *Proquest Newspaper Database* lists 25,856 articles going back to 1971.

---

[4] The current Merriam-Webster website incorrectly claims that the first known use of the term occurred in 1951.

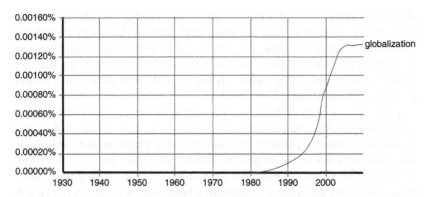

Figure 2.1 The use of 'globalization', 1930–2010 (using Google *Ngram*)

Despite the immense intellectual attention expressed in these quantitative records, it is striking that, until recently, this multitude of articles
and books remain largely silent on the history or etymology of the concept
(Figure 2.1). Similarly, in the many dictionaries and encyclopaedias
devoted to globalization, there is no entry for 'globalization, the concept
of'. One high-profile dictionary devoted to the subject of globalization
with the subtitle *The Key Concepts* does not even feature an entry for
'globalization' as such (Mooney and Evans, 2007). Organized broadly
around the theme of globalization, Andrew Jones's (2006) dictionary
contains little more than a page and a half of a general discussion of
'globalization' that is confined to listing various approaches to the phenomenon rather than offering even the briefest of genealogies of the
concept. The massive and well-organized *Encyclopaedia of Global Studies*
(Anheier, Juergensmeyer, and Faessel, 2012) has two major entries on
globalization—'Globalization: Approaches'   and   'Globalization,
Phenomenon of'—but there is no entry on the etymology and historical
evolution of the keyword. Scholars thus have taken for granted one of the
very tools of their trade. The core concept we use today to carry our
intuitions, histories, arguments, politics, and considerations about the
global social imaginary has been left shrouded in mystery. One can find
no equivalent to David Forgacs' (1984) elegant genealogy of the concept
of 'national-popular' or Guido Zernatto's (1944) classic historical investigation of the keyword 'nation'.

The poverty of genealogical research on globalization represents too
large a vacuum in the pertinent academic literature to be shrugged off
as a mere curiosity and inconsequential oversight. Our genealogical
examination of the keyword aims not only at helping to fill this

conceptual void, but also at contributing to an investigation of the social underpinnings of how we come to imagine our increasingly interconnected world. The first thing that can be said by way of explanation is that key writers on the subject have studiously worked on proper definitions of the concept (Robertson, 1992; Appadurai, 1996; Scholte, 2005; Roudometof, 2016), yet they have deferred what should have been an equally important task: namely, an investigation of the ways in which the concept came to mean what it now does. Delving into its intricate dynamics of meaning formation seems to have been set aside as the urgency of explaining the objective dimensions of the intensifying global interdependence—especially its economic and political aspects—eclipsed the genealogical imagination of globalization theorists.

The Many-Branched Tree of Globalization: Early Imaginings of the Global

Our research findings suggest that early uses of the keyword were complicated and discontinuous and involved a multiplicity of intellectual entry points and influences. Perhaps most surprisingly, they go back to meaning constellations and discursive orbits that did not always endure on the long road to academic (and public) prominence. Like the emergence of *Homo sapiens* as a species during which, over many millennia, different kinds of hominids thrived side by side for some time before nearly all of them became extinct, some globalization strains turned out to be evolutionary dead ends. We found that the meaning formation of the concept was many-branched, and that the shoots of its development were often fractious, intermittent, and, buffeted by ferocious winds of change, encountered unanticipated twists and reversals.

As Philippe Bourbeau (2018: 21) observes, the historical evolution of major concepts and issues can best be characterized as 'a disparity and diversity of meanings; some interpretations are forgotten, set aside, or defeated, while others become integrated into the construction of the dominant narrative. This narrative can be broad: two positions at the top of the genealogical "tree" might be quite distant from each other'. Embracing Bourbeau's pluralistic spirit, we also adopt the popular genealogical 'tree' metaphor—with the proviso that we envisioned it as sprouting diffuse roots and many branches in exceedingly complex patterns. Indeed, early uses of 'globalization' involved a multileveled canopy of understandings and associations that included notions of interregional connections, the act of being systematic, an early childhood development phase, and a general dynamic of linking the entire world together.[5]

Although 'globalization' did not appear prominently in academic and popular discourses until the early 1990s, imaginings of the 'global' and the 'globe' had already been popular for centuries. Going back as far as the early sixteenth century, for example, an emergent class of intellectuals —cartographers, philosophers, and writers—used cosmographic images of the *globus* in competing narratives. One lineage used spherical images to associate the early Atlantic empires with the past cultural glory of imperial Rome. Early map-makers projecting incipient forms of cosmopolitanism with cartouches of cultural difference that might be considered as stylized precursors to the 'Family of Man', a photographic exhibition first displayed in 1955 at the Museum of Modern Art in New York City. It comprised photographs of the human condition from 68 countries and toured the world for eight years (Cosgrove, 2003).

But the early decades of the twentieth century witnessed a clear shift in people's perceptions of the global, as the modern media and communications industries were becoming acutely aware of their own transnational networks serving mass audiences. A number of newspapers around the world, particularly in Britain, the United States, and Canada, were using 'globe' in their titles, such as *The Boston Globe*, *The Globe* (London), and the *Globe and Mail* (Toronto). From the 1920s onwards, some newly constituted commercial airlines featured globes in their advertising projections. Founded in 1927, Pan American World Airways flew under a blue globe logo until its economic collapse during a very different period of global competition in the 1990s. The *Daily News*—later the inspiration for the *Daily Planet* of *Superman* movies' fame—proudly displayed a gigantic rotating globe in the massive lobby of its New York headquarters at its opening in 1930.

Already in the 1910s, a number of Hollywood movie studios had seized upon globes as a vital component of their corporate image. The first logo for Universal Pictures from 1912 to 1919 incorporated a stylized Earth with a Saturn-like ring. It was called the Trans-Atlantic Globe or the Saturn Globe. In the 1920s, its revised logo was planet Earth floating in space with a biplane flying around it and leaving in its wake a trail of white vapour. Built in 1926, Paramount Picture's New York headquarters were topped by an illuminated glass globe, which was later blackened in response to anticipated perils linked to World War II. In the immediate

---

[5] Another early use of 'globalization' to denote 'generalization' or 'totalisation' occurs in Clifford Geertz's work (1964: 207). The prominent anthropologist used the term in 1964 to criticize what he saw as the increasing generalization of the key concepts of 'culture' and 'identity', which, in his view, would result in a blunting of intellectual discernment.

aftermath of the war—and in the spirit of celebrating the global reach of the communications industry—the Hollywood Foreign Correspondents Association initiated a series of media presentations and receptions they called the Golden Globe Awards.

People's dominant social imaginary changed dramatically in the mid-twentieth century. World War II (the first truly global war), fascism, totalitarianism, and a techno-scientific experiment that culminated in the dropping of nuclear bombs on civilians had begun the serious process of reflection on the dark side of modernity. In the case of World War II, a global military catastrophe had shuddered across the whole world, causing reverberations in faraway villages in the Global South—villages otherwise barely aware that a war was in progress. But this was not enough in itself. Rather, it was changes during the 'peacetime' years that provoked a series of different authors, all writing from the Global North, to respond actively to the globalization of warfare. Their aspirations for a different world, their dismay at intensifying adverse developments, and their concerns regarding ideological contestation met with a relativizing ontological disruption to their existential verities.

As part of this relativizing process, older senses of the world came under assault. The 1950s, supercharged by the enhanced destructive capacity of thermonuclear weaponry, destroyed the sense of the Earth as an unassailably stable platform upon which humans could flourish. Still, when Hannah Arendt (1958) published *The Human Condition*, there was no familiar concept to describe the process of intensifying social relations that were busily stitching together humanity as an interconnected, yet uneven, entity. Although the German–American political philosopher never employed the term 'globalization' in her book, she nonetheless opened the prologue with the 'global' image of an 'Earth-born object'—the Soviet-launched satellite Sputnik—projected out into the universe. Describing the launching of the first satellite as an event 'as important as any other in history', her story serves to introduce her thesis of the Earth now constituted the 'very quintessence of the human condition' (Arendt, 1958: 2). Sensing the emerging gestalt of a planetary social whole in the late 1950s, she spoke of an incipient global society 'whose members at the most distant points of the globe need less time to meet than the members of a nation a generation ago' (Arendt, 1958: 257).

Indeed, nothing captured the rise of the global imaginary as starkly as the dawning space age. Most of all, the awesome pictures of 'Earth Rising'— taken by Apollo 8 astronaut William Anders after the first ever manned orbit around the moon on 24 December 1968—did much to enhance people's awareness of our collective journey on Spaceship Earth. These photos showed a small, vulnerable blue planet floating in a vast sea of black, with the moon in the foreground providing a destabilizing horizon of reference. This relativizing of the place of planet Earth in relation to the universe had a profound impact, confirming the 'obviousness' of an emerging global imaginary. Fifteen months later, the first Earth Day was celebrated (Poole, 2008). Long before the invention of the term 'Anthropocene'— the post-Holocene age of human impact discussed in much detail in Chapter 9—the early environmental movements suggested that life on the planet was threatened by multiple anthropogenic degradations.

This idea of planet Earth as vulnerable was reinforced by an ontological jolt that hit the world's populations as photographs of the Earth taken from outer space circulated around the globe. While 'Earthrise' conveyed the fragility of our blue globe suspended in the vast cosmos, it fell short of presenting the complete, unobstructed view of Earth that allows for a full appreciation of our interdependent existence. Apollo 17 astronauts achieved this difficult feat four years later in their magnificent image of our unshadowed globe floating in the blackness of space. Given the number AS17-22727 by NASA, the 1972 picture quickly achieved the status of the most widely reproduced photograph in history. To this day, it is the sharpest of only four whole round Earth pictures ever taken by human beings. With Earth nearing winter solstice at the time, Apollo 17's optical lens revealed a brilliantly white South Pole tilting sunward. White clouds over Antarctica were swirling north across the Great Southern Ocean, penetrating as far as the middle of the great African continent and the tiniest visible slivers of Australia and South America. The deserts of Arabia and the Horn of Africa take up the top of the earthly sphere, and the vista reaches its limits at the small, barely visible oval of the Mediterranean basin. This so-called Blue Marble Shot revealed to the human eye the full panorama of our terrestrial home in blue–brown–white hues without political boundaries or a privileged Western geographical centre. Most importantly for our purposes, the photo reinforced the linguistic figure of the 'global' configured around concepts of circulation, connectivity, and communication. As the human geographer Denis Cosgrove pointed out, the Blue Marble Shot helped fuel 'a universalist, progressive, and mobile discourse in which the image of the globe signifies the potential, if not actual, equality of all locations networked across frictionless space' (2001: 263).

No doubt, the remarkable Apollo images of the globe taken from outer space also loomed large in the emergence of the transnational and countercultural revolutions of the 1960s. Though still a long way from a genuine condition of globality, the world was clearly becoming more integrated. The growing presence of the adjective 'global' in the news, science, advertising, policy circles, and the entertainment industry reflected the remarkable rise of a global imaginary. It punctuated the language of nationalism and its exclusivist claims to the management of modern societies. It was in this transformative context of becoming worldwide—in both an objective and subjective sense—that the global ceased to be the accidental quality of the 'international' and became something *in and of itself*.

While such examples of historical contextualization are both important and necessary in tracing the formation of 'globalization', they are not sufficient to give specificity to the actual process of meaning formation. Moreover, since these dynamics usually travel in many different directions, they don't congeal easily into a single word or phrase—with Marshall McLuhan's powerful image of the 'global village' being one of the very few mid-century exceptions that merely confirm the rule (Carpenter and McLuhan, 1960; McLuhan, 1964).[6] On the one hand, the prevalence of these kinds of phrases and images is strong testimony to the power of 'the global' as a logo or icon long before the concept of 'globalization' began to be used regularly by journalists and academics. On the other hand, however, the enhanced visibility of the global made it all the stranger that much of the late-twentieth-century writing on globalizing communications lacked a historical consciousness of anything prior to the immediate 'communications revolution' and the broader process of globalization that these commentators were struggling to understand. The discursive explosion of the keyword in the 1990s notwithstanding, this dissonance suggests that the dominant national social imaginary of the twentieth century became only very gradually overlaid with a thickening sensibility of global interdependence.

The Many-Branched Tree of Globalization: The Long Incipient Period (Late 1920s to Early 1980s)

To recapture, then, it was in this critical period from the Roaring Twenties to the Revolutionary Sixties that the linguistic shift from 'globe' and 'global' to the explicit use of 'globalization' slowly progressed. Our research reveals the existence of at least four major genealogical branches in the explicit meaning formation of the concept prior to its 'conceptual convergence' phase during the 1980s. The first meaning

---

[6] It appears that McLuhan's famous coinage of the phrase was slightly preceded by the German philosopher Günther Anders (1972), who noted in a 1959 public lecture that '*Der Globus ist zum Dorf geworden*' ('The globe has turned into a village').

strain is rooted in the fields of education and psychology; the second in society and culture; the third in economics and business; and the fourth in politics and international relations (IR).[7]

The pedagogical–psychological meaning branch appears to be the oldest of the four and relates primarily to notions of universalization and integration of knowledge acquisition. Dating back to 1930, one of our earliest snapshots shows the Scottish educator William Boyd employing the concept throughout his work.[8] He associated 'globalization' with a holistic approach to education: 'Wholeness, ... integration, globalization ... would seem to be the keywords of the new education view of mind: suggesting negatively, antagonism to any conception of human experience which over-emphasizes the constituent atoms, parts, elements' (Boyd and MacKenzie, 1930: 350). In this usage, 'globalization' has hardly anything to do with the world understood as planetary. It simply articulates a 'universal' learning process by moving from the global to the particular. Boyd, in turn, acquired the term by translating the French word *globalisation* as used by the Belgian educational psychologist Jean-Ovide Decroly (1929).

This even earlier snapshot from the 1920s shows Decroly using the concept in reference to what he called the 'globalization function stage' in early childhood development. Within a few years, 'globalization' became an important concept in his early-twentieth-century 'new education' movement. Decroly and some like-minded colleagues were eager to introduce a holistic pedagogical system for teaching children to read and learn—*la méthode globale* ('whole-language teaching'). This method is still used in Belgian and French schools that bear Decroly's name. However, over the next decades, this educational and psychological meaning trajectory largely diminished—save for one notable exception. In 1953, C.W. de Kiewiet (1953: 13, 70), president of Rochester University, published a short article that called for the creation of a 'globalized curriculum' reflecting the 'realities of world conditions'. But the author's fervent appeal to 'globalize' American universities used the concept only in its verb form, not as a noun.

Still, one is struck by the topicality of Kiewiet's demand to globalize the curriculum, especially in light of its sudden reappearance in the 1970s

---

[7] To reiterate, some conceptual strains never developed and others materialized outside our four-branched genealogical framework. For example, the mathematician Arthur Kruse introduced the concept of 'residual globalization' in 1969 (Kruse, 1969). In this instance, the reference was to abstract equations and systematic relations. A generation later, 'residual globalization' was discussed at length in an electrical engineering doctoral dissertation without any reference to Kruse's study (Herndon, 1995: 54).

[8] Boyd's immensely successful classic, *The History of Western Education* (1921), went through ten editions between 1921 and 1972.

and 1980s.[9] These later initiatives eventually took root in the changing higher education environment of the 1990s and led to significant academic innovations, including the establishment of the transdisciplinary field of global studies (Steger and Wahlrab, 2017). Thus, it would be fair to say that this early pedagogical branch of meaning formation thinned out and sputtered before mutating into its contemporary discursive field of the 'globalization of education'. This topical phrase signifies in the contemporary context the study of various objective globalization dynamics such as the transnationalization and rejuvenation of educational systems worldwide (Mittelman, 2017). Moreover, 'globalization' has also become an important term in the growing pedagogical literature dedicated to the exploration of the dramatic changes that impact higher education as a result of new forms of digital technology, global rankings, and growing student flows across national borders (Wildavsky, 2012; Altbach, 2016; Mittelman, 2017).

Organized around cultural and sociological meanings, the second genealogical branch of 'globalization' made its appearance in the 1940s. Our initial snapshot depicts an early case that is remarkable for its isolated occurrence, unusual context, and the mode in which it was delivered. In 1944, Lucius Harper, an African–American editor, journalist, and early civil rights leader, published an article that quoted from a letter written by an African–American soldier based in Australia. In the letter, the GI conveys his impressions of the global dissemination of problematic American cultural–political views about 'Negroes':

The American Negro and his problem are taking on a global significance. The world has begun to measure America by what she does to us [the American Negro]. But—and this is the point—we stand in danger ... of losing the otherwise beneficial aspects of globalization of our problems by allowing the 'Bilbos in uniform' with and without brass hats to spread their version of us everywhere. (Harper, 1944: 4)

'Bilbos in uniform' is a snappy reference to Theodore G. Bilbo (1877–1947), a mid-century governor and US senator from Mississippi who was an avid advocate of segregation and an openly racist member of the Ku Klux Klan. As David Runciman (2013: 13) explains, Bilbo brazenly echoed Hitler's sentiments expressed in *Mein Kampf* by asserting that merely 'one drop of Negro blood placed in the veins of the purest Caucasian destroys the inventive genius of his mind and strikes palsied his creative faculties'. At the time, nationally elected representatives of the segregated South had successfully blocked a series of legislative attempts

[9] See, for example, Kerr (1979) and Anderson (1982).

to clamp down on lynching. Arguing that such practices were a matter for individual states to regulate, they insisted that the necessity of lynching was something that Northerners simply could not understand. To be sure, Southern racists like Bilbo realized what was at stake and sought to complement their obstructionist legislative efforts by spreading rumours about an 'international Jewish conspiracy' aiding what they saw as aggressive Northern interference: 'The niggers and Jews of New York are working hand in hand' (Bilbo, quoted in Runciman, 2013: 13–16).

By quoting the 'globalization letter' from an African–American soldier serving his country in the Pacific theatre, Harper's article allowed for political mediation that increased the verisimilitude of the passage. Despite Australia's nationally closed and race-based, white-only immigration policy, black soldiers in World War II were often greeted abroad with a relative openness that confronted their sensibilities formed in the United States. Harper's article appeared in the *Chicago Defender*, a Chicago-based newspaper for primarily African–American readers and probably the most influential newspaper of its kind in the United States. As the executive editor of that weekly, Harper regularly addressed an estimated readership of 100,000 (Cooper, 1999). Moreover, he helped to establish the Bud Billiken Club and Parade— the oldest and largest African–American parade in the United States. Harper also ghost-authored the successful autobiography of Jack Johnson, America's first black heavyweight boxing champion. Some years later, the editor's civil rights activities came under intense scrutiny by McCarthy's infamous subcommittee of the US Senate Committee on Foreign Relations. Overall, though, it appears that the impact of Harper's use of 'globalization' on the American press in general and the African–American community in particular must have been negligible, since virtually no English-language periodicals picked up the term for decades after the 1940s.

A second important snapshot corresponding to the sociocultural genealogical branch of globalization occurred in an academic context that corresponds to the rise of modernization theory and structural–functionalist 'social systems' approaches in the social sciences spearheaded by the American sociologists Talcott Parsons (1951) and Robert K. Merton (1949). The popularity of such macro-level sociological perspectives ultimately inspired Marxist critics like Immanuel Wallerstein (1974) to develop their alternative 'world-systems' paradigm. In 1951, Paul Meadows, a notable American sociologist who never received mention in the pantheon of globalization pioneers, contributed an extraordinary piece of writing to the prominent academic journal, *Annals of the American*

Academy of Political and Social Science. His article stands out for reasons that will become quickly apparent:

The culture of any society is always unique, a fact which is dramatically described in Sumner's concept of *ethos*: 'the sum of the characteristic usages, ideas, standards and codes by which a group is differentiated and individualized in character from other groups'. With the advent of industrial technology, however, this tendency toward cultural localization has been counteracted by a stronger tendency towards cultural universalization. With industrialism, a new cultural system has evolved in one national society after another; its global spread is incipient and cuts across every local ethos. Replacing the central *mythos* of the medieval Church, this new culture pattern is in a process of 'globalization', after a period of formation and formulation covering some three or four hundred years of westernization. (Meadows, 1951: 11)

This passage is worth quoting at length, not only because it represents one of the earliest pieces of sustained writings that use the concept in a more contemporary sense, but also because Meadows' analysis puts 'globalization' in a conductive relationship with other pivotal terms such as 'industrialism', 'localization', 'universalization', and 'Westernization'.[10] Meadows' act of putting the process of globalization in inverted commas suggests that he was either uncertain or self-conscious about using the term relationally. But the synergy formed by the American sociologist between such crucial spatial signifiers as 'globalization' and 'localization'—extended by later globalization researchers such as Roland Robertson (1992) and Saskia Sassen (1991)—suggests that he was far ahead of his time. The difference is that later globalization pioneers usually did not use the two terms to indicate countermanding processes. As George Modelski emphasized in a long interview, 'the local level . . . always has to be connected to the other levels' (Modelski, in Steger and James, 2015: 24).

Another remarkable achievement of Meadows' article lies in its uncanny recognition of the strong nexus connecting 'globalization' with 'ideology' and 'industrial technology'. As he pointed out at the end of the introductory section, 'The rest of this paper will be devoted to a discussion of the technological, organizational, and ideological systems which comprise this new universalistic culture' (Meadows, 1951: 11). Although resisting the pull of the 'religion of the first occurrence' as described at the outset of this chapter, we are tempted to note that Paul Meadows probably comes closest to deserving the

---

[10] The German historian Hanno Kesting (1959: 306) draws a similar early connection between 'globalization' and 'industrialism' when he notes, '*Die Industrialisierung der Welt ist nicht notwendigerweise eine Globalisierung des Industrialismus in seiner kapitalistischen Form*' ('The industrialization of the world is not necessarily a globalization of industrialism in its capitalist form').

questionable recognition of perhaps being the first scholar within this sociocultural strain of 'globalization' to use the concept in a way that would become its dominant mode two generations later. Using Google citations and other reference indices, however, we could not find any subsequent articles or books that directly attribute their own work to Meadows' innovative practice of linking other key sociological concepts to 'globalization'. But given the place and form of its publication, there is no doubt that his essay must have been widely read. Readership and library subscriptions for *Annals of the American Academy of Political and Social Science* were extensive.

Meadows' pioneering cultural–sociological efforts to engage 'globalization' remained largely dormant until the 1970s and early 1980s when other sociologists occasionally used the concept to describe what they saw as an irreversible expansion of the Anglo-American disciplinary paradigm across national borders. As Harry H. Hiller put it, 'We cannot expect national sociologies to be mere transitional devices in the globalization of sociology' (1979: 132). A more extended application of the cultural aspects of the concept—some of which Meadows had already pioneered in the early 1950s—occurred 25 years later when the German anthropologists Wolfgang Rudolf and Peter Tschohl (1977: 298) discussed what they saw as a rapidly accelerating, worldwide process towards cultural homogenization. In their view, this dynamic was so significant that it required the introduction of a 'new' descriptive concept: 'globalization' ('*Globalisierung*'). Similarly interested in cultural dynamics, the American theologian Roger Haight (1982: 436) described the 'growing interdependence of all humanity' as 'the globalization of human culture'.

The third genealogical branch of globalization articulates economic and business meanings. Here, too, the keyword had a rather tenuous start and was used rarely and intermittently. A snapshot from the late 1950s relates the term to the possible extension of the European Common Market. The article (Anonymous, 1959) was published in the journal *International Organization*, a periodical that, a few decades later, would carry hundreds of references to globalization. The 1959 article, however, limited the scope of the term to regional and administrative matters by suggesting that European Community countries could take a series of concrete steps towards their common market goal, which included the 'globalization of quotas'. But the geographic framework invoked by the term 'globalization' did not extend beyond six European countries and thus merely served to describe a process of regionalization.

Another snapshot from 1962 features the use of 'globalization' by François Perroux, a prominent critic of dominant capitalist financial and economic policies towards the Third World. Sympathetic to a Marxist-influenced dependency theory approach to economic development, the French political economist often situated his critique of such Eurocentric practices to the larger geopolitical framework of the Cold War. Commenting on the emerging space race between the United States and the USSR in the 1960s, he placed the intensifying dynamics of global interdependence at the core of his expressed concern for the survival of our species:

The conquest of space and nuclear achievement belong to the two super-powers which they reinforce and oppose: their peaceful and warlike consequences are global, whether the powers wish it or not. For the moment, the two superpowers are resisting this globalization, which is also universalization, because it is of interest to humanity and to the entire being of each man. (Perroux, 1962: 10)

Most importantly, Perroux also used the concept in a context clearly more akin to the contemporary dominant meaning related to the formation of integrated economic markets on a planetary scale. As Stéphane Dufoix (2013b: 2) points out, Perroux (1964: 265) refers explicitly to the '*mondialisation de certains marches*' ('globalization of some markets') nearly a generation before Theodore Levitt's alleged invention of the term 'globalization', and from a decidedly more critical perspective than the Harvard business professor. However, we need to tread carefully here. Perroux's original essay was written in French and the term in question was a translation from the French *mondialisation* ('worldization')—a word in use at least since the early 1950s (Bach, 2013: 91). Dufoix (2013b: 2) informs us that the Belgian lawyer Paul Otlet had used this term in 1916 when he argued for taking strong 'steps of *mondialisation*' in the industrial quest for finding and exploiting natural resources. Again, it should be noted that the contextual meaning of Otlet's *mondialisation* was quite different from the one that is now usually translated as 'globalization'. The legal scholar connected *mondialisation* to *internationalisation*, with the former being the ultimate extension of the latter. The normative connotation of the term *mondial* was 'what is good for all nations' (Otlet, quoted in Dufoix, 2013b: 2). But the translation of Perroux's *mondialisation* as 'globalization' was not the only such case occurring during the 1960s.[11] But such occasional journalistic attempts to conflate the terms had petered out by the 1980s when *mondialisation* received its precise English equivalent—'mundialization', not 'globalization' (Dufoix, 2013b: 2).[12]

[11] See, for example, Cerami (1962: 495). Some authors, like the British Labour politician Denis Healey (1961: 155), chose to absorb *mondialisation* into the English language without attempting a translation.

[12] 'Mundialization' is still in use today. See, for example, the website of the Mundialization Committee in Hamilton (Canada): http://mundialization.ca. We are very grateful to Stéphane Dufoix (2013b) for sharing his pertinent unpublished article, 'Between Scylla and Charybdis: French Social Science Faces Globalization'.

Once established by Perroux, this semantic nexus linking 'globalization' to 'markets' and 'business' managed to stay alive over the next few decades. For example, the business section of *Time Magazine* (29 December 1967) featured a cover story titled 'The Long-Term View from the 29th Floor'. It cited the optimistic views of Michael Haider, then CEO of Standard Oil Company of New Jersey, who saw 'no limit to the globalization of American business'. Celebrating the 'fact' that 'globalization' was 'stretching out to developing markets in Africa, Latin America and the Far East', Haider advanced the following claim: 'U.S. companies have stopped thinking in terms of borders . . . Together, they are rocking the world. Their globalization is an inevitable showdown between modern technology and old-style nationalism. The pace of globalization is so vigorous that other nations are increasingly concerned and cantankerous'. The CEO's conflation of globalization with a US-led global market expansion would become ultimately the core claim of neoliberal market globalism: namely, that globalization was about the liberalization and global integration of markets (Steger, 2009: 61).[13]

The fourth genealogical branch of globalization is rooted in meaning clusters related to politics and IR. An early 1952 snapshot reveals the use of the concept in support of a further expansion of the activities of newly established international organizations. Acting as a representative of the United Nations (UN), the international law scholar Sigmund Timberg (1952) advocated the formation of so-called international govcorps, which he envisioned as institutions mediating between the foreign policy strategies of national governments and increasingly globally operating corporations. Timberg's rationale for their creation was his belief in the prevention of international conflict among nations by means of increasing transborder political and economic activities such as international trade and customs accommodations. For the legal expert, the development of cooperative structures among nations would transform what he called 'happenstance globalization' into a deliberate, rational planning process rooted in modern management techniques. Such a planned form of globalization would not only ease 'national passions and conflicts', but also improve the efficiency and productivity of bureaucrats working in foreign ministries (Timberg, 1952: 747–50).

Similarly reflecting on the positive effects of the intensification of IR, the American political scientist Inis Claude published a widely read article

---

[13] Already by the early 1970s, American business executives had found in leading business magazines enthusiastic promoters of what CEO William I. Spencer called the mindset of the 'new globalists' who recognized that, 'The political boundaries of nation-states are too narrow and constricted to define the scope and sweep of modern business' (Spencer, cited in Silk, 1972: 63).

in 1965 on the future of the UN. Equating universalization and globalization, the leading international organizations expert mentioned the concept of 'globalization' only once under a chapter heading of 'The Movement toward Universality', where he argued, 'The United Nations has tended to reflect the steady globalization of international relations' (Claude, 1965: 837).[14] In other words, rather than envisioning the creation of new organizational structures and institutions such as Timberg's 'international govcorps', Claude considered the UN as a whole as the most appropriate model for a rationally planned globalization of international cooperation. Aurelio Peccei, an Italian industrialist, philanthropist, and co-founder of the Club of Rome, saw things differently. He considered Claude's 'movement toward universality' as a 'slow, unsystematic movement' towards what he called a 'multicontinental unity in diversity'. Peccei then forged an innovative link between globalization as 'mentality' and globalization as 'social structure', thus connecting the concept's political and sociocultural meaning branches: 'The important thing, however, in my opinion is that this *process of progressive globalization or planetization* has itself the germ and appeal of an idée-force, because its foundations are cast in the triumphant realities of this age' (Peccei, 1969: 148, emphasis in original).

Around the same time, and with no reference to Claude or Peccei, an extraordinary article appeared that had the potential to change the entire field of IR. Penned by the Polish–American political scientist George Modelski, the 1968 essay discussed the connection between 'globalization' and 'world politics' in a comprehensive way:

A condition for the emergence of a multiple-autonomy form of world politics arguably is the development of a global layer of interaction substantial enough to support continuous and diversified institutionalization. We may define this process as globalization; it is the result of the increasing size, complexity and sophistication of world society. Growth and consolidation of global interdependence and the emergent necessities of devising ways and means of handling the problems arising therefrom support an increasingly elaborate network of organizations. World order in such a system would be the product of the interplay of these organizations, and world politics an effort to regulate these interactions. (Modelski, 1968: 389)

[14] In the 1950s and 1960s, Claude and Modelski were joined by only a handful of fellow IR scholars like Trygve Mathisen (1959) and Michael Brecher (1963) in the use of the phrases 'globalization of international relations' or 'globalization of politics'. But the frequency of these terms increased markedly during the 1970s; see, for example, Kolodziej (1971), Senghaas (1973: 165), and Garrett (1976: 392). Moreover, in the context of the ongoing Cold War, these phrases began to sprout new permutations such as 'globalization of US power', 'globalization of Chinese foreign policy', and 'globalization of the Cold War'; see Slater (1976: 74), Walli (1976: 461), Cook (1976: 707), and Byung-joon (1980).

In the same year his article appeared, Modelski led a team of social science researchers at the University of Washington in drafting an application to the US National Science Foundation, which, for the first time, used 'globalization' in the title of a comprehensive research project: 'The Study of Globalization: A Preliminary Exploration'. Unfortunately, this highly innovative application was soundly rejected, halting Modelski's efforts on the subject for two decades. As it turned out, this politics and IR trajectory of 'globalization research' had to be revised and reconfigured several times before the first grant to study 'globalization' was finally awarded. In the end, Modelski's sophisticated rendition of a complex process had surprisingly little academic impact, even though the author defined 'globalization' in a way that prefigured the heated 1990s' discussions on its political dimensions. For years, no citations appeared that linked the article to other discussions of globalization. In fact, a Google Scholar search reveals that Modelski's 1968 essay was only cited a total of seven times. The IR scholar William R. Thompson, for example, referred to the article in 1981, but failed to mention the term 'globalization' around which Modelski's original article was framed. Ironically, Thompson would later go on to write extensively on the process of globalization—including as Modelski's co-author.

Still, Modelski's conceptualization of world order and world politics as 'globalization' foreshadowed later challenges to the canonical status of the 'international' in IR that were launched in the 1970s and 1980s by political scientists like James Rosenau (1976; 1990), Robert Keohane, and Joseph Nye (Keohane and Nye, 1977). These scholars employed terms and phrases like 'complex interdependence' and 'transnationalism' to emphasize the changing dynamics of the international system and the roles played by reconfigured states and a growing variety of non-state actors. Recognizing the rapid transformation of the power and authority of national governments under globalizing conditions, Robert Keohane (1984) eventually argued for a revision of IR's key concept of sovereignty from a territorially defined barrier to a bargaining resource for politics characterized by complex transnational networks. As Barrie Axford (2013: 38) notes, this new 'transnational' theoretical orientation in IR partly corresponded with the more fluid approaches of 'international political economists' and 'regime theorists' who, some years later, would examine the workings of institutionalized systems of co-operation in 'global' issue areas such as economic development, climate change, surveillance, and digital technology.

There is no question that, during the 1970s and early 1980s, the use of globalization as related to all four of its principal meaning branches increased and intensified markedly. There is also clear evidence for the proliferation of new areas of application, such as:

'globalization of modern technology' (Brucan, 1975: 64); 'globalization of food markets' (Nau, 1978: 776); 'globalization of sports' (Mazrui, 1977); 'globalization of the social environment' (Tiryakian, 1982: 353); and 'globalization of social, economic, and financial problems' (Brucan, 1984: 108). But these references to new fields of application were not always linked to substantive discussions designed to deepen the meaning of the concept. Take, for example, an article penned by the sociologist Paul Lamy (1976) with the promising heading, 'The Globalization of American Sociology: Excellence or Imperialism?' Except for the title, perhaps given by an editor, the concept was not once used in the text. The closest the author came to implying a specific meaning of globalization was in the article's abstract, which links the general spatial concept of 'international expansion' to his thesis of the disciplinary expansion of American-style sociology to other countries. In the overall schema of the article, then, 'globalization' was not given any pressing analytical significance and ultimately disappeared inside a different conceptual framework.

At the same time, however, an increasing number of observers in the early 1980s consciously used the term in a much more significant way to indicate the dawn of a new historical epoch. For example, in his analysis of the brief border war between Vietnam and China in 1979, the British IR scholar Les Buszynski (1980: 829) links the conflict explicitly to a new 'era of globalization'. Additional evidence for this qualitative shift in the use of the concept was reflected in the creation of new terms that represented variations on 'globalization'. A particularly relevant 1980 snapshot shows the largely unsuccessful attempt by the American world-system scholar Albert Bergesen to introduce the term 'globology' as a general signifier for a new sociological paradigm dedicated to the study of interdependent world social relations (Bergesen, 1980).[15] Less than two decades later, a reconfigured and methodologically more diverse 'global studies' permutation of Bergesen's 'globology' initiative found its permanent place in the academy as a new transdisciplinary field (Steger and Wahlrab, 2017).

The Many-Branched Tree of Globalization: The Short Period of the Conceptual Convergence, Early 1980s–Early 1990s

By the 1980s, the economistic meaning association of globalization with a worldwide integration of markets was experiencing a noticeable

---

[15] Similarly, but independent of Bergesen's work, the term 'globalistics' emerged at the turn of the twenty-first century in the Russian academic context to denote a cross-disciplinary integrative field of social scientific research devoted to the study of globalization (Chumakov, 2008).

upswing. As we noted above, however, business-orientated meanings had regularly surfaced during the three decades preceding the publication of Theodore Levitt's immensely influential *Harvard Business Review* article. What was once a rather modest bough of the many-branched genealogical tree of globalization—exemplified in François Perroux's offhand remark in 1964 about the 'globalization of markets'—gained a more secure place in the growing literature on the rise of the multinational corporation and international business management popularized in the 1970s by the Austro-American management guru Peter Drucker (1969: 74–5) and other advocates of what came to be called 'the new world economy'. Ultimately, the neoliberal revolution of the Thatcher–Reagan era helped turn the globalization-as-market narrative into the dominant meaning cluster.

Levitt's 1983 essay imbued the concept with strong neoliberal meanings, allowing it to escape its academic business school context and infiltrate the public discourse for good. Global power elites disseminated Levitt's neoliberal ideological perspective of 'globalization' as a beneficial process driven by the new digital technologies that were destined to lift millions out of poverty while furthering the spread of democracy and freedom around the globe. For example, without acknowledging the reference, American globalization guru Thomas Friedman (2007) adopted one of the subheadings in Levitt's essay as the title of his bestseller, *The World Is Flat*. Indeed, Levitt's article had a strong impact on the popular depiction of globalization as 'inevitable'—an 'inexorable' economic process mediated by new technologies and destined to give birth to a 'global market for standardized consumer products on a previously unimagined scale of magnitude'.

But the description of what the Harvard scholar considered 'indisputable empirical trends' was inseparable from his neoliberal ideological prescriptions. For example, he insisted that multinational companies had no choice but to transform themselves into global corporations capable of operating in a more cost-effective way by standardizing their products. The necessary elimination of costly adjustments to various national markets depended, according to Levitt, on their swift adoption of a 'global approach'. What the author had in mind was the willingness of CEOs to think and act 'as if the world were one large market—ignoring superficial regional and national differences ... It [the global corporation] sells the same things in the same way everywhere' (Levitt, 1983: 92–100).

Levitt's stated imperative of economic homogenization along the lines of the Anglo-American neoliberal model inspired hundreds of similar pieces in business magazines and journals that sought to convince leading companies to 'go global'. The advertising industry, in

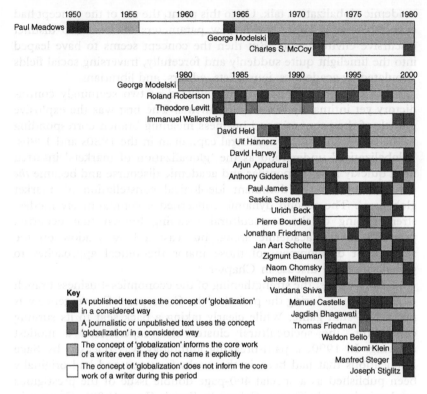

Figure 2.2 The use of 'globalization' by select authors, 1950s–2000

particular, set about creating 'global brands' by means of worldwide marketing campaigns. Hence, it is hardly surprising that the founder of the advertising giant Saatchi and Saatchi was one of Levitt's most fervent disciples. As we noted in Chapter 1, the collapse of the Soviet Bloc less than a decade later supercharged the seamless merger of Levitt's mantra of the 'inevitable globalization of markets' with an American political triumphalism that celebrated the relegation of communism to the 'dustbin of history'.

Our critical genealogical investigation reveals the occurrence of a leap in the meaning formation of the keyword towards the end of the decade. As Figure 2.2 shows, the relatively short period from the early 1980s through the 1990s constitutes the richest yet at the same time most challenging segment of the many-branched meaning tree that is 'globalization'. These years mark a pivotal time characterized by what we think of as the 'Conceptual Convergence' involving popular and academic globalization talk. Up to this point, the use of the concept had occurred largely within the narrow parameters of these two distinct discursive environments. But then the concept seems to have leaped into the limelight quite suddenly and forcefully, traversing social fields populated by academics, journalists, editors, and librarians.

The Conceptual Convergence consisted of two seemingly contradictory yet intimately related movements. The first was the explosive growth of the economic and business meaning branch corresponding to the take-off phase of neoliberal capitalism in the 1980s and 1990s. 'Globalization' understood as the 'globalization of markets' inserted itself quickly into the popular and academic discourse and became *the* core concept of the dominant ideological constellation of 'market globalism'. The second dynamic concerned a comparatively modest strengthening of the sociocultural meaning branch that occurred primarily in the academic arena, but cast a long shadow on the subsequent development of those major theoretical approaches to globalization we discuss in Chapter 3.

In other words, the strengthening of the economics–business branch of globalization during the period of the Conceptual Convergence was not a zero-sum game. While clearly taking a back seat to its surging competitor, the sociocultural cluster also experienced a modest upswing. In 1990, a path-breaking anthology was released by Sage Publications that had been in the works for years and had originally been published as a special 400-page double issue of the prestigious academic journal, *Theory, Culture & Society* (June 1990). Created in 1982 as an interdisciplinary project working across the borders of sociology and cultural studies, the periodical's editors endeavoured to establish *the* prime forum for cutting-edge social theorists eager to overcome the long-standing divide between the social sciences and the humanities. Titled *Global Culture: Nationalism, Globalization and Modernity*, the 1990 volume succeeded admirably in this objective by bringing together a group of authors who were to become some of the most important writers on the global: Arjun Appadurai, Zygmunt Bauman, Peter Beyer, Jonathan Friedman, Ulf Hannerz, Anthony King, Roland Robertson, Bryan Turner, and Immanuel Wallerstein. All went on to write on globalization in depth and some became pioneers of the fledgling transdisciplinary field of global studies.[16] The anthology was the brainchild of the journal's editor-in-chief, the British sociologist Mike Featherstone (1990), who assumed a pivotal role in globalization

[16] On the difference between globalization studies and global studies, see our discussion in Chapter 7, as well as Steger and Wahlrab (2017).

studies, although he did not contribute any major scholarly mono-graphs on the subject. As we noted in Chapter 1, Robertson's and Appadurai's critical reflections generated more interest in global cul-tural dynamics and stimulated established social theorists like Ulf Hannerz (1996), John Tomlinson (1999), and Ulrich Beck (2000) to make vital contributions to the development of cultural approaches to globalization.

Gathering even more force in the growing popular discourse on globa-lization, the concept eventually made the leap into the consciousness of the masses, where it assumed a prominent position as *the* new keyword of its time. As Jan Aart Scholte (2005: 51) noted some years later, the proliferation of global talk seemed unlikely to be accidental. The growing popularity of the term arguably reflected a widespread intuition that contemporary social relations were undergoing an important shift in character. Interviews with a dozen academic globalization pioneers of the 1990s shed light on this short but crucial period of the Conceptual Convergence (Steger and James, 2015). Constituting an indispensable element in our systematic effort to understand the genealogical dynamics of the keyword, these substantive interviews confirm that the Conceptual Convergence seems to have occurred quickly and without much fanfare. As it turned out, nearly all of the globalization pioneers we interviewed did not remember a distinct 'eureka' moment at which the concept took an axiomatic hold upon their minds or whether they absorbed it from the popular discourse or their own academic environments. What our con-versations show, however, is that the entire discursive environment of the late 1980s and early 1990s was becoming increasingly laden with 'globa-lization'. It is not clear whether these globalization pioneers absorbed the term from the mass media or thought that they had produced it from their own literary imaginations. But it seems that the concept was somehow 'already there' and ready to be deployed in more specific ways related to their own academic interests.

For example, Arjun Appadurai noted that he 'probably' came upon the concept 'in the very late 1980s—most likely sometime between 1989 and 1991. I would say it was after the fall of the Berlin Wall. The context? Most likely, I read about "globalization" in the press, rather than encoun-tering the term through an academic route'. Religion scholar Mark Juergensmeyer concurred: 'I also remember a lot of talk about "globaliza-tion" in the immediate aftermath of the fall of the Berlin Wall. So that would put my encounter with the concept sometime around 1989 or 1990'. Likewise, Nobel Prize-winning economist Joseph Stiglitz con-fessed, 'I don't remember the context or the first time I heard "globaliza-tion". Perhaps it was around the publication of Thomas Friedman's book, *The Lexus and the Olive Tree* [1999] or a bit earlier'. Similarly, the social anthropologist Jonathan Friedman found it hard to date his first encounter with the concept: 'The media were starting to use "globalization" and business got into the act as well. And I remember a lot of talk about the "end of the nation-state" [in the 1990s], which was very much linked to this new buzzword "globalization"'. The same goes for global historian Nayan Chanda: 'I don't recall exactly the first time I encountered "globalization", but it must have been in the early 1990s'. Saskia Sassen joined the chorus: 'I cannot remember the exact moment when it happened. All I know is that I found myself at some point using it' (Steger and James, 2015: 44–125).

Roland Robertson represents the notable exception to these voices, asserting that he had actually coined the term in 1979 when he had been in the process of rethinking the key sociological concept of 'modernization'. As he recalls, 'Consciously, I first heard it ["globalization"] from my own mouth ... I said to myself, "Modernization is not just about a particular society—it's the modernization of the world". So if it is clumsy to call it "modernization of the whole world", so what should I call it? So, I called it "globalization", and that's how it all began' (Robertson, in Steger and James, 2015: 31). Robertson's sincere—yet mistaken—conviction that he had 'invented' a brand-new concept *ex nihilo* reflects not only his unawareness of the term's long genealogical evolution, but also its low profile in the academic community at the time. Still, Robertson's early articles on the subject in the 1980s resurrected the sociocultural branch of 'globalization' that had largely withered after Paul Meadows' initial musings in the 1950s.

As the conceptual career of globalization took off in the 1990s, the academic careers of most of these globalization pioneers followed suit. Again, we employ the pointed phrase 'career of a concept' (Carver, 2004) in a critical sense to flag our intention to attend to the important contextual and professional dynamics of power and interests with regard to the burgeoning use of the term. The rise of globalization can hardly be separated from the careers of numerous persons and collectivities— academics and others—who endowed the concept with specific meanings that entered into the intensifying swirl of the discourse. And yet, the concept gathered too much force too quickly to be controlled by any single person or specific intellectual current or lineage. As Figure 2.2 shows, academics and journalists from social backgrounds and affiliated with different ideological perspectives engaged in a self-conscious process of career building through accruing valuable cultural capital associated with the rising concept. After all, a person's reputation in academia and journalism often depends on his or her ability to name crucial phenomena or invent new terms with the potential of gaining traction. But in relation to coining or claiming concepts as a way of advancing in the academic status game, the assertion of maintaining a privileged relationship with globalization did not always or immediately lift the professional standing of some of the main scholars in the fields who we interviewed.

Concluding Reflections

Tracing the erratic emergence of the keyword 'globalization' across four distinct genealogical branches from the 1920s to the 1990s, we argued in this chapter that a careful genealogical mapping of the concept represents an indispensable preliminary task in the attempt to expand our understanding of why and how it came to matter so much in the 1990s and beyond. Ultimately, then, the central aim of our discussion was to respond to the four critical questions raised at the outset of this chapter in more substantive ways. Our genealogical enquiry offers better explanations of how it happened that such an inelegant and unwieldy word as 'globalization' began to define the twentieth-century sense of social change in the English-speaking world and beyond.

While its meaning formation occurred in interaction with objective processes unfolding in the materially globalizing world that it described, neither a purely analytic delineation nor a broad historical contextualization of those processes is sufficient in itself to gauge the full genealogical scope of the concept's emergence and contemporary use. Our critical investigation suggests that, across the middle quarters of the twentieth century, 'globalization' generally figured as little more than a 'loose descriptor with little analytical shape' (Scholte, 2016: 223). It was deployed with a surprising variety of meanings and in different social contexts. As the popular and academic discourses on the subject converged in the 1980s, however, the term began to function as a powerful 'condensation symbol', capable of compressing a whole coterie of ideas and notions into a single keyword. As Doris Graber (1976: 134) suggests, condensation symbols are crucial concepts, buzzwords, phrases, emblems, and stereotypes capable of injecting intense emotional and affective power into what is said about a phenomenon and how it should be understood in specific historical settings. Our mapping exercise confirms that 'globalization' functioned in the early 1990s as a 'well connected condensation symbol in a network of meaning primed by the context' (Kaufer and Carley, 1993: 202). It stimulated a whole host of evaluations, cognitions, and feelings about what people increasingly perceived as a shrinking world.

Indeed, the concept gained traction from the successful condensation of associations across four analytic levels of the formation of social meaning, all of which we discuss in much detail in Chapter 4. On the most palpable level of ideas, the concept engendered some momentum as key academics, librarians, editors, and journalists attempted to explain large-scale social change and its associated altered fields of understanding. As our discussion has shown, however, such mediated meaning formations occurred along distinct genealogical branches and sometimes resulted in indeterminate and discontinuous meaning trajectories. Individual articulators like Paul Meadows or George Modelski were crucial to developing richer meaning orbits, but the staying power and spread of concepts depended upon deeper levels of meaning formation in subsequent decades.

At the second level of ideologies, contestation over understandings and explanations took these specific circulations and consolidations of meaning further into applied political territory. This chapter suggests that the burgeoning of the concept of 'globalization' benefitted greatly from various advocates of neoliberal capitalism who placed it within a conceptual framework that provided the ammunition for their free market-orientated political programs and agendas. As some of our historical snapshots demonstrate, one especially powerful ideological understanding of globalization originated in the field of business studies and economics. Moreover, our interviews with globalization pioneers in the 1990s clarified how the concept entered the arena of ideological contestation, which fuelled an emerging globalization debate characterized by the Conceptual Convergence of popular and academic discourses on the subject (Steger and James, 2015).

At the even deeper meaning layer of social imaginaries, 'globalization' framed the pre-reflexive background understandings of intensifying social interdependence. Concepts tend to take off when they are capable of articulating a changing subjective and objective sense of the social whole. Across most of the course of the twentieth century, and despite alternative ideologies of cosmopolitanism and internationalism, a predominantly national imaginary had prevailed as the common sense of what people projected as the 'natural home' for their communal longings and imaginings.

As we discussed at the outset of the chapter, in the second half of the twentieth century, a new global imaginary slowly and erratically emerged from within the old background understanding. At the same time, new ideas of the 'global' were forced to come to semantic compromises with the previously dominant national imaginary. Even today, discussions of the global carry forward parts of this conceptual inheritance as reflected in related terms such as inter*national* relations, trans*national* connections, or '*a* world system'. Our genealogical enquiry explains why these terms continue to exert a strong but anachronistic hold on the public imagination—a process aptly named by Raymond Williams (2005) as moving between being 'dominant' and 'residual'.[17] Moreover, during the two middle quarters of the twentieth century, academic careers were being built on the keyword and its associated fields of 'international relations' and 'international studies'. Still, our interviews with globalization pioneers capture how influential IR scholars like George Modelski or James Mittelman grappled for decades with the dissonance between their academic career expectations tied to the 'international' paradigm and their growing conceptual affinity for the 'global' in ways that gradually facilitated their fertile encounter with 'globalization' (Steger and James, 2015).

Concepts resemble the tip of the iceberg sitting on the larger ontological level of meaning formation. Our genealogical research suggests that, at this deepest level of the 'human condition', the keyword tapped into a core of social meanings about contemporary shifts in time, space, embodiment, and other profound dimensions of social relations, including what it meant to be 'modern'. Although generations of academics had used the concept 'modernity' long before 'globalization', both terms experienced a remarkable discursive revitalization in the 1980s, not least by means of the strong postmodern challenge to the 'grand metanarratives' of modernity (Lyotard, 1979; Habermas, 1990). What is telling about the revitalization of the 'modernity debate' is that many of the globalization pioneers we interviewed drew explicit connections between this dynamic and their fledgling attempts to make sense of the global. Thus, globalization came to be associated with processes of modernity that were—and still are—changing the world in fundamental ways. Popular and academic language use was forced to catch up with transformative social change and its associated social practices and meanings. As it did, the unfolding career of the keyword 'globalization' contributed significantly to interpreting these social dynamics at all four levels of meaning formation.

---

[17] Across the course of this book, we use the terms developed by Raymond Williams —'dominant', 'emergent', 'residual', and 'archaic'—as adjectives to signal the complex interweaving of dominant and subordinate meanings and practices. Moreover, we employ these adjectives in our discussion the intersection of ontological formations. For example, 'modernity' constitutes the dominant contemporary formation, yet it faces challenges from emergent postmodernism and the persistence of subordinate traditional and customary ways of life. In this context, we introduce a fifth term to Williams's schema: 'enduring'. Still, 'enduring' practices do not need to be oppositional in order to exert continuing influence.

3 Rethinking the Dominant Framework of Globalization Theory

As we demonstrated in Chapters 1 and 2, both the frequency and intensity of the use of the keyword 'globalization' increased dramatically during the last two decades of the twentieth century. So did the production of thematic studies of globalization as a set of *objective processes*, many of which attempted to map and explore its major domains.[1] The ensuing springtime of scholarship on global-scale processes and their social impacts marked the first period of sustained academic investigation of globalization and how it should be conceptualized and analysed. But what was it that made these pioneering academics at the fin de siècle think that globalization added significant value to the understanding of contemporary social dynamics and thus mattered so much that it had to be examined as an objective phenomenon *in itself*?

We suggest that a significant part of the answer can be found in a major systemic shift that occurred in social enquiry and intellectual practice, in part as a result of intensifying globalization processes.[2] Coupled with other significant technological developments across the second half of the twentieth century, the rapid expansion of social relations and consciousness contributed to an unsettling of older certainties about traditional social norms and the relationship of humans to God and nature (Turner, 1994; Juergensmeyer, 2000; 2008; Taylor, 2007; Christoff and Eckersley, 2013).[3] These destabilizations amounted to much more than

---

[1] To a lesser extent, these works also explored new forms of subjectivity linked to the rise of the global imaginary. See our discussion on the subjective dimensions of globalization in Chapter 4.

[2] Similarly, Roland Benedikter (2013) refers to a 'global systemic shift' in key dimensions of modern societies. By contrast, Peter Dicken's (2015: 3) notion of a 'global shift' is more narrowly confined to economic and technological aspects. See also our pertinent discussion in Chapters 1 and 2.

[3] We use the concept of *relativism* to denote a dominant valence of the postmodern, while we refer to the dominant valence of the modern as *constructivism*. In constructivist terms, the basic categories of human existence such as time and space become the terrain of different projects. Bodies, landscapes, genome systems, nation-states, and political systems become projects for *construction* and *reconstruction*. In relativist terms, (re)construction is displaced by *deconstruction*, which allows for new appeals to what in the age of Trump is called 'post-truth'.

the periodic disorientations in the evolution of modern societies. They involved a profound transformation of local relations, affecting the dominant valences of everyday social life. The associated destabilization of the modern national imaginary by global-scale dynamics fuelled a fierce intellectual assault on the hegemonic status of modernity in social and political theory.[4]

In a rush of philosophical exuberance, one influential social thinker even went so far as to argue that humanity was exiting the modern era and heading into a fundamentally altered 'global age' (Albrow, 1996; 2007). Here, Martin Albrow's argument runs into trouble for a number of reasons. First, it makes a singular epochal claim, assuming the singularity of the global imaginary—perhaps because it presents itself as such—and it leaves out the tensions and contradictions that ensue in the overlaying of multiple ontological formations. Second, it involves a category mistake by treating a spatial concept—globalization—that signifies the extension of social relations and consciousness across world-space and world-time as if it were an ontological condition or formation in the same way that 'the modern' or 'the postmodern' might be conceptualized. On the upside, however, Albrow's work made a significant contribution to social theory by advancing an extremely provocative thesis that foregrounded the magnitude of the ways in which modern living and knowing were being destabilized—including in the privileged Global North.

Albrow was not alone in thinking that something profound was happening to the modern social order. Scores of social thinkers in the early 1990s argued that social change had entered an unprecedented phase that required novel vantage points and innovative ways of theorizing (Beck, 1992; Lash and Friedman, 1992; Beck, Giddens, and Lash, 1994; Featherstone, Lash, and Robertson, 1996). As we discussed in Chapter 2, some of them adopted the term 'globalization' to describe the fundamental shift associated with people's acute and profound sense of discontinuity and change. In the process, these scholars constructed a discrete body of 'globalization theory' that framed the vigorous globalization debates of the 1990s and beyond. While Marx and Engels' reflections on the subject might appear quite dated, we submit that their notion of the liquidity of modernity astutely prefigured our current era of

---

[4] A number of thinkers came to describe this shift as the supersession of the epoch of modernity by postmodernity (Jameson, 1991). We approach this question less epochally. In our terms, while our present unsettled age remains dominated by the modern, it has become overlaid by an emergent formation of the postmodern, intersecting with subordinate customary and traditional relations. In the ensuing chapters, we work with four basic ontological formations in our analysis—customary, traditional, modern, and postmodern. We treat these categories as layers of social life rather than successive, separate epochs.

enhanced reflexivity about humanity's globalizing existence: 'All that is solid melts into air, all that is holy is profaned, and man is at last forced to face with sober senses, his real conditions of life, and his relations with his kind' (Marx and Engels, 1848: 17).[5]

The proliferating scholarly forays into these intensifying liquidity dynamics of the waning twentieth century resulted in the publication of landmark surveys of globalization by Malcolm Waters (1995), James Mittelman (1996; 2000), Tony Spybey (1996), Robert Schaeffer (1997), Alan Scott (1997), Robert Holton (1998), David Held (Held et al., 1999; 2007), Ulrich Beck (1999, 2000), Colin Hay and David Marsh (2000), Frank Lechner and John Boli (2000), Jan Aart Scholte (2000), Richard Langhorne (2001), El-Ojeili and Hayden (2006), and others. Guiding their readers through the thicket of the proliferating globalization literature, these primers introduced remarkably similar conceptualizations of objective global-scale processes that still dominate the field of global studies today. The most significant feature that most of these formative works had in common was their representation of scholarship on the global by means of a diachronic 'three-wave' classification scheme. The corresponding tripartite division of globalization theory into competing 'camps' or 'schools of thought' was widely embraced and reproduced in numerous studies on the subject and soon became the conceptual foundation of the dominant framework of globalization theory (Kofman and Youngs, 1996; Held et al., 1999; Hay and Marsh, 2000; Martell, 2007). It shaped the debate on the subject for the next two decades by providing what came to be seen as an unofficial 'gold standard' of informed enquiry on the subject. In fact, the three-wave model became so deeply ingrained in academic globalization debates that periodic attempts to facilitate theoretical innovation were reflexively interpreted within the dominant model as more or less successful 'third-wave efforts' to move beyond the critical insights of second-wave sceptics (Martell, 2007).

Picking up the globalization story in the 1990s where we left off in our previous discussion, this chapter shifts from genealogical enquiry to an assessment of the main currents of globalization theory. The bulk of our exposition is taken up with a critical overview of the conventional three-wave model, followed by the introduction and explication of our alternative classification scheme that frames our own theoretical model elaborated in Chapters 4 and 5. We end this chapter with our contention that the desired evolution of global theory should not depend upon the

---

[5] 'Liquid modernity' is also the central metaphor in Zygmunt Bauman's influential reflections on globalization (Bauman, 1998; 2000).

realization of a superior third-wave position built primarily on the exposure of the conceptual shortcomings alleged to inhere in representations associated with the previous two waves. Rather, global theory must balance the necessary critical impulse directed at existing accounts with an appreciative absorption of the rich insights contained in the four interconnected conceptual approaches identified in this chapter.[6]

The Dominant Framework of Globalization Theory

For the last two decades, the hegemonic narrative of globalization theory has been organized around a conceptual model that postulates the existence of three competing main currents. Usually presented as 'waves' or 'phases' of globalization theory, these intellectual streams have been portrayed in authoritative texts as comprising distinct groups of competing scholars widely referred to as 'hyperglobalizers', 'sceptics', and 'transformationalists' (Kofman and Youngs, 1996; Held et al., 1999; Hay and Marsh, 2000; Martell, 2007; Chirico, 2014; Dicken, 2015). This dominant representational model contains two additional propositions. The first is the diachronic temporal claim that three distinct waves of scholarship on the global have followed each other in quick succession during the 1990s and beyond. The second proposition is the qualitative claim that three corresponding 'broad schools of thought' represent antagonistic and mutually incompatible perspectives on globalization. At the same time, however, the dominant accounts posit conceptual homogeneity within these theoretical currents by insisting that each 'reflects a general set of arguments and conclusions about globalization with respect to its conceptualization, causal dynamics, socio-economic consequences, implications for state power and governance, and historical trajectory' (Held et al., 1999: 2–3).

The relatively small but influential group of 'hyperglobalizers' has been portrayed as making up the bulk of the initial wave of globalization theory. These writers are said to have elevated the current compression of time and space to the status of the primary driver of contemporary social change (Reich, 1991; Ruggie, 1993; Barnet and Cavanagh, 1994). According to the dominant interpretation, first-wave accounts emphasize an epochal shift in the constitution of contemporary societies that has ushered in a fundamentally new period in history: the global age (Albrow, 1996; Gray, 1996). Adopting a teleological perspective similar to the

---

[6] Like Jan-Aart Scholte (2016), Barrie Axford (2013), and many other globalization scholars, we consider 'global theory' and 'globalization theory' to be interchangeable designations for social thought focused on the global.

determinism of early market globalists like Theodore Levitt, many of the writers associated with the first-wave category employ a sweeping economistic narrative. As Held and his collaborators assert, 'Hyperglobalizers argue that economic globalization is bringing about a "denationalization" of economies through the establishment of transnational networks of production, trade, and finance' (Held et al., 1999: 3).

The hegemonic framework of globalization theory usually identifies the influential Japanese management guru Kenichi Ohmae as one of the prime examples of first-wave thinkers. In his influential books, Ohmae (1990; 1995) celebrated new forms of techno-economic interconnectivity as the indispensable central nervous system of a hypercompetitive 'borderless world'. He envisioned transnational investment and commodity flows directed by globally interlinked electronic stock markets operating 24/7 as the catalysts for the imperative jettisoning of the last vestiges of antiquated trade protectionism. He expressed the hope that 'archaic' nationalist sentiments at the core of crucial modern legal notions such as 'state sovereignty' would soon be eclipsed by the border-traversing logic of global capitalism (Guéhenno, 1995; Ohmae, 1995).

Offering a far more nuanced and politically sophisticated account than Ohmae, international relations scholar Susan Strange, too, is frequently included among this category of first-wavers. She argued that intensifying globalization processes meant that nation-states could no longer dodge the threat of obsolescence: 'Where states once were masters of markets, now it is the markets which, on many crucial issues, are the masters over the governments of states' (1996: 4). Criticizing hyperglobalizers for their 'misleading simplifications', 'uncritical assertions', and the 'general thinness' of their empirical evidence, dominant accounts of the globalization debates in the 1990s and beyond assert that the earliest wave of globalization theory was losing much of its momentum by the turn of the century (Hay and Marsh, 2000: 4; Martell, 2007: 174).

The dominant conceptual model places the two remaining camps of 'sceptics' and 'transformationalists' into the category of 'second-wave globalization theory' that is said to have emerged in response to earlier hyperglobalist accounts (Hay and Marsh, 2000; Martell, 2007). Allegedly committed to the production of more 'sober', 'sophisticated', and 'empirically orientated' globalization research, the group of sceptics is presented as a relatively united camp populated by theorists who emphasize the continuing significance of nation-states and regional dynamics. Warning their readers to beware of 'the more enthusiastic of the globalists and transnationalists', sceptics charged their hyperglobalist competitors with lacking a sense of history, which, in turn, led to their exaggerations of the decline of the nation-state and their associated failure to appreciate the enduring centrality of the post-war *international* system (Mann, 1997; Waltz, 1999; Keohane and Nye, 2000). At the core of the dominant portrayal of such sceptical second-wavers, one finds the firm rejection of the hyperglobalist thesis of an intensifying 'world society' in favour of the claim that today's expanding social networks contain 'no singular, relatively systemic principle of interaction or integration' (Mann, 1997: 494).[7]

Paul Hirst and Grahame Thompson (1996) represent the prime example of sceptical second-wavers cited in nearly all authoritative overviews of the globalization debate. Building on David Gordon's (1988) earlier insights, the British political scientists argued that the world economy has never been a truly *global* phenomenon. At best, it amounted to just another wave of internationalization in the form of a limited *regional* dynamic confined to North America, Europe, East Asia, and Australia. Without a genuine worldwide economic system, there could be no such thing as 'globalization'. Hirst and Thompson linked their sceptical case against the existence of economic globalization to their criticism of the hyperglobalist misuse of the term 'globalization' in both the popular and academic discourse: 'As we proceeded [with our economic research], our scepticism deepened until we became convinced that globalization, as conceived by the more extreme globalizers, is largely a myth' (Hirst and Thompson, 1996: 2).

Similarly, neo-Marxist critics Immanuel Wallerstein (2000) and Justin Rosenberg (2000; 2005) are often mentioned as examples of second-wave sceptics committed to the view that globalization hardly represents an epochal transformation. Rather, they saw it as amounting to little more than an empty signifier given to the latest phase in the evolution of capitalism. Wallerstein (2000), for example, rejected the generalizing force of the concept of 'globalization' as 'meaningless'. What others called 'globalization', he suggested, was just the epiphenomenon of a contemporary transition period in the world economy. As the concept enjoyed a long phase of popularity, however, Wallerstein (2011) eventually incorporated it into his world-systems theory as a lower-level background term. A final group of academics cited as exemplars of the sceptical approach includes scholars who engaged in a systematic analysis of the risks posed by even limited forms of international economic integration. These sceptics took hyperglobalist economists to task for downplaying obvious systemic dangers such as the looming threat of social

---

[7] The concept of a 'world society' has been linked to globalization debates by the sociologist John W. Meyer (2000; 2007) and other social theorists influenced by his work (Krücken and Drori, 2009).

disintegration as a result of unfettered economic globalization (Rodrik, 1997; Scott, 1997).

The third perspective on the subject is associated in conventional accounts with theorists who consider globalization as a profoundly transformative set of deterritorializing processes capable of moving human societies towards unprecedented levels of interconnectivity (Castells, 1996–98; Held et al., 1999; Sassen, 1999; Scholte, 2005). As David Held and his co-authors (1999: 7) explain:

In comparison with the sceptical and hyperglobalist accounts, the transformationalists make no claims about the future trajectory of globalization; nor do they seek to evaluate the present in relation to some single, fixed 'globalized world', whether a global market or a global civilization ... Such caution about the exact future of globalization is matched, nonetheless, by the conviction that contemporary patterns of global economic, military, technological, ecological, migratory, political and cultural flows are historically unprecedented.

This passage reveals that the transformationalist position is typically portrayed as showing a penchant for macroanalytical approaches and for confining research efforts to only one or two major dimensions of globalization. With regard to its cultural aspects, transformationalists explored the tensions between sameness and differences in transnational formations (Hannerz, 1996; Jameson and Miyoshi, 1998; Tomlinson, 1999). At the same time, however, transformationalists are said to have accepted the sceptical claim that globalization should not be seen as a single, monolithic process, but as a complex, often contradictory, and uneven set of processes involving sub-global scales as well. International relations scholar James Rosenau (2003: 11) used the term 'fragmegration' to describe such 'pervasive interaction between fragmenting and integrating dynamics unfolding at every level of community'.

This alleged willingness of transformationalists to incorporate sceptical insights into their position led to conflicting interpretations among the authors of influential three-wave accounts. Some insist that the partial acceptance of sceptical views by the transformationalist camp is not significant enough to undermine its theoretical distinctiveness and therefore does not endanger its status as a separate school of thought (Held et al., 1999). Others suggest that partial overlap between sceptics and transformationalists indicates that their theoretical differences have been exaggerated (Hay and Marsh, 2000). These conflicted assessments of the distinctiveness of the transformationalist position beg the question as to what extent the latter camp actually constitutes a 'third wave'. Consequently, some scholars propose that there have only been two waves of globalization theory, since transformationalists have been unable to advance beyond the conceptual ground staked out by second-wave sceptics (Kofman and Youngs, 1996; Hay and Marsh, 2000). In an attempt to split the difference, later commentators like Luke Martell (2007: 194) propose that the transformationalist position has progressed beyond the second wave, yet it has fallen short of staking out a genuine third position: 'Transformationalists share many of the doubts of the sceptics in practice and express them in their own analyses but move away from them when coming to more globalist conclusions'.

Today, this once-lively third-wave debate has grown stale, exposing the limitations of the dominant framework. To be sure, waves and corresponding schools of thought are accessible metaphors that possess descriptive utility, especially for introductory surveys of major approaches to globalization.[8] But they have less value for the development of global theory beyond such entrenched and rather petrified positions. For this reason, we introduce an alternative framework that breaks down the existing camp mentality of the dominant three-wave model by presenting complementary insights drawn from multiple perspectives. We seek to theorize the complexity of shifting globalization dynamics in ways that draw out shared patterns of practice and overlapping historical trajectories. The conceptual progress in scholarship on the global depends on rethinking the dominant theoretical framework built on the simplistic and misleading proposition of successive waves and chronic divisions.[9]

A New Typology of Globalization Theory

Our typology takes as its point of departure a critique of the dominant three-wave model. In particular, we object to its aforementioned temporal and qualitative claims. Departing from the diachronic narrative of three successive waves that have defined the globalization debate, our synchronic framework conveys a much messier picture of simultaneous and frequent interactions among four analytically distinct modes of theorizing the global: *neoclassical theorists, domain theorists, complexity theorists*, and *generalizing theorists*. To be clear, these are intersecting modes of theorizing, not ideal types. These mutually reinforcing approaches developed their profile throughout the 1990s and beyond in a complex

[8] Indeed, we have used the hyperglobalist/sceptical/transformationalist template for descriptive purposes in our own introductory work on globalization. See, for example, Steger (2014; 2017a) and Steger and James (2015).

[9] Thus, we applaud Barrie Axford's observation that the time has come to 'move on' from what he calls 'the hackneyed trinity of hyperglobalism, transformationalism, and scepticism' (2016: 7). Nick Bisley (2007: 18), too, criticizes Held's tripartite classification scheme, but replaces it with another rather conventional 'domain' typology of economic, political, and sociological perspectives on globalization.

interplay of both contrasting and overlapping discourses on various dimensions of globalization.

Although the works of major globalization theorists tend to cut across all of these four categories, their special affinity for one or two of these modes makes it possible to associate them *primarily* with one or two of the specific modes of our fourfold model. While our typology confirms the existence of disagreements and differences among those four theoretical tendencies, it deviates from the dominant three-wave framework by emphasizing strong synergies not only within but also among these four interrelated groups of globalization scholars. In what follows below, we explicate these modes of thinking about globalization by analysing the contributions of influential exemplars.

The Neoclassical Mode

The neoclassical mode of theorizing the global emphasizes the salience of approaches and insights offered by classical social and political thinkers, especially the 'Big Three': Karl Marx, Max Weber, and Emile Durkheim. Roland Robertson (1992), for example, developed his globalization perspective with explicit reference to the structural–functionalist framework pioneered by Durkheim and later modified by Talcott Parsons and his Weberian affinities. Anthony Giddens' main works on the subject (1990; 1999), too, are heavily indebted to the ideas of Weber and Durkheim, with Marxist elements doing significant work in the background. George Ritzer (1993; 2007) drew copiously on Weber's analysis of modern rationality to arrive at his celebrated formulation of the 'McDonaldization' of globalizing societies.

While Immanuel Wallerstein might not fit the rubric of 'globalization theorists', his Marx-inspired world-systems framework influenced many writers on the subject, including Christopher Chase-Dunn (1989), Samir Amin (1997), Barry Gills (2000), William Tabb (2001), Leslie Sklair (2002), Ash Amin (2004), Valentine Moghadam (2008), Jackie Smith (2008), and others. Two influential thinkers whose early works were acutely piqued by Wallerstein's thought, Jan Aart Scholte (2000) and Roland Robertson (1992), ultimately eschewed world-systems theory and instead developed alternative ways of understanding 'the world as a whole'. In addition, neo-Marxist spinoffs like Antonio Gramsci's revisionism or Karl Polanyi's culturist approach to capitalist development served as the catalysts for vital contributions made by notable globalization scholars such as Robert Cox (1996), James Mittelman (1996; 2000), Justin Rosenberg (2000; 2005), Mark Rupert (2000; Rupert and Solomon, 2005), Martin Shaw (2000), Ankie Hoogvelt (2001),

Ronaldo Munck (2002; 2007), William Robinson (2004; 2014), and others.

William Robinson's work is especially significant and innovative in that it proceeds in dialogue with both world-systems theory and Gramscian revisionist Marxism while at the same time developing 'a particular theory of globalization, one based on the global capitalism approach' (Robinson, 2004: xiii). For Robinson, globalization represents a qualitative stage, a momentous threshold marking the transition from different world economic systems to global formations. Articulated in exceptionally lucid prose, Robinson's perspective is anchored in the classical Marxist proposition that it is the economy, or, more technically, the mode of production, which remains the structurally determinant dynamic (Robinson, 2014: 10).[10] To some extent, then, Robinson seeks to theorize global capitalism from a Marxist perspective rather than exploring globalization in its own right. In other words, his work presents globalization as the contested outcome of the intensifying spread of capitalism in the late twentieth century. Indeed, Robinson's key concepts of a powerful 'transnational capitalist class' and an emerging 'transnational state' are directly linked to his core claim that 'globalization represents a new stage in the evolving world capitalist system' (Robinson, 2004: 2; 2011: 349).

But perhaps the most exemplary case of neoclassical theorizing can be found in David Harvey's Marx-inspired reflections on globalization. If Roland Robertson should be recognized for initiating a 'cultural turn' in globalization studies, then Harvey deserves a nod for facilitating a 'spatial turn'. Influenced by the writings of the neo-Marxist French philosopher Henri Lefebvre, Harvey coined the immensely influential phrase 'time–space compression'—the forerunner to Robertson's related phrase 'compression of the world'—to capture the crucial role of spatial and temporal dynamics in this process (Harvey, 1989). During the 1990s, the British political geographer developed his space-centred perspective further by claiming a central position for 'globalization' in the social science vocabulary as a 'key word for organizing our thoughts as to how the world works' (Harvey, 1995: 1). Reminding his readers that globalization processes have always been integral to capitalist development because the accumulation of capital had always involved profoundly geographical and spatial dynamics, Harvey (1995: 12) proposed a spatial redefinition of

---

[10] Here, our approach builds upon such a 'modes of practice' method, but instead of confining our analysis to the mode of production, we work with multiple modes as foundational to human practice: production, exchange, organization, communication, and enquiry. Sometimes we add the modes of consumption and mobility to give a classical sevenfold matrix.

'globalization' as an ongoing 'process of production of uneven temporal and geographical development'.

Harvey's elaboration of the significance of globalization selected key passages in Marx and Engels's *Communist Manifesto*, which aided his explanation of capitalism's growing ability to provide a new 'spatial fix' to its current neoliberal phase of expansion. Such a spatial remedy involved, crucially, the creation of a global historical geography of capital accumulation, which allowed the bourgeoisie to 'get a foothold everywhere, settle everywhere, establish connections everywhere' (Marx and Engels, 1848). Following Marx, Harvey (1995) postulated that the intensification of late-twentieth-century production and exchange of commodities—aided by new communication technologies—required new spatial strategies to overcome national barriers. In short, the study of the contemporary phase of globalization benefitted directly from Marx and Engels' classical insights into the geographical dynamics of capital accumulation and class struggle on a *worldwide* scale. To bolster his argument, Harvey quotes another key passage from the *Communist Manifesto*:

Through the exploitation of the world market the bourgeoisie has made the production and consumption of all countries cosmopolitan. It has pulled the national basis of industry right out from under the reactionaries, to their consternation. Long established national industries have been destroyed and are still being destroyed daily. They are being displaced by new industries—the introduction of which becomes a life-and-death question for all civilized nations—industries that no longer work up indigenous raw materials but use raw materials from the ends of the earth, industries whose products are consumed not only in the country of origin but in every part of the world. In place of the old needs satisfied by home production we have new ones, which demand the products of the most distant lands and climes for their satisfaction. In place of the old local and national self-sufficiency and isolation we have a universal commerce, a universal dependence of nations on one another. As in the production of material things, so it also with intellectual production. (Marx and Engels, 1848)

Harvey's selection of this paragraph left no doubt as to the link between classical social thought and his contemporary investigations of the global: 'If this is not a compelling description of globalization, then it is hard to imagine what would be. And it was, of course, precisely by way of this analysis that Marx and Engels derived the global imperative "working men of all countries unite" as a necessary condition for an anticapitalist and prosocialist revolution' (1995: 2). Elevated as the prototypical 'globalization passage', this textual fragment would be repeated over and over again by various global theorists as 'irrefutable confirmation' that Marx should be seen as 'the theorist of globalization *avant la lettre*' (Tomlinson,

1999: 76). It was also paraded as 'clear evidence' for the relevance of this most famous of all Marxist texts for current globalization scholarship.[11]

Harvey's Marx-inspired spatial turn both influenced and interacted with the writings of other space-centred globalization theorists such as Manuel Castells (1996–98), Neil Brenner (1999), Mike Douglass (2000), Jan Aart Scholte (2000), Saskia Sassen (2001), and John Agnew (2009). In particular, these thinkers adopted Harvey's key insight that globalization should be understood as a protracted spatial process of capitalism rather than a recent political–economic condition—as asserted by neoliberal commentators like Theodore Levitt and Thomas Friedman. Moreover, Harvey's strong emphasis on the geographical sophistication of the nineteenth-century founders of scientific socialism provided a strong antidote to the potent 'Marx is dead' charge made by neoliberal market globalists in the aftermath of the collapse of Soviet communism. Far from relegating Marxism to the dustbin of history, the rise of globalization had made this classical sociological tradition more relevant in the global age than ever before.

To sum up, the neoclassical mode of theorizing possesses the considerable virtue of situating scholarship on the global within currents of social thought whose insights have withstood the test of time. In particular, it connects global analyses to some of the enduring categories and issues of social development such as capitalism, industrialization, the division of labour, state–society relations, social stratification, and, of course, the evolution of modernity/postmodernity. Still, the construction of globalization theory with reference to specific classical thinkers produces a variety of perspectives on the subject. With regard to the perennial modernity debate, for example, Giddens (1990) drew on classical sources to construct his thesis that globalization represents a consequence and extension of modernity. Albrow (1996) utilized classical insights to argue the opposite: namely, that globalization fuels an epochal shift away from modernity. In other words, both of these contradictory positions—modernity as inherently globalizing and globality as inherently postmodernizing—were articulated in a neoclassical mode of theorizing the global.

On the downside, however, this mode often remains overly attached to the key concepts and problematiques of its nineteenth-century European philosophical and geographical origins. In addition to their expressed antipathy towards post-structuralist perspectives, the writings of most neoclassical globalization theorists rarely offer a sustained engagement with crucial contemporary identity categories such as race, gender, and

---

[11] See, for example, Waters (1995: 9), Tomlinson (1999: 76), Beck (2000: 22), and Hersh and Brun (2000: 107).

sexual orientation. References to postcolonial theory and non-Western philosophical frameworks are sporadic. If they do occur, these engagements are usually confined to defensive responses to legitimate demands for the greater incorporation of knowledge produced outside the Euro-American academy.[12]

The Domain Mode

From the early 1990s on, globalization pioneers recognized the difficulty of developing a comprehensive theoretical framework that presented the compression of the world as a differentiated set of processes that could not be reduced to a single dynamic yet remained attentive to its manifestations in specific aspects of social life. In most cases, the first step in resolving this conundrum consisted of assembling a 'lay of the land' by identifying the most pivotal 'domains' or 'dimensions' of the phenomenon. These discreet aspects were supposed to be brought together again in the holistic depiction of globalization as a 'highly differentiated phenomenon involving domains of activity and interactions as diverse as the political, military, economic, cultural, migratory, and environmental. Each of these domains involves different patterns of relations and activities' (Held et al., 1999: 23). This 'rebundling' of domains under the signifier 'multidimensional' served two important objectives. First, it made it easier for globalization researchers to accomplish their analytical task of breaking up the phenomenon's enormous proportions. Second, it allowed them to work collectively on the overarching project of understanding globalization in its totality while at the same time bringing each researcher's special academic expertise to bear on its specific domains.

Thus, the domain mode of theorizing the global was born. From the start, it attracted scores of interested scholars trained in conventional disciplines and enticed them to explore particular aspects of globalization nestled under the fledgling transdisciplinary umbrella of global studies.[13] The most frequently studied domains—linked here to a short selection of influential publications—include the following:

• The *economic*, referring to the intensification and stretching of economic connections across the globe (Ohmae, 1990; 1995; Reich, 1991; Sassen, 1991; 1999; Dicken, 1992; 2015; Helleiner, 1994; Hirst and Thompson, 1996; Rodrik, 1997; Gowan, 1999; Luttwak,

---

[12] For example, Anthony Giddens (1990) associates modernity (in the singular) with a specific European historical period and geographical origin.

[13] For our examination of the evolution and current state of global studies as a transdisciplinary field of enquiry, see Chapter 7.

1999; Bhagwati, 2000; 2007; Gilpin, 2000; Micklethwait and Woolridge, 2000; Tabb, 2001; Soros, 2002; Stiglitz, 2002; 2018);

- The *political and governmental*, dealing with the intensification and expansion of political, governance, and citizenship interrelations criss-crossing the world (Bauböck, 1995; Held, 1995; Sassen, 1996; Strange, 1996; Archibugi, Held, and Kohler, 1998; Gray, 1998; Weiss, 1998; Clark, 1999; Hurrell and Woods, 1999; Hardt and Negri, 2000; Shaw, 2000; Baylis and Smith, 2001; Patomäki, 2001; Kaldor, 2003; Keane, 2003; Rosenau, 2003);
- The *cultural*, exploring the intensification and expansion of cultural flows across the globe (Featherstone, 1990; Hannerz, 1992; Robertson, 1992; Ritzer, 1993; Beyer, 1994; Canclini, 1995; Appadurai, 1996; Barber, 1996; Latouche, 1996; Wilson and Dissanayake, 1996; Jameson and Miyoshi, 1998; Tomlinson, 1999; Berger and Huntington, 2002; Pieterse, 2015; Yudice, 2003);
- The *ideological*, tackling the expansion of political belief systems across world-space and world-time (Cox, 1996; Bourdieu, 1998; Chomsky, 1999; Falk, 1999; Rupert, 2000; Steger, 2002; 2008; 2009; Mittelman, 2004; Harvey, 2005).

Over the years, new major domains and subdomains were rapidly added to this list, which included ecology, technology, communications and the media, art, law, religion, democracy, education, military and war, race and ethnicity, gender, human rights, diplomacy, social movements, citizenship, postcolonialism, urbanization, security, migration, and so on. The rapidly intensifying dynamic of global climate change in particular spawned the publication of major studies on the subject after the turn of the century (Jorgensen and Kick, 2006; Giddens, 2009; Newell, 2012; Eckersley and Christoff, 2013). Moreover, the two most visible academic book series on globalization now contain dozens of volumes covering a broad spectrum of dimensions.[14]

Attentive readers might notice that our selective list of domain scholars reveals two crucial features, both of which are especially relevant for the purpose of contrasting our alternative typology with the dominant three-wave model. First, it contains the names of some of the thinkers we previously categorized as neoclassical theorists. These double entries suggest that our four modes are neither mutually exclusive nor incompatible. Rather, the overlap reflects the intertwined evolution of globalization theory as a collective enterprise populated by scholars who employed

---

[14] See Rowman and Littlefield Publishers: https://rowman.com/Action/SERIES/_/GLO/G lobalization; and Routledge: www.routledge.com/Rethinking-Globalizations/book-series/RG.

multiple modes of theorizing to produce knowledge of the global. The interconnectivity of our four intersecting modes will become even clearer in our discussion of the remaining approaches. Second, even at this early stage of introducing our alternative typology, it seems rather obvious that the conventional diachronic depiction of three successive waves finds itself at odds with empirical reality, which favours representations of the synchronic production of globalization theory. Further evidence for the simultaneity of scholarship on the global is provided by the overlapping dates of major publications associated with each of our four intersecting modes. In short, the conventional three-camp model employs a faulty timeline, for there is little evidence that hyperglobalizers preceded sceptics, who, in turn, were followed by transformationalists. Rather, different perspectives emerged simultaneously and in constant interaction with each other at all stages of the unfolding globalization debate during the 1990s and beyond.

One of the most unorthodox and innovative examples of domain thinking can be found in Michael Hardt and Antonio Negri's study of the political dimension of globalization. Hailed by sympathetic reviewers as the 'Communist Manifesto for our time' and condemned by scathing critics as an 'impenetrable work of absolute abstraction', their unexpected bestseller Empire (2000) focused on the emerging political world order of the new century. The book transcended the narrow walls of the ivory tower and thrust its authors into the glaring public spotlight that only rarely shines on social theorists or political philosophers. Hardt and Negri's analysis of the political domain of globalization is characterized by their remarkable ability to paint in transdisciplinary strokes, in the process drawing on a plethora of materials from legal studies, politics, economics, philosophy, anthropology, cultural studies, comparative literature, and critical theory.

At the core of the study, one finds the authors' insistence that Empire represented a radically new paradigm of *political* authority and control—a 'new global order' composed of a series of national and supranational organisms that supersede old, nation-state-centred forms of sovereignty. Empire is not merely a metaphor but a theoretical concept signifying a 'political subject that effectively regulates these global exchanges, the sovereign power that governs the world'. In their view, this single logic of globalization operated in all spheres of social life, and perhaps most visibly in the regulation of human interaction, the formation of global markets, the creation of new technologies, the expansion of vast circuits of material and immaterial production, and the generation of gigantic cultural flows. No longer opposed by an extra-systemic 'outside', this new form of sovereignty constituted a regime that effectively encompassed the 'spatial totality' of the entire globe (Hardt and Negri, 2000: 353, 413). Wielding enormous powers of oppression and destruction, Empire neither established a territorial centre nor relied on fixed boundaries, but 'manages hybrid identities, flexible hierarchies, and plural exchanges through modulating networks of command. The distinct national colours of the imperialist map of the world had merged and blended in the imperial global rainbow'. As a regime 'with no temporal boundaries and in this sense outside of history or at the end of history', Empire thus dwarfed any particular imperialist project previously undertaken by single nation-states (Hardt and Negri, 2000: xii–xv).

After a descriptive analysis of the present features of Empire and a long interpretation of the historical transition from imperialism to Empire, Hardt and Negri (2000: 210) concluded on an optimistic note, suggesting that the creative forces of the exploited and subjugated producers that sustain Empire were also capable of autonomously constructing a 'counter-Empire'—an alternative political organization of global flows and exchanges fuelled by the multitude's 'will to be against'. Struggling for global mobility, global citizenship, a guaranteed social wage, and the right to the reappropriation of the means of production, this subjugated 'multitude' was said to invent new forms of democratic expression as well as novel manifestations of constituent power.

In this context, Hardt and Negri (2000: 396–400) offered an insightful discussion of the subversive effects of a political demand for global citizenship. A direct response to a globalizing world, mass migration and increasing mobility were alleged to contain the revolutionary political potential to undermine economic inequalities and asymmetrical power relations that are rooted in an anachronistic defence of fixed boundaries and spatial divisions separating the Northern and Southern hemispheres. Calling for subversion, insurrection, and bio-political self-organization, Hardt and Negri (2000: 413) ended their study by introducing the heroic political figure of the 'militant'—a cross between St Francis of Assisi and a Wobbly organizer—as the one who best expresses the revolutionary potential of the multitude.

Once again, this unorthodox yet sophisticated example of domain thinking reaffirms the interconnectivity of all four modes of globalization theory. After all, one of the greatest virtues of Hardt and Negri's study lies in its ability to explore the political aspects of globalization by incorporating select insights from relevant classical thinkers, especially Marx and Weber. In addition, their theoretical approach feeds on perspectives associated with anarchism, existentialism, poststructuralism, critical theory, critical race theory, subaltern studies, and feminist theory.

However, their engagement also exemplifies one of the main short-comings of the domain mode of theorizing: the difficulty of reassembling a 'big picture' of globalization that gives other domains as much weight as the one serving as the primary analytical prism. In the case of Hardt and Negri's analysis, its political focus on the decline of national sovereignty results in the projection of a 'systemic totality' called Empire whose dynamics are said to explain the phenomenon of globalization *in general*. In other words, their projection of this evolving new space of authority and control reduces globalization to a *political* project of superseding old, nation-state-centred forms of sovereignty. What is usually missing in such domain approaches, then, is a more balanced movement from the parti-cular to the general characterized by a proper rebundling of various globalization domains that reaffirms the 'multidimensionality' of the phenomenon emphasized by domain thinkers in the first place.

The Complexity Mode

The complexity mode of theorizing approaches globalization as an intri-cate, changeable, and highly contingent phenomenon whose study requires close encounters with multiple forms of complexity and differ-entiation. As John Tomlinson (1999: 1–2) argued in his influential book on cultural globalization, the notion of 'complex connectivity' captures in a 'simple and relatively uncontentious way' a basic understanding of globalization as a 'rapidly developing and ever-densening network of interconnections and interdependencies that characterize modern social life'.[15] Major thinkers employing the complexity mode include Ulf Hannerz (1992; 1996), George Ritzer (1993), Jonathan Friedman (1994), Barrie Axford (1995; 2002; 2013), Manuel Castells (1996–98), Scott Lash (Featherstone, Lash, and Robertson, 1996), Zygmunt Bauman (1998), Saskia Sassen (1999; 2000), and John Urry (2003).

From the beginning, these social thinkers sought to connect their analytic focus on complexity to what eventually came to be seen as the 'Holy Grail' of global studies embodied in the ideals of transdisciplinarity and multidimensionality. As Barrie Axford (2013: 8, emphasis in origi-nal) puts it, the challenge was to the present the real-life complexity of globalization by means of a coherent yet non-reductive account of 'the analytically separate but interconnected and perhaps mutually constitu-tive dynamics of economics, politics, and culture, delivered through

---

[15] At one level, Tomlinson could be characterized a domain thinker, for he makes the cultural domain of globalization the focus of his analysis. Still, his intricate theoretical discourse stretches his position into the complexity mode.

a robust *interdisciplinarity* or *transdisciplinarity*. To some extent, then, complexity theorists endeavoured to complete the 'rebundling' process left unfinished by domain thinkers—but without the modernist 'grand theory' ambitions of some generalizing thinkers eager to systematize a unitary approach to globalization.

Since global complexity appears in many forms and pervades different social arenas, globalization scholars approached it from different angles and through multiple levels of analysis. These included representatives from all three camps conventionally associated with the dominant three-wave model. Their early research efforts often involved empirical mappings of complexity that drew heavily on the new discourse of 'networks' and 'flows', which had intensified in the early 1990s as a result of the Information and Communications Technology Revolution.

Manuel Castells is an intriguing exemplar here because, at one level, he could be seen as a domain theorist focusing on the domain of communications, but he takes on complexity thinking as his primary mode of analysis. In particular, he played a pivotal role in the academic attempt to situate the technological complexity discourse centres on 'electronically processed information networks' within the emerging globalization debate configured around 'social interdependencies'. Examining complex globalization processes operating in economic, social, and cultural domains, he offered an empirically grounded account capable of explaining the changing social and organizational arrangements of what he called the 'network society'. Castells (1996–98) presented the new communication and information networks as open structures capable of infinite expansion and integration of a large number of new nodes and ties. The Spanish social scientist claimed that the global 'Information Age'— embedded in interconnected networks of production, power, and experience—was replacing the Industrial Age and its centrally organized, vertical chains of command and control geared towards the production and distribution of power. While Castells aimed at constructing a coherent theoretical perspective, he stopped just short of proposing the sort of general, unitary theory of society that generalizing thinkers like David Held and his collaborators tried to assemble.

Castells insisted that the key to understanding the evolving network society—and the diffusion of its logic of interconnectivity across *all* social domains—lay in an in-depth analysis of the globalizing forms of social complexity in the contemporary context. Indeed, the unprecedented combination of flexibility and task implementation inherent in networks allowed for superior coordination and management of the growing social complexity. Networks appeared in the contemporary context in myriad forms and dynamics, most importantly as the capitalist world economy greased by transnational financial flows that are directed by 24/7 stock exchange markets, globally connected webs of civil society and their proliferating nodes of information-sharing non-governmental organizations, Internet-based mobile digital devices generating, transmitting, and receiving signals in interlinking global media systems, expanding crime cartels and drug-traffic routes cutting across national and regional geographies, and so on. As Castells (2000: 6, emphasis in original) explained:

[D]igital networking technologies, characteristic of the Information Age, powered social and organizational networks in ways that allowed their endless expansion and reconfiguration, overcoming the traditional limitations of networking forms of organization to *manage complexity* beyond a certain size of the network. Because networks do not stop at the border of the nation-state, the network society constitutes itself as a global system, ushering in the new form of globalization characteristic of our time.

In particular, Castells sought to unlock the complexities of the global network society by concentrating on the 'flows'—purposeful and repetitive sequences of exchange and interaction involving such things as language, data, money, or drugs—that pass through nodes along the ties of the network. However, under conditions of increasing complexity, flows could assume many different forms, characteristics, and qualities. Castells recognized this difficulty and acknowledged that his empirical analysis of specific flows in the network society could not proceed without a prior consideration of larger space–time transformations in the human experience resulting from the new patterns of connection and mobility. Introducing his influential notion of the 'space of flows', he argued that microelectronics-based digital communication, advanced telecommunication networks, and computerized information systems had transformed conventional forms of social space by 'introducing simultaneity, or any chosen time-frame, in social practices, regardless of the location of the actors engaged in the communication process'. Unlike a 'space of places'—conventionally bounded space linked to specific locations such as delineated suburbs, villages, towns, and the nation-state—Castells' space of flows referred to a new interrelationship of knowledge, power, and communication that 'involves the production, transmission, and processing of flows of information'. To be sure, the space of flows on the Internet still relied on the production of localities as nodes of expanding communication networks, but the primary function of such 'places' consisted of providing 'material support of simultaneous social practices communicated at a distance' (Castells, 1996–98: xxxii).

Building on Castells' notion of 'space of flows' and Zygmunt Bauman's (2000) idea of 'liquid modernity', John Urry emerged in the 2000s as one of the most influential academic voices urging the reconfiguration of sociological and social scientific research around the 'liquid' nature of 'complexity'. Citing the transformative impact of globalization—reflected especially in the increasing mobility of people, commodities, technologies, and ideas—the British sociologist attempted to connect social enquiries into the nature of the global with the 'complexity sciences' and 'chaos theory' in order to capture these new transnational dynamics. In particular, he argued that new concepts and methods borrowed from physics and biology had the capacity to expand our understanding of the global as a complex system or series of interdependent systems. Appreciative of Castells' innovative examination of intersecting global networks as the new framework for studying globalization, Urry (2003) nonetheless criticized his colleague for lacking a sufficiently broad range of theoretical terms necessary to illuminate the intensification of global complexity. As he saw it, Castells' notion of 'network' was 'too undifferentiated a term' to capture the dynamic properties of global processes and worldwide connections. Hence, his basic premise was to overcome the 'limitations of many globalization analyses that deal insufficiently with the *complex* character of emergent global relations' (Urry, 2003: 15, 39, emphasis in original).

As his starting point, Urry proposed that emergent global systems should be conceptualized as interdependent and self-organizing 'global hybrids'. Combining both physical and social relations in curious and unexpected ways, these formations were capable of evolving towards both disorganization and order. Teetering 'on the edge of chaos', global hybrids often moved away from points of equilibrium and stability, thus exhibiting the qualities of unpredictability, contingency, non-linearity, irreversibility, and indeterminacy that have long been described and analysed in natural sciences devoted to the study of complexity, such as quantum physics, thermodynamics, cybernetics, ecology, and biology (Urry, 2003: 14). He cited informational systems, automobility, global media, world money, the Internet, climate change, health hazards, and worldwide protests as examples of such global hybrids.

Next, Urry (2003: 56–9) introduced the concept of 'globally integrated networks' consisting of 'complex and enduring networked connections between peoples, objects and technologies stretching across multiple and distant spaces and times'. Their purpose was to manage global complexity by introducing regularity and predictability into the chaotic multiplicity of emergent globality. For example, global enterprises like McDonald's, American Express, or Sony were organized through globally integrated networks that interweaved technologies, skills, texts, and brands to ensure that the same service or product was delivered in more or less the same way across the entire network. This made outcomes predictable, calculable, routinized, and standardized. Under conditions of advanced globalization, however, globally integrated networks often exhibited insufficient flexibility and fluidity to implement appropriate modes of organizational learning.

Thus, Urry introduced another key concept for the purpose of advancing our understanding of globalization as complexity: 'global fluids'. While these highly evolved manifestations of global hybridity undoubtedly involved networks, the term 'networks' did not do justice to the 'uneven, emergent and unpredictable shapes' that global processes might take. Structured by the various dimensions and domains of global order, global processes travelled along network ties from node to node, but their movements were much less stable and predictable than Castells suggested when he introduced the notion of 'space of flows' within 'global networks'. Urry (2003, 60–1) argued that global fluids 'may escape, rather like white blood corpuscles, through the "wall" into surrounding matter and effect unpredictable consequences upon the matter'. For example, powerful 'fluids' of travelling people or health hazards such as global pandemics travelled across national borders at changing speeds and 'at different levels of viscosity with no necessary end state or purpose'. For Urry (2003: 61), the notion of global fluids (of different viscosity) was superior to the 'networks' metaphor in explaining how the 'messy power of complexity processes' was organized in the global age.

For all its virtues—such as its insistence that globalization was neither unified nor could be presented as a linear and orderly set of processes unfolding in separate domains—the complexity mode of theorizing exemplified in the works of Urry and Castells suffers from at least three serious weaknesses. First, it relies on multiple and overlapping concepts to describe complexity in abstract ways that make it extremely difficult to understand how metaphors like 'globally integrated networks' and 'global fluids' are related. Second, these rather dense and abstract sets of concepts are employed in the service of arguments that provide little by way of real-world illustration and specification, thus obscuring the theory–practice connection that is vital for the engagement of global problems.[16] Thirdly, the post-structuralist emphasis on fluidity overemphasizes

[16] By contrast, our *engaged theory of globalization* places the metaphors of 'flows' and 'fluids' within complex relations of viscosity and stickiness, discontinuity and continuity—and what we call modes of integration and differentiation. It only takes a moment of reflection on the very different mobilities of commodities and refugees in this world of border crossing and border security to realize that the metaphors of 'flows' or 'liquidity' can only serve as partial descriptors of the real-life complexity of globalization. Such metaphors also tend to diminish vital questions of structural power, including the power to stop others moving across borders.

discontinuities, contingency, and surface flows at the expense of also understanding continuities, determinations, and deeper structures. Finally, the investigation of globalization through the prism of growing complexity demands researchers' willingness to accept the impossibility of closure in the analysis of the global. The resulting imperative of intellectual modesty that comes with one's recognition of the limits to knowledge tends to be obeyed by only the rarest of academics—globalization scholars not exempted.

The Generalizing Mode

The generalizing mode of theorizing approaches globalization as a systematic phenomenon. Thus, it aims for nothing less than the construction of a unified and generalizable theory. Such efforts are typically associated with modernist social scientific thinking along structuralist lines; that is, the conceptualization of global interdependencies as the interaction of relatively stable structures such as institutions and classes that cut across multiple spatial scales. There are only a handful of social theorists who have attempted this feat, yet some of them have disavowed consciously embarking on such an ambitious quest. The thinkers who came closest to employing such 'grand theory' designs include Anthony Giddens (1990; 1999), Roland Robertson (1992), David Held and his collaborators (Held et al., 1999; Held and McGrew, 2007), Jan Aart Scholte (2000, 2005), Peter Sloterdijk (2013, 2014), and, to a somewhat lesser extent, Manuel Castells (1996–98, 2009, 2012).[17]

Perhaps the most impressive example of the generalizing approach can be found in Global Transformations: Politics, Economics, and Culture, a massive, 500-page transdisciplinary study that presented readers with the impressive results of collective academic globalization research stretching over the entire decade of the 1990s. The book was co-authored by four British domain thinkers dedicated to extending their specialized research expertise across the main dimensions of globalization. The team leader was David Held, a political theorist who had previously analysed the changing nature and form of democratic nation-states in the context of intensifying global relations. He was joined by Anthony McGrew, an international relations specialist who approached domestic politics as a product of more powerful interstate forces; David Goldblatt, a social theorist with a strong background in environmental

---

[17] Justin Rosenberg (2000) offered one of the earliest comprehensive critiques of this generalizing mode of theorizing globalization.

policy; and Jonathan Perraton, a political economist and international finance expert.

Combining their expertise to engage in a holistic analysis of the major domains of globalization, these scholars also showed some affinity for the complexity mode of theorizing globalization as an extremely intricate and differentiated set of processes to be grasped in its totality only through a generalizing model attentive to the demands of multidimensionality.[18] Thus, the authors attempted to 'develop a more comprehensive explanation of globalization which highlights the complex intersection between a multiplicity of driving forces, embracing economic, technological, cultural and political change' (Held et al., 1999: 12). For Held and his co-authors, each of the major domains of social life contained different patterns of relations and activities. Though connected to all of the other dimensions, various globalization dynamics operated at times largely autonomously according to impulses and forces that were internally created and applied. Hence, the success of their comprehensive approach to unravelling global complexity by means of a general explanatory theory depended to a significant degree on overcoming the inherent limitations of the domain mode that required intricate delineations of the main dimensions of globalization.

Moreover, *Global Transformations* firmly embraced and further developed the conventional waves model of globalization theory by introducing the corresponding categories of 'camps' populated by 'hyperglobalizers', 'sceptics', and 'transformationalists'. While useful in describing significant currents in the intensifying globalization debate of the 1990s, this typology set the problematic precedent of shackling theoretical innovation to a narrative of contesting perspectives emerging from three opposing forces. As we noted earlier, the association of third-wave approaches with theoretical innovation served to reify the dominant framework of globalization theory within which informed scholarly debate was supposed to take place.

Other problems that were not obvious during a first reading developed as their analysis proceeded. Firstly, while Held and his co-authors wisely opted for a cross-domain approach, they failed to stabilize the analytical basis of their domain structure. Their book's subtitle lists three major domains—politics, economics, and culture. Yet at times they used the deviating triple-bottom-line list of social, political, and economic domains (Held et al., 1999: 7). At other times, they resorted to a longer

---

[18] In terms of our engaged theory of globalization, their work was conducted at the level of 'empirical generalization'. This is the first level of what we nominally distinguish as four levels of analysis moving from the most concrete to the most abstract levels: (1) empirical generalization; (2) conjunctural analysis; (3) integrational analysis; and (4) categorical analysis. See our discussion in Chapter 5.

domain list of overlapping and different inclusions (Held et al., 1999: 12, 24, 27), which brought together political, military, economic, cultural, labour, migration, environment, legal, criminal, and technological dimensions. In other words, the domain structure introduced in their book tended to work as an empirical set of changing themes rather than as part of a larger analytical framework.

The authors then expanded their unstable domain framework of globalization by adding four 'spatiotemporal dimensions' to the variable lists of social domains: (1) the extensity of global networks; (2) the intensity of global interconnectedness; (3) the velocity of global flows; and (4) the impact of global interconnectedness. Their adoption of Castells' 'network' and 'flows' terminology linked these four spatiotemporal dimensions to the complexity mode. But their notion of 'global flows' was simplified to signify the general 'movements of physical artefacts, people, symbols, tokens and information across space and time'. Similarly, 'global networks' were reduced to 'regularized or patterned interactions between independent agents, nodes of activity, or sites of power' (Held et al., 1999: 16). Once again, the spatiotemporal dimensions operated as empirical analytics, which could be tested by measuring indicators. They did not, as David Harvey (1989) had accomplished, layer their analysis in a way that allowed them to identify different social forms of space and time.

Still working on the empirical plane, Held and his team complicated their framework by adding yet another set of four 'organizational dimensions' necessary for sketching the broad shape of globalization: infrastructures, institutionalization, stratification, and modes of interaction. In other words, their attempts to tame global complexity within a general explanatory framework ultimately led them to add two analytically distinct sets of 'dimensions' to the variable sets of domains, with both operating at the same level of *empirical generalization* as the domain lists. And herein lies the problem. The relation between the analytical parts remained empirical and cumulative—just like an ever-expanding single-storey abode with rooms added without a clear architecture. When applied to concrete social dynamics, the distinction between 'social domains', 'spatiotemporal dimensions', and 'institutional dimensions' became blurred, thus inviting conceptual confusion.

Consequently, Held and his colleagues encountered the same obstacle that had bedevilled complexity thinkers: their grand theory architecture introduced multiple cross-cutting categories that sat alongside each other as an accumulating series of analytical entry points. Placed at the same level of abstraction, they lacked an integrating framework capable of indicating why each of these analytical entry points was important and how they related to each other. For instance, why were 'institutional dimensions' added as a separate cross-domain set when they pertained primarily to the political domain? Why was the labour domain not made a subset of the economic domain? Similarly, the law domain never appeared as a subset of the political domain. Moreover, and connected to this problem, when they discussed globalization *in practice*, their elaboration of the analytical entry points—domains and dimensions—tended to do little more than thematically organize their descriptive focus. Despite these limitations, however, Held, McGrew, Goldblatt, and Perraton came closer than any previous attempt to present a systematic and integrated theory of globalization.

Let us briefly consider another—quite unique—example of theorizing globalization in a generalizing mode: the grand *philosophical* project of Peter Sloterdijk. The maverick German philosopher and charismatic television personality recently published a massive tome on how, from ancient times to the present, humans made their worlds in relation to three major variants of 'spheres': 'orbs', 'globes', and 'foams' (2011; 2014; 2016). Each of these three types of sphere is treated in a separate volume. Without entering into a sustained dialogue with any of the major globalization theorists we introduced in this chapter, Sloterdijk's trilogy represents the most ambitious philosophy (and history) of globalization ever written. In *Spheres, Volume 2: Globes*, the author highlights the connection between spherical permutations and globalization throughout human history: 'Globalization can only be understood by opening up to the realization that the thought figure of the orb is an ontologically, and thus technically and politically, serious matter ... This serious history is the history of being' (Sloterdijk, 2014: 47).[19]

Still, Sloterdijk's generalizing narrative commits the reductionist error of narrowing the very basis for being human to the gestalt of 'spheres'—and spheres alone. Instead of treating a particular figure of speech associated with spatiality as the point of departure for a careful exploration of ontological complexity (as we attempt to do), the various permutations of 'spheres' become *the* means by which all meaning of globalization is mediated. In other words, globalization becomes the central dynamic through which spherical permutations fuel various stages of 'world-making'.

At the first stage of 'classical' and 'traditional' world-making, for example, the form of globalization is 'metaphysical' and represented by the

---

[19] As we emphasize in the Chapters 4–6, the ontological level of analysis is, indeed, critical to theorizing globalization and its history.

spherical figure of the 'orb'. At the second stage of 'modern' world-making, the circle of 'immunity' that bound humans to God is ruptured and the orb becomes transformed into of the modern spherical figure of the 'globe'. This rupture ushers in 'terrestrial globalization', starting with a mercantile form of 'encompassing the globe' reflected in the fifteenth- to sixteenth-century European voyages of discovery, the imperialist and colonialist ventures of the ensuing centuries, and the world wars of the twentieth century.

For Sloterdijk (2011: 66), the modern 'encompassing' dynamic of globes has given way to a third stage of contemporary world-making that is manifested in the spherical figure of 'foaming bubbles'. The corresponding social formation of digital globalization appears in today's electronic simultaneity and social heterogeneity that dissolves the modern globe of geography into postmodern bubbles of virtuality. Sloterdijk consciously advances the spherical metaphor of 'foam' as the necessary replacement for the supposedly inadequate, non-spherical figure of 'liquidity' (Bauman, 2000). At this point, his philosophical grand narrative engages for the first time with the extant literature on globalization, albeit in very general and critical terms:

One of the main characteristics of conventional views about globalization is, to be frank, a discreet comic element ... The monopolization of the discourse on globalization by political scientists and sociologists, to whom we owe the continuation of journalism by morose means, would be quite bearable on the whole— were it not for the fact that the basic concepts of these debates are almost all unrecognized philosophical terms whose amateurish use leads to insinuations and distortions of meaning ... Pirated copies of cluelessness circulate freely in the whole world. (Sloterdijk, 2013: 6–7)

Indeed, there seems to be somewhat of a phenomenological obsession at the core of Sloterdijk's generalizing mode of theorizing—and historicizing—the global, for everything about being human can be understood only through his fixation on spheres. The various permutations of spherical dynamics are associated with different forms of globalization, which, in turn, become the master concepts for explaining the social evolution of humanity. Hence, Sloterdijk finds spheres, orbs, and circles everywhere: from circular villages to mediaeval walled towns to the global village of planet Earth; from the Garden of Eden to the shape of a woman's womb or even in a cartoonish 'thought bubble'. In the process, however, his philosophical attempt to revive the 'grand narrative' as method becomes an oblique and idiosyncratic form of theorizing a certain kind of spatial shape and its permutations rather than probing the ontologically changing nature of globalizing spatiality across the centuries.

To summarize, we identified a number of influential examples of the generalizing mode of theorizing the global, all of which possess the virtue of seeking to develop a holistic conceptual framework for understanding the compression of the world in its full complexity. Scholars writing in this mode keep alive the possibility of assembling a general and systematic framework for conceptualizing what globalization is and how it unfolds across a wide range of domains and in specific geographical and historical contexts.

On the downside, however, generalizing thinkers of globalization often find themselves bogged down by the preliminary task of mapping out in much detail the various dimensions of the phenomenon. These are then brought together either metaphorically or by adding categories that often remain unconnected and insufficiently explained. As Andrew Jones (2010: 88, 239) rightly observes, grand theories of globalization remain vulnerable to criticism concerning the capacity of *any* generalizing theoretical framework to universally and adequately capture every possible aspect of global interconnectedness. Thus, the generalizing mode of theorizing the global is prone to reducing multiple complex changes in the contemporary world to a single inadequate conceptual framework.

Concluding Remarks

Our critical examination of the dominant three-wave framework of globalization theory introduced an alternative typology designed to lay the groundwork for our own theoretical contribution outlined in the Chapters 4 and 5. Like the representatives of the four intersecting and complementary modes of theorizing the global, the authors of the present study are firmly committed to moving globalization theory into new conceptual territory. But we suggest that the necessary labours of intellectual innovation are more likely to succeed outside of the narrow parameters of the dominant three-camp mentality. Well intentioned as the quest for a vanguard third-wave position might be, it remains captive to an antiquated template tainted by intellectually rigid and empirically questionable demarcations between rival camps and consecutive waves. Rather, we hope to encourage new attempts to rethink the dominant framework of globalization theory in fundamental ways for the purpose of expanding our understanding of the global.

As Jan Aart Scholte (2016: 223) reminds us, the first two decades of the twenty-first century have witnessed a significant expansion of the 1990s' globalization debate, resulting in a 'substantial library of explanatory and normative global theory'. On the flip side of the coin, however, a central weakness of understanding goes back to our earlier discussion of a global systemic shift affecting the dominant valences of social life. Paradoxically, the Great Unsettling has brought questions of the global to the fore, while, at the same time, the rise of the corresponding postmodern mood has mitigated against the possibility of developing general explanatory theories of globalization. In other words, major approaches to the study of globalization emerged precisely at a moment when once highly valued attempts to construct generalized and singular embracing social theories found themselves under severe attack from postmodern and postcolonial forces. Similarly, neo-Marxist critics like Immanuel Wallerstein or Justin Rosenberg clung to their macro-level structuralist framework while at the same time criticizing what they identified as the major 'folly' of striving for a generalized understanding of the phenomenon. The fashionable post-modern sensibilities critical of modernity, together with objective challenges within the continuing dominance of modernity, came together to push pioneering thinkers like David Harvey or Anthony Giddens towards an examination of globalization as an objective phenomenon in itself. Their growing attention to the intensifying compression of space and time grew out of their intuition that the conventional categories of analysis were no longer adequate for explaining this systemic shift.

Globalization may simply be a blanket name given to a matrix of processes that extend social relations and consciousness across world-space and world-time (Nairn and James, 2005). But, as our critical examination of globalization theory in this chapter has demonstrated, the way in which people experience these stretching relations is incredibly complex, changing, and difficult to explain. This suggests that globalization continues to matter a great deal as both an *explanandum* and an *explanans*—a dynamic of space–time compression that is to be explained as well as a phenomenon that provides explanation of our changing world. For this reason, theorists of the global remain in search of an integrated set of methodologies—and not necessarily a singular grand theory—that can sensitize us to empirical complexities while enabling us to abstract patterns of change and continuity. Ideally, these same methodologies should simultaneously be able to contextualize and explain the nature of the very enquiry that goes into this task. The next two chapters confront this difficult challenge.

4   Considering the Subjective Dimensions of Globalization

Since the conceptual convergence of popular and academic globalization discourses in the early 1990s, *objective* phenomena of time–space compression have been the focus of most of the major approaches to globalization we evaluated in the Chapter 3. These patterns, processes, and impacts of global-scale processes have been studied in extraordinary detail. As we discussed, major works have been written on the empirical aspects of the phenomenon, ranging from the consequences of containerization for global trade to the redefining effects of the global intersection of biotechnology and genomic sequencing and DNA editing. Much discussion has centred on cutting-edge digital devices like tablets and smartphones that hook into sprawling social media networks. One can also find new studies on how human body parts, second-hand clothing, the English language, news cartels, and pineapples, among many other things, have become increasingly part of global systems of production, trade, communication, and enquiry. In the relatively short span of barely three decades, thousands of books and articles have been devoted to the economic, technological, infrastructural, and political dimensions of globalization.

By comparison, the *subjective* dimensions of globalization have not received the level of attention that has been paid to the objective aspects of global interchange.[1] This is especially true for the study of the thickening of people's consciousness of the world as an interconnected place. These subjective aspects include meanings, ideas, discourses, moods, sensibilities, identities, and understandings that arise in tandem with material processes of space–time compression. While examinations of various aspects of subjective globalization have not been entirely absent in scholarship on global-scale processes, they have remained undertheorized. As Roland Robertson (2009; 2015) noted, it remains a major puzzle as to how the investigation of 'consciousness' has been so consistently overlooked or marginalized in research on the global.

---

[1] For our earlier and less extensive discussion of subjective globalization, see Steger and James (2013).

However, there are some notable exceptions, including some innovative studies on the culture of economics. For example, an anthology titled *Frontiers of Capital* documents ethnographically the emergent subjectivities of finance capitalism, including the rise of symbolic risk analysts who have shouldered a large part of the social assessment work of big banks and insurance companies (Fisher and Downey, 2006). Another edited volume titled *Savage Economics* explores what it calls 'the cultural constitution of political economy' (Blaney and Inayatullah, 2010). Most of the authors featured in this insightful collection of essays carry forward the pioneering analysis of Angus Cameron and Ronan Palan (2004). These British social scientists suggested that the narrations and stories about global economic relations should be considered as *constitutive* of social practices, rather than being relegated to second-class status as mere 'dependent variables' or 'superstructural epiphenomena'. Thus, highlighting the performative element in globalization discourse, the authors rightly consider globalization as a cultural practice in the form of meaning-making processes that have real material consequences. Obviously, their insights into the subjective contributions to the making of the global in the world 'out there' can easily be applied to other objective domains of globalization, such as global governance and digital networks.

Our explicit recognition of the relevance of globalization's subjective dimensions resonates with the overall theme of the present study and constitutes the starting point of this chapter. Here, we show why and how subjective dynamics of globalization matter just as much as global trade flows, investment transfers, or the transnational movement of goods, technologies, and people. This chapter brings the subjective aspects of globalization into sharper focus by situating our discussion within a larger theoretical framework that draws on insights emanating from the four modes of theorizing globalization introduced in the Chapter 3. We explore subjectivities expressed in ideologies, narratives, descriptions, claims, and other forms of meaning-making about the global that are both contested and embraced in contemporary societies. Ultimately, Chapter 5 will bring together the objective and subjective dimensions of globalization in our outline of an *engaged theory of globalization*.

Subjective Dimensions of Globalization: Four Levels of Meaning and Analysis

The thickening of global consciousness can be analysed across four interrelated levels of social life. The first level encompasses meanings in the form of ideas, images, and narratives. *Ideas* are mental images, impressions, concepts, metaphors, narrated thoughts, beliefs, or opinions that form the building blocks of social meaning. They may or may not gain social purchase. While an individual can hold an idea without ever expressing it, it is always already framed socially—to the extent that humans are social beings.

The second layer includes meanings as contested and decontested by various *ideologies*. *Ideologies* are patterned public clusters of normatively imbued ideas, metaphors, narratives, and concepts, including particular representations of power relations. These conceptual maps help people navigate the complexity of their political universe and carry claims to social truth. Ideologies of globalization now pervade social life almost everywhere across the globe (Steger, 2008). At the end of the second decade of the twenty-first century, this might be a relatively uncontentious claim, but there is still much theoretical work left for globalization theorists willing to map the clusters of ideas that feed into today's competing 'globalisms'. In particular, they need to find more systematic ways of tracking the lines of historical development involving the globalization of ideas, values, and culture.

The third level contains meanings as felt in largely taken-for-granted *imaginaries*. These deep-seated modes of understanding are patterned convocations of the social whole that provide the largely pre-reflexive parameters within which people imagine their social existence. They are expressed in conceptions of 'the global', 'the national', or 'the moral order of our time' (Taylor, 2004; Steger, 2008). During the last three or four decades, the rising global imaginary has become articulated by competing globalisms, which, in turn, are now part and parcel of intensifying ideational and material networks enveloping our planet.

The fourth layer encompasses meanings as embodied in relation to deep-seated *ontologies*. Patterned ways-of-being-in-the-world, these existential categories refer to lived experiences that provide the grounding conditions of the social such as linear time, territorial space, and individualized embodiment (James, 2006). In order to understand the subjective power of the modern in the making of globalization, for example, we need to gain a historically sensitive understanding of ontological dynamics, including the intersection of the modern with the tribal-customary, the traditional, and the postmodern.

In Chapter 5, we present our theoretical approach in much more detail by schematically plotting the four levels of social meaning to corresponding levels of analysis. At this stage, we offer a simple preview of our analytical strategy with regard to the subjective dimensions of globalization. The first level, *empirical* analysis, is foundational to making any claims about the world. This requires collecting data about ideas and attending to the conceptual details of change. However, to understand the complexity of the complex patterns of those ideas, our analysis moves

Levels of the social	DOING	ACTING	RELATING	BEING
Levels of analysis	I. Empirical	II. Conjunctural	III. Integrational	VI. Categorical
	Increasing epistemological abstraction of the standpoint of analysis			
Objects of analysis: I Levels of social MEANING	Instances and patterns of social IDEAS	Patterns of social IDEOLOGIES	Patterns of social IMAGINARIES	Patterns of social ONTOLOGIES

Figure 4.1 Four levels of social meaning and theoretical analysis[2]

to study ideologies as embedded in *conjunctures* of history and relates these ideologies to patterns of practice and meaning in terms of 'ways of acting'. In order to study ideologies in the context of patterns of subjective inter-relationships, we must examine deeper, pre-reflexive patterns of social meaning—hence our focus on social imaginaries. This works at a more abstract level of *integrational* analysis, where we attempt to map social background understanding. Finally, we arrive at the deepest level of human existence, which requires us to consider ontologies or foundational *categories* of existence: time, space, embodiment, and so on. Each of these four facets of lived subjectivity is constituted in social practices at an ever-greater degree of generality, durability, and depth (Figure 4.1).

While we recognize that the separation of these four layers only works for analytical purposes, such abstractions nonetheless constitute a useful methodological tool that enables us to track the changing, contradictory, and overlapping nature of subjectivities of globalization. Thus, our attempt to analyse these interdependent levels of social meaning in the next section of this chapter moves from examining ideologies of globalization to arguing that these shared mental maps can be understood more broadly as contributing to the emergent dominance of a global social imaginary, which, in turn, calls for an analysis of the ontological dominance of the modern. Finally, by linking the contemporary social context of globalization to ideological contestation, we hope to reinforce why and how various subjective aspects of contemporary space–time compression matter just as much as transnational investment flows (Figure 4.1).

Levels 1 and 2: Ideas and Ideologies

Let us begin our analysis at the first two levels of ideas and ideologies. Like other major social phenomena, globalization is associated with patterns of

---

[2] See also Appendix 2, which puts our analysis of *levels of social meaning* in the larger context of the overall *engaged theory of globalization* approach.

ideas related to and about forms of material practice. As we have already expressed in various ways, the relationships between those practices and ideas are extraordinarily complicated and mutually constitutive. Just as the formation of nations is associated with the ideologies of the national imaginary—that is, politically contested ideas about who should achieve the desired end of forging the 'natural' connection between nation and state—processes of globalization are associated with ideologies expressing the global imaginary that both influence and make sense of practices. Here our key notion is that full-blown ideologies are patterned and conceptually thick enough to form relatively coherent and persistent articulations of the underlying social imaginary. One or two statements of contention do not an ideology make. Ideas, values, and statements of contention must come together into a mature conceptual constellation to count as ideology.

But when does a political belief system warrant the designation of a separate 'ideological family'? What criteria should be used to determine that a relatively enduring constellation of ideas constitutes an ideology? Political theorist Michael Freeden suggests that political ideologies display unique features anchored in distinct conceptual morphologies. Resembling large rooms containing various pieces of furniture uniquely arranged in proximity to each other, ideologies are assembled around 'core concepts', 'adjacent concepts', and 'peripheral concepts'. The resulting conceptual patterns constitute the unique 'fingerprint' of political ideologies such as liberalism or socialism. Freeden then introduces three useful criteria for determining the degree of 'maturity' that sets a full-blown ideology apart from a fledgling ideational cluster: first, its degree of uniqueness and complexity; second, its context-bound responsiveness to a broad range of political issues; and third, its ability to produce effective claims in the form of conceptual chains of decontestation. 'Decontestation' is the process by which ideas are taken out of the contest over meaning and thus are seen as truths by many people. In other words, these ideas become naturalized through attempts to reduce the indeterminacy and multiplicity of their linguistically expressed meanings to fixed, authoritative definitions and statements. Crucial in the formation of thought systems, such decontestation chains thus arrange core concepts in a pattern that links them to adjacent and peripheral concepts (Freeden, 1996; 2003: 54–5). The ideological function of 'fixing' the process of signification around specific meanings was discussed as early as the 1970s by the French linguist Michel Pecheux and other intellectuals associated with the French semiotic journal, *Tel Quel* (Eagleton, 1991: 195–7).

Playing a key role in the ongoing social process of decontesting core concepts, the elite codifiers of competing globalisms generated pressing and contested claims about what it means to live in a globalizing world. It may sound counterintuitive to suggest that ideologies of global interconnection were prevalent even before the overt and contested recognition (the naming) of the importance of globalization as a condition of our age, but this is just to emphasize that ideas are not always directly expressed in relation to a self-reflexively named set of practices. What we can say, however, is that today's competing globalisms, like the previously dominant 'grand ideologies' of the national imaginary—liberalism, conservatism, socialism, communism, and fascism—remain always contingent, arguable, and in tension with each other. Thus, they resist any easy analysis of their affective power.

In the course of the 1990s, 'globalization' became a core concept—one of few powerful signifiers at the centre of any given political belief system. Thus, it contributed significantly to the articulations of the emerging global imaginary in new ideological keys that corresponded to the thickening of public awareness of the world as an interconnected whole. This meant, of course, that the conventional 'isms' of the last two centuries were coming under full-scale attack by 'globalization', whose impact was rendered visible, among other things, by a remarkable proliferation of prefixes adorning conventional ideologies (Steger, 2008). 'Neo' and 'post', in particular, managed to attach themselves to existing 'isms', turning them into hyphenated hybrids such as 'neo-liberalism', 'neo-conservatism', 'neo-anarchism', 'post-Marxism', and so on. The multiplying 'post' prefix attested to the growing recognition that mainstream discourses were moving 'post' the familiar ideational categories of the nineteenth and twentieth centuries anchored in the national imaginary. The proliferation of the 'neo' prefix suggested that people recognized that the world was entering a new ideological era in which conventional political belief systems no longer neatly applied. Inextricably linked to these material processes of 'time–space compression' (Harvey, 1989), the transformation of the ideological landscape in the late twentieth century occurred along the lines of a rising global imaginary whose core concept of globalization was articulated by a growing number of competing new ideologies we call 'globalisms'.

Our past research on the ideological dimensions of globalization demonstrates that some ideational clusters configured around the keyword have succeeded in forming coherent and durable ideological formations (Steger, 2005; 2008). Specifically, three variants are conceptually thick enough to warrant the status of mature ideologies. To start with the dominant strain, *market globalism* emerged as the ideological standard in the 1990s. As we noted in Chapter 1, however, it has come under sustained attack by ideological challengers on the political left and right. Its chief codifiers were corporate managers, executives of large transnational corporations, corporate lobbyists, high-level military officers, journalists and public relations specialists, intellectuals writing to large audiences, state bureaucrats, and politicians. These global power elites asserted that, notwithstanding the cyclical downturns of the world economy, the global integration of markets along laissez-faire lines was not only a fundamentally good thing, but also represented the given outcome and natural progression of the human condition. As we discuss below, the morphology of market globalism was configured around a number of interrelated central claims: that globalization is about the liberalization and worldwide integration of markets (neoliberalism); that it is powered by neutral techno-economic forces; that the process is inexorable; that the process is leaderless and anonymous; that everyone will be better off in the long run; and that it furthers the spread of democracy in the world.

Among the numerous elite codifiers of market globalism we introduced in Chapter 1, *New York Times* syndicated columnist Thomas L. Friedman stands out not only because of the enormous impact of his writings or his personal relationships with political and economic elites on all five continents, but also for his ability to speak to his millions of readers in easily digestible soundbites that bring conceptual order to the threatening complexity and unevenness of their rapidly integrating world. Friedman presented his ideological claims for the first time in systematic fashion in *The Lexus and the Olive Tree: Understanding Globalization*. This 1999 international bestseller was lionized by scores of reviewers as the 'official narrative of globalization'. Francis Fukuyama, for example, hailed the expanded paperback edition as 'A powerful volume that comes as close as anything we now have to a definition of the real character of the new world order' (Friedman, 1999: cover review).

So, what then was this 'real character of the new world order'? For Friedman, it boiled down to 'The One Big Thing' people should focus on: 'I believe that if you want to understand the post–Cold War world you have to start by understanding that a new international system has succeeded it—globalization'. Taking the entire globe as his frame of reference, the journalist proceeded by juxtaposing 'division' as the central aspect of the Cold War system with 'integration' as the overarching feature of the 'globalization system'. This fundamental dichotomy underpinned his frequent challenges to the legitimating discourses of the national imaginary: 'The world has become an increasingly interwoven place, and today, whether you are a company or a country, your threats and opportunities increasingly derive from who you are connected to'.

For Friedman, globalization was both a new phase in the unfolding of modernity and an objective, interconnected system. Possessing an all-encompassing structure and logic, the rules of the globalization system 'today directly or indirectly influence the politics, environment, geopolitics and economics of virtually every country in the world'. Serving as a leading metaphor for the 'greased' and 'turbo-charged globalization system', the Lexus was chosen as a central metaphor because it allegedly defied the limitations of time and space much in the same manner as globalization 'shrinks the world from a size "medium" to a size "small"' (Friedman, 1999: pp. ix–xii, xxi).

Citing a 1998 full-page advertisement run by the global investment firm Merrill Lynch in major American newspapers, Friedman declared that 9 November 1989—the day the Berlin Wall fell—marked the 'birthday' of the globalization system. Three statements made in the advertisement best characterized the dynamics underpinning the ten-year-old global age: the auspicious 'liberalization of markets' following the collapse of the 'walled-off world'; the 'spread of free markets and democracy around the world permitting more people everywhere to turn their aspirations into achievements'; and the 'awesome power of technology'—'properly harnessed and liberally distributed'—to 'erase not just geographical borders but also human ones' (Friedman, 1999: xvi). 'Global market integration' clearly represented *the* core idea in Friedman's decontestation of globalization, and he left no doubt as to what he had in mind: 'The relevant market today is the planet Earth and the global integration of technology, finance, trade, and information in a way that is influencing wages, interest rates, living standards, culture, job opportunities, wars and weather patterns all over the world' (Friedman, 1999: 27).

This neoliberal interpretation of free-market dynamics served as the ideological foundation for the principal market globalist claims Friedman weaved together in his book. First, he argued that globalization is primarily about the information and communications technology-fuelled liberalization and global integration of markets. The increased flow of goods, services, and people across conventional national boundaries enervated nation-states while invigorating global corporations and a few 'super-empowered individuals'. Second, he insisted that globalization, in the long run, would benefit everyone. On balance, he assured his readers, it generated prosperity and spread liberal democratic principles that provide for greater political stability in the world. Third, Friedman considered the liberalization and global integration of markets as inextricably intertwined with the global diffusion of American values, consumer goods, and lifestyles. Although he saw the world becoming increasingly 'Americanized', he did not present these values as unalterable entities tied to a political territory called the United States. Universal in its appeal and application, he noted, American culture could be absorbed and modified by any culture in the world without necessarily destroying cultural diversity.

What made Western-centric ideological codifiers like Friedman 'globalists', however, was their ideological orientation towards the world as a single, interdependent place that commanded more attention than the nation-state. But making the 'globalization system' their frame of reference did not mean that the national imaginary no longer exerted a significant influence—especially on Americans who took great pride in their nation's unchallenged post–Cold War hegemony. Friedman's way to square the circle was to treat the United States as 'the world's great geopolitical shaper'—with the shaky proviso that 'it would be too much to say that the United States is in charge of globalization' (Friedman, 1999: 204). He seemed to suggest that, culturally speaking, 'globalization' was actually 'Americanization'; that is, the global diffusion of American values, consumer goods, and lifestyles. While gaining steam throughout the 1990s, this perspective had also received its fair share of criticism from commentators who condemned the 'McDonaldization' (Ritzer, 1993) or 'McWorldization' (Barber, 1996) of the planet's diverse cultures. Friedman (1999: 474–5), on the other hand, closed fittingly with an unapologetic paean to America and its unique role in the globalizing world: 'And that's why America, at its best, is not just a country. It's a spiritual value and role model ... And that's why I believe so strongly that for globalization to be sustainable America must be at its best— today, tomorrow, all the time. It not only can be, it must be, a beacon for the whole world'.

In contradistinction to market globalism, *justice globalism* is configured around core concepts such as distributional justice, equity, rights, transnational solidarity, sustainability, and diversity (Steger, Goodman, and Wilson, 2013). Championed by forces of the political left, this political belief system articulates a very different set of claims suggesting that the process of globalization is powered by neoliberal corporate interests that produce global crises; that market-driven globalization has increased worldwide disparities in wealth and well-being; that, because liberal democracy tends to be thin and procedural, enhanced democratic participation is essential for solving global problems; that a more just world is possible and urgently needed; and that existing power relations in the world—especially the unequal North–South relationship—must be fundamentally altered to benefit the global poor and the ailing planet.

During the 2000s, these claims, disseminated by a new 'global justice movement', had begun to cohere around the time of massive anti-free trade protests in Seattle and elsewhere around the world. Social activists started to engage in what sociologist Sidney Tarrow (2005: 40–60) called 'global framing'; that is, a flexible form of 'global thinking' that connects local or national grievances to the larger context of 'global justice', 'global inequalities', or 'world peace'. In addition to articulating their particular concerns and demands within a global framework, justice globalists increasingly engaged in multi-issue framing—the ability to grasp how certain issues like environmental protection or the struggle against AIDS related to other issues such as patriarchy, race, or the debt burden of the Global South. Tarrow also argued that most of these transnational activists could be characterized as 'rooted cosmopolitans' because they remained embedded in their domestic environments while at the same time developing a global consciousness as a result of vastly enhanced contacts with like-minded individuals and organizations across national borders. With the 2001 creation of the World Social Forum in Porto Alegre, Brazil, the Global South became a central organizing space for tens of thousands of justice globalists who delighted in their annual 'counter-summit' to the January meeting of the market-globalist World Economic Forum in the exclusive Swiss ski resort of Davos.

The social activist and writer Susan George participated in most of these demonstrations as a key organizer and featured speaker. Her widely read articles and books soon earned her a reputation as one of the premier idea-persons of the global justice movement—the counterpart to market globalism's chief ideological codifier, Thomas Friedman. Indeed, George offered a spirited rebuttal of the common accusation made by Friedman and other market globalists that justice globalists were reflexively and unthinkingly 'anti-globalization'. She reminded her readers that those who refer to themselves collectively as the global justice movement strongly objected to the rather insulting label 'anti', preferring instead the less loaded prefixes 'alter' or 'counter'. As she emphasized, 'The movement is not "anti" but internationalist and deeply engaged with the world as a whole and the fate of everyone who shares the planet. It also has plenty of concrete proposals to offer, making it easily more "pro-globalization" than its adversaries'. What united people who felt themselves part of the movement, she insisted, was their belief that another world was possible and that today's pressing social problems could 'no longer be solved individually, locally, or even nationally' (George, 2004: xi–xx).

At the core of George's extensive critique of market globalism lay her unshakable conviction that the liberalization and global integration of markets led to greater social inequalities, environmental destruction, the escalation of global conflicts and violence, the weakening of participatory forms of democracy, the proliferation of self-interest and consumerism, and the further marginalization of the powerless around the world. Hence, she assigned her alter-globalization movement two fundamental tasks. The first was ideological, reflected in concerted efforts to undermine 'the premises and ideological framework' of the 'reigning neoliberal worldview' by constructing and disseminating an alternative translation of the global imaginary. This alternative was to be based on the core principles of the World Social Forum, particularly social justice, diversity, democracy, solidarity, ecological sustainability, and planetary citizenship. The second task was practical, manifested in the attempt to realize these principles politically by means of mass mobilizations and non-violent direct action targeting the core structures of market globalism: international economic institutions like the World Trade Organization (WTO) and the International Monetary Fund, globalizing corporations and affiliated non-governmental organizations, large industry federations and lobbies, the mainstream corporate media, and the 'present United States government' (George, 2004: 100–7).

George then proceeded to lay out in some detail concrete proposals offered by justice globalists in support of their ideological vision. The programmatic core of these demands was a 'global Marshall Plan' that would create more political space for people around the world to determine what kind of social arrangements they wanted: 'Another world has to begin with a new, worldwide Keynesian-type programme of taxation and redistribution, exactly as it took off at the national level in the now-rich countries a century or so ago. Such a programme would need to be administered democratically so that citizens would share the responsibility for choosing and overseeing programmes for each country' (George, 2004: 137–8). The author envisioned that the necessary funds for this global regulatory framework could come from the profits of globalizing corporations and financial markets—through the introduction of the global short-term investment tax. Other justice-globalist proposals included: the cancellation of poor countries' debts; the closing of offshore financial centres offering tax havens for wealthy individuals and corporations; the ratification and implementation of stringent global environmental agreements; the implementation of a more equitable global development agenda; the establishment of a new world development institution financed largely by the Global North and administered largely by the Global South; the establishment of international labour protection standards, perhaps as clauses of a profoundly reformed WTO; greater transparency and accountability provided to citizens by national governments and global economic institutions; making all governance of globalization explicitly gender sensitive; the transformation of free trade into fair trade; and a binding commitment to non-violent direct action as the sole vehicle of social and political change (George, 2004: chs 6–10).

Finally, key ideological codifiers of justice globalism challenged the Western-centric model of globalization articulated in Friedman's vision of an American-led expansion of social relations across world-space and world-time. For George, the global diffusion of American values, consumer goods, and lifestyles was *not* inherent in contemporary globalization processes. Rather, Friedman's call for the 'Americanization' of the planet represented a false universalism that served the interests of market globalists in the United States and their allies around the world eager to augment the power of neoliberal capitalism and its associated culture of consumerism. In the wake of September 11 and the intensifying 'Global War on Terror', George criticized the 'American model' as an aggressive, 'imperialist' version of market globalism (George, 2004: ch. 5).

The third ideological strain includes various *religious globalisms*— usually, but not always, associated with the political right. Evident in some variants of all three monotheistic religions, its most spectacular strain over the last two decades has been the jihadist form of Islamism represented by al-Qa'ida, ISIS, Boko Haram, and other transnational actors. Its tremendous influence around the world points to the rise of new political ideologies resulting from the ongoing deterritorialization of Islam. Indeed, Islamist globalism constitutes the most successful ideological attempt yet to articulate the rising global imaginary around its core concepts of *umma* (Islamic community of believers in the one and only God), *jihad* (armed or unarmed struggle against unbelief purely for the sake of God and his *umma*), *kufr* (unbelief), and *tawhid* (the absolute unity of God).

Let us briefly consider the major ideological claims of al-Qa'ida's version of religious globalism. The bulk of writings and public addresses by leaders like the late Osama Bin Laden or Ayman al-Zawahiri emerged in the 1990s in the context of a 'virtual world' moving from print to the Internet and from wired to wireless communication. As Islamism scholar Bruce Lawrence (2005: xvii, xi) notes, Bin Laden's 'messages to the world' were deliberately designed for the new global media. They appeared on video and audiotapes, websites, and handwritten letters scanned onto computer discs and delivered to Arabic-language news outlets, including the influential Qatari satellite television network Al Jazeera. Indeed, the al-Qa'ida leaders managed to inject themselves regularly into a transnational political discourse by appearing on the TV screens of a global audience as some of the world's chief critics of market globalism.

Taking as his point of departure the Islamic doctrine of *tawhid*, Bin Laden followed the interpretation of his Egyptian teacher Sayyid Qutb, who argued that all worldly power belongs to the one and only Lord of the Worlds whose single, unchanging will is revealed in the Qur'an. Unconditional submission to Allah's will entailed the responsibility of every member of the *umma* to prevent the domination of humans over humans, which violated the absolute authority of God. According to Qutb, the highest purpose of human existence was 'to establish the Sovereignty and Authority of God on earth, to establish the true system revealed by God for addressing the human life; to exterminate all the Satanic forces and their ways of life, to abolish the lordship of man over other human beings' (Qutb, quoted in Moaddel and Talattof, 2002: 240). Qutb's version of political Islam greatly influenced al-Qa'ida's understanding of the *umma* as a single global community of believers united in their belief in the one and only God. As Bin Laden (2005: 119) emphasizes, 'We are the children of an Islamic Nation, with the Prophet Muhammad as its leader; our Lord is one, our prophet is one, our direction of prayer is one, we are one *umma*, and our Book is one'.

Thus, Bin Laden and his followers regarded the restoration of the *umma* as no longer a cosmologically universalizing process effected locally, nationally, or regionally; that is, the cosmos as existing in every instantiation. Rather, its meaning was located above all in a concerted *global* effort, spearheaded by a jihadist vanguard operating in various localities around the world. Al-Qa'ida's desired Islamization of modernity took place in global space emancipated from the confining national territoriality of 'Egypt' or the region of the 'Middle East' that used to constitute the political framework of religious nationalists fighting modern secular regimes in the twentieth century. Religion scholar Olivier Roy (2004: 19) comes close to how we would understand it when he says, 'The Muslim *umma* (or community) no longer has anything to do with a territorial entity. It has to be thought of in abstract and imaginary terms'. We would say that the *umma* comes to be framed by a new imaginary, the global, which brings the older cosmology down to earth, this time unconstrained by modern territories. By this same process, although al-Qa'ida members embraced the Manichean dualism of a 'clash of civilizations' between its imagined global *umma* and global *kufr* (unbelief), their religious globalism transcended clear-cut civilizational fault lines. Their desire for the restoration of a worldwide *umma* attested to the globalization and Westernization of the Muslim world just as much as it reflected the Islamization of the West. Constructed in the ideational interregnum between the national and the global, jihadist-globalist claims still retained potent metaphors that resonate with people's national or even tribal solidarities while remaining consistent with the overarching imperative of taking the war against Islam's enemies global.

Al-Qa'ida's simple ideological imperative—rebuild a unified global *umma* through global *jihad* against global *kufr*—resonated with the dynamics of a globalizing world. It held a special appeal for Muslim youths between the ages of 15 and 25 who lived for sustained periods of time in the individualized and deculturated environments of Westernized Islam or an Islamized West (Roy, 2004). If the restored, purified *umma*— imagined to exist in global space that transcended particular national or tribal identities—was the final goal of their globalism, then *jihad* surely served as its principal means. For our purposes, it is not necessary to engage in long scholastic debates about the many meanings and 'correct' applications of *jihad*. Nor must we excavate its long history in the Islamic world. It suffices to note that Islamist globalists like Bin Laden and al-Zawahiri endorse both 'offensive' and 'defensive' versions of *jihad*. Their decontestation of this core concept draws heavily on interpretations offered by Qutb, for whom *jihad* represented a divinely imposed *fard 'ayn* (individual obligation) on a par with the non-negotiable duties of prayer and fasting. Likewise, Bin Laden (2005: 69, 202, 218) celebrated *jihad* as the 'peak' or 'pinnacle' of Islam, emphasizing time and again that armed struggle against global *kufr* is 'obligatory today on our entire *umma*, for our *umma* will stand in sin until her sons, her money, and her energies provide what it takes to establish a *jihad* that repels the evil of the infidels from harming all the Muslims in Palestine and elsewhere'. For al-Qa'ida, *jihad* represented the sole path towards the noble goal of returning the *umma* to 'her religion and correct beliefs'—not just because the venerable way of *da'wa* (preaching; admonishing) had failed to reform the treacherous Muslim elites or convert the hostile crusaders, but, most importantly, because Islam was 'the religion of *jihad* in the way of God so that God's word and religion reign supreme' (Bin Laden, 2005: 61).

His rhetoric notwithstanding, Bin Laden never lost sight of the fact that Islamist globalists were fighting a steep uphill battle against the neoliberal forces of market globalism. For example, he discussed in much detail the ability of 'American media imperialism' to 'seduce the Muslim world' with its consumerist messages. He also made frequent references to a 'continuing and biased campaign' waged against jihadist globalism by the Western corporate media—'especially Hollywood'—for the purpose of misrepresenting Islam and hiding the 'failures of the Western democratic system' (Bin Laden, 2007). The al-Qa'ida leader left little doubt that what he considered to be the 'worst civilization witnessed in the history of mankind' had to be fought for its 'debased materialism' and 'immoral culture' as much as for its blatant 'imperialism'. He repeatedly accused the United States of trying to 'change the region's ideology' through the imposition of Western-style democracy and the 'Americanization of our culture' (Bin Laden, 2005: 167–8, 214). Thus, jihadist globalists were not choosy about the means of struggle: anything that might weaken the infidels sufficed. Such tactics included large-scale terrorist attacks, suicide bombings, and the public killing of hostages: 'To kill the Americans and their allies—civilians and military—is an individual duty incumbent upon every Muslim in all countries' (Bin Laden, 2005: 61, 166).

Decontesting their core concepts of *umma, jihad,* and *tawhid* in potent ideological claims, Bin Laden and al-Zawahiri develop a powerful narrative predicated upon globalization's destabilization of the national imaginary. One of the defining features of religious globalisms is that they draw on the intersection of two ontological formations —the modern and the traditional. It has been this contradictory intersection of grounding forms that has given religious ideologies their extreme intensity. Less radical forms of 'moderate' Islamist globalism, often linked to Recep Erdoğan's 'Turkish model', gained ground during the Arab Spring in Tunisia, Egypt, Yemen, Libya, and Syria, where political movements searched for new combinations of Islamism and modern democracy.

Still, religious globalism functions in a mode that contrasts sharply with the defensive attempts by national populists like Donald Trump and Marine Le Pen to hold on to a declining national imaginary.[3] Despite its chilling content, jihadist Islamism imagines community in unambiguously global terms. And yet, for all their complexity as ideologies, and despite the obvious tensions between them and differences across different settings, these three main globalisms are part of a complex, roughly woven but patterned ideational fabric that increasingly figures the global as a defining condition of the present while still remaining entangled in the national. People who accept the central claims of globalism—whether from the political right or left—internalize the apparent inevitability and relative virtue of global interrelationality and mobility across global time and space. However one might seek to understand global history and whatever reversals we might face in our current moment of anti-globalist populism, the perception of intensifying social interconnections—and the struggles against it—still defines the spirit of our times.

---

[3] For our analysis of anti-globalist populism as a challenge to all three variants of globalism, see our discussion in Chapter 8.

Level 3: Imaginaries

Let us now move on to the third subjective level of globalization. As we noted, the various ideologies associated with globalization have come to coalesce around a new sense of a global social whole—a global social imaginary of profound, generalizing, and deep impact. A number of prominent social thinkers have long grappled with the notion of 'imaginary', which is more than an ideologically contested representation of social integration and differentiation. Claude Lefort (1986: 197), for example, argued that, 'In this sense, the examination of ideology confronts us with the determination of a type of society in which a specific regime of the imaginary can be identified'.

As we discussed in Chapter 2, established notions of 'spirit of the times' or zeitgeist were challenged in the second half of the twentieth century by the new conception of the 'imaginary'. In common use, the concept of the imaginary came to refer to something invented or not real, projected into the future, and imagined beyond it. However, for many writers ranging from philosophers to psychoanalysts, even this imaginary projection of invented possibilities had to have a place to stand on, a place from which to project imaginations. The notion of the 'imaginary' provided a locus from which to begin to understand the complexity of human beings. This was precisely where the French psychoanalyst Jacques Lacan (1949) used the notion of 'imaginary' (and the *imago*) to describe the basis for relating an 'unresolved human organism' to her or his reality. Lacan's imaginary was established most firmly through the mirror stage as a child came to see itself as a whole person—perhaps prompted by the physical act of looking in a mirror. In other words, the imaginary was that which made us human. However, treating the imaginary as the basis of everything was as theoretically unsustainable as the grounding of the human in the metaphysical and arguing that humans made their own worlds.

Written at the same time as these early lectures of Lacan, Jean-Paul Sartre's *The Imaginary* (1940) came out of a completely different theoretical lineage with a stronger emphasis on the social. Sartre similarly distinguished between the 'imaginary' and the 'real'. However, while these categories were usually seen as only two analytical sides of an integrated subjective–objective world, Sartre's existentialist project allowed them to come together across an abyss of tension as the antithetical expressions of feeling and conduct. It was out of this background that the social theorist Cornelius Castoriadis offered his critique that made it abundantly clear that the notion of the 'imaginary' could not be confined to the psychoanalytic or the shallow psychosocial. It had to be seen as a 'social imaginary'. As Castoriadis (1975: 3) emphasized, 'The imaginary of which I am speaking is ... the unceasing and essentially undetermined (social-historical and psychical) creation of figures/forms/images, on the basis of which alone there can ever be a question of "something". What we call "reality" and "rationality" are its works'. He then moved from the defensible position that a generalizing social imaginary developed in Western capitalist society to suggesting that, because it occurred alongside the 'disenchantment of the world' and 'the destruction of previous forms of the imaginary', it 'has, paradoxically, gone hand in hand with the constitution of a new imaginary, centred on the "pseudo rational"' (Castoriadis, 1975: 130–1). But the introduction of this term raised more questions than it provided answers for. Why did the characterization of the present depend upon the formation of 'pseudo-rationality'? And even if we provisionally accepted the notion of the pseudo-rational, how could individuals analytically stand outside the imaginary in order to understand a phenomenon that encompassed them completely in all its pseudo-rationality?

What was required was a more direct formulation of the social imaginary. Canadian philosopher Charles Taylor (2007: 156) made a pivotal contribution by defining the social imaginary as 'the ways we are able to think or imagine the whole of society'. Indeed, Steger's formulation of the 'global imaginary' (2008) drew directly upon Taylor's focus on these common-sense 'background understandings' of lived social experience. For both writers, a social imaginary was determined by current ideas *and* practices constituted in relation to meanings and practices of the past. This, for example, avoided the common misinterpretation of Benedict Anderson's (1983) conception of nations as imagined communities, which put the emphasis on the ideas and images that people hold in their minds. Secondly, both Taylor and Steger viewed the imaginary not as totalizing, but rather as a culturally dominant framework, layered across prior and emerging imaginaries. This interpretation dovetailed to some extent with Antonio Gramsci's (1971) notion of 'cultural hegemony'. Thirdly, both social theorists considered the imaginary not as particular ideas or beliefs held by people, but as a collation of ideas rooted in a larger social frame. Finally, both argued that the imaginary could be informed by theoretical developments and thus be analysed conceptually. Still, it was not primarily an intellectual schema such as Lacan's conceptions of the imaginary—symbolic and real—but constituted a lived and generalizing sensibility held by individuals and groups across existing social hierarchies. 'What I'm trying to get at with this term', noted Taylor, 'is something much broader and deeper than the intellectual schemes people may entertain when they think about social reality in a disengaged mode' (2007: 171).

In a way, Taylor's use of the term appeared to be more akin to Pierre Bourdieu's conception of the pre-reflexive habitus; that is, 'systems of durable, transposable dispositions, structured structures predisposed to function as structuring structures, that is, as principles which generate and organize practices and representations' (Bourdieu, 1990: 53). In our view, however, Bourdieu's 'habitus' is too normatively driven, while 'social imaginary' imparts a stronger sense of the social whole or the general 'given' social order. What we take from Bourdieu's theoretical insights, however, is a sense of how patterns of practice and ideas can be seen to be objectively outside of the particular practices and ideas of persons, even as those patterns were generated subjectively by persons acting in and through the habitus.

While Taylor's work on the social imaginary proved to be immensely valuable, there remain a number of problems. For example, he sometimes describes the social imaginary as *the* framing base of meaning, and sometimes as one of a number of frames of meaning. For instance, Taylor also uses the notions of 'moral order' and 'cosmic imaginary' alongside 'social imaginary', as if our normative claims or understanding of our place in a *traditional* cosmology or *modern* universe are not social. Moreover, the concept ends up becoming *everything* to do with the social meaning of people as they relate to each other. As Taylor (2004: 23; 2007: 171) put it, '[It is] the ways in which they imagine their social existence, how they fit together with others, how things go on between them and their fellows, the expectations which are normally met, and the deeper normative notions and images which underlie these expectations'. This conflation is fine as description, but analytically it leads to confusion by broadening the concept to encompass three different elements, all of which we carefully treat as analytically separate in our work: the complex layering of imaginaries (our 'convocations of the social whole'); the practices associated with the (re)producing of those imaginings; and the lived categories of existence such as time, which sometimes reach across different social imaginaries (Steger and James, 2013). For example, *modern* time frames both nineteenth-century national and contemporary global imaginaries.

Indeed, our layering of *ideas*, *ideologies*, and *imaginaries* works more precisely both in relation to each other and as an integrated set of levels of social engagement with meaning. To reiterate: ideas are beliefs expressed by individuals; ideologies collate ideas as comprehensive belief systems composed of patterned ideas and claims to truth; and imaginaries are convocations of the social whole that frame different ideological contestations. Hence, our understanding of the social imaginary contains another crucial insight: namely, that it constitutes patterned convocations of the lived social whole. The concept of 'convocation' refers to the calling together of an assemblage of ideas—explicit and tacit—that people experience as self-evidently connected. It is akin to Louis Althusser's (1971) central concept of 'interpellation', but does not entail the French philosophe's association of ideologies with self-consciously defending or actively naturalizing activities.

Related to 'convocation', our concept of 'the social whole' points to the way in which certain apparently simple terms such as 'our world', 'us and them', and 'the market' carry taken-for-granted and interconnected meanings. To be sure, the terms of connection could be framed by a national imaginary or a global imaginary, or a tension between both. But the notion of 'the social whole' allows us to define the imaginary as broader than the dominant sense of community. A social whole, in other words, is not necessarily coextensive with a projection of community relations or the ways people imagine their social existence. Nor does it need to be named as such. It can encompass a time, for example, when there exists only an inchoate sense of global community, but there is today paradoxically an almost pre-reflexive sense that at one level 'we' as individuals, peoples, and nations have a common global fate. Put in different terms, the medium and the message—the practice of interrelation on a global scale and the content of messages of global interconnection and naturalized power—have become increasingly bound up with each other.

As recently as 40 years ago, implicit notions of the social whole—including 'the market'—were stretched across relations between nation-states and would therefore have been seen as coextensive with the nation-state, hence the then-widespread use of the term 'international relations'. When most sociologists and political scientists analysed 'society', they tended to assume the boundaries of the nation—in the relevant literature this is referred to 'methodological nationalism'. In other words, the social whole was a national imaginary that tended to be equated with the community of the nation-state. Now we find that such concepts as 'society' have become terms of ambivalence because they have become stretched between two contesting yet interdependent imaginaries: the national and the global.

Level 4: Ontologies

What is the relationship between a social imaginary and an even deeper *ontological* formation such as modernity? And, related to this, how can we track the existential meaning of what Taylor called the transition from the dominance of a cosmological (traditional) imaginary to a universalizing (modernizing) imaginary? In Taylor's exposition, the *modern* social imaginary was built by three dynamics. The first was the separating out of *the economy* as a distinct domain, treated as an objectified reality. The second was the simultaneous emergence of *the public sphere* as the place of increasingly mediated interchange and (counterposed to) the intimate or *private sphere* in which 'ordinary life' is affirmed. The third was the sovereignty of *the people*, treated as a new collective agency even as it is made up of individuals who see self-affirmation in the other spheres (Taylor, 2004).

The problem with Taylor's argument is not that it is wrong, but that it has no conceptual frame to make sense of the different dynamics. Moreover, it is just a set of factors without providing a way of working through their interrelationship except by rubbing them together in long historical narratives. We might ask: why these three dynamics rather than many others? In other words, these highlighted historical developments are certainly relevant to what might be called the *modern* ontological formation that has seen the shift from a national to a global imaginary, but so are many other developments: the transformation in the dominant mode of organization from patrimonial engagement to the abstraction of bureaucratic governance that began to name collective categories of 'people' and 'citizens'; the rise to dominance of capitalist production systems that reconstituted the meaning of 'the economy' and opened both codified time discipline and time choice for people who had previously lived in the frame of cosmological time and value; the change in the dominant mode of communication from script to print; the digital interchange that gave us the contemporary emphasis on global connectivity; or the emergence of analytical science as the dominant mode of enquiry that, in its most recent phase, has given us both techno-science and the technical realization that we live in the global Anthropocene. Listing specific dynamics as Taylor does neither helps us to define a social imaginary in general nor gives us an answer to the crucial question of how to elaborate modes of social practice that determine the lived reality of an ontological formation such as modernity without simply adding factor to factor in a flat, descriptive elaboration.

We use 'ontologies' here as a shorthand term referring to the most basic framing categories of social existence: temporality, spatiality, corporeality, epistemology, and so on. These are categories of being-in-the-world, historically constituted in the structures of human interrelations. To talk of 'being' in this way does not imply a given or unchanging human essence, nor is it confined to the generation of meaning in the sphere of selfhood. If questions of ontology are fundamentally about matters of being, then everything involving 'being human' is ontological. Still, we are using the concept of 'being' more precisely than categories of existence such as 'space' and 'time' that, on the one hand, are always talked about, and, on the other, are rarely interrogated, analysed, or historically contextualized except by philosophers and social theorists. A brief illustration of the themes of time and space will help bring this largely taken-forgranted connection between ontological categories and globalization to the surface.

Let us start with the ontological category of *spatiality*. It is crucial, since 'globalization' is obviously a spatial concept. Indeed, the academic observation that to globalize means to 'compress time and space' has long been part of public discourse. However, to be more historically specific, contemporary globalization is predominantly lived through a modern conception of spatiality linked to an abstracted geometry of territory and sovereignty, rather than as a traditional cosmological sense of spatiality held together by God, Nature or some other generalized Supreme Being (Sassen, 2006). This is a claim about forms of dominance rather than a simple epochal shift from or replacement of an older form of temporality. It accords with Jan Nederveen Pieterse's (2015) view of globalization generating new 'hybrid' or 'mélange' modernities anchored in changing conceptions of time and space. For example, those ideological codifiers who espouse a jihadist or Pentecostal variant of religious globalism tend to be stretched between a modern-territorial sense of space and a 'neo-traditional' sense of a universalizing *umma* or Christendom, respectively. In this neo-traditional understanding, then, the social whole exists in, prior to, and beyond modern global space (Gill, 2002: 177–99).

On the other hand, we also find instances of ambiguous modern spatialities sliding into 'postmodern' sensibilities that relate to contemporary globalization. Take, for example, airline advertising maps that are post-territorial (postmodern) to the extent that they show multiple abstract vectors of travel—lines that criss-cross between multiple city-nodes and travel across empty space without reference to the conventional mapping expressions of land and sea, nation-state, and continental boundaries. Against such a backdrop and with no global outline, an advertisement for KLM Airlines assures potential customers that, 'You could fly from anywhere in the world to any destination'. Our point here is that one comfortably knows how to read those maps despite the limited points of orientation, and one also knows that they are global before reading the fine print—'anywhere in the world'. At the same time, dominant representations of global spatiality such as Google Earth often retain some modern features. However, at the start of the third decade of the twenty-first century, we no longer need the old-style icons of planet Earth to know that the local and the global are deeply interconnected. People living at the transition from a national to a global imaginary simply 'know' how to read these images.

The ontological category of *temporality* is especially important with regard to the contemporary global imaginary, even if the notion of 'time' does not seem to be contained in the concept of globalization. Modern time is the demarcated, linear, and empty time of the calendar and clock. But the ontological sense that time passes second by second is a modern convention rather than being intrinsically natural, scientifically verifiable, or continuous with older cosmological senses of time. Modern time is abstracted from nature and verifiable only within a particular mode of modern scientific enquiry—the Newtonian treatment of time as unitary, linear, and uniform. It reached one of its defining moments in 1974 when the second came to be measured in atomic vibrations, allowing the post-phenomenal concept of nanoseconds—one-billionth of a second.

This sense of time-precision has been globalized as the regulative framework for electronic transactions in the global marketplace. It drives the billions of transactions on Wall Street just as much as it imposes a non-regressive discipline on the millions of bidders on eBay. A modern sense of time has been globalized and now overlays older ontologies of temporality without fully erasing them. Another important point is that ideological codifiers tend to draw upon an assumed connection between modern time and globalizing processes to project their truth claims, which linked together such concepts such 'progress', 'efficiency', 'perfectibility', and 'just in time'. Indeed, market globalists commonly use concepts of 'time' and 'the global' to sell high-end commodities, ranging from expensive watches and clothes to computers, mobile phones, and other digital devices. Take, for example, a garish advertisement for New York's Columbus Circle clothing stores: '6.10pm. Think globally. Act Stylishly'. These words are linked to an image framed by the outlines of a clock that show a woman jumping out of a taxi to go shopping. This image-text makes sense when you consider that the eight most commonly used words in the English language today are time, person, year, way, thing, man, and world. And, of course, English itself is being globalized (Crum, 2011).

In this context, let us note that we employ the concepts of 'the customary', 'the traditional', 'the modern', and 'the postmodern' as provisionally useful designations of ontological difference. *Customary* tribalism is defined by the dominance of particular socially specific modalities that can be characterized by analogical, genealogical, and mythological practices and subjectivities. This, for example, would include notions of genealogical placement, the importance of mythological time connecting past and present, and the centrality of relations of embodied reciprocity. *Traditionalism* can be characterized as carrying forward prior ontological forms from customary tribalism, but reconstituted in terms of universalizing cosmologies and political–metaphorical relations. An example here is the institution of the Christian Church. It may have modernized its practices of organization and become enmeshed in a modern monetary economy, but the various denominations of the Church, and most manifestly its Pentecostal variations, remain deeply bound up with a traditional cosmology of meaning and ritual. The truth of Jesus is not analytically relative or a question of modern proof. In this sense, a 'return' to traditionalism characterizes many of the expressions of contemporary religious globalisms.

Modernism carries forward prior forms of being, but fundamentally reconstituting (and sometimes turning upside down) those forms in terms of technical-abstracted modes of time, space, embodiment, and knowing. Time, as we noted above, becomes understood and practiced not in terms of cosmological connection with a capital 'C', but through empty, linear timelines that can be filled with the details of the past and present as well as events made by us with an eye towards a 'better' future. Indeed, one of the key dynamics of modernity is the continuous transformation of present time by political designs for the future. The consciousness of modernity arose as a vision that human beings can create community in a new image (Delanty, 2009: 8). What has changed with the emergence of the global imaginary is not this 'modernist' vision itself, but the sense that 'community' or 'society' now refers to the entire 'world' as much as to a particular 'nation'. As we discuss in the next section of this chapter, modern space is territorialized and marked by abstract lines on maps—with places drawn in by our own histories. Modern embodiment becomes an individualized project separated out from the mind and used to project a choosing self. And modern knowing becomes an act of analytically dismembering and resynthesizing information. In practice, modernism is associated with the dominance of capitalist production relations, commodity and finance exchange, print and electronic communication, bureaucratic-rational organization, and analytic enquiry.

Postmodernism, too, carries forward modern forms of being while at the same time relativizing older ontological categories in the direction of sensibilities of mobile simultaneity, time transversal, deterritorialization, virtuality, and changing assemblages of self-identity. We thus resist linear considerations of postmodernity as a stage that replaces the modern. We agree with Nestor Garcia Canclini's suggestion that it is preferable to conceive of postmodernism as problematizing the ideologies, imaginaries, and ontologies of modernity established within the traditions it attempted to exclude or overcome (Canclini, 1995: 9). In today's globalizing world, we find different formations of traditionalism, modernism, and postmodernism in complex intersection with each other. In spite of these continuities, however, it would be a serious mistake to close one's eyes to the global formation of qualitatively new ideas, meanings, and sensibilities.

The Significance of Modernity and Nationality

Our attention to globalizing consciousness across these four levels includes reflections on the significance of modernity and nationality in contemporary societies. After all, the historical codification of political ideologies developed hand in hand with the master concept of 'modernity'. We understand this concept as a contingent periodizing term and an ontological formation, which refers to an uneven dominance of subjectivities and practices of 'the modern' within and across overlapping spatial settings. To be clear, we reject the common understanding of modernity as the totality of a period within a particular spatial (usually Eurocentric) setting.[4] Still, the specific attributes of the initial *meaning* of modernity derive from the French and American revolutions (Steger, 2008). The Enlightenment dichotomization of the sacred and the profane greatly aided this development. The carving out of a distinct secularizing space for politics buttressed liberalism's successful assault on the Church's monopoly on shaping ideational structures of order. It would be a mistake, however, to accept ideology's self-conscious image as secular. As Mark Juergensmeyer (2008: 20) has pointed out, there are significant structural and functional similarities between political and religious belief systems, as both represent 'ideologies of order' imparting coherence and authority on social life.

Competing with religious belief systems over political legitimacy, the principal ideologies of modernity evolved hand in hand with what John Stuart Mill called the 'sentiment of nationality' (Steger, 2008: 44–57). As has been well documented, the new conceptual framework of the nation constituted a powerful modernizing force. At the same time, the social form that the nation-state took was founded on a modern sense of spatiality, temporality, and embodiment (James, 2006). Modern spatiality framed the landscape in terms of demarcated, bounded territories. Modern temporality allowed the nations to move forward as communities

---

[4] While agreeing with the rationale for developing the notion of 'multiple modernities', we do not necessarily accept the particular theorization associated with this attempt to understand the unevenness of modernity (Eisenstadt, 2003).

of fate in calendrical time, with or without God. Nationhood found its embodied political expression in the transformation of subjects into abstract modern citizens who laid claim to equal membership in their imagined community and institutionalized their autonomy within the modern nation-state.

These features petrified into ontological 'certainties' about what a nation was. Although the national imaginary had not risen to world dominance until the turn of the twentieth century, this did not spell the end of political ideologies. Quite to the contrary, questions about who really counted as part of this citizenry and what, exactly, constituted the essence of the nation became the subjects of fierce ideological debates and social struggles. Issues of where the boundaries of each territory lay became the bases of violence and war. Seeking to remake society according to the rising national imaginary, the restless citizen experienced a simultaneous being-in-the-world with other citizens while at the same time exhibiting a 'forward-looking' attitude that became the hallmark of modernity (Anderson, 1991). What this narrative from contemporary history evinces is that ideologies tend to move in and out of contestation. Imaginaries move at a deeper level and, in different ways, enter the common sense of an age. Ontologies—such as how we live temporally or spatially—constitute the relatively enduring ground upon which we walk.

In order to be legitimate within the increasingly *inter-national* political formation of modernity, political communities had to be nation-states. Even the tribal and traditional communities at the edge of empire—still in significant ways constituted through other ontological forms than the modern—took on a layer of the modern and sought to become nation-states. The national gave the modern social imaginary its distinct flavour in the form of factual and normative assumptions and taken-for-granted understandings in which the nation—plus its affiliated or to-be-affiliated state—served as the necessary framework of the political. By the end of the nineteenth century, the national imaginary had acquired alluring banner headlines and truth claims that resonated with people's interests and aspirations. It thus bound them to specific ideological visions of community. Like-minded individuals were organizing themselves into clubs, associations, movements, and political parties with the primary objective of enlisting more people to their preferred vision of the national.

As we noted previously, the ethico-political translation of the national imaginary occurred in terms of the competing grand ideologies of modernity. Liberalism, for example, articulated the national imaginary as concrete political programmes and agendas valorizing the profit-orientated production of mass commodities and the generation of meaning primarily on the basis of industrialization, consumption, individualism, and rational legalism. This is not to say that discursive frameworks of earlier modern periods did not generate narratives, metaphors, and framings of the global. By the early twentieth century, however, it was the national that framed the sense of the social whole. Today, competing ideologies of globalization articulate a tangled but generalizing global imaginary, which, more readily than ever before, cuts across national, class, gender, race, state-based, geopolitical, and cultural differences, postcolonial divides, and other social boundaries. While a high degree of generality and self-reflexivity was inconceivable in the nineteenth century or earlier, this does not mean that the contemporary phase of globalization has become uncontested, homogenous, and totalizing.

Concluding Reflections

Globalization was never merely an objective process of increasing capital and commodity flows across national borders. It also contains crucial subjective dimensions that have remained undertheorized in globalization research. Ideas, ideologies, imaginaries, and ontologies of globalization matter as much as its economic and technological dynamics. The acceleration and multiplication of global material networks occurs hand in hand with the intensifying recognition of a shrinking world. Such heightened awareness of the compression of time and space influences the direction and material instantiations of global flows. Indeed, the compression of the world into a single place increasingly makes the global the frame of reference for human thought and action (Robertson, 1992: 6). Globalization involves both the macrostructures of community and the microstructures of personhood. It extends deep into the core of the self and its dispositions, facilitating the creation of new identities nurtured by the intensifying relations between the individual and the globe (Elliott and Lemert, 2006: 90; Bayart, 2008).

In this chapter, we have argued that social imaginaries name constellations of different ideologies that are otherwise lived as competing, complementary, or disconnected regimes of meaning. For example, market globalism, justice globalism, and religious globalisms may all have competing normative orientations to the world, but at the same time they all depend upon a global imaginary for their discursive power. The rising global imaginary finds its political articulation not only in the ideological claims of contemporary social elites who reside in the privileged spaces of our global cities; it also fuels the hopes, disappointments, and demands of migrants who traverse national boundaries in search of their piece of the global promise. Thus, the global is nobody's exclusive property. It inhabits class, race, and gender, but belongs to none of these. Nor can it be pinned down by carving up geographical space into watertight compartments that reflect outdated hierarchies of scale (Sassen, 2007).

The three currently dominant ideologies of globalization—market globalism, justice globalism, and religious globalism—make up an ideological family that translates a generalized global imaginary into competing political programmes and agendas. Despite the existence of multiple points of contestation, these globalisms function as the political translators of an emergent global imaginary riding on slow-moving and intersecting ontologies. We contend that people from various socioeconomic backgrounds around the world are developing a sense that their basic social categories, including 'the person' and 'the nation', exist within a social whole called 'planet Earth', 'the world', or 'the globe.' The global imaginary remains in continuing intersection with prior dominant imaginaries such as 'the national' and 'the sacred order of things', but is slowly reframing them. As the eruptions of the global continue to sear these conventional modes of understanding, they not only change the world's economic infrastructure, but also transform our sense of self, identity, and belonging. This has profound consequences for politics, including the politics of protest and contention.

However, this is not to suggest that we are witnessing an 'emerging global normative synthesis' (Etzioni, 2004: 214–44). Our perspective is much less utopian. As today's unexpected 'populist explosion' (Judis, 2016) has demonstrated, normative contestations around the national have the potential to intensify. At the same time, different ontological formations intersect in complex ways. Older traditional and customary ontological formations continue to ground the lives of many people, and a postmodern layer of temporality–spatiality has slowly and powerfully emerged. Certainly, the modern—read and reinterpreted through processes of globalization as both an objective and subjective set of social processes—continues to provide the dominant evolving social frame through which people around the world make sense of their complex lives. However, it is in the ontological tensions and contradictions of this globalizing intersection of formations that we can understand the Great Unsettling of the current period.

Perhaps one of the most difficult questions of our global age is how to balance our ontological needs and our desire for social integration. The global justice movement is yet to address the layers of subjective globalization in reflexive and systematic ways that shed light on the nature of the global imaginary and, most markedly, the continuing ontological dominance of the modern. It is this uncontested subjective and objective ground that, until recently, has given neoliberal market globalism much of its strength. Unless global justice movements address these deeper subjective levels—and not only the objective practices associated with them—they will limit themselves to a mere expression of utopian hopes for the overthrow of what they do not like. Moreover, they may open the way for even stronger manifestations of anti-globalist populism. Positive emancipatory politics (as opposed to more limited liberation politics) requires justice-globalist activists to set up the ideological, imaginary, and ontological conditions that are indispensable for the creation of 'another world'.

This means that the rise of the global imaginary is neither inevitable nor irreversible. We do not expect it to progress in linear fashion towards history's telos of globality, destined to change people's consciousness for good. The best way of characterizing what we have in mind is to speak of a destabilization of the national consciousness that goes hand in hand with the spotty and uneven eruption of the global imaginary. Social theorists Ulf Hedetoft and Mette Hjort (2002: 15) put this well:

'Globality'—for want of a better term—spells significant changes in the cultural landscapes of belonging, not because it supplants the nation-state . . . but because it changes the contexts (politically, culturally, and geographically) for them, situates national identity and belonging differently, and superimposes itself on 'nationality' as a novel frame of reference, values, and consciousness, primarily for the globalized elites, but increasingly for 'ordinary citizens' as well.

Today, the national and global imaginaries rub up against each other in myriad settings and on multiple levels, producing new tensions and compromises within a changing sense of modernity/postmodernity. Putting the analytic spotlight on the subjective dimensions of globalization not only yields a better understanding of the changing ideological landscape of our time, but also helps us make sense of the profound and multidimensional processes that go by the name of globalization. This chapter's discussion—together with our critical evaluation of the dominant theoretical framework of globalization offered in Chapter 3—has prepared us for the next step in our reappraisal of globalization matters: outlining our own comprehensive theoretical framework.

5   Outlining an Engaged Theory of Globalization

This chapter presents a first outline of an engaged theory of globalization that builds on the approaches and methods discussed in the previous chapters. As Jan Aart Scholte (2016: 222) points out, global theory is about conceptualizing social relations with a focus on intensifying transplanetary interdependencies, both concrete and imagined. We consciously use the descriptor 'engaged' to signal our intent to link explanatory and normative concerns. Indeed, our theoretical affinity lies with forms of critical social theory committed to making a positive difference in the everyday lives of ordinary people, both locally and globally. Moreover, our theoretical project is 'engaged' in the sense of nurturing a sensibility of critical reflexivity that comes with the recognition of the historical specificity of existing social arrangements. We seek to advance action-orientated interpersonal understanding while contesting various forms of domination, inequality, and injustice within contemporary social formations.

This cultivation of critical reflexivity also entails a responsibility to work with the nuances of theorizing about social practice and meaning rather than indulging in simplistic or reductionist judgements. It also requires a willingness to subject the epistemological basis of our explanations to critical scrutiny. To be sure, maintaining a high degree of engaged reflexivity is difficult because it involves the dual process of entering into the world to make critical claims about what is happening while simultaneously stepping back from it to abstract larger social patterns. In other words, an engaged exploration of the conditions and limits of global knowledge demands that scholars plant one foot firmly in the practical world of processes and things while keeping the other in the analytical world of ideas. Consequently, the analysis of our globalizing world must be predicated upon a humbling recognition of the growing complexity of our life-worlds without abandoning the philosophical commitment to drawing out the broad patterns of practice and meaning. The ultimate aim of our theoretical approach is to orientate social research towards the concrete global problems that frame our era of the Great Unsettling.

We begin this chapter by introducing some general principles of engaged social thought such as reciprocity, mutuality, transcalarity, transculturalism, difference, and transdisciplinarity. We then provide an outline of our particular theory of *globalization* in the form of five specific propositions discussed in response to central questions that have framed the globalization debates since the 1990s. We chose this dialectical approach to facilitate the better discernment of significant patterns of practice related to both objective and subjective aspects of globalization. Moreover, posing specific propositions allows us to develop the foundation of a conceptual and methodological framework capable of analysing the complexity of globalization in as much depth as possible.

Pushing back against the scepticism of postmodern and post-structuralist critiques of systematic theory formation, our approach experiments with a mixture of two of the ways of theorizing the global we introduced in Chapter 3: the complexity and generalizing modes. This is not to say that we desire to return to a modernist 'grand narrative' of understanding global social change. Nor do we dismiss the value of middle-range contributions to globalization scholarship characterized by their attention to empirical detail. Rather, this chapter takes the first step towards the much larger objective of constructing a systematic and comprehensive theory of globalization based on multiple levels of analysis. Ultimately, our framework aims to include empirical causal analysis; a model of multidirectional historical development; new historical periodizations and theoretical typologies; clarification of the conceptual conditions of glocal dynamics; analysis and evaluation of the different forms of globalization; and a commitment to and justification of an active global politics rooted in an engaged normative agenda.[1]

General Principles of an Engaged Theory of Globalization

Engaged theory begins with a consideration of relations of *reciprocity* and *mutuality*. To some extent, reflective thinking is always a solitary process. But the act of writing down one's thoughts also entails a dimension of relationality by requiring the researcher to draw on the work of many scholars who have come before, as well as those who work currently in pertinent fields of enquiry. In assembling our theoretical framework, we are acutely aware of our massive debt of relationality. Accordingly, we

---

[1] Thus, our theoretical efforts both draw from and extend the agenda of a 'critical global studies' advanced by Mittelman (2000; 2004: 40–1), Robinson and Appelbaum (2005), Sassen (2007), Browning (2011), Axford (2013), Pieterse (2013a), Scholte (2016), and Darian-Smith and McCarty (2017). See also Chapter 7 for our examination of the transdisciplinary field of global studies.

continue to make explicit references to pertinent scholarship—a mode of relational writing we have already embraced in the earlier chapters of this book discussing genealogical and theoretical globalization matters. Our collaborative style also extends to the everyday world of practice and ideas that envelops different communities, social movements, civil administrators, political leaders, popular commentators, and fellow academics.

As discussed in Chapter 4, another general principle involves the importance of *transcalarity* in globalization theory. Questions of place and spatial orientation are crucial to understanding global social change in the twenty-first century. Thus, our engaged theory treats processes of globalization as conducted in relation to lived places. Since global relations are always lived in local places, this means that globalization is experienced in and through its localization. All places are now increasingly 'glocal' and involve geographical scales that cannot be reduced to vertically nested separations, but stretch across local, national, regional, and global dimensions. This kind of spatial thinking is particularly important in breaking the still-dominant association of globalization research with phenomena and processes that are explicitly global in scale (Sassen, 2003). Such 'methodological globalism' can be as pernicious as those forms of methodological nationalism that global theorists seek to overcome in their work. As Jan Aart Scholte (2016: 217) has pointed out, reifications of the 'global', the 'national', or the 'local' must give way to transcalar approaches that emphasize spatial complexity in ways that do not 'distribute causality between discrete spaces, such as the global determines the national, the local determines the regional, or whatever'. Similarly, Robert Holton (2008: 199–200) calls for the development of 'methodological glocalism'—a non-reductionist account of interactions across multiple often overlapping spatial scales and dimensions at which social action takes place in our globalizing world. Indeed, broad generalization about global patterns need to be conceptualized across all spatial scales while being grounded in particular and specific references. In the spirit of both of these contributions, we argue for a methodological tension between the local and the global—what might be called 'methodological dialectics'—treating the global and the local as distinct analytical categories, but in practice related though increasing tensions and contradictions across human history.

However, as we elaborate in Chapter 7, this task of reorientating globalization theory must avoid being framed by Eurocentric themes and concerns and instead embrace the ethical imperative for the negotiation of transcultural codes for global engagement (Mignolo and Schiwy, 2003; Scholte, 2016). Recognizing global patterns of dominance emanating from the Global North, our engaged social theory nonetheless puts this ethical search for common ground in the context of relations of difference, contingency, and contestation. For example, European imperial expansion was fundamental to the global process of nation formation, but this does not mean that Europe provided the blueprint for making nation-states. Rather, imperial expansion provided the constitutive context for a globalizing relation that saw nation-states formed across the world in relation to each other, in particular through a global process of contestation, including local assertions of sovereignty, independence, decolonization, and difference.

Hence, engaged theory recognizes multiple manifestations of *difference* —and the terms on which difference is negotiated—as key to engaging our evolving human condition in the context of globalization. Rather than dissolving difference in abstract universals, we attempt to work through difference by moving across different disciplines, different fields and domains of practice and meaning, and different forms of practice. In addressing difference, attention to the ontological dimension of globalization is crucially important. In particular, we take care not to assume the one-dimensional homogenization of modernity, even though the globalization of modern processes and meaning is central to understanding the current dominant form of globalization. This ontological aspect also relates to the way in which we approach power.

Globalization has deeply challenged many prevailing ideas and practices in the social sciences and humanities. The resulting imperative to globalize the research imagination has put pressure on conventional academic landscapes and architectures shaped by Western disciplinary logics developed in the previous two centuries. As Jane Kenway and Johannah Fahey (2009: 4) put it, mobilizing this global imagination 'becomes a form of "disciplinary urging" encouraging those in the field to move beyond its impasses and absences, even beyond inherited ways of thinking'. But such an intellectual enterprise of globalizing our research methodologies stands in stark contrast to established forms of academic boundary maintenance that discourage relationships and exchanges between different disciplines.

Engaged theory proceeds from the general premise that understanding the profound changes affecting social life in the global age requires the development of *transdisciplinary* approaches. Since global complexity appears in many forms and pervades different social arenas, it makes sense to approach it from different angles and through multiple levels of analysis. As discussed above, one way of illuminating these intensifying complexities involves a transcalar approach that rejects the reification of the global as an ontologically discrete space. A related second perspective emphasizes that globalization dynamics can no longer be approached through Western modes of producing and disseminating knowledge that favoured the organization of modes of social existence into discreet spheres of activity. But the necessary task of tackling global issues such as climate change, pandemics, terrorism, digital technologies, market-ization, migration, urbanization, and human rights conflicts with the conventional disciplinary organization of knowledge that was institutio-nalized for the first time in nineteenth-century European universities and still shapes contemporary academic settings around the world.

As the complexity theorists introduced in Chapter 3 have pointed out, the compression of space and time has added many layers of intricacy to social life. This means that intellectual innovation needs to be capable of creating new epistemic paradigms that counteract the compartmentaliza-tion of knowledge while at the same time stimulating new forms of sub- and multi-disciplinary differentiation. Transgressing disciplinary space means establishing relationships to knowledge that are more open to the perpetual intellectual demands for change and reflexive alteration. Hence, our theoretical framework aims at the transdisciplinary integra-tion of multiple knowledge systems and research methodologies.

The concept of 'transdisciplinarity' is configured around the Latin prefix 'trans' ('across' or 'beyond'). It signifies the systemic and holistic integration of diverse forms of knowledge by cutting *across* and through existing disciplinary boundaries and paradigms in ways that reach *beyond* each individual discipline. If interdisciplinarity can be characterized by the mixing of disciplinary perspectives involving little or moderate inte-gration, then transdisciplinarity should be thought of as a deep fusion of continuing disciplinary knowledge that produces new understandings capable of transforming or restructuring existing disciplinary paradigms. Often an elusive goal, full transdisciplinarity involves at least four major dynamics: the dialogical integration of knowledge in a never-ending con-versation between different epistemological forms and knowledge con-tents; the transgression of (continuing) disciplinary boundaries; the transcendence of the scope of particular disciplinary views by articulating them in a holistic framework; and an issue-driven focus on problem-solving in life-worlds that elevates concrete research questions and prac-tices over disciplinary concerns (a variation on Alvargonzález, 2011: 394–5).

The formulation of possible responses to such complex on-the-ground problems as poverty, inequality, violence, or environmental degradation requires the deep integration of a broad range of perspectives from multi-ple disciplinary backgrounds. As we discuss below, our engaged theory approaches global complexity and links abstract theory to case-specific knowledge in order to develop knowledge and social practices that promote the common good. By favouring issue-driven projects based on shared concerns, we adopt a critical stance vis-à-vis the requirements of 'normal science' and existing organizational arrangements. Our criticism seeks to be constructive in the sense of supporting common definitions and holistic frameworks that might stake out new knowledge territories with an explicit focus on social complexity. Thus, our engaged theory embraces transdisciplinarity as a potent means to combat knowledge fragmentation and scientific reductionism while facilitating an understanding of the 'big picture', which is indispensable for stimulating the political commitment needed to tackle pressing global problems. As we discuss in Chapter 6, transdisciplinary activities have become especially closely associated with the emergence of integrative fields such 'global studies'.

Specific Propositions of an Engaged Theory of Globalization

Having sketched the broad general principles of our theoretical framework, we can now move on to the specifics of our outline. Since any genuinely *engaged* theory must demonstrate the ability to critically reach beyond itself, we begin the main section of this chapter with the premise that adequate theorizing requires a prior generalizing social theory or approach. Again, this necessary first step should not be confused with a classical quest for a singular framing Grand Theory. We set ourselves the less ambitious task of building, in a gradual and careful fashion, what we hope will become an *integrated* conceptual approach to a complex world in which globalization constitutes a key matrix of interconnected processes. As we noted earlier, our task requires a *systematic* method that is able to take into account the contradictions and tensions, discontinuities and continuities, and agencies and structures linked to the extension and intensification of social relations and consciousness across world-time and world-space.

Consequently, we seek, first and foremost, to expand our understanding of the complex matrix of processes that shape the social formations of our time, including their objective and subjective dimensions grounded in practices and meanings unfolding in different world-times.[2] But let us reiterate that there can never be an all-encompassing theory of globalization-in-itself. What we are attempting is not a single theory, but

[2] For us, the concepts of 'subjective' and 'objective' serve as analytical terms of orientation —two different perspectives from which an analysis of the global takes place. They are not opposites or alternating absolutes. Comprehensive understandings of globalization always require both perspectives.

a systematic way of approaching theory. In other words, our theorizations take place in tandem with a methodological framework that takes into account the contradictory and uneven layering of different practices and subjectivities across all social relations. Thus, our discussion assumes the form of five substantive propositions elaborated in response to central research questions that have emerged consistently in the academic globalization debates of the last three decades:

1 How should globalization be conceptualized?
2 Should globalization be equated with material interconnectivity?
3 What dominant forms has globalization assumed throughout history?
4 What is the relationship between globalization and relations of power, domination, and subjection?
5 What is the relationship of globalization theory to social practice?

Question 1: How should globalization be conceptualized?

Proposition 1: Globalization is a complex matrix of processes characterized by the extension and intensification of social relations and consciousness across world-space. Here, we refer to 'world-space' in terms of the historically variable ways that it has been practised (objectively) and socially understood (subjectively) across changing world-time.

Proposition 1 offers a definition that is basic to our understanding of globalization as both an objective and subjective dynamic, now and throughout human history. To begin with, a general definition needs to acknowledge that the reality of conflicting understandings of the phenomenon should not detract from the importance of capturing its essential character in precise yet non-reductionist language. Some degree of specificity is required to describe what lies at the heart of globalization without neglecting its historical variability. As we described in Chapter 2, before we were confronted with planetary suchness in the stunning 1968 Earthrise photograph of the partially occluded globe, there were already different practices and conceptions of world-space (Cosgrove, 1994). This accords with our principle concerning ontological difference, including non-modern forms of globalization. In earlier times, people on this planet have never come as close as today to the condition of globality—an unprecedented development in human history.[3] Still, both intended and unintended processes of globalization and its associated subjectivities were occurring to the extent that these comprehensive social dynamics—together with their ecological consequences—had global reach.

---

[3] We return to the crucial distinction between 'process' and 'condition' towards the end of our discussion of Proposition 1.

As we discuss in more detail in our historical Chapter 6, subjective and ideological projections of the globe—the earliest form of globalism— emerged with the incipient development of a technical–analytical mode of enquiry developed by the ancient philosophers of major civilizational centres around the world. In the Mediterranean region, for example, an understanding of the inhabited world-space called the *Oecumene* was conceptualized and debated during the sixth and fifth centuries BCE. This conception combined understandings both from phenomenal experience such as oral testimony and from abstracted principles such as geometry and astronomy (Jacob, 1999). Lines of objective global extension further evolved in the early empires of Eurasia and Africa. For example, at its height in the first two centuries CE, the Roman Empire imagined itself in control of most of the known world, although it was not 'global' as we currently understand that concept.

The definition of globalization offered by our proposition attempts to be concise without being reductive. By contrast, many existing definitions of globalization are one-dimensional, often showing a tendency to reduce globalization to the economic basis of global relations or focus on the information and communications technology (ICT) revolution as its defining characteristic. In this regard, Thomas Friedman's popular defi- nition of globalization is symptomatic. For him, globalization is the 'inexorable integration of markets, nation-states and technologies to a degree never witnessed before—in a way that is enabling individuals, corporations and nation-states to reach around the world farther, faster, deeper and cheaper than ever before' (1999: 7–8).

But let us examine a more sophisticated and highly influential academic definition. Offered by David Held and his collaborators, it escapes such common reductionism:

Globalization is a process (or set of processes) which embodies a transformation in the spatial organization of social relations and transactions, assessed in terms of their extensity, intensity, velocity and impact—generating transcontinental or interregional flows and networks of activity, interaction and the exercise of power. (1999: 16)

The first key definitional point made by the authors is that globalization is a process, not a state of being. This characterization is also a central feature of our Proposition 1. Still, we detect a lack of precision in their definition. For example, it is unclear what level of 'transformation' is required to associate the modalities of 'extensity, intensity, velocity and impact' with the larger category of 'globalization'. Or alternatively, why is the 'interregional' or even 'transcontinental' reorganization of space suf- ficient to be categorized as an essential feature of 'globalization'? Finally,

why do the authors designate changes in the mode of 'spatial organization' as the defining basis of globalization? Unfortunately, the definition
and subsequent discussion offered by Held and his co-authors fail to
resolve these questions.

Conversely, our Proposition 1 avoids a characterization of globalization
in terms of interregional reorganization of space. Nor does it contain
related phrases found in many other definitions such as the 'annihilation
of space', the 'death of geography', the 'overcoming of distance', the 'end
of the nation-state', or the positing of any other 'end state' that will finally
be reached when local, national, and regional configurations have become
subsumed by the global.[4] While it is quite possible that globalization
might become far more totalizing than it is now, we hold that it can
never annihilate sub-global spatial scalings—at least as long as humans
remain bound to their physical bodies and immediate social relations.
Rather, as our definition suggests, globalization at its core is about the
extension and intensification of social practices and consciousness *across*
world-space.[5] We further suggest that the concept of 'world-space' must
itself be defined in historically variable terms across changing world-time.
This important qualification relates to our concern with historicity and
placement—a crucial point we elaborate in Propositions 2 and 3. In short,
we consider globalization as a multilayered, multi-scalar, and uneven
matrix of space–time-altering processes that are historically specific yet
constantly changing.

To further illustrate our definitional intent, let us consider another
characterization. Malcolm Waters defines globalization as '*a social process
in which the constraints of geography on economic, political, social and cultural
arrangements recede, in which people become increasingly aware that they are
receding and in which people act accordingly*' (2001: 5, emphasis in original).
At a first glance, Waters' description avoids reductionism and appears to
be quite comprehensive. Still, it lacks any reference to the crucial notion
of 'world-space', which lies at the heart of *globali*zation. As we argue in
Chapter 6, the first objective form of embodied globalization was
reflected in the completion of human settlement of this planet from
Africa to the Americas circa 10,000 years ago. However, this form of
globalization by customary peoples occurred with no recorded awareness
that the 'constraints of geography' were 'receding'. Surely, *objective* forms
of embodied globalization can occur without *subjective* awareness, and
vice versa. For this reason, our definition specifies globalization as the

---

[4] For a short overview of influential definitions of globalization, see Al-Rodhan and
Stoudman (2006).
[5] Our term 'intensification' is meant to contain the related terms 'acceleration' and 'multiplication' that are sometimes featured in other definitions of globalization.

extension and intensification of consciousness *and* social relations *across world-space*. In short, Waters' definition clings to a subjectivist understanding of the spatial integration of social relations rather than resorting to a more layered understanding of globalization.

Overall, then, Proposition 1 of our outline responds directly to two widespread criticisms raised repeatedly in the pertinent literature: first, a lack of definitional precision on what constitutes globalization (Bisley, 2007); and second, the unreflective lexical conflation of 'processes' and 'conditions' of growing interconnectivity (Rosenberg, 2000; Axford, 2013). We agree that one major obstacle standing in the way of producing useful definitions of 'globalization' is the imprecise way in which the term has been variously used in both academic literature and popular discourse to describe different phenomena such as a process, a condition, a system, a force, and an age. Given that these concepts have diverse meanings, their indiscriminate usage furthers obscurity and confusion. For example, a sloppy conflation of process and condition leads to circular definitions that explain little. This can be seen in the familiar truism that globalization (the process) leads to more globalization (the condition)—a statement that does not allow the drawing of meaningful analytical distinctions between causes and effects (Rosenberg, 2000).

Conversely, our definition highlights dynamics of 'extension' and 'intensification' at the core of a complex *matrix of processes* while at the same time emphasizing the significance of social *praxis* and historical context. We consciously selected the term 'matrix' for our definition of globalization to acknowledge the sense of conceptual confusion that is associated with it. This conceptual haziness is nicely captured in a key dialogue in the popular Hollywood film trilogy, *The Matrix*: 'No-one can conceive it ... No-one can be told what it is ... It has to be seen ... to be understood'.

Let us then clarify the meaning of 'matrix' by considering a fuller range of connotations. In its most general sense, a matrix is a setting in which something takes form, has its origin, or is enclosed. In obstetrics, for example, 'matrix' refers to the body of the womb. By contrast, in mathematics, it points to a regularized array of abstract elements. And in engineering—our personal favourite given the current populist backlash against globalization—it refers to a bed of perforated metal placed beneath an object in a machine press against which the stamping press operates. The concept of a matrix thus carries in its multiple meanings the contradictory intersection of embodied and abstracted social relations, contingent events, and—crucial for our definitional purposes—systematic processes.[6]

---

[6] For a detailed discussion of the emergent 'global matrix' and its relationship to nationalism, see Nairn and James (2005).

By 'processes' we mean observable sequences of social change that gradually transform the *dominant* social condition of nationality into one of globality. As we noted previously, however, this does not mean that the national or the local are becoming extinct or irrelevant. In fact, the sub-global settings remain important arenas that are constantly changing their appearance, functions, and character as a result of increasing global inter-relations. In contrast to our process-orientated understanding of globaliza-tion, we adopt the term *globality* to signify a *social condition* characterized by extremely tight global economic, political, cultural, and ecological relations reaching across national borders and civilizational boundaries (Steger, 2017a). 'Globality' signifies a future social condition of extraordinarily high social interdependencies beyond the currently existing nation-state system and its associated national imaginary.

At its core, then, globalization should be conceptualized as a complex matrix of processes fuelling shifting forms of human interrelation. Such global social change implies three fundamental assumptions. First, we are slowly moving away from the dominance of the modern condition that gradually came to frame the world from the eighteenth century onwards. Second, we are moving towards a dominant postmodern con-dition in which processes of globalization are increasingly blanketing the world.[7] Third, we have not yet reached globality. Hence, we should neither assume that globality is already upon us nor that it is tantamount to a determinate end point that precludes any further development. One could easily imagine different social manifestations of globality. One might be based primarily on values of individualism, competition, and free-market capitalism, while another might encompass more commu-nal and cooperative norms and institutions. These multiple alternatives point to the fundamentally indeterminate character of globality.

Like 'modernization' and other verbal nouns that end in the suffix '-ization', 'globalization' suggests a sort of dynamism best captured by the notion of 'development' along complex but discernible pat-terns. While such unfolding may occur quickly or slowly, it always corresponds to the idea of global social change and therefore denotes a complex matrix of processes of transformation reflected in our definition of globalization as the extension and intensification of social relations and consciousness across world-space and world-time.

---

[7] As we noted in Chapter 4, our understanding of 'postmodernity' carries forward modern forms of being while at the same time relativizing older ontological categories in the direction of sensibilities of mobile simultaneity, time transversal, deterritorialization, virtuality, and changing assemblages of self-identity. We thus resist widespread linear considerations of postmodernity as an era in human history replacing modernity.

Question 2: Should globalization be equated with material interconnectivity?

Proposition 2: We resist the common equation of globalization with material forms of interconnectivity such as mediated communication systems and financial exchange systems. Our alternative analytical approach proceeds from our definition of globalization as a complex matrix of both objective *and* subjective processes—practice and consciousness—which brings us into *relation* with human and non-human 'others' across the globe. The concept of 'relation' is used here more broadly than 'connectivity'.

Across the globalizing world, the notion of 'interconnectivity' has been normalized as the contemporary condition of being and acting as a 'person-in-the-world'. Even discerning scholars of cultural globalization like John Tomlinson (1999) insist that globalization *is* 'complex connectivity'. Being connected across boundaries of all sorts has assumed multiple meanings; most of them are positive. Who, but perhaps a few customary villagers, traditional monks, and conservative eccentrics, are happy to be relegated to a communications 'backwater' of relative reclusiveness? 'Parochialism' and 'isolation' are nouns that conflict with those desirable places where modern and postmodern networks of connectivity dominate. In globalizing cities across the world, hyperconnected individuals might complain about the intense demands extracted from them by their numerous ICTs, but none of them want to be disconnected.

Today's intensification of interconnectivity has both important and banal consequences. For a new generation, mediated connectivity is basic to their identity—with significant consequences for their patterns of consumption and attachments to new commodities and brands. Being an acolyte of social media like Twitter or Facebook has become a precondition for the construction of such an identity. In Hong Kong, London, New York, and Sydney, people queue outside Apple stores, willing to wait hours and days for the commercial release of new versions of the iPhone or iPad. Extremely useful for marketing purposes, such street scenes are also depressing images of a changing world of 'connectivity fetishism'.

Indeed, since the arrival of the World Wide Web and the spread of mobile communications, mediated connectivity has been quietly normalized as central to a consolidating global imaginary. In conjunction with the concept and practice of the 'network' and 'networking', 'interconnectivity' has become foundational to an era of intensifying globalization— both objectively and subjectively. While communications-based and networked forms of connectivity represent, objectively, only one aspect of globalization, subjectively these forms have assumed an unprecedented centrality. Both this phenomenal sense and the practical consciousness of the importance of 'being connected' have borne back upon mainstream writing in fields as diverse as sociology and the digital humanities—and not always in helpful ways.

As we pointed out in Chapter 4, in spite of the considerable analytical attention given to the current intensification of patterns of interdependence (Castells, 2010), the subjective dimensions of connectivity have received little critical scrutiny. Rather, interconnectivity tends to be treated as the way of the present, with its objective dynamics to be mapped in ever-greater detail. These mapping exercises follow predominantly empirical methodologies, because much of the globalization literature considers the extensiveness and intensiveness of mediated and networked connections to be direct empirical matters: you have it or you don't; it can be measured by degree and across distances or it doesn't exist; and so on. Objective connectivity has become *the* process that is used to measure 'globalization' in general. Thus, it has become the overriding proxy that stands in for the much more complex set of objective *and* subjective globalizing relations. Such reductionist statements have led to considerable confusion in mainstream social theory.

As a result, 'interconnectivity' tends to be linked in the globalization literature to mediated communication systems and financial exchange systems. This is where the emphasis is put on the delivery processes provided by ICTs. At the same time, in empirical or experiential terms, the notion of 'connectivity' becomes stretched across all modes of practice to mean all interactivity and interchange at a distance. This ambiguity is problematic for understanding globalization. The problem is compounded by a second recently introduced ambiguity. Both corporate descriptions and personal testimonies regarding the role of social media platforms such as Facebook, Instagram, or Twitter tend to emphasize the personal, even intimate possibilities of connecting to others more effectively. However, social media platforms are *at the same time* objectively abstract and automated platforms using algorithms to codify data and channel consumption choices (Van Dijck and Poell, 2013).

It only takes a moment to realize that the objective lines of communication and exchange that carry such connection are as important as the subjective experience of global interconnectivity and the feelings associated with it—and that these are often in tension with each other. But because both the sensory experience of connectivity and the structures of technological connection are so 'obvious', they tend to be reduced to the natural outcome of what is now simply referred to as 'the network'. The concept of 'network' has thus assumed a sophisticated but uncritical pre-eminence. Many social theorists actively conflate all social relations into it

(Castells, 2010; Latour, 2010), which has led to much confusion on the subject.

We argue that an adequate understanding of globalization needs to recognize that connectivity is only one possible outcome of increasing the extension and intensification of social relations across global space and time—even if it is experienced differently from a subjective point of view. An increasing dynamic towards localization or even rupture is an equally possible outcome of intensifying globalization. As we noted in our discussion of transcalarity, it is actually very possible to have both increased connectivity and increased localization simultaneously. It is also possible to have a globalizing communications system of intensifying connectivity that leads to uneven patterns of isolation. In political terms, for example, the Cold War constituted a global system that led to decreasing or demarcated connectivity for some states while supercharging others. In personal terms, it is now being recognized that globalizing social media systems work both to connect some and to isolate others—intensively in both extremes (Quartiroli, 2011). Moreover, to reiterate a point we made in Chapter 4, it is possible to have a rather thick consciousness of globalization—for example, the classical Greek and Roman consciousness of a terrestrial 'globe'—while at the same time the objective relations of globalization remain thin and undeveloped.

Our recognition of the pivotal role of subjective aspects of globalization with regard to questions of interconnectivity echoes Roland Robertson's (2009; 2015) keen observation that the investigation of consciousness has been consistently overlooked or marginalized in globalization theory. But the realization of the significance of subjectivity demands further specification. Hence, the following typology helps us to distinguish between different forms of 'consciousness'.

The first form of consciousness is *sensory experience*, the phenomenal sense that something exists in relation to or has an impact on a person. The concept of 'affect' attests to this kind of consciousness, as does 'sense data'. But 'sensory experience' is less technically conceived than those abstract expressions. It is consciousness as embodied experience—felt, but not necessarily reflected upon. The modern experience of connectivity envelops sensory experience. It is potentially everywhere, even when the Internet is down. In part, this is what gives connectivity its power.

The second form is *practical consciousness*. This involves knowing how to do things, knowing how to 'go on'. As writers as different as Wittgenstein and Marx have elaborated, it is basic to human engagement. The practical consciousness of connectivity is constantly self-confirming. The globalization of systems of ICTs has delivered unprecedented practical possibilities of connection, and a generation of people have assimilated the communicative techniques of the World Wide Web, the Internet, and various social media platforms as practical consciousness.

The third form is *reflective consciousness*, the modality in which people reflect upon the first two forms. It is the stuff of ordinary philosophy and day-to-day thinking about what has been done and what is to be done. With the dominance of modern subjectivity, this form involves the socially mediated production of the ego as the phenomenal, impermanent self, which knows the world experientially as it subjectively appears to it. However, as neuroscientific experiments have demonstrated, the unitary sense of self is a subjective representation. Citing these studies, German philosopher Thomas Metzinger (2010) argues that the ego can be likened to a 'tunnel that bores into reality' and thus gives apparent 'substance' to the ego by limiting what can be seen, heard, smelled, and felt.

The fourth form is *reflexive consciousness*—reflecting on the basis of reflection—which interrogates the nature of knowing in the context of the constitutive conditions of being. While some globalization theorists have variously made reflexivity the condition of contemporary subjectivity (Beck, Giddens, and Lash, 1994), we treat it as much more than situations where an actor recognizes processes of socialization, with this recognition bearing back upon and changing such processes. The reflexive process of interrogating the conditions of existence is tenuous, recursive, and always partial.

Specifying these different forms of consciousness also allows us to put 'interconnectivity' in its place *ideationally*, but this is no easy feat. Connectivity differs from old, more ideologically contested concepts such as 'freedom' or 'equality'. Conventional ideological clusters such as liberalism present us with ideals such as 'freedom', 'liberty', and 'autonomy' as conditions for normative ideals to which we should aspire. However, for all their naturalization as lifelong objectives, these ideals remain contested and debated. Liberalism's freedom is juxtaposed to the conservative claim about the importance of obligation and the authority of the state. Liberalism's core concept of 'liberty' is qualified in the social-democratic tradition by its emphasis on 'equality' (Bobbio, 1996 Freeden, 1996). And the current dominant desire for autonomy is in some political traditions still set against the constraints of reciprocity and mutuality.

By contrast, the concept of connectivity appears to be unmoored from such constraining qualifications. As we noted at the outset, it is equated with objective dimensions of globalization that appear in the form of networked relations as a predominantly positive form of social relations: affinity, community, accordance, association, and inclusion. Somehow— through a multilevel process worth investigating closely—the notion of 'connectivity' missed out on the process of political philosophical dialogue that produces 'essentially contested concepts' (Gallie, 1955). When the condition of connectivity is juxtaposed against other conditions, it tends to be posed in opposition to an uncomfortable set of antonyms that nobody aspires to anyway: disjuncture, separation, detachment, isolation, closure, and exclusion.

Our way out of this reductive tendency is to establish an alternative analytical foundation anchored in our definition of globalization as both objective *and* subjective processes that bring us into *relation* with human and non-human 'others' across the globe. The concepts 'relation' or 'interrelation' are used here more broadly than 'connectivity' or 'interconnectivity'. A 'relation' can be spatially close and proximate or involve substantial absence—including through death. It can be layered across more embodied to more abstracted connections *and* disconnections. Social (inter)relations range from the embodied relations of friends and family-connected diasporas to more abstract systemic relations carried by different modes of social practice that will be discussed in more detail in Proposition 3.

Question 3: What dominant forms has globalization assumed throughout history?

Proposition 3: Globalization can usefully be understood in terms of four dominant forms. These historically changing forms overlay each other in complex patterns of practice (objective) and meaning (subjective). Understanding these forms requires, in our approach, moving across four levels of analysis.

We argue that globalization has taken diverse forms throughout world history.[8] Even within a particular historical moment there are always multiple forms in operation. At the present time, for example, globalization ranges from embodied extensions of the social, such as the intensifying movements of refugees and migrants, to the disembodied extensions of abstracted connectivity, as can be found in instant communications through new technologies of textual or digital encoding. Crucially, then, we distinguish between the following four dominant forms of globalization:

1 *Embodied globalization* refers to the movement of peoples across the world. It is the oldest form of globalization, and remains enduringly relevant in the contemporary movements of refugees, emigrants, travellers, entrepreneurs, and tourists. Refugees crossing the

---

[8] For our extended reflections on the 'long history of globalization', see Chapter 7.

Mediterranean or the Rio Grande today continue to put their bodies on the line as they move in search of sustainable lives.

2 *Agency-extended globalization* corresponds to the lines of global extension mediated through the agents of institutions such as empires, corporations, and states. Its history can be traced back at least as far as the expansionist empires of Rome and China and the proselytizing of the agents of Christendom. Again, it continues to the present, even if it is no longer the dominant mode of extension. For example, it is not insignificant that the United States currently has more than half a million military personnel located across the globe.

3 *Object-extended globalization* refers to the global movement of objects, in particular traded commodities, as well as those most ubiquitous early objects of exchange and communication such as coins and notes. It takes us from the ancient Silk Road to the development of the modern shipping containers crossing the world's oceans and the digitally controlled delivery system of amazon.com. Traded global commodities today range from pre-loved pairs of Levi's jeans to the relics and treasures of antiquity such as the Ram in the Thicket from Ur. Representing an ancient deity, this statue survived 4,600 years only to vanish from the Iraq National Museum in the aftermath of one of those digitalized 'virtual' wars that have become a hallmark of the global age.

4 *Disembodied globalization* is characterized by the extension of social relations through the movement of immaterial things and processes, including words, images, electronic texts, and encoded capital such as cryptocurrencies. It has its earliest beginnings in the capacity for transcending time and space through the written word, but disembodied globalization has taken an enormous qualitative leap with the digital revolution and is emerging as the dominant form of globalization in the twenty-first century.

Examining these intersecting forms of globalization and understanding their real-world impacts requires researchers to move across the four levels of analysis we introduced in Chapter 4. These are only *analytical* distinctions, and the notion of 'levels' serves only as a metaphor designed to avoid the problem of conceptual conflation (see Appendix 2 at the end of the book).

1 *Empirical analysis*—surveying the detailed empirical instances of globalizing processes and activities.

2 *Conjunctural analysis*—mapping the globalizing patterns of ideological meaning *and* social practice, the conjunctures of different *modes of practice* at particular times in history.

3 *Integrational analysis*—delineating the dominant global imaginary *and* associated *modes of social integration*.

4 *Categorical analysis*—laying out the deeper ontological formations enveloping globalization such as world-time, world-space, and new manifestations of corporeality. These are categories of being-in-the-world, historically constituted in the structures of globalizing human interrelations.

As we have emphasized previously, our analysis must be extended into the subjective dimension of globalization composed of ideas and meanings. In general, moving across these four levels of analysis suggests that the closer that researchers focus on the empirical details of globalization processes, the more complicated and messy these dynamics appear. But as scholars abstract from the immediacy of particular empirical contexts, more coherent patterns become discernible. In our work, we do not always specify the particular level from which certain theoretical claims emanate, but we always take into consideration the aforementioned dual process of reflexivity, which requires both getting close and standing back from the world. The simultaneity of these dialectical moments of (dis)engagement is nicely captured in the Greek term *theoria*, which means both 'contemplation' and 'speculation'. Indeed, working across these four layers of analysis in a dynamic way requires the frequent shifting of analytical standpoints by engaging very closely with the massive empirical detail of social life ('contemplation') while also interrogating it in a rather detached fashion ('speculation').

We begin the necessary analysis of these dominant forms of globalization with extensive *empirical* documentation. However, problems on the level of empirical analysis often arise over either using the same term to describe different things or presenting partial versions of the same phenomenon. Hence, we appreciate the aptness of the Buddhist parable of the blind scholars attempting to grasp the full contours of a large animal by merely groping at its various body parts (Steger, 2017: 14). Unfortunately, the globalization debate is rife with generalizing descriptions that confuse parts with the whole. As we noted in Chapter 3, some thinkers argue that globalization does not exist *as such* (Hirst and Thompson, 1996) or, alternatively, that it is an all-embracing phenomenon (Waters, 2001). Sometimes globalization is described as an ongoing historical process of extremely long duration (McNeill, 2008) or, alternatively, that it has ushered in an entirely new epoch characterized by the wholesale replacement of modernity (Albrow, 1996).

We suggest that these 'all-or-nothing' and 'either/or' styles of interpretation should be avoided. It is imperative to recognize that globalization cannot be reduced to a single domain (usually economics), a single mode of practice (usually production or communication), or, conversely, a definitive list of 'dimensions'. Moving between different levels of analysis allows a more refined approach of mapping the complexity of intersecting levels and patterns of social practice that affirms the multiplicity of domains without precluding the development of research foci on specific aspects. Hence, we disagree with Justin Rosenberg (2000) and other critics whose insistence on specifying measurable indicators of globalization to generate hypotheses capable of being set against 'hard evidence' remains stuck on the level of empirical analysis.

At the second and more abstract level of *conjunctural* analysis, we engage a fuller range of questions across the broad spectrum of 'globalization matters'. This type of analysis also facilitates a more nuanced understanding of sprawling power networks. We examine globalization by tracking the networks of social interchange in relation to some major *modes of social practice*: production, exchange, communication, organization, and enquiry. These dominant ways of people acting in the world are related to globalization in that they serve as its principal 'drivers' and thus determine the various forms it has assumed in both contemporary and historical contexts. We also suggest that this correspondence between forms of globalization and modes of social practices needs to be analysed in a non-reductionist and holistic manner.

For example, the dominant mode of *production* has become mediated by digital technologies and is thus less dependent on labour-in-place or single-site integration. *Exchange* has become increasingly dominated by the proliferating processes of commodity marketing and abstracted capital trading. *Enquiry* has become a techno-scientific exercise of rationally decontextualizing locality and specificity. *Organization* relies increasingly upon abstract rational-bureaucratic modes centred on the institutions of the entrepreneurial state and the transnational corporation. *Communication* has become dominated by electronic interchanges and networked mass self-communication (Castells, 2012: 7), including mass broadcasting with content sourced from across the globe. While difficult to control by governments and private enterprises, the major hubs and nodes of these horizontal networks of digitally mediated communication tend to be organized in relation to the United States.

Some globalization researchers have attempted to make this conjunctural move towards modes of practice, with varying degrees of success. Richard Langhorne's (2001) work, for example, illustrates the limitations of concentrating on only one mode of practice. He begins with the tautologous claim that globalization is made possible by *global* communications. This sentence is then rephrased in the form of a single determinative statement: the 'communications revolution is *the* cause of globalization' (Langhorne, 2001: 2, emphasis added). Continuing in this mode of reductionist technological determinism, Langhorne (2001:

2) adds: 'The real beginning of the globalizing process came when the steam locomotive revolutionized the transport of people, goods and information, particularly newspapers, and at much the same time, the electric telegraph first divorced verbal communication from whatever was the speed of terrestrial transport'. Ultimately, Langhorne's focus on technology is too narrow to cover the intensifying real-life complexity of social practice in the global age.

Ultimately, then, the level of conjunctural analysis contributes to a better understanding of how various modes of social practice contribute—often unevenly—to the extension and intensification of social relations across world-space and world-time. It also makes it easier to identify and analyse global social formations. Global *capitalism*, for example, is a social formation based on an accelerating electronic mode of production and an expanding mode of commodity exchange and financial interchange. Global *mediatism*—the systemic interconnectivity of a mass-mediated world—is a social formation anchored in a mode of electronically networked communication. And global *techno-scientism* is a social formation of practice based on a new intersection between the mode of production and the mode of enquiry. For example, satellite transmission, cable networking, and the Internet were all developed in a techno-scientific mode as means of communication within state-supported capitalist markets that rapidly carried globalization to a new dominant level of technological mediation (Briggs and Burke, 2002).

Adding to the levels of empirical and conjunctural analysis, our engaged theory framework incorporates a third level of *integrational* analysis, which is well suited for probing more deeply into the nature of the relations in which these intersecting modes of social practice occur. As we noted in Chapter 4, integrational analysis should be part of a comprehensive analysis of the different modalities assumed by globalization across human history that begins with the empirical investigation of its dominant forms. Indeed, it is analytically important to differentiate between various forms of globalization conceptualized as overlapping modes of integration, which refer to the various ways in which social relations interact with each other across world-space and world-time. These modes of integration range from relations held together *and* separated by the embodied movement of people to more abstract relations where the bodies of people cease to be the defining condition of the particular mode of globalizing relations.

The ontological changes inherent in globalization processes become visible through *categorical analysis* and suggest a new, 'postmodern' level of production and exchange characterized by both the relativization of time and space and the reconstitution of prior elements of modern industrial capitalism (Hinkson, 1993). Indeed, this fourth and final level of our analytic approach emphasizes the changing nature of the various categories of being, including temporality and spatiality, embodiment, and epistemology. Here, we are interested in the *nature* of the space that people move in, relate across, or set up systems to manage or transcend. The definition provided in Proposition 1 suggests that globalization involves the extension of social relations across world-space. However, this does not mean that globalization can be explained in terms of the abstraction of spatiality in itself. This point parallels an influential argument offered by globalization critic Justin Rosenberg:

> It is not only space and time, which partake of these qualities of uniformity and abstraction. On the contrary, for classical social theory, it was precisely the generalising of these properties across the totality of forms of social reproduction (mental and material), which define the key question—the question of modernity itself. Abstraction of individuals as 'individuals', of space and time as 'emptiable', of states as 'sovereign', of things as 'exchange-values'—we moderns, wrote Marx, 'are now ruled by *abstractions*'. (2000: 63, emphasis in original)

Categorical analysis allows us to make visible what prominent globalization critics like Rosenberg or Hirst and Thompson omit: changes in the very nature of the way that space and time become reconfigured in the 'global age'. For all the substantial facts and figures that Hirst and Thompson accumulate, they completely miss the significance of these ontological changes. By focusing exclusively on the alleged continuities in the international integration of the economy from the 1870s to the present, they ignore the deep ontological differences that call for a categorical analysis of globalization (Level 4 in our approach) in favour of quantitative generalizations conducted on the empirical level (Level 1 in our approach). For example, they overlook Level-4 changes affecting the very character of economic globalization and instead emphasize empirical dynamics like 'a switch to short-term capital' from the longer-term capital of the gold standard period. Some of 'the capital flows of the present', they suggest, 'could thus be accounted for by significant differences in the pattern of interest rate variation' (Hirst and Thompson, 1999: 29).

Our engaged theory framework is capable of capturing a much broader spectrum of social change. At the same time, it identifies significant strains of continuity on a much subtler level than a Hirst–Thompson Level-1 analysis, which remains confined to empirical generalization. Rather than amassing tons of empirical data that allegedly 'prove' that the world economy was neither more nor less 'globalized' in 1910 as in 1995, our theoretical framework adds the value of expanding social analysis to deeper levels of abstraction that refine our grasp of global dynamics. Thus, empirical analysis must be supplemented by a categorical analysis capable of capturing the novel forms of abstraction inherent in globalization dynamics. For example, many derivative exchanges today are conducted as 'over-the-counter' transactions on private digital networks as exchanges of the temporally projected value of value-units that do not yet exist! Such disembodied forms of change *and* continuity are the hallmarks of contemporary economic globalization.

Overall, then, our Proposition 3 suggests that the higher the level of abstraction in the form of integrative relation—from embodied to disembodied relations—the easier it becomes to overcome obstacles to global flows. For example, the more materially abstract globalization processes are, the easier it is for them to cut across national borders. Surprisingly, many globalization theorists miss this rather obvious point. While it is true that the movements of bodies, objects of exchange, and processes of disembodied interrelation are increasingly 'globalized', it is absolutely crucial to note that they are globalized in different ways. On the empirical level, we may find that finance capital tends to flow quite easily across 'deterritorialized' national borders—a movement made possible by the combination of neoliberal political decisions and processes of exchange and organization. Conversely, the embodied flow of political refugees is often impeded by border agents who apply heavy-handed forms of state control and unprecedented degrees of surveillance in the service of particular nativist cultural preferences.

Linked to the four dominant forms of globalization, our fourfold analytical approach guides our *systematic* efforts to outline an engaged theory of globalization that is both critical and comprehensive.[9] Indeed, our method can be applied to the study of *any* particular historical period of globalization. Moreover, as we argue in later chapters, our theoretical framework is especially helpful in identifying the shortcomings of contemporary charges of 'deglobalization' that have buttressed the influential claim that globalization—both the idea and the process—matters far less in the current populist moment.

Question 4: What is the relationship between globalization and relations of power, domination, and subjection?

Proposition 4: Globalization is structured as relations of power, linked to different levels of practice and meaning. Manifestations of asymmetrical power relations, domination, and subjection operate differently across the various forms of globalization ranging from the embodied

---

[9] For a visual representation of our engaged theory of globalization, see Appendix 2.

to the disembodied. Over the last few decades, a framework of globalizing connections has emerged as the dominant form of geographical extension through which power is exercised, but it remains contested.

Power is a central category of analysis in all of our work on globalization. As Michael Mann (1986) and Michel Foucault (1991a; 1991b) have suggested, questions of power reach far beyond the political as conventionally understood and are thus relevant across all of aspects of social life. Over the last half century, in particular, there has been an extension of power relations across the globe that affects the emerging dominance and increasing penetration of social formations of practice, including global capitalism and global mediatism as discussed in Proposition 3. Our engaged theory recognizes that enquiry is bound up with power and knowledge practice on both the epistemological and normative levels. Thus, it is sensitive to the fact that the methodological choices of the globalization researcher have significant ethical and practical consequences in our globalizing world. Still, the structuring dynamics of globalization as relations of power have not been sufficiently theorized in the pertinent literature.

Dependency theory, for example, tends to become self-contradictory by statistically documenting dependency and subjection in terms of state-bounded development while simultaneously treating the 'world-system' as the primary object of enquiry. World-systems theory attempts to tackle this problem by designating 'the region' as the primary subunit of the world economy. Such a move, however, overly restricts the analysis while also leaving the category 'world economy' as a definitional totality characterized by a single mode of practice—economic production at the expense of cultural factors. Indeed, dependency theory and world-system theory tend to reify the capitalist mode of production or exchange as the basic determinant of contemporary international relations. This strikes us as a rather reductive account of social practice that treats capitalism as a system of economics that reconfigures and replaces everything that came before it.

Conversely, our theoretical framework avoids turning globalizing capitalism into a one-dimensional system of power relations. If we accept that contemporary capitalism has completely replaced prior modes of production, then we would have no way of understanding why the penetration of capitalism, as extensive and intensive as it is, has not produced a homogenization of cultures and economies. Globalization is neither a clear-cut process of disorder, fragmentation, or rupture, nor a coherent force of homogenization that inevitably sweeps all before it. Writers as sophisticated and concerned about the structures of the 'social whole' as

Fredric Jameson (1991) and David Harvey (1989) have argued that the 'postmodern world' has become increasingly fragmented without having an account of the level at which rupture takes place and the level at which reintegration is occurring. While both thinkers have made brilliant contributions to theorizing the structures of the changing world, they make the mistake of reifying the postmodernist language of fragmentation without providing us with an account of the levels at which fragmentation actually occurs. A similar problem of positing a social whole based on fragmentation is found in the argument about a shift from 'organized' to 'disorganized capitalism' (Offe, 1985; Lash and Urry, 1987). World capitalism has not recently become disorganized—and it was not uniquely *organized* in the first place, and certainly not when the Austrian social democratic theorist Rudolf Hilferding (2010) first coined the term at the beginning of the twentieth century.

As we emphasize throughout this study, there is no doubt that the pace of social change has accelerated in the last few decades. Most people around the world experience their life-worlds as increasingly unsettled and volatile. But this does not mean that we must surrender to the postmodern narrative of rupture and arbitrariness by disavowing the possibility of ascertaining generalizable patterns of social change. Both postmodernists (Lyotard, 1979) and their critics (Giddens, 1990) may be right to point to the subjective *experience* of social fragmentation. However, they have done very little to theorize the relationship between the increasing interconnection of power relations at a more abstract level —open to generalization when viewed from afar—and the confusing, variable pastiche of often fragmented networks of resistance apparent when viewed at close hand.

Thus, we promote an understanding of shifting power relations as an expanding and intensifying dialectic of rupture *and* continuity. As we emphasized previously, all that is solid does not necessarily melt into globalized air. For example, nation-states are still formidable power players. Processes of globalization may eventually undermine the sovereignty of the nation-state, but there is no inevitability about such an outcome, neither in logic nor in reality. It is salutary to remember that the institutions and structures of modern globalization and the modern nation-state were born during the same period. They were formed through concurrent processes, with the tension between them operating over specific phenomena such as boundary formation and sovereignty rather than in general terms. Our argument goes directly against those who would treat nation formation and global formation as the antithetical outcomes of respectively a 'first and second modernity', or those who narrowly define globalization as that which undermines the nation-state and thus misrepresent globalization as 'the processes through which sovereign national states are criss-crossed and undermined' (Beck, 2000: 11).

Recent attempts to understand domination and subjection in a globalizing world often struggle with the fact that the increasingly abstract nature of (dominant) power as discussed earlier does not mean that it is any less structured. This tension serves as a point of departure for the theoretical interventions of previously discussed domain theorists like Michael Hardt and Antonio Negri (2000; 2005), who analyse social structure as the patterned instantiation of people doing things. Our approach, however, parts company with their attempt to bring back the concept of 'empire' as 'a single power that over-determines them all, structures them in a unitary way, and treats them under one common notion of right that is decidedly postcolonial and post-imperialist' (2000: 9). Our Propositions 1 and 2 suggest that globalization—and thus global domination and subjection—should be treated as socially contingent, historically specific, and spatially layered processes; practices and meanings usefully explored by means of our 'four levels' analytical framework. It carries forward the Marxist principle that people make history, but not under conditions of their own choosing. While emphasizing that global capitalism constitutes the dominant dynamic of our time, we nonetheless argue in equally strong terms that global subjection needs to be understood as a relational process fostering a condition of subjection—used in both senses of that word—within a dominant pattern of social practices and institutional frameworks.

Unlike Hardt and Negri, we do not consider 'subjection' to be predominantly based upon 'imperial' exploitation and domination. The dominant social formations of practice—global capitalism, global techno-scientism, and global mediatism, not 'Empire'—now frame the various forms of dependency, marginalization, and exploitation. By using the term 'framing', we intend to emphasize the reconstitutive and delimiting processes of social reproduction in which historic dynamics such as colonialism or imperialism remain, to some extent, relevant to the contemporary evolution of social formations such as 'corporate globalization'. For example, despite emerging postmodern global configurations at the turn of the twenty-first century, 'older' expressions of power and collective actions that reflect the modernist logic of imperialism continue to occur with unfortunate regularity. At the same time, we *do* concur with Hardt and Negri's assessment that the conventional modern forms of state-based imperialism no longer determine the structures of world politics. Acts of domination for extending national interest claims now have to be socially legitimated, politically rationalized, and ethically defended against ever more acerbic scrutiny. Increasingly, they have become ethically ambiguous and unreflective, reactionary attempts to ameliorate problems exacerbated by earlier activities of modern imperialism. Despite such obvious continuities, much has changed. Classical imperialism, from the ancient and traditional empires to early-twentieth-century colonialism and mid-century neocolonialism, was based largely upon control of territory—however uneven that might have been—as well as the direct exploitation of material resources. It entailed forms of agency extension; that is, the presence on the ground of agents of the empire.

With the development of electronic trading, computerized storage of information, and an exponentially increasing movement of capital, there has been an abstraction of the possibilities of control and exploitation, an abstraction of the relationship between territory and power, and an abstraction of the dominant level of integration. To some extent, Susan Strange's (1986) term 'casino capitalism' partly captures this process. But when used together with terms such as 'fictitious capital formation'—that is, capital produced without a growth in the production of material objects—it gives the misleading impression that this abstraction is less real than gunboat diplomacy or factory production. In fact, when, for example, global electronic markets sell futures options on agricultural goods not yet produced and transnational corporations speculate on the basis of satellite weather forecasting, both the unfolding social relations and the power effects are very real: interests other than the importance of feeding people are framing production choices.

Question 5: What is the relationship of globalization theory to social practice?

Proposition 5: Globalization theory must be critical. We understand 'critical' in both its analytical and ethico-political sense as: (1) questioning the logic and evidence base of arguments; and (2) engaging concrete global problems and seeking to improve the everyday lives of people around the world.

Our engaged theory of globalization holds that *critique* has a crucial role to play in guiding social practice in our globalizing world. Thus, we promote an engaged, ethically charged understanding of critical thinking that exposes the harms caused by dominant global practices while offering constructive visions for more positive global futures. The term 'critical' derives from the ancient Greek verb *krinein*, which translates in various ways as 'to judge', 'to discern', 'to separate', and 'to decide'. From an epistemological perspective, then, the compound concept 'critical thinking' signifies a discerning mode of thought capable of judging the quality of a thing or a person by separating its constitutive form from mere attributes. While modern social thinkers have pointed to a strong philosophical affinity between 'critical' and 'thinking', the conceptual connection between these terms goes back for millennia. Both Western and Eastern cultural traditions have celebrated the ethical virtues of critical thinking as epitomized in such heroic tomes as Plato's *Republic* or the *Bhagavad Gita*. Indeed, most global philosophical traditions do not understand 'critical' solely in analytic terms as 'value-free' operations of the discerning mind, but insist that it also entails a normative commitment to justice.

Undoubtedly, these analytical capabilities of objectivity, balance, and problem-solving should be the foundation of any form of critical thinking. Still, the well-meaning efforts of pedagogues to enhance the educational effectiveness of their vocation should not remain unconcerned with political and ethical reflexivity, lest they reduce the activity of critical thinking to a mere analytical 'skill'. Here, intellectual training subsumes and consumes the possibility of an intellectually reflexive culture. The presentation of critical activity as a form of cognitive dexterity betrays a rather impoverished social and ethical imagination (Sharp, 1985). After all, confined to such a value-free analytic framework, critical thinking connects to the life-world only in rather instrumental ways. For example, it resonates with the exhortations of many business leaders who demand from schools to improve their students' 'critical thinking skills' in the hope of taking material advantage of a 'well-educated workforce'. Other than making more profitable work-related judgements, however, the notion of 'well educated' in this neoliberal context has no explicit ethico-political connection to the social world. Rather, it refers to economic efficiency, productivity, flexibility, and other instrumental skills highly valued in advanced capitalist societies.

Conversely, an ethico-political understanding of critical thinking emphasizes the crucial link between thinking and its social practices. Thought processes should not be isolated from the entire spectrum of the human experience. It is not enough to engage things merely in terms of how they are, but also how they might be and should be. And to be mindful of this socially engaged dimension of thinking also means to be aware of the connection between contemplation and action, as well as between interrelated analytical and ethico-political forms. This emphasis on the connection between thinking and doing has served as common ground for various socially engaged currents of critical thinking that have openly associated themselves with different critical theories.

Originally used in the singular and upper case, Critical Theory was closely associated with mid-twentieth-century articulations of Western

Marxism as developed by thinkers of three generations of the famous 'Frankfurt School' of Social Research (Bronner, 2011). In recent decades, this original Critical Theory tradition has been subsumed under the pluralized framework of critical theories—in the plural and lower case. Thus, critical theories now stretch across an extremely wide intellectual terrain covering conventional class-based perspectives as well as identity-centred enunciations of social critique including feminist theory, LGBTQ theory, psychoanalytic theory, critical race theory, postcolonial theory, indigenous theory, and so on. In spite of their tremendous methodological diversity and philosophical eclecticism, today's critical theorists share a vital normative concern with analysing the causes of current forms of domination, exploitation, and injustice.

Focusing on global social change, our work on globalization finds strong affinity with the concerns and approaches of these new critical theories. In particular, it has become increasingly obvious that dominant neoliberal modes of globalization have produced growing disparities in wealth and well-being within and among societies. They have also led to an acceleration of ecological degradation, new forms of militarism and digitalized surveillance, previously unthinkable levels of inequality, and a stupefying intensification of consumerism and cultural commodification. Seeking to expose the negative consequences of such a corporate-led 'globalization from above', critical reflexivity assumes intellectual responsibility in the global age. We agree with Pierre Bourdieu (2003), who argued that intellectuals must engage in a permanent critique of all of the abuses of power or authority committed in the name of intellectual authority. Such critical thinking is especially important in a globalizing world where 'scholars have a decisive role to play in the struggle against the new neoliberal *doxa* and the purely formal cosmopolitanism of those obsessed with words such as "globalization" and "global competitiveness"' (Bourdieu, 2003: 24–5). Accepting their ethical responsibility meant that academics had to breach the 'sacred boundary' inscribed in their mind that separated scholarship from social commitment. Ultimately, Bourdieu likened scholarly intervention on the world stage on behalf of the powerless to an indispensable act of giving symbolic force to critical ideas and analyses.

When applied by Bourdieu's 'public intellectuals' or Antonio Gramsci's 'organic intellectuals', critique lies at the heart of our engaged theory of globalization, for it serves the ultimate goal of attaining 'self-knowledge of global society through active theorizing and political work' (Appelbaum and Robinson, 2005: 14–17). In particular, it seeks to contribute to a research agenda for public intellectuals and academic activists committed to exposing the social and environmental damage inflicted by neoliberal globalization. Bourdieu called the production of alternative forms of knowledge 'realistic utopias', and James Mittelman (2004: 98) refers to them in a similar manner as 'grounded utopias' that express emancipatory interests in scrutinizing the language used to frame globalizing processes, revealing the institutions in which knowledge and ideology are created, locating an analysis within definite cultural contexts, listening to different voices, and engaging in embodied and lived experiences in concrete social contexts.

Conclusion

The general principles and five propositions fleshed out in this chapter form the backbone of our engaged theory of globalization. They explicitly respond to the charge of insightful critics that because global theory has only partly delivered on its promise, significant challenges remain even after a quarter-century of concentrated work. These perceived shortcomings include imprecise definitions of what constitutes 'globalization'; elusive transdisciplinarity; a lack of transcalarity; missing ontological analyses of the globalizing world; insufficient attention to the necessary construction of post-universalist global ethics; an inability to break the stranglehold of knowledge hierarchies situated in the Global North; inadequate critical reflexivity; and a thin engagement with concrete political struggles for progressive institutional reform and structural transformation (Jones, 2010; Scholte, 2011; Axford, 2013; Pieterse, 2013a; Darian-Smith and McCarty, 2017).[10]

We have developed our theoretical model by explicitly recognizing, firstly, how the nature of our analysis depends upon adequate definitions and the place of abstraction from which we begin our conceptual enquiry into the dominant forms of globalization. We argued for the utility of moving across several theoretical levels, starting from on-the-ground detailed description to generalizations about modes of social practice and global social formations. And we inveighed against privileging any one of these intersecting levels of analysis. A careful application of our theoretical approach reveals that the world is becoming increasingly interconnected at the most abstract level of integration. On that level, for example, the disembodying networks of electronic mass communication are shown to function as a tremendously integrating force, even though an analysis at the level of the face to face clearly shows their potential to accentuate social difference and cause social disruption.

---

[10] We return to some of these points in Chapter 6, which examines the promise of the growing academic field of global studies.

Let us end this chapter on a caveat. Our outline is intended to serve only as a first step in the long process of improving its theoretical design and methodological sophistication. At this early stage, our theoretical framework leaves as many questions to be explored as it has answered. For example, our efforts to capture the complexity of the globalization matrix incline our approach towards building the sort of detached abstractions we decried in Chapter 3 with regard to complexity theories. Mindful of the questionable viability of assembling a generalized meta-theoretical framework for understanding globalization, we nonetheless endeavour to develop a systematic approach capable of theorizing the multiple and complex dynamics of today's intensifying interrelations. Thus, we seek to chart a precarious middle way that presents globaliza-tion as a systemic matrix of transformative processes, yet remains atten-tive to the risks associated with the abstract theoretical propositions of modernist grand narratives that do not bear detailed empirical scrutiny (Jones, 2010: 239).

Moreover, we need to address more directly the significance of various social actors and institutional regimes in the attempted production of new transnational configurations such as the incipient structures of global governance or state–civil society networks. Indeed, building a systemic and general framework for the analysis of global structural transformation requires a profound understanding of pertinent governance apparatuses and their attached policy instruments. The first steps towards a new theoretical model are always inadequate; our outline is no exception. Still, we believe that our discussion has managed to demonstrate that globalization remains a compelling element of contemporary social the-ory. The appropriation of the concept in so many theoretical discourses reflects its enduring appeal and purchase on the social imagination (Axford, 2013: 177). Indeed, its continued relevance as *engaged theory* is capable of inspiring innovative and critical enquiries into the complexities of contemporary social change.

Returning to the practice-orientated concerns of our outline, we wish to conclude this chapter by reiterating a key political purpose of our engaged theory of globalization: the study of the major power differentials and social inequalities that operate across the supposedly free and open world-wide exchanges and interdependence that dominant neoliberal forces place at the heart of 'globalization'. What is left out in these sanitized techno-economic versions of contemporary space–time extension are growing levels of violence and suffering experienced by billions of ordin-ary people around the world—not to speak of the myriad non-human sentient beings and the deteriorating condition of our planet itself. It is this very ambiguity of growing wealth and well-being for the few and stagnation and misery for the many that the neoliberal proponents of corporate globalization find so hard to admit. Blindness to the connection between global garlands and worldwide scenes of horror has greatly contributed to the political rise of emergent anti-globalist populists desperate to rekindle the weakening flames of the national imaginary. It is in our crisis-ridden context of the Great Unsettling that the development and refinement of the theoretical considerations of globalization become even more imperative.

6   Excavating the Long History of Globalization

The thickening of interdependencies between the social and natural worlds contains a crucial temporal component reflected in the acceleration of moving materialities across the globe. How far back in history do processes of globalization go? And why does the periodization of globalization matter? These are the two guiding questions of this chapter that deepen our discussion of the historical matters offered Chapters 2 and 5. We live in an unsettled world that accentuates the new and relativizes time and space by orientating us to 'the global now'. While the rising global imaginary makes it hard for us to understand the past as a foreign country, mainstream understandings of globalization tend to be captured by the present. Working in and across our globalizing world is a future-orientated endeavour that begins with an analysis of pertinent contemporary phenomena while taking seriously the constitutive importance of the past. In light of the current fragmentation of the alterglobalization movement and the relative ebbing of its associated ideology of justice globalism, popular accounts of deglobalization often present equally fractured alternatives to contemporary forms of free-market globalization. Consider, for example, various emerging national populist arguments for new tariffs and protective walls that call for the deceleration of the movement of goods and people while more abstract forms of digital globalization actually gain in both volume and frequency of usage.

As we hope to demonstrate in this chapter, the long history of globalization tells a similar story of great complexity. Large-scale processes of space–time compression certainly go back long before the 1980s, a decade when an increasingly recognized name for increasing interconnectivity emerged. Taking the long perspective, we argue in this chapter that we can discern different trajectories of growing interrelations that are qualitatively distinct and thus require careful periodization schemes. As we noted in Chapter 2, processes of globalization predate the time when, according to a common contemporary myth still taught in many educational settings, the Renaissance astronomer Nicolaus Copernicus 'first' showed ignorant humans that an erstwhile flat earth should be understood as a heliocentric sphere. It is a too-often misunderstood historical fact that the sensibility of living in a world-space conceived of as an all-encompassing 'orb' or 'globe' existed many centuries before modern science projected a planet moving in the relative blackness of space around a yellow dwarf star at the margins of the Milky Way.

Hence, the processes of globalization through which the world-as-known became global need to be conceptualized in terms of the variable ways in which they have been lived across world-time.[1] This is the basis of our definition of globalization offered in Chapter 5—the extension and intensification of social relations and consciousness across world-space and world-time. 'World-space' is understood here as a dynamic configuration cutting variably across changing world-time. As we have been keen to underscore in Proposition 1 of our engaged theory of globalization, our definition thus recognizes the importance of variable objective and subjective relations; that is, variable forms of practice and consciousness. However, variability does not mean that 'anything goes'. In the contemporary world of 'post-truth', too many responses to history vacillate between arrogant dilettantism based on sampled reading and grand pronouncements swayed by the sense of the new. The task of this chapter is to sketch a sensible way that eschews presentism while allowing for understanding both the historical continuities and discontinuities of globalization. As Jan Nederveen Pieterse writes:

First, because of its presentist leanings, much research treats globalization unreflexively, may overlook structural patterns, present as novel what are older features and misread contemporary trends. Second, a presentist view implies a Eurocentric view and thus recycles the massive cliché according to which world history begins with the 'rise of the West'. Conventional cutoff points in globalization history, 1500 and 1800, echo old-fashioned Eurocentric history. Third, this view of globalization is not global. It ignores or downplays nonwestern contributions to globalization, which does not match the record and makes little sense in times of growing multipolarity when multicentric readings of world history have become more meaningful. (2012: 1)

In addition to his important warning about the pitfalls of presentism, Pieterse's last two points are especially useful in light of the postcolonial critique of global studies, which we will elaborate in Chapter 7. Save for

---

[1] Here, the concept of the 'world-as-known' does not necessarily have to mean known directly through voyages of discovery or scientific verification. To focus only on that way of knowing would be to cast a modern analytical sensibility back across all history, as if we have always understood the planet in the same way. The practice of knowing can take many forms, from analogical and cosmological *ways of knowing* to analytical and relativizing ways.

a few exceptions of early planetary thinking in the West, it was not until the aftermath of the decolonization process that we witnessed the rise of sweeping critiques of the nineteenth- and twentieth-century Eurocentrism from a global and multilinear perspective. The European or Western bias was based on a simple and yet false assumption: namely, that important concepts, practices, technologies, and capacities were said to have emerged from Europe or from Europeanized parts of the world. Originating in Europe, these crucial capacities were then allegedly diffused in unilinear fashion to the rest of the world. The semiotic prominence of 'Western values' or 'European civilization' in such Eurocentric narratives reveals their cultural embeddedness in powerful diffusionist and orientalist models. Imagined as the permanent navel of the world due to its recent (and probably already fading) success in relation to others, the West was inscribed with a superior cultural essence that must be diffused to the inferior, 'backward' periphery. It represented the active masculine principle, whereas the East appeared as a passive feminine vessel waiting to be filled with occidental knowledge. James Blaut (1993), for example, refers to this hegemonic conceptual regime as 'the colonizer's model of the world'—a biased worldview constructed by Europeans and their American descendants to explain, justify, and assist their colonial expansion. Rather than being grounded in geographical and historical diversity, such mental models amount to imperialist and colonialist translations of the national imaginary.

An instructive example of the contemporary persistence of such pejorative and historically flawed strains of Eurocentric diffusionism can be found in the writings of influential American foreign policy experts. For example, Michael Mandelbaum (2002) asserts that 'the ideas that conquered the world'—peace, democracy, and free markets—were 'invented' in Great Britain and France in the seventeenth and eighteenth centuries. Claiming that 'it was natural for Britain and France to lead the world into the modern age', Mandelbaum never acknowledges that these countries owe much of their 'meteoric rise' to the previous scientific and cultural contributions and achievements made by the great Eurasian civilizations of Arabia, China, India, Japan, and Persia (Diamond, 1997), not to speak of similar developments in Africa, the Americas, and the Pacific.

Conversely, the non-Eurocentric evolutionary model of globalization presented in this chapter dovetails with a holistic planetary approach. Often referred to as 'big history', this perspective calls upon the education of a new generation of global historians to link various periods in the history of our species with the history of the cosmos, the solar system, and our planet. Big history pioneer David Christian (1991: 223) formulates this task in respect to globalizing scales of space and time:

What is the scale on which history should be studied? The establishment of the *Journal of World History* already implies a radical answer to that question: in geographical terms, the appropriate scale may be the whole of the world. ... I will defend an equally radical answer to the temporal aspect of the same question: what is the time scale on which history should be studied? ... [T]he appropriate time scale for the study of history may be the whole of time. In other words, historians should be prepared to explore the past on many different time scales up to that of the universe itself—a scale of between ten and twenty billion years. This is what I mean by 'Big History'.

In short, non-Eurocentric periodizations of globalization share an affinity with big history perspectives by drawing on a series of mutually strengthening metaphors and concepts that envision the place of our species in the larger framework of a 'global', 'planetary', or even 'cosmic' time–space continuum. Hence, this chapter's task of excavating the long history of globalization requires new periodization schemes cognizant of a new geological era—the *Anthropocene* (see Chapter 10). This most recent period in the Earth's history involves human activities that have a significant impact on the Earth's climate and ecosystems.[2] Expressing the global imaginary in such ways contributes to the acceptance of ideas emphasizing that humans are living today in a geological–social age of our own partial making. Thus, the creation of a whole range of new ideas and images becomes necessary, most importantly the articulation of the global imaginary as explicit affirmations of belonging to the Earth—our collective home.

Similarly, the engaged theory we outlined in Chapter 5 rejects common treatments of globalization as a recent phenomenon, just as it counters those that suggest that nothing qualitatively has changed over the past century (or centuries). Humans are not, as some writers loosely suggest, now living in the 'Global Age' (Albrow, 1996). Rather, expressed more precisely, we can say that we are now living in a period in which globalization has become increasingly (even overwhelmingly) dominant as a process of intensifying interconnection, interchange, and impact—in economic, political, cultural, and ecological ways. Earlier examples of objective global connection—for example, the Silk Road trade transversals (Abu-Lughod, 1989)—have now changed in their dominant form and become a blanket of connections, albeit thin at some points. Similarly, earlier lineages of subjective recognition of emerging globality —for example, the focused excitement about circumnavigation in the early modern period (Chaplin, 2012)—have become a generalized global

---

[2] The term was coined by Paul Crutzen and Eugene Stoermer (2000), who regarded the influence of recent human behaviour on the Earth as so significant as to constitute a new geological era. See our discussion of the Anthropocene in Chapter 10.

imaginary. Yet, as we noted in Chapter 5, this thickening convocation of the social whole is shot through with numerous contradictions and challenges.

To give a comparative illustration, the world of Claudius Ptolemy (c. 100–c. 170 CE), imagined by his Hellenic belief in the Pythagorean theory of a spherical globe, was substantially different from that projected by George W. Bush when he initiated the Global War on Terror (2001–13).[3] Both conceptions take the world to be a spherical globe. Both projections were directed towards spatial extension. However, the nature of that sphere and the practices of how a particular empire or state can reach across world-space were understood and practiced in fundamentally (ontologically) different ways. Most of the classical empires such as Athens, Rome, and the Celestial Empire intended to rule their known world *cosmologically* as an 'orb' (Sloterdijk, 2014). Despite common contemporary caricatures, their key astronomers did not believe the world was flat: neither in geographical nor spiritual terms. Extending power required being in place. In comparison, by the time of George W. Bush, the US Empire was post-territorial and, for all the critiques of a new imperialism, did not seek to rule the world by spatial expansion. Rather, it sought to wrangle a new 'global order', one that accorded with US national interests but was always largely beyond its direct spatial control.[4]

By analytically defining globalization in this variable way, we can say simply that the phenomenon of globalization has been occurring across the world for millennia, but in qualitatively changing ways. Looking back across history, globalization has involved the extension of uneven relations between people in far distant places through such processes as the movement of people, the exchange of goods, and the communication of ideas. We can track a long history of different kinds of globalization, even if people did not name it as such or study it as a phenomenon in itself. In the late nineteenth century, for example, pivotal social thinkers such as Karl Marx and Frederick Engels (1848) presciently wrote that international interdependence and the revolutionizing of production were bringing about world-historical changes of global significance—even if it took another century for the phenomenon to be named 'globalization'.

[3] For a sensitive discussion of the changing forms of US imperialism, see *American Empire: A Global History* (Hopkins, 2018).
[4] Ironically, during that period, one of capitalism's key philosophers wrote a book that proclaimed that the world is now flat (Friedman, 2007). Friedman's extended shock-horror joke, reversing Copernicus, was not even accurate in its own terms, but it did illustrate the contested ideological projection that social difference had flattened out across the world, an idea that Copernicus or Ptolemy would never have entertained.

Processes of global extension, interconnectivity, and impact intensified significantly in the late twentieth century and into the present century. Increasing awareness of this intensification gave rise to two concurrent developments that condensed in the twentieth century. As we noted in Chapter 2, a popular sense of a globalizing planet swept across the world as finance capitalism, electronic media, and techno-science tightened the connections between people into an integrating, if uneven, layer of globalizing economics, ecology, politics, and culture. This is the period of globalization we call the Great Unsettling. Indeed, developing a better historical understanding of the changing nature of globalization up to our own volatile times greatly matters.

Conceptualizations of Globalization across Different Periods of History

There have been several attempts at periodizing the phases of globalization. Twenty years ago, Roland Robertson (1992) developed the earliest influential mapping of the history of the globalization process by delineating the following five phases:

> Phase 1: The Germinal Phase: in Europe from the early fifteenth to mid-eighteenth centuries—characterized by the accentuation of ideas about humanity as a whole and the development of scientific theories of the world as a planet.
>
> Phase 2: The Incipient Phase: mainly in Europe from the mid-eighteenth century to 1870s—characterized by the formalizing of conceptions of international relations and standardized citizenry.
>
> Phase 3: The Take-Off Phase: 1870s to mid-1920s—characterized by the 'rush' to an integrated form of globalization and a relatively unified conception of humankind.
>
> Phase 4: The Struggle for Hegemony Phase: 1920s to late 1960s—characterized by conflict and war, but still extending the globalization process.
>
> Phase 5: The Uncertainty Phase: late 1960s to present.

When Robertson presented this schema, his mapping of the historical phases of globalization constituted a significant breakthrough. Most importantly, it challenged a dominant tendency in both the scholarly literature and in popular representations to treat globalization as if it had only just emerged during the past couple of decades. However, there were several problems with this historical mapping that still bedevil the field of global studies and make it instructive to return to Robertson's breakthrough study. In particular, there is an overemphasis on Europe as the originating source of the phenomenon of globalization. Secondly, Robertson's periodization scheme infers a teleology of development whose categories such as the 'Take-Off Phase' are associated with a particular kind of market-based development theory.[5] Thirdly, Robertson seems to confuse the act of periodizing itself with contingent naming of the dominant form of globalization at a particular historical juncture. To be sure, it is not a bad thing to recognize crucial patterns of practice and to put dates around them. But such a mode of naming reflects a problematic tendency in global studies to substitute epochalism—the reduction of a given period to a certain form of practice and vice versa—for the more discerning task of multiple historical referencing.

One group of historians brought together by Anthony Hopkins (2002; 2006) made a powerful attempt to overcome the major problems with globalization and reductive epochalism. Firstly, they explicitly sought to avoid the tendency towards Eurocentrism by examining the multicentric patterns of globalization across different regions of the world. Unfortunately, Eurocentrism is still found in much of the extant literature, despite attempts by well-meaning authors to write otherwise. In the worst examples, Europeans supposedly initiated the processes of globalization, just as the European Industrial Revolution is treated as the diffusionist source of a global 'take-off'. More recently, Western-centrism has replaced Eurocentrism, as the 'United States' is often used to name periods of globalization at the very time when any single nation-state has much less overall impact on the globe than ever before (Taylor, 2016).

Secondly, Hopkins and his collaborators challenged the continuing neoliberal or economist tendency to conflate globalization with market dynamics. Their targets of criticism are political economists exemplified most recently by Richard Baldwin (2016) who recognize the long-run history of globalization but then proceed to reduce it to questions of different modalities of economic production and consumption. The names of Baldwin's four phases of globalization, except for the first one, reflect the centrality of economic processes in his periodization scheme:

Phase 1: Humanizing the Globe: 200,000–10,000 BCE
Phase 2: Localizing the Global Economy: 10,000 BCE–1820 CE
Phase 3: Globalizing Local Economies: 1820–1990
Phase 4: Globalizing Factories: 1990–present

[5] Roland Robertson has since revised this conception and has done a lot of work on ideas of globalization during the Greek and Roman Empires, in effect pushing his schema back to 2,000 years ago. See Inglis and Robertson (2005; 2006).

Such a framework would be defensible if Baldwin prefaced it by emphasizing that he was interested in *economic* globalization. Instead, he uses example after example that treat 'economic development' and 'globalization' as interchangeable terms. Moreover, Baldwin uses a key period of globalization—the 'Phase 3' globalization of the modern period that gave us two world-encompassing wars—as if political globalization was simply irrelevant: 'The confrontation', he writes dramatically, 'which comes in Act II as the classic rules of drama tell us it should—sees the hero faced with daunting setbacks that leave theatregoers wondering whether globalization is doomed' (Baldwin, 2016: 47). In other words, Baldwin treats a period in which the effects of war were first globalized as its exact opposite: namely, a period in which globalization was severely curtailed. While this narrow characterization might work for limited economic aspects such as declining trade volumes during the 1930s and 1940s, we must keep in mind that trade represents but one aspect of the much more complex phenomenon of economic globalization. Thus, Baldwin's periodization scheme does not even work for economic globalization.

The pitfalls of Eurocentrism and reductive economism are two of significant reasons why working through the question of history matters to the contemporary conceptions of globalization. However, for all of the work the Hopkins' scholars put into traversing this treacherous terrain, their account still leaves us with a number of problems. Most critically, like Robertson, they project a stage theory of development that gives the impression of a movement from incipient towards proper globalization. Hopkins (2002; 2006) identifies four principal forms: archaic globalization, proto-globalization, modern globalization, and postcolonial globalization. While his descriptions of the complexity of history break new theoretical ground, none of these categorizations work very well. *Archaic globalization*, the first phase, refers to the kind of globalization that occurred long before the period of 'modern globalization'. However, the category of the 'archaic' suggests a kind of closure that conflicts with Hopkins' recognition of 'archaic globalization' actually containing some strikingly modern features. Without developing an ontological claim about the meaning of 'archaic', this characterization lacks the necessary attention to inherent contradictions and anomalies of globalization dynamics.

As its name implies, Hopkins' second category of *proto-globalization* contains strong teleological tendencies, for it presumes that what comes after this period is the basis for describing the phenomenon at this earlier, different stage. The prefix 'proto' effectively links proper globalization to the present, whereas proto-globalization represents a stage where time–space compressions have not yet reached their telos. Indeed, this 'proto' stage is reductively defined in terms of two developments: changing state systems and the rise of the finance systems with pre-industrial manufacturing. As we elaborate below, however, much more was happening during this period than just these intensifying dynamics of social organization and exchange.

Hopkins' third stage, *modern globalization*, is likewise defined in reductive terms through the rise of the nation-state and the Industrial Revolution. As we will show, both are important developments, but both are part of a larger matrix of social changes. The final phase, *postcolonial globalization*, possesses the virtue of selecting a more descriptive term for the contemporary form of globalization than Robertson's 'Uncertainty Phase'. Still, Hopkins and his collaborators define 'postcolonial' largely with respect to one particular nation-state: the United States of America. Paradoxically, however, this emerging superpower did not make that much difference to the decolonization process. While it is true that many scholars have similarly made the United States the core locus of contemporary globalization, we wish to point to empirical problems with such a claim, just as we are careful to distinguish 'globalization' from 'Americanization'.

Let us offer one more example that exposes the many pitfalls of defining and tracking the history of globalization. There is a tendency among neo-Marxist writers to link globalization unreflectively to capitalism—either as a recent stage in the social form of capitalism (Robinson, 2014; Kotz, 2015) or as being historically shaped by capitalism. As Peter Taylor, a theorist of global cities working within this neo-Marxist paradigm, puts it, 'Globalization is a manifestation of capitalism' (2016: 132). Despite its admirable parsimony, however, Taylor's statement conflates a multidimensional process of spatiotemporal extension with a particular mode of economic production and exchange. This move is not only problematic from a theoretical perspective, but also impairs political practice. Indeed, political alternatives to the alleged time-bound nexus of capitalism and globalization become limited to hardening national boundaries to the flow of goods and renegotiating trade relations à la Donald Trump or to dissolving all borders as advocated by the No Borders Network (Bauder, 2014). Both alternatives ignore non-capitalist forms of globalization expressed, for example, in the slogan of the local–global food movement La Via Campesina: 'Globalize the struggle, globalize the hope'. Moreover, locking globalization into capitalism makes economics, understood as the modes of production and exchange, the basis of all social change.

Taylor (2016), too, proposes distinct historical stages of globalization: (1) imperial globalization, culminating in the late nineteenth century; (2)

American globalization, bourgeoning in the mid-twentieth century from 1945 to 1970; and (3) corporate globalization, the contemporary form starting in the 1970s. Here, some of the problems we discussed above reappear and compound. Why, across all of human history, does Taylor select a four-decade-long period of globalization associated with the power of one particular nation-state? In fact, Stage 2 conflicts with his expressed 'long-held frustration' that too many enquiries into globalization are framed by the unexamined primacy of the state that are then lifted to a global level. Moreover, why does he assume that the economic imperialism of evolving capitalism constitutes the dominant characteristic of Stage 1 globalization? After all, empires across history have shown globalizing tendencies, which does not mean that all empires were capitalist. Moreover, in the period in question, not all globalization dynamics were coextensive with imperialism.

For example, the different histories of classical Rome or the Celestial Chinese Empire tell stories of the multicentric and enduring lineages of globalization that predate Taylor's account by many centuries. Although imperial Rome was profoundly restricted in its reach and intensity in comparison to modern globalizing empires, it was nonetheless a genuine empire that drew lines of connection across vast expanses of their known world. The evidence that points to it being a globalizing empire is overwhelming, even if the forms of global orientation are not what some contemporary globalization theorists might think of as significant (Hingley, 2006). Moreover, most of the evidence for globalized extension has been historically transmitted in the form of specific modes of enquiry—such as a cosmological interrogation of the universe—rather than practical connections on the ground judged from a contemporary perspective.

Poets, in particular, emerged as important agents of such specific modes of enquiry. The Roman bard Ovid's *Metamorphoses*, for example, begins with a description of 'the god, whatever god it was', who moulded 'the earth into the shape of a great ball, taking care to make it perfectly round' (8 CE: 10). Ovid is also credited with the well-known aphorism: 'To all other peoples, fixed boundaries are set in the world; for Rome, the bounds of city and globe are one' (*urbis et orbis idem*). Writing shortly thereafter, Claudius Ptolemy, born as a Roman citizen with 'Greek' parents in what is now known as 'Egypt', developed an eight-volume *geographica* in which he writes systematically about the known 'world' stretching from Caledonia and Anglia to what became known as Java Minor. Significantly, Ptolemy recognized that he did not know everything about the globe, but this was not just a theological point. In knowing that vast stretches of the world existed beyond his mappings, he not only imagined the known and unknown global, but established the abstracting framework of grid lines for filling in those spaces that was later the basis of the cartographical globalism for the sixteenth-century revolution in map-making (Cosgrove, 2003).

Thus, the basic challenge we confront in this chapter concerns the valid question of the best timing of globalization from a variety of social perspectives. Some scholars consciously limit the historical scope of globalization to the post-1989 era in order to capture its contemporary uniqueness (Robinson, 2011). Others are willing to extend this time frame to include what they consider to be 'groundbreaking developments' of the last two centuries (Langhorne, 2001). Still others argue that glo-balization really represents the continuation and extension of complex processes that began either with the emergence of modernity and the capitalist world system in the 1500s (Robertson, 2003) or the changes across the 1000s brought on by interregional travel and trade and cultural outreach (Bentley, 1993; Stearns, 2010). And a few researchers refuse to confine globalization to time periods measured in precisely defined dec-ades or centuries (Frank and Gills, 1993; Scholte, 2005). Rather, they suggest that these processes have been unfolding in uneven and complex ways for many millennia.

There is little doubt that each of these contending perspectives contains important insights. The advocates of the first approach have marshalled impressive evidence for their view that the dramatic expansion and accel-eration of global interchange fuelled by cybercapitalism since the 1980s represents a quantum leap in the history of globalization. The proponents of the second view correctly emphasize the tight connection between contemporary forms of globalization and such developments as the Industrial Revolution. The representatives of the third perspective rightly point to the significance of the time–space compression that occurred in the sixteenth century when Eurasia, Africa, and the Americas first became connected by enduring trade routes. Finally, the advocates of the fourth approach advance a convincing argument when they insist that any truly comprehensive account of globalization—understood in its remarkable variability across world-time—falls short without the incorporation of ancient developments and the significance of their enduring dynamics for our planetary history.

Our Historical Framework

Is it possible to set up a comprehensive historical periodization that incorporates the strengths of all of these positions? This task animates our chronology introduced below. In addition to authors already discussed in this volume such as Roland Robertson and A.G. Hopkins, the works of Kenneth Pomeranz (2001), Robbie Robertson (2003), Jürgen Osterhammel and Niels P. Petersson (2005), Bruce Mazlish (2006), Nayan Chanda (2007), Dominic Sachsenmaier (2011), and Akira Iriye (2012) have been important in reacting strongly against the Eurocentric bias inherent to most of the conventional world history approaches. As we noted above, these 'global historians' and 'big historians' served as the catalysts for the birth of 'global history' (Conrad, 2017), which forms the basis of our own historical perspective.

While any brief discussion of global history such as ours is necessarily marred by the unavoidable tendency to overgeneralize, we identify four dominant historical periods that are distinguished from each other by significant accelerations in the pace of social interchange as well as the widening of their geographical scope. Most importantly, these periods represent new layers of social formation in terms of qualitative changes. Thus, we can say that globalization is an ancient process stretching back into the mists of time, and, over many millennia and centuries, it has crossed distinct qualitative thresholds. Our chronology does not imply a linear unfolding of history, nor does it advocate a conventional Eurocentric or Western-centric perspective of world history. Rather, we seek to excavate a long history of globalization that provides ample evidence for remarkable continuities and enduring patters as well as unanticipated surprises, violent twists, sudden punctuations, and dramatic reversals. Finally, our multicentric historical account of globalization involves all major regions and cultures of our planet.

Our task of excavating the long history of globalization is guided by our identification of the four different *social forms* of globalization we discussed in Proposition 3 of our engaged theory of globalization: (1) *embodied globalization*, referring to the movement of peoples across the world; (2) *object-extended globalization*, referring to the global movement of objects, in particular traded commodities; (3) *agency-extended globalization*, corresponding to the lines of global extension mediated through the agents of institutions such as empires, corporations, and states; and (4) the most abstract form, *disembodied globalization*, characterized by the extension of social relations through the movement of immaterial things and processes.

In practice, these forms are entangled in a web of globalizing extensions. However, as we suggested in our genealogy of 'globalization' presented in Chapter 2, it is important to recognize that these different forms can be enduring, emergent, residual, and dominant at different times and places in history (Williams, 2005). This point is crucial to avoiding the kind of epochalism criticized earlier. Our historical framework allows us

to argue, for example, that embodied globalism is not the defining condition of contemporary globalization, even though it remains ever-present
and critically important. Contrary to the work of some writers on the post-
war changes in migration patterns, the statistical evidence suggests that,
in terms of sheer numbers and proportions, the century after 1815 was at
least as important a period of embodied global resettlement as the present
refugee upheaval. Because of the strictures of national borders, the twentieth century after 1915 saw a sharp decrease in transnational migration
between the world wars and, then again, an upsurge after 1945. However,
in relative terms, global migration and even refugee movement have been
increasingly constrained by ever more restrictive immigration laws. What
is new about processes of migration and asylum-seeking in the last few
decades is the increased diversity and spread of immigrant destinations
across the globe and the numbers of internally displaced persons—not the
simple fact of massive movement.

Similarly, object-extended globalization should not be seen as the
defining condition of the present, though it contributes to what we have
called the blanketing effect of contemporary globalization. There has
been a significant increase in the global movement of goods across the
mid-to-late twentieth century based on the development of such new
techniques as shipping containerization (Levison, 2006). Changes across
the first half of the twentieth century in the techniques and technologies of
production and exchange, including in transportation and factory
mechanization (often described as Fordism, after the particular form of
Henry Ford's mechanization of the automobile industry), meant that in
the post-war period, globalizing exchange and production burgeoned.

As we note in Chapter 11, the defining dominant condition of contemporary globalization is the movement of abstracted capital and culture
through processes of disembodied interchange. The nineteenth century
saw a revolution in the means of globalization. Previously, the extension
of communications beyond face-to-face and oral communication had
been effectively limited to messages carried at the rather slow speed of
available transport or across relatively short distances by unwieldy and
limited transmissions techniques such as semaphore, pigeons, smoke
signals, beacons, and reflected light signals. Writing and print had, from
a much earlier stage, enabled the storage of complicated meanings and
messages and provided a medium for their slow dissemination across the
world, but the development of telegraphy and telephony in the nineteenth
century became part of one of the most fundamental changes in extending
communications. Telegraphy was developed in crucial conjunction with
the layering of undersea telegraph cables across the Atlantic from the
1850s to the 1870s, and by 1902, with the laying of the Pacific cables, the

globe had been circled. This was a substantially new phenomenon, and it has since taken on a new and intense generality with the intersection of electronic communications, computerized exchange, applied science, and techno-capitalism.

Using this fourfold set of analytical distinctions, together with the distinction between customary, traditional, modern, and postmodern ways introduced in Chapters 4 and 5, we can now excavate a series of overlapping tracks of globalization across history that begin with the emergence of human beings as a terrestrial species inhabiting the entire planet.[6] Alongside our narration of spatial extension and social integration, we will simultaneously tell a story of the overlaying of customary relations with traditional relations and, ultimately, modern (and postmodern) ways of life. Here, we define the contested concept of 'the modern' by the way in which prior social relations were reconstituted through a *constructivist* reframing of social practices in relation to basic categories of existence common to all humans. In recent decades, we have seen a newly emergent formation that requires further consideration—a relativization of social relations, including time and space. This process leads us to identify a period we call the 'Great Unsettling'.

Thus, our careful excavation of the long history of globalization occurs within a conceptual framework that distinguishes between four periods of globalization, all of which are associated with the *dominance* of specific ontological formations:

> Period 1: The Great Divergence (customary)[7]
> Period 2: The Great Universalizing (traditional)
> Period 3: The Great Convergence (modern)[8]
> Period 4: The Great Unsettling (postmodern)[9]

We resolved to these periods contingently and conditionally, neither downplaying the consequences of that dominant form of globalization nor ignoring that it coexists with other ways of life, even as it dominates them. Dominant formations are thus understood as always in tension with other enduring, emergent, and residual ways of relating to others—

---

[6] Recently, Bruno Latour (2018) made the 'terrestrial' a key concept in his discussion of globalization and ecology. In Chapters 9 and 10, we address some key similarities and differences between Latour's perspective and ours.

[7] This category comes from David Northrup (2005) and was put forward in perhaps the most radical yet incredibly simple temporal model of global history. He proposes that global history can be divided into just two periods: one dominated by dynamics of 'divergence' and the other by forces of 'convergence'.

[8] This concept comes from Kenneth Pomeranz (2001) and Richard Baldwin (2016), but is reworked to take it beyond a narrower emphasis on economics.

[9] Here, two key theorists provide inspiration to our approach: David Harvey (1989) and Fredric Jameson (1991).

sometimes creatively, but also destructively. The history of globalization is thus one of both periodical rupture *and* long-term continuities.

The Great Divergence: The Period in which Humanity Spread Across the Globe

The first phase of globalization was characterized by people moving (in effect) to colonize the planet ecologically. It involved the apparently simple embodied extension of persons across world-space. If Africa is currently understood as the place from which humans first emerged, the first phase of globalization can be said to have been marked by the period 12,000 years ago when small bands of hunters and gatherers reached the southern tip of South America. This 'event' marked the end of the long process of settling all five continents that was begun by our hominid African ancestors approximately 125,000 years ago. Although some major island groups in the Pacific and the Atlantic were not inhabited until relatively recent times, the global dispersion of our species was effectively achieved. Completed by South American nomads, the success of this endeavour rested on the migratory achievements of their Siberian ancestors who had crossed the Bering Strait into North America at least 1,000 years earlier.

Some writers argue that this form of global colonizing was not globalization at all. This is because they define globalization more narrowly than we do, equating globalization with connectivity—arguably only one of the bases for extending social relations across world-space. It is certainly true that during this earliest phase of globalization, connectivity between the thousands of hunter–gatherer bands was localized and face to face—that is in part why we call it 'the Great Divergence'. And there was certainly no subjective sense of the global. But our argument here is that the gradual (objective) human settlement of almost the entire globe needs to be included in any comprehensive analysis for a meaningful understanding of ecological globalization (see Chapter 9).

Localized social interaction between genealogically bound communities changed dramatically about 12,000 years ago when humans took the crucial step of systematically producing their own food. The early part of this period was still dominated by customary relations, but it involved what can be called a slow 'traditionalization' of the mode and means of agricultural production, associated with the development of a cosmological understanding of nature. As a result of several factors, including the natural occurrence of plants and animals suitable for domestication, as well as continental differences in area and total population size, only certain regions located on or near the vast Eurasian landmass proved to be ideal for these growing agricultural settlements (Diamond, 1997). These areas were located in the Fertile Crescent, north-central China, North Africa, north-western India, and what is today called 'Papua New Guinea'. In summary, the dominant dynamic of this earliest phase of globalization was *embodied* divergence—people and social connections originating from a single region but moving and culturally diversifying over time and space.

The Great Universalizing: The Period of Traditional Globalization in which Empires as Universalizing Polities Began to Treat Their Worlds as Cosmologically Integrated

Gradually, across the period from around 4,000 BCE, settled tribes, chiefdoms, and, much later, states based on agricultural production, patrimonial organization, and cosmological enquiry emerged, with the latter to become, for a time, the most powerful polity-communities on the planet. In certain nodes in particular alluvial regions, continuing hunter–gatherer groups were *partly* displaced by centralized and stratified patriarchal social structures headed by chiefs and priests. This is not to suggest the usual 'ascent of man' story, with domesticating agriculture and sedentarism inevitably giving rise to civilizing polities. These new agricultural settlements were difficult places to live. They had to domesticate their denizens—people, animals, and plants alike (Scott, 2017). Nevertheless, for the first time in human history, agricultural societies were able to support social classes whose members did not participate in food production. Thus, a globalization of *traditional* relations, and in particular imperial polities, overlaid and, in many places, began to complicate and reconstitute earlier *customary* relations.

This form of slow globalization, with many points of origin, was characterized by the emerging dominance of what we have called *agency extension*—the agency of polities, sodalities, and other organizations effected by designated agents. This kind of power was in turn extended by the use of writing as an *emergent* means of *disembodied extension*. The invention of writing in Mesopotamia, Egypt, and central China between 3,200 and 2,500 BCE roughly coincided with other changes such as the introduction of the wheel around 3,000 BCE in Southwest Asia. Marking the overlaying of the customary period, these monumental techniques and technologies contributed to profound social changes that moved globalization to a new level. Thanks to the auspicious east–west orientation of Eurasia's major continental axis—a geographical feature that had already facilitated the rapid spread of crops and animals suitable for food production along the same latitudes—the diffusion of these new technologies to distant parts of the continent occurred within only a few centuries (Diamond, 1997).

Writing greatly facilitated the coordination of complex social activities and thus enabled large state formations. But it also contributed to remaking the dominant sense of the social whole (Goody, 1986). This phenomenon was most apparent in the rise of an intellectual class and the impulse to abstract from local particularities and write universal histories. This impetus can be seen across many cultural backgrounds, such as the ancient Greek philosopher Herodotus (484–425 BCE), the Hellenistic historian Polybius (200–118 BCE), the Chinese historian Sima Qian (145–90 BCE), the Persian chronicler Tabari (839–923 CE), and the North African thinker Ibn Khaldun (1332–1406 CE), to mention but a few of these early pioneers. They all used documents, testimonies, and artefacts to investigate stories, mythologies, and traditions that cut across what they perceived to be different 'cultures' or 'civilizations'.

The period of the Great Universalizing also became an age of imperial states. Empires were universalizing in the sense that they framed their relations to others and to nature in all-embracing cosmological terms. This was the period in which the world religions were formed. As some states succeeded in establishing permanent rule over other states, the resulting vast territorial accumulations formed the basis of the Egyptian Kingdoms, the Persian Empire, the Macedonian Empire, the American Empires of the Aztecs and the Incas, the Roman Empire, the Indian Empires, the Byzantine Empire, the Islamic Caliphates, the Holy Roman Empire, the African Empires of Ghana, Mali, and Songhay, and the Ottoman Empire. All of these empires fostered the multiplication and extension of long-distance communication and exchanges of culture, technologies, commodities, and diseases that are now firmly associated with the term 'globalization'.

The most enduring and technologically advanced of these vast traditional conglomerates was undoubtedly the Chinese Empire. A closer look at its history reveals some of the early dynamics of universalizing globalization. After centuries of warfare among several independent states, the Qin Emperor's armies in 221 BCE finally unified large portions of northeast China. For the next 1,700 years, successive dynasties known as the Han, Sui, T'ang, Yuan, and Ming ruled an empire supported by vast bureaucracies that would extend its influence to such distant regions as Southeast Asia, the Mediterranean, India, and East Africa. The codification of law and the fixing of weights, measures, and values of coinage fostered the expansion of trade and markets. The standardization of the sizes of cart axles and the roads they travelled on allowed Chinese merchants for the first time to make precise calculations as to the desired quantities of imported and exported goods.

The most extensive of these routes of object extension was the Silk Road. It linked the Chinese and the Roman Empires with the Parthian domain and other trading communities that served as skilled intermediaries. Even 1,300 years after the Silk Road first reached the Italian peninsula in 50 BCE, a truly multicultural group of Eurasian and African globetrotters—including the famous Moroccan merchant Ibn Battuta and his Venetian counterparts in the Marco Polo family—relied on this great Eurasian land route to reach the splendid imperial court of the Mongol Khans in Beijing.

In summary, then, traditional empires were not in the modern sense 'global', but they were globalizing. There are important indications also of a globalizing ethos that went beyond the intellectual groupings of philosophers, poets, and architects to practices of everyday organization. The Peutinger Table, an early Roman map known from a thirteenth-century copy, draws geometric lines that stretch across the Empire and beyond to the known world, from Rome to Gaul in the west and (in the Ptolemaic description) the Ganges in the east. It is a stylized map, about 6.8 metres long and rolled out like a narrow scroll. In modern cartographical terms, its straight-line connections distort the world unrecognizably, but they give a clear sense of the practical connections—roads and ports—that integrate the farthest known reaches of the world. What was new about the Roman Empire was not that it had a sense of a 'world-space'. This had already occurred more than 2,000 years earlier, as demonstrated by a Mesopotamian clay tablet with a circular map centred on Assyrian territory that shows the Euphrates joining the Persian Gulf and surrounded by the 'Earthly Ocean'. Rather, what was new was that it was intended to represent an ongoing—and globalizing—set of interconnections of exchange and organization. It is indicative that Trajan, the early second-century CE Roman emperor who presided over the Empire at its greatest geographical spread, came from the Iberian Peninsula rather than from Rome or the Apennine Peninsula. Almost 2,000 years later, Catholics were still debating whether the Pope should come from the Apennine Peninsula, although there was general agreement that 'he' needed to speak Italian.

Despite common contrary arguments in the pertinent literature, the Chinese empires from about 1,000 years ago were globalizing. There is little doubt that, despite the contradictory nature of their engagement, a series of Chinese empires did contribute to the slow globalization of social relations across that period. Though at one stage the Chinese withdrew from the world—formalized by the 1436 imperial decision to prohibit the construction of seagoing ships that had taken Chinese traders as far as Malindi on the east coast of Africa—this prohibition did not mean that the Chinese Empire successfully extricated itself from a gradually globalizing world. Their court negotiated treaties with and therefore recognized other empires, even conceding other rulers' ranks as emperors. This was handled within the traditional framework of the 'Mandate of Heaven' by subordinating other rulers in established terms as 'younger brothers' or 'nephews'.

The Celestial Empire produced printed atlases that date to long before the European Ortelius's supposedly first historical atlas, and even though the very early maps of China show the world as fading off beyond the 'natural extent' of territory, mediaeval maps by cartographers such as Zhu Siben (1273–1337) included phonetic designations for European place names and gave the shape and orientation of Africa. In 1267, the Persian geographer Jāmal al-Dīn brought a terrestrial globe to Kublai Khan, the expansionist Mongol leader who ascended to the throne in China in 1260. Under Kublai's patronage, Arab geography and cartography flourished at the imperial court.

While some of the evidence remains fragmentary, the historical pattern in this period is one of expanding global knowledge and expanding military and trade relations, particularly in East Asia and Central Asia down to South Asia. By the sixteenth century, particularly through Jesuits acting as globalizing agents of Christianity, globalizing Chinese cartography was strengthening, with a version of the world map called the Ricci Map (1584) being reproduced by the thousands. The point being made here is a relative and qualifying one—a ban on globalizing shipping does not mean that China dropped out of the worldwide dynamics of intensifying interconnectivity. Moreover, the 1436 ban was lifted by the middle of the sixteenth century during the time of the capture of the Americas by feuding European states. The subsequent period of the Ming–Qing transition is associated with significant trade in silver and sugar beyond the Empire, including possibly as much as half of the silver mined in the Spanish Americas. Similarly, the subsequent Qing ban on maritime trade in 1661 was imposed as a response to the power relations effected by objective global connections (Van de Ven, 2002).

This story of the imposition and subsequent lifting of the shipping ban in China is still relevant as an enduring pattern of globalization today. Consider, for example, the current Chinese policy of 'One Road, One Belt', as Xi Jinping's authoritarian government is seeking to re-establish the old Silk Road as it attempts to shift its export-orientated economic strategy to one favouring large transnational infrastructure projects. China is still chasing after a favourable 'global order' in a world that is still largely beyond its control except for particular moments in particular places, and at significant cost.

The Great Convergence: The Period When Modern Relations Came to Dominate the Planet

The term 'modernity' has become associated with the eighteenth-century European Enlightenment project of developing objective science, projecting a generalizing ethic of justice and law, and liberating rational modes of thought and social organization from the perceived irrationalities of myth, religion, and political tyranny. By contrast, we emphasize the valence of constructivism that came to overlay traditional valences of cosmology and metaphor (James, 2018). This allows us to acknowledge the existence of multiple expressions of modern ways of being that developed in various parts of the world, both independently and in resistance to European modernity. But this complex set of processes needs to be unpacked very carefully. While Europe was a key player in global process of modernization, including globalizing modernity itself, it was not *the only* locus of modernity.

To be sure, the rise of European metropolitan centres and their affiliated merchant classes represented an important factor in strengthening globalizing tendencies during the early modern period. Embodying the new values of unlimited material accumulation, European economic entrepreneurs laid the foundation of what later scholars would call the 'capitalist world system'. However, these fledgling capitalists could not have achieved the global expansion of their commercial enterprises without their engagement beyond Europe. By the early 1600s, national joint stock companies like the Dutch and British East India companies were founded for the express purpose of setting up profitable trade posts outside Europe. (Agency extension was crucial here.) As these innovative corporations grew in size and stature, they acquired the power to regulate most intercontinental economic transactions, in the process implementing social institutions and cultural practices that enabled later colonial governments to place these foreign regions under direct political rule.

Related embodied developments such as the Atlantic slave trade and forced population transfers within the Americas—increasingly extended and intensified through more abstract means of organization such as double-entry accounting—resulted in the suffering and death of millions of non-Europeans while greatly benefiting white immigrants and their home countries. Religious warfare within Europe also created its share of dislocation and displacement for Caucasian populations. Moreover, as a result of these protracted armed conflicts, military alliances and political arrangements underwent continuous modification. This highlights the crucial role of both warfare and imperialism as catalysts of globalization, a process often forgotten in the literature.

In political terms, territorial nation-states began to emerge in the late eighteenth century in Europe and the Americas as the modern *globalized* container of social life. Here, it should be said that European imperial expansion, in the context of fundamental shifts in the dominant modes of practice across the world, was fundamental to nation formation. But this does not mean that Europe provided 'the blueprint' for nation-state formation. Rather, it was imperial expansion that provided the context for a deeply contested globalizing relation that saw nation-states formed as part of a global system in relation to each other.

In economic terms, the volume of world trade increased dramatically between 1850 and 1914. Guided by the activities of multinational banks, capital and goods flowed across borders relatively freely as the sterling-based gold standard made possible the worldwide circulation of leading national currencies like the British pound and the Dutch guilder. On the eve of World War I, merchandise trade measured as a percentage of gross national output totalled almost 12 per cent for the industrialized countries, a level unmatched until the 1970s. Global pricing systems facilitated trade in important commodities like grains, cotton, and various precious metals.

However, this apparent economic dynamic cannot be separated from its interacting cultural matrix. Brand-name packaged goods like Coca-Cola drinks, Campbell soups, Singer sewing machines, and Remington type-writers made their first appearance. In order to raise the global visibility of these corporations, international advertising agencies launched the first full-blown, transborder commercial promotion campaigns. AT&T coined advertising slogans in celebration of a world 'inextricably bound together'. The twentieth-century arrival of mass-circulation newspapers and maga-zines, film, and television further enhanced a growing cultural conscious-ness of a rapidly shrinking world in which mass consumption, violence, risk, poverty, and aspiration all came together in the same horizon. High mass consumption met with new expressions of cosmopolitanism. New forms of political control met with passionate globalizing movements of liberation politics. In summary, a global imaginary was emerging that carried the spores of its own unsettling.

The Great Unsettling: The Period When Postmodern Globalization Emerged in Tension with Continuing Modernization

The dramatic acceleration of worldwide interdependencies and global impact at a distance that has occurred since the mid-twentieth century represents yet another quantum leap in the history of globalization. It is appropriate to call this latest wave 'the Great Unsettling'. It is the period in which the rapid development of abstracted and disembodied connectivity came to relativize—to unsettle—relations between people, machines, regimes, objects, and nature. Today, the Great Unsettling stretches into every aspect of social life. It has emerged into contention at different speeds and with different time markers across different domains of social life: ecological, economic, political, and cultural. This multidimensional globalization dynamic makes it useful to elaborate the period in terms of those different domains, at least in the first instance.

In ecological terms, the splitting of the atom and the Hiroshima bombing marked the crossing of the threshold in which nature was being taken apart rather than just dug up, cut down, manipulated, and refabricated. It had begun earlier in theory and experimentation and sped up across the twentieth century. Niels Bohr's quantum theory unsettled modern laws of dynamics and spatial measurement, just as Albert Einstein's theory of temporal–material relativity signalled an emergent way of rethinking (and unsettling) the nature of time itself. In a completely different field, a number of scientists, including Norbert Weiner and Claude Shannon, were meeting in a series of annual Conferences on Cybernetics (1943–54) to unsettle the distinction between humans as natural beings and computerized machines as cybernetic organisms. In yet another field, genetic scientists were working through the implications of being able to map and manipulate the basic building blocks of life. What began as a project that linked all of life on earth turned into a global scramble for the control of exploitable genes (Thacker, 2005). As Donna Haraway (1997: 58–9) observed, a new kind of 'species being is technically and literally brought into being by transnational, multibillion-dollar, interdisciplinary, long-term projects to provide exhaustive genetic catalogs'. For both good and ill, social life was tumbled and transmuted. But let us be careful here. Ours is a different argument from that made by Will Steffen and his colleagues (2015), who empirically document the acceleration of the human impact upon the planet. Without contesting their point, their concept of 'the Great Acceleration' remains a set of empirical measures concerning human impact (see our further discussion of this point in Chapter 10). It signals the current dominance of scientific object-orientated *quantitative* thinking. We are adding a *qualitative* dimension, thus making our argument far more encompassing.

In economic terms, techno-science, bioscience, fiduciary capital, new algorithmic coding of exchange processes, and the emergence of platform capitalism (Srnicek, 2017) all came together to foundationally unsettled the relation between production and the accumulation of value. While modern capitalism continues to bring about a spatial convergence of global economic relations, the new layer of postmodern capitalism works to relativize that dominant way of practicing time and space. Finance capital provides a powerful illustration of this relativizing. Across the course of the twentieth century, concomitant with the development of electronic codification as a new dominant means of communication, we witnessed the overlaying of paper money and the gold standard by electronic exchange systems that unevenly but fundamentally began to change the nature of global financial exchange. It was something that classical social theorists such as Karl Marx or Georg Simmel could not have envisaged despite their understanding of money as a material abstraction—mobile and apparently fluid, and acting to universalize the comparability of value.

Although many of the globalizing tendencies had slow antecedents, the changes multiplied quickly in the late twentieth century. In the area of personal finance and investment, the first globally linked credit cards such as American Express, MasterCard, and Visa expanded across the 1960s; electronic cheque-clearing systems were developed in the 1970s; and electronic funds transfer systems and automatic teller machines came into regular use in the 1980s. Electronic banking through global browsers such as Netscape, Internet Explorer, and Google took hold in the 1990s, as did new schemes for electronic marketing, merchandizing, and computer-assisted share trading such as through the NASDAQ system (1971), the London Stock Exchange Automated Quotation system (1986), and the Hong Kong Automatic Order Matching and Execution System (1993). New financial instruments were built upon older processes and sped up processes of temporal convergence while unsettling their earlier bases. This, however, remains a description as the level of empirical generalization. It can be taken much further.

As we noted in Chapter 5, perhaps the key moment in relativizing the mode of exchange was the shift towards traded derivatives—esoteric contracts specifying future outcomes based upon the *relative* performance of another instrument or investment. It is hard to say when the threshold was passed, but post-risk options as a primary way of accruing value developed quickly from the 1970s and grew exponentially from the mid-1980s. By the turn of the century, derivatives amounted to an estimated US$70 trillion, or eight times the annual gross domestic product of the United States. Hedge funds increased significantly over the first years of the new century, growing annually at approximately 15–20 per cent. The vagueness of the figures is testament to both the abstraction of the process and the superseding of older forms of institutionalization that measured monetary exchanges. Derivative exchanges, for example, are conducted 'over the counter' on private digital networks as the exchange of the temporally projected value of value-units that do not yet exist except as projections. This, at one level, is time relativized and space collapsed.

These new derivative exchanges became the basis of the 2008 Global Financial Crisis. Hedging, once a modern means of offsetting risk, effectively comes down in this new relativizing world to a process of gambling on the future by collapsing time and trading in options on the future now. In short, derivatives collapse modern time–space into a postmodern present–future of eternal duration—a *global now* of relativized possibilities for further accruing exchange value. Let us note that the enduring relevance of object extension continued as globally branded objects flourished, but the key to economic and political power shifted to abstracted disembodied relations. Algorithmically based data mining, code management, and micro-directed mass communications—with Cambridge Analytics and its role in the 2016 US presidential election serving as a prominent example—became the dominant means of accruing value and power.

To use the terms introduced earlier, these dynamics are related to a generalizing shift in the nature of how time–space is constituted. The modern 'empty' space–time of trading in objects and services—with value directly connected to the objects and services being traded—has been overlaid by a level of postmodern time–space in which the objects and services are subordinated to the more abstract exchange. Value, at least at one level, has become thoroughly relativized. As derivatives markets show, value-orientated and abstracted time/spaces have become the constitutive context in which abstracted 'items' such as possible future changes in the value of an object are traded alongside the objects themselves.

The political consequences of the Great Unsettling are profound. The phenomenal world of producing and moving goods around the world had now been framed by a new layer of the economy—ironically ushered in through the legislation of nation-states—that now operates largely beyond the reach of democratic influence.[10] While the atomic bomb was a figure of ecological unsettling, in political terms it initially worked differently, contributing to the continuing Great Convergence. The explosion of two powerful atomic bombs that killed 200,000 Japanese, most of them civilians, provided a crisis point that contributed to a series of international attempts in the immediate post-war period to integrate

---

[10] Various responses to this shift have taken up the idea of taxing such financial exchange; see Heikki Patomäki's *Democratising Globalisation* (2001). Interestingly, Joseph Stiglitz, in his 2006 book on reforming the global economic system, completely ignores this emergent and increasingly dominant level of the global economy.

(not relativize) world politics. Nothing did more to convince people around the world of their linked geographical and political fate than the atomic bomb. However, it was an associated Cold War doctrine, rationalized by the possibility of global nuclear war, that signalled the relativizing shift: mutual assured destruction (MAD). Saving the planet from nuclear winter—another ecological unsettling—supposedly entailed defending the contradiction of being prepared to launch the destruction of a thousand suns upon the earth. An emerging global imaginary had found horrifying expression in the fitting Cold War MAD acronym. This is elaborated in Chapter 10 on the Anthropocene and the new insecurities.

Political contradictions in the Great Unsettling abound. The 1991 collapse of the Berlin Wall, for example, intensified the orientation of global politics around ideologies of freedom. But across the world, concepts of 'freedom' and 'liberty' were claimed variously by both the left and right as their own, and this occurred just as the data surveillance of people's lives became more and more intrusive upon that personal freedom. Politics saw the multiplying of ideological perspectives, and new material contradictions emerged. For example, neoliberal attempts to remake the global market involved deregulating its older integrating mechanisms while increasing the intensity of multiple corporate centres of interconnected control, such as through algorithm-driven data logistics (Rossiter, 2017). In turn, these logistics, most prominently in the form of Facebook and other social media platforms, became one of the new management tools for both selling things and conducting electoral politics.

In cultural terms, expressions of difference and positions of identity have become increasingly relativized and contested. Meaning has become more and more perspectival; that is, dependent on the intersection of social places where one stands. In this context, the new anti-globalist forms of populism we discuss in Chapter 7 seek to return to past certainties while further unsettling the meaning of social life. Thus, the period of the Great Unsettling is reflected in both the public and the personal cultural realms. The Internet, wireless communication, digital media, and online social networking sites overlay and remake older forms of social interchange. These unprecedented and encompassing networks of interactive communication tightly connect the local and global in new ways, but these interactions are experienced in contradictory ways as offering individualized and relativized portals onto a world of apparently open possibilities—even as the process is carried by an intense global integration of a corporate-controlled platform of tools and services that seek to channel those possibilities. In short, we live in an unsettling period when globalization has been kicked into a far more intense quantitative and qualitative gear.

Conclusion

In this chapter, we emphasized that globalization has had a long history and unfolds in both long journeys and intensive spurts. But it is only by showing its changing dominant forms that we can truly understand the present, including its continuities and discontinuities or ruptures with the past. Globalization matters historically because it is woven into the fabric of the evolution of our species and its myriad activities leading to its settlement of the entire planet. It also matters because, throughout human history, processes of globalization have been inlaid with dynamics of power, identity, meaning, connectivity, impact, and everyday exchanges between people. During the period of the Great Universalizing, globalization was associated with the imaginaries and integrating practices of empires and sodalities, expressed forcefully by intellectuals and leaders rather than affecting everything about everyday life. During the era of the Great Convergence, it began unevenly to affect everybody on the planet, both objectively and subjectively. The difference between the present period of the Great Unsettling and earlier periods is that globalization processes have been vastly intensifying while also spawning new forms of social relations. This is not to say that globalization itself is new. Rather, we are suggesting that we are now facing unprecedented forms of global connectivity and impact in a world blanketed by globalizing processes ranging from techno-capitalism and data mining to climate change and satellite-connected mediation. At the same time, these dynamics are continuously contested by relativized social movements that no longer can expect an enduring existence or inhabit a single generating locale.

Finally, we linked the Great Unsettling to the emergence of the 'postmodern', because the current period is characterized by the emerging dominance of processes and events that *relativize* meaning and practice. At one level, these processes reconstitute the ways in which time and space are lived. But since they do not change *everything*, they generate deep contradictions that further unsettle social life. Given the complexity of this global systemic shift, we focused on some key examples—techno-science, finance capital, MAD—to carry a sense of these emerging, contradictory, and quickly dominating changes. In summary, then, our historical scheme culminated in our account of the unsettling of the ontologically changing dominant nature of time and space—not merely an elaboration of different intersections and scales of spatiality.

Global reconfigurations of space and time enable the billions of transactions on Wall Street just as much as they impose a non-regressive discipline on the millions of bidders on eBay, at a local real-estate auction, or waiting at a motion-sensitive red traffic light. And yet, both modern and traditional modalities of space and time have become overlaid by the relative time–space without erasing those prior forms. Instantaneity and proximity have become the cutting-edge spatiotemporal modes in our age of unsettlement, but they continue to cohabit our globalizing world with older forms of space and time.

In summary, then, the complex matrix of processes we call 'globalization' has had a long and changing history, which includes irregular fluctuations in its dominant forms. The future trajectory of our period of the Great Unsettling will reflect the sum total of myriad individual and collective decisions made on a daily basis, and especially how we choose to live locally. The emergent dynamics of globalization will depend on how much we consume, how often we travel, whether we welcome refugees, what media we attend to, whether we maintain the current inhospitable regime of 'national borders', and how we choose to relate to other terrestrials—human and non-human.

7   Examining the Promise of Global Studies

All of the theoretical and historical globalization matters discussed in the previous chapters fit into the overarching academic framework of 'global studies'. Seeking to expand our understanding of recent and long-term social change, this initiative emerged in the late 1990s and has since been institutionalized in many universities around the world. According to prominent global studies scholars such as Mark Juergensmeyer and Eve Darian-Smith, the growing field of enquiry holds out the grand promise of moving 'beyond the disciplinary and cultural limitations of the past and not only illumine facets of the global era but also give the worldwide academic enterprise a more global dimension' (Juergensmeyer, 2013: 768–9). In other words, global studies aspires to nothing less than a paradigm shift in the human and natural sciences by aiming for a systematic reordering of human knowledge around global–local dynamics. At the same time, it seeks to facilitate the education of reflective global citizens through the establishment of innovative transnational learning and teaching environments.

However, as Barrie Axford notes, the difficulty with realizing global studies' ambitious promise 'lies in part in the sheer naivety of an all-embracing concept like globalization and partly in the obduracy of existing systems of knowledge as these have construed the world' (2013: 184). One necessary ingredient for overcoming such engrained attachments to the dominant academic paradigm is the exploration of globalization in as much complexity as possible. As we discussed in Chapter 3, global studies scholars have sought to attend to the thickening forms of social interrelationality, the profound reconfigurations of space and time, the uneven impacts of novel digital technologies, and the enhanced forms of mobility reflected in intensifying flows of people, goods, services, ideas, and communication across a multitude of geographic and social barriers (Juergensmeyer, 2014; Steger, 2014; Juergensmeyer, Steger, and Sassen, 2019).

The emerging field's research focus on fluidity and instantiations of interconnectivity (for good and ill) means that the national no longer commands centre stage. Consequently, scholarship on the global has paid much attention to the recent transformation of the conventional functions of the nation-state that have tended to weaken modernist forms of state sovereignty. Refusing to treat the state as the primary mover in world politics, many researchers consider it as but one important actor in the web of today's material and ideational interdependencies alongside proliferating non-state entities, non-governmental organizations, and transnational social movements. For this reason, global studies proponents are especially critical of methodological nationalism—that is, taken-for-granted assumptions of the naturalness and givenness of a world divided into societies along nation-state boundaries—an assumption that still underpins much of conventional international relations thinking, as well as some neo-Marxist state theory.[1] As globalization scholar Thomas Eriksen suggests, 'Transnationalism must be the premise [of global studies], not an afterthought' (2014: 78).

Overcoming methodological nationalism—and not simply replacing it with methodological globalism—depends to a large extent on the ability to develop analytical approaches and methodologies that are not tethered to a single discipline. Hence, globalization proponents cite the advancement of transdisciplinarity and transnationalism as two of the most pressing tasks of global studies (Axford, 2013; Darian-Smith and McCarty, 2017; Steger and Wahlrab, 2017). Hoping to carve out novel transdisciplinary paths, such scholars have sought to incorporate insights generated by previous interdisciplinary initiatives pioneered in the 1970s and 1980s, such as world-systems analysis, postcolonial studies, cultural studies, environmental studies, and women's studies (Darian-Smith and McCarty, 2017). Like these older alternatives that managed to attract scores of marginalized scholars dissatisfied with the disciplinary status quo, global studies has been fuelled by many academics' growing disaffection with the conventional higher education enterprise. The contemporary trend towards compartmentalization and specialization of knowledge means that universities tend to be divided into disciplinary silos reflected in insulated department structures. For this reason, global studies scholars have endeavoured to combine their ambitious quest to blaze new trails of social enquiry with their efforts to transform these tight disciplinary compartments into more cross-cutting intellectual fields.

Finally, leading global studies researchers have pledged to develop problem-centred programmes and issue-relevant research projects that respond to the concrete opportunities and specific challenges of global

---

[1] For a recent academic exchange of conflicting perspectives on the role of the state in global studies, see Barrow and Keck (2017) and Steger (2018).

interdependence as they unfold in the daily lives of billions of people. Global studies researchers like the present authors have striven to connect their theoretical work to cutting-edge public policy initiatives such as ecologically sustainable modes of global problem-solving that contain the real potential of bridging the academic arena and relevant public forums. In other words, scholarship on the global emphasizes the imperative of tackling the pressing transnational issues of the twenty-first century, all of which call for a renewed relationship between sustained theoretical reflection and committed in-the-world engagement (Mittelman, 2004; Robinson, 2005; Steger and Wahlrab, 2017). This self-reflexive task of linking theory and practice requires both critical global thinking and applied projects shaping the education of global–local citizens.

Has Global Studies Delivered on Its Promise?

As we shall demonstrate below, it is not too difficult to provide substantial empirical support for our contention that global studies matters in the global landscape of compartmentalized knowledge production. But it seems less certain whether this new field of study has delivered on the most central aspects of its ambitious promise. Barrie Axford (2013: 8) and Richard Appelbaum (2013: 547), for example, represent two influential voices in a sizeable chorus of global studies proponents who have suggested that the quest for the Holy Grail of critical globalization scholarship—the study of globalization's multiple dimensions delivered through a robust transdisciplinarity—has proven an 'elusive' and 'largely aspirational' objective, as only a very small number of pertinent studies have come close to this ideal. But before we explore in more detail the extent to which global studies has actually lived up to its grand promise, let us first consider the existing evidence for its relevance in the international academic environment.

For starters, it is hard to deny that academic projects bearing the designation 'global studies' have been both expanding and multiplying. For example, there has been a highly visible proliferation of global studies programmes, departments, research institutes, and professional organizations in major universities around the world, including the Global South. As the demand for pertinent courses and undergraduate and postgraduate degrees has skyrocketed, so has the institutional support for global studies scholarship offered by many institutions of higher education. Even less research-orientated liberal arts colleges and occupationally orientated community colleges have begun to articulate global studies components in their more applied teaching and learning missions.

In the United States alone, there are now over 300 undergraduate and graduate programmes that have adopted the indicator 'global studies'—either as a stand-alone label or in combination with more established terms such as 'international' or 'transnational'.[2] Some pioneering public research universities like the University of California, Santa Barbara (UCSB), the University of North Carolina at Chapel Hill, and Arizona State University house gigantic programmes that serve thousands of global studies undergraduate majors. Outside the United States, large institutions like Shanghai University, RMIT University in Melbourne, Australia, the University of Leipzig, Moscow State University, Roskilde University in Denmark, Sophia University, Tokyo, and the University of Gothenburg in Sweden accommodate hundreds of global studies graduate students, in addition to their sizeable undergraduate programmes.[3]

In 2015, UCSB launched the first global studies doctoral programme at a Tier-1 research university in the United States—an innovative scheme also pursued by the University of California, Irvine, and other research-orientated institutions.[4] New global studies teaching programmes and research units have drawn considerable funding from major government institutions and the philanthropic sector. For example, in 2015, Northwestern University announced that it had received a donation constituting the largest single private gift in its history. The US$100 million endowment came from Roberta Buffett Elliott, the sister of the US billionaire investor Warren Buffett, who supported the establishment of a new 'Buffett Institute for Global Studies' at her alma mater. And a final body of evidence indicating the strength of global studies points to the phenomenal growth of new journals, book series, textbooks, handbooks, encyclopaedias, academic conferences, and professional associations—like the Global Studies Consortium or the Global Studies Association—that have embraced the novel umbrella designation of 'global studies'.[5]

To be sure, the growth of global studies in the United States has also been crucially connected to the redirection of funding practices by the federal government and established philanthropic organizations, such as the Ford Foundation or the MacArthur Foundation, from the residual nation-state-centred frameworks of international studies and

---

[2] For a listing of these colleges and universities, see https://bigfuture.collegeboard.org/college-search.

[3] For a representative selection of large graduate programmes in global studies in universities around the world, see https://globalstudiesconsortium.org/member-programs.

[4] There are also Tier-2 institutions in the United States, such as the University of Massachusetts Lowell, which offer PhD degrees in global studies.

[5] For a representative overview of these resources and institutions, see Steger and Wahlrab (2017) and Darian-Smith and McCarty (2017).

area studies—dominant during the Cold War—to the newcomer global studies. As Isaac Kamola's (2014) pioneering work on the subject demonstrates, starting in the mid-1990s, a number of important funding bodies announced their new plans to replace 'national' and 'area' structures with a 'global' framework. For example, the American Social Science Research Council recommended defunding 'discrete and separated area committees', which were reluctant to support scholars interested in global developments and 'policy-relevant global issues'. When conventional area studies experts realized that traditional sources of funding were in danger of drying up, many joined the newly emerging global studies cohort of scholars centred on the study of globalization in its many dimensions.

Major US research universities embraced this trend while reducing the level of support for area studies teaching and research programmes. At the same time, they developed new investment schemes and strategic plans that provided for the creation of new global studies or global affairs programmes and centres. Kamola (2014) argues that influential professional organizations like the National Association of State Universities and Land Grant Colleges and the American Association of Colleges and Universities eagerly joined these efforts to synchronize market-orientated initiatives of 'globalizing the curriculum' and 'recalibrating college learning' with the shifting opportunity structures of the 'new global century'. Part and parcel of this changing higher education environment, global studies was thus nurtured by the dominant ideology of market globalism that articulated the rising global imaginary in concrete pro-market agendas and programmes. During the last three decades, this powerful logic of neoliberalism has thoroughly penetrated the academic world (Mittelman, 2017). The fortunate recipient of these material and ideational transformations, global studies owes much of its success to this global systemic shift in favour of 'globalization matters'.

To sum up, there exists strong empirical evidence buttressing our contention that global studies has and continues to matter in the global landscape of knowledge production. Clearly, the fledgling field has come a long way in a relatively short period of time. But has it delivered on its grand promise? Has it, indeed, offered 'new ways of thinking about global-scale processes and problems' (Darian-Smith and McCarty, 2017: 30)? Moreover, has the much-touted 'global turn' in the global academic environment been successfully instituted in the form of substantive programmes that represent much more than just the opportunistic adoption of the trendy label 'global studies'? While it is still too early in the development of the emerging field to arrive at definitive answers to these questions, this chapter offers an interim assessment of its status by considering a number of important reservations that have been expressed in recent years not only by critical voices outside the field, but also by largely sympathetic global studies insiders.

Responding to Major Criticisms of Global Studies

Criticisms of global studies can be organized under four major headings. To start with, global studies stands accused of failing to generate a necessary scholarly consensus on what constitutes its central features and essential components. Lacking agreed-upon definitions and comprehensive delineations of its analytical framework, global studies has allegedly been unable to acquire a coherent intellectual profile that would facilitate the development of a distinct research and teaching agenda. As a result, the field is said to have remained a diffuse and underdeveloped project-in-the-making that relies heavily on murky generalizations and cobbled-together methodologies.

Second, there has been significant disagreement among global scholars on the proper relationship between globalization studies and global studies. Far from amounting to an abstract exercise in semantic hairsplitting, this dispute addresses crucial issues at the heart of global studies such as the status of the master concept 'globalization'. This ongoing quarrel has been exacerbated by a clash of conflicting historical narratives about the stages and conditions of the emergence of global studies as a new field, especially the extent to which conventional logics and disciplinary moorings have influenced its academic evolution.

Third, a number of detractors claim to have identified a profound theory–practice gap involving the programmatic content of global studies—its analytical promise—and a lack of empirical substance reflected in inadequate institutional manifestations. As evidence for the existence of this wide gulf, critics have pointed to the mushrooming of refurbished international studies and area studies programmes, most of which are said to have donned the coveted mantle of 'global studies' for primarily instrumental reasons. Hence, many of the 'actually existing' global studies academic instantiations are deemed as falling considerably short of the field's programmatic scope and vision.

The fourth objection comes from influential postcolonial thinkers located both within and without global studies who have offered incisive critiques of what they see as the field's troubling geographic, ethnic, and epistemic attachments to hegemonic knowledge frameworks developed and anchored in the Global North. Pointing to the spectre of philosophical parochialism lurking behind the field's supposed global theoretical and practical concerns, these critics suggests that the evolving global studies paradigm has not paid enough attention to the postcolonial imperative of both contesting and decentring dominant Western ways of seeing and knowing.

In what follows below, we examine the promise of global studies—and the current state of the field—by responding to these four major objections.

The First Criticism: Lack of Consensus and Conceptual Fuzziness

Perhaps the most common charge advanced against the emerging field is its alleged lack of consensus on basic approaches and definitions. This is one of the reasons why Proposition 1 of our engaged theory of globalization emphasizes the importance of clear and concise definitions. This first criticism of global studies can be boiled down to the contention that the failure to delineate its main contours and central features has stifled the formation of a general agreement on the actual and desirable scope and composition of the new field. Hence, a number of critics have complained about its lack of focus and conceptual clarity, which makes global studies appear to be the study of 'everything global'. Like many other interdisciplinary programmes developed between the 1980s and 2000s, the field is said to invite the impression of a fuzzy and rather confusing combination of widely different approaches operating on various levels of analysis.

As global studies proponent Philip McCarty asserts, 'In Global Studies there was, and remains, a strong tendency to revel in the mesmerizing complexity of it all' (2014: 284). Similarly, Fredric Jameson and Masao Miyoshi characterize global studies as an academic 'space of tension' framed by multiple disagreements in which the very problematic of globalization itself is being continuously produced and contested (1998: xvi). In summary, then, these largely sympathetic critics see global studies as lacking a clear conceptual framework, which warrants their use of unfavourable adjectives like 'underdeveloped', 'incoherent', 'immature', and 'uneven' to characterize the new field (Pieterse, 2013a: 500, 504; Scholte, 2016: 223).

As we noted in Chapter 5, such hard-hitting characterizations strike us as correct insofar as they identify enduring disagreements among globalization scholars over authoritative definitions and analytical distinctions. Axford makes the same point when he notes that the 'field of global studies is a welter of contrasting positions on the generation and nature of knowledge about concepts with a global root. Overall, it remains a highly contested science' (2016: 5). Jan Nederveen Pieterse argues similarly: 'There is no consensus on the definition of globalization, its effects, and periodization' (2013: 503). This existing discord within global studies might be partly to blame for its difficulties (but only until recently, as we shall argue) in clearly articulating and conveying the field's scope and methods to interested students and faculty. Likewise, the advocates of this first criticism rightly draw our attention to the persistence of methodological quarrels over what approaches should be favoured.

The lack of scholarly consensus on the 'right way' to study globalization corresponds to the field's larger problem of generating widely shared definitions or formulating precise hypotheses capable of being set against empirical evidence (Axford, 2013: 188). In short, the doggedness of these debates underscores the fact that global studies constitutes a large tent that has perhaps stretched too far to accommodate an amalgam of globalization scholars hailing from multiple disciplines and linked to diverging theoretical perspectives and methodological preferences. In this regard, Jameson's characterization of global studies as an unsettled and contested 'space of tension' contains more than just a grain of truth.

At the same time, however, we contend that this criticism has been taken too far. A more balanced assessment would also unearth the field's compensating strengths. For example, what strikes detractors as conceptual 'fuzziness' could be interpreted by advocates as a refreshing breeze of innovation imbued with the sort of energetic openness to different perspectives that tends to characterize most academic newcomers. Thus, the obvious weakness of the field's institutional inexperience coexists with its strength of thinking outside the box—a valuable quality exhibited by an impressive number of global studies researchers. It is precisely such bold defiance of academic conventions and the invigorating refusal to bow to the intransigent dictates of dominant knowledge paradigms that opens the doors to new insights and practices.

A 2013 issue of the leading journal *Globalizations* provides clear evidence for this coexistence of inexperience and innovation that has framed the emerging field. Containing a special exchange forum around the question, 'What is global studies?', the high-profile collection featured eight insightful contributions. It opened with a lead article on the subject penned by Jan Nederveen Pieterse, a discerning critic hailing from UCSB's Global Studies Department—the most successful of its kind in the United States. His provocative essay drew six substantive reaction papers authored by global studies insiders, which, in turn, were followed by a final response by the lead author. As the journal editors note at the outset of the issue, their intention was to facilitate the conceptual and methodological evolution of the field by 'opening the widest possible space for discussion of alternative understandings of globalization', while also 'encouraging the exploration and discussion of multiple interpretations and multiple processes that may constitute many possible globalizations, and many possible alternatives' (Pieterse, 2013a: 497). Since the special forum drew a strong and positive reaction from its readers, the journal editors decided to publish several additional response essays in a subsequent issue. These new interventions provided further arguments on and insights into the ongoing debate over the proper content, scope, and methods of the evolving field.

The diversity of opinions and perspectives expressed in these scholarly exchanges demonstrates that global studies is framed by *both* significant disagreements *and* major agreements. This mixture of views and perspectives—rather typical for most academic fields—suggests that the deeper problem with the substance of global studies might not lie with its alleged 'fuzziness', but with a widespread *presumption of its incoherence*. In fact, the latter tends to be levelled against *all* new objects of study, domains, approaches, or subjects and sensibilities that did not exist or were not recognized at the time in which the major disciplines took shape. New academic programmes usually known by the denotation 'studies'—environmental studies, urban studies, cultural studies, ethnic studies, black studies, poverty studies, development studies, sustainability studies, internet studies, and, of course, global studies—represent, by virtue of their very recent origins and intellectual novelty, fundamental challenges to the conventional academic superstructure. To better cope with such unorthodox intruders, established disciplinary discourses frequently assign these 'studies' an inferior intellectual role, one that alleges a lack of coherence, structure, evenness, depth, and sophistication compared to 'real' academic disciplines like sociology, political science, or biology.

But what about the related allegation of the missing authoritative delineations of global studies' main contours and central features? As Pieterse (2013a: 500) asserts, 'books with the phrase "global studies" in their title are few and mostly introductory textbooks or readers'. In light of recent attempts to develop precisely such works, we submit that this charge can no longer be sustained. A significant number of global studies scholars have not only offered comprehensive outlines of what they consider to be the essential features and main characteristics of the evolving field, but also provided clear rationales as to why their efforts are so important for understanding the profound patterns of social change in the global age (Anheier, Juergensmeyer, and Faessel, 2012; Juergensmeyer, 2013; Sparke, 2013; Smallman and Brown, 2015; Darian-Smith and McCarty, 2017; Steger and Wahlrab, 2017; Gunn, 2018; Juergensmeyer, Steger, and Sassen, 2019). In fact, without the existence of such substantive macro-mappings of the field, it would have been impossible for us to identify the contents of the grand promise of global studies at the beginning of this chapter.

Moreover, recent publications of such works have provided a much-needed response to the growing demands from students and faculty to be properly introduced to the scope and methods of the field. Usually articulated in terms of central pillars or characteristics, these framings show much analytical overlap. This is reflected in their matching adjectives to describe the main features and components of the field: 'transdisciplinary', 'transnational', 'reflexive' and 'critical', 'multicultural', 'contemporary' and 'historical', 'multiscalar', 'multilevel', 'multidimensional', 'holistic', 'transgressive' and 'integrative', 'problem-orientated', 'globally responsible', and 'socially engaged'. Even inveterate critics such as Pieterse have begun to acknowledge the significance of these mapping efforts. In fact, the last section of his *Globalizations* article attempts an ambitious delineation of what he calls 'Global 3.0' or a 'value-added global studies' (2013a: 505; 2013b: 551–6).

Finally, as Eve Darian-Smith (2015: 165) points out, such comprehensive delineations not only hold out the hope for a slowly emerging consensus on central concepts and features of the field, but also serve important institutional goals conducive to its further development:

For bureaucratic and institutional purposes, it is important to arrive at some general consensus about what 'global studies' entails. This is necessary in order to formalize an intellectual community of scholars and students, and to garner resources and funding for research agendas. Having a general idea about what the field of global studies encompasses is essential in order to hold conferences, submit grants, and to have one's work published, read, cited, and taught in classrooms. Moreover, articulating what constitutes 'global studies' today makes it possible to think about its future directions in the years ahead as an emerging field of inquiry.

But what about the charge related to the field's allegedly 'cobbled-together methodologies' (Appelbaum, 2013: 548)? While this observation was probably not too far off the mark only a few years ago, it no longer applies today. The publication of new books and articles offering distinct global studies toolkits has raised expectations that the inadequate methodological state of affairs is finally in the process of being remedied. Eve Darian-Smith and Philip McCarty's *The Global Turn: Theories, Research Designs, and Methods for Global Studies* (2017) represents the most impressive of these new substantive studies dedicated to systematically engaging methodological issues and outlining concrete research projects on global-scale issues. Introducing readers to the design and execution of global studies research, the authors provide an overview of cutting-edge analytics, methods, and pedagogics specific to their young field. Their innovative 'global transdisciplinary framework' relies on what they call 'multidimensional methodology', which makes it possible to design and implement viable global studies research agendas (Darian-Smith and McCarty, 2017: 10).

Accordingly, the core chapters of *The Global Turn* offer students and faculty interested in global studies a step-by-step outline towards realizing these tall objectives. Firstly, they propose new ways of asking provocative questions that help distil global studies research into a unique set of methodological enquiries. Secondly, they walk their readers through the specifics of designing a global studies research project. Thirdly, they introduce mixed-method and global methodological strategies. Fourthly, they discuss the specific advantages of global case studies—a method that enables the reader to analyse and engage with the complexity of global issues using manageable research toolkits. Fifthly, the authors provide and describe specific examples of global studies research that successfully deploy a global case study method in innovative transnational studies such as Bishnupriya Ghosh's *Global Icons* (2011), Paul Amar's *The Security Archipelago* (2013), and Mark Juergensmeyer, Dinah Griego, and John Soboslai's *God in the Tumult of the Global Square* (2015).

The rich discussion provided in *The Global Turn* goes a long way in deflecting the charge of the field's methodological cobbled-togetherness. Rather, the study presents a distinct global studies research framework composed of 'a synthesis of new global perspectives, transdisciplinary theoretical approaches, and methodological and analytical implications of those elements' (Darian-Smith and McCarty, 2017: 225). Such successful articulations of global studies' methodology have also contributed to the formation of a more cohesive field populated by researchers who 'ask distinctly global research questions, design viable research projects and empirically engage global issues, and produce research that is relevant to contemporary challenges' (Darian-Smith and McCarty, 2017: 225). Still, to what extent such elevated analytical ambitions have been realized in actually existing global studies programmes around the world remains an open question we will engage in more detail in our response to the third criticism. For the moment, however, we must keep in mind that even a possibly insufficient empirical fulfilment of Darian-Smith and McCarty's programmatic vision has no bearing on the present criticism related to the field's alleged *conceptual* and *methodological* shortcomings.

Overall, then, we find that this first criticism of global studies only partially holds. While it is true that the young field constitutes an evolving space of tension, the emergence of substantive agreements alongside comprehensive delineations has added considerable empirical evidence to our impression that the analytical evolution of the field has been steadily progressing. Given the recent enhancement of global studies' conceptual and methodological profile, the charges of 'lacking consensus' and 'conceptual fuzziness' appear to be exaggerated, unbalanced, and outdated.

The Second Criticism: Global Studies versus Globalization Studies

The second criticism levelled against global studies concerns its alleged inability to progress from its early phase of globalization studies associated with scholars who are said to have remained anchored in their specific disciplines while keeping a narrow focus on the study of globalization in its various aspects. At stake in this seemingly scholastic debate are not merely the prospects for the formation of an authoritative genealogy of the field, but the very significance of globalization as the conceptual focus of the field. Mark Juergensmeyer, for example, advances a historical narrative that presents globalization studies as an early form of globalization research moored in single-discipline perspectives when he argues that global studies amounts to a field much 'larger' than the 'limited' study of globalization processes:

Put simply, the difference between 'globalization studies' and 'global studies' is this: the first is a subject and the second is a field. Globalization studies are the combined instances in which globalization is studied from various disciplinary perspectives. Global studies is the emerging transdisciplinary field that incorporates a variety of disciplinary and new approaches to understanding the transnational features of our global world. (2013: 765–6)

Approvingly citing Juergensmeyer's separation of globalization studies from global studies, Eve Darian-Smith and Philip McCarty, too, embrace his 'difference thesis' when they assert the need to move beyond globalization studies as a 'discipline-anchored project' associated with 'an earlier preoccupation with defining historical and contemporary phases of globalization and analyzing its many processes, facets, and impacts' (2017: 25).

The initial articulation of this 'difference thesis' can be found in Pieterse's (2013a) previously mentioned *Globalizations* lead article, which asserts that global studies emerged from a qualitatively different earlier wave of 'uneven' and 'discipline-bound' globalization studies. For Pieterse (2013a: 500, emphasis in original), global studies is different from studies of globalization in that it 'adds value *beyond* studies of globalization and international studies'. He then operationalizes this 'added value' in terms of 'interdisciplinarity', 'multicentrism', and 'multilevel thinking'.

Although the very rationale of his essay rides on his difference thesis, Pieterse (2013a: 511) surprisingly downplays its significance in the concluding paragraph: 'The difference between studies of globalization/global studies should not be overdrawn. There are analytical differences but they exist more as a potential than as reality. The issue isn't belabouring the difference between globalization/global studies, which is partly semantic; the issue is advancing the understanding of globalization, no matter the heading'. Note that Pieterse describes the differences between studies of globalization and global studies as both 'analytic' and 'partly semantic'. But what qualifies as 'analytic'? Earlier in his essay, the author does offer a clue as to what he seems to have in mind: 'Global studies are different from studies of globalization; they differ just as *global sociology* differs from the *sociology of globalization* and *global history* differs from the history of globalization' (Pieterse, 2013a: 505, emphasis in original).

In other words, 'the global' before the disciplinary marker makes all the difference: 'Most history has been national, regional, or civilizational, and global history represents a more comprehensive and advanced perspective' (Pieterse, 2013a: 505). While this observation might explain the difference between conventional history and global history, it hardly sheds light on the 'analytic' differences between the 'history of globalization' and 'global history'. It simply assumes that the comparison will also hold in the global studies case, meaning that studies of globalization must be as nationally and regionally focused as global history. However, Bruce Mazlish—the very scholar approvingly cited by Pieterse as an authority on 'global history'—has repeatedly affirmed the reverse: namely, that the history of globalization lies at the very heart of the academic enterprise of global history: 'New Global History (NGH), the name taken to set off the study of present-day globalization from previous manifestations of the process, has been reluctantly embraced by some of my colleagues and myself as a necessary demarcation of inquiry' (2006: 2). Contra Pieterse, then, Mazlish not only equates the study of globalization with global history, but also limits the latter to the study of the present-day historical phase of globalization.

It seems to us that global studies works much the same way. The proper reassertion of the significance of the master concept 'globalization' at the heart of global studies leads to the breakdown of Pieterse's difference thesis—even in its supposedly 'analytic' formulation. This conceptual collapse means that the author's admission of the 'partly semantic' nature of the difference thesis must become 'fully semantic'; that is, a difference in wording only. And this conclusion reinforces our impression that the alleged differences between global studies and globalization studies are of a purely semantic nature.

Moreover, Pieterse ties his difference thesis to a historical narrative that suggests a discipline-bound wave of globalization studies preceding global studies. But this account misses the fact that it was not until the mid-to-late 2000s that the designation 'global studies' became more widely adopted in the academy—usually as a pragmatic umbrella label appropriated by many globalization researchers around the world. Let us offer a personal story to further illustrate this point. One of the present authors—Manfred Steger—arrived in 2005 as the new Head of the School of International and Community Studies at RMIT University in Melbourne, Australia, where he was charged with setting up a larger transdisciplinary school organized around the study of global-scale processes. After some discussion, the involved faculty settled on the name 'School of Global Studies, Social Science, and Planning'—even though Steger had at first suggested 'School of Globalization Studies, Social Science, and Planning'. But he agreed to 'Global Studies' after being told that the new school name was far too long and required shortening. He did so without a second thought because, in his mind, these terms signified the same thing: namely, the collective and conscious academic effort to advance the study of globalization as a transdisciplinary and transnational project.

Many globalization scholars from around the word have shared similar stories about how they came to rely more exclusively on the label 'global studies'. Equally pragmatic reasons tend to dominate their accounts. They have used the related terms 'global studies' and 'globalization studies' loosely and without much system-building ambition in the pursuit of their transdisciplinary globalization projects (Turner, 2010). Alternative accounts offered by global studies proponents like Victor Roudometof (2012) and Kevin Archer (2013) have confirmed that 'global studies' was one of several labels available to emerging globalization researchers during the last 20 years or so. Likewise, in their introduction to their important reader, *Critical Globalization Studies*, Richard P. Appelbaum and William I. Robinson (2005: xi–xii) use 'global studies' and 'globalization studies' interchangeably. As one of the present authors noted years ago, 'Studies of globalization and, more generally, studies in the broad and loosely defined field of global studies did not become conscious of themselves as such until the 1990s' (James, 2012: 753). A number of academics employed the term 'global studies' as early as the late 1990s to refer to both their work and newly established programmes or centres at their respective universities. Others experimented with the labels 'globalization studies', 'critical globalization studies', 'global affairs', or 'transnational studies' before settling on 'global studies'.

Indeed, some of these designations still exist, which shows that 'global studies' has not been universally adopted.

Finally, let us address the assertion of globalization studies' alleged single-disciplinary moorings. It is true that most global studies scholars emerged, necessarily, from conventional disciplinary backgrounds in the social sciences and humanities. But this does not mean that their global imagination was colonized by a mono-disciplinary logic. Quite to the contrary, nearly all of the major globalization scholars writing between 1995 and 2005—the period in which global studies emerged—emphasized inter-, multi-, and trans-disciplinarity as defining hallmarks of globalization research. Here are some examples: David Held et al.'s *Global Transformations* (1999), John Tomlinson's *Globalization and Culture* (1999), Ulrich Beck's *What Is Globalization?* (2000), James Mittelman's *The Globalization Syndrome* (2000), Jan Aart Scholte's *Globalization* (2005), and, indeed, Jan Nederveen Pieterse's *Globalization and Culture* (2004). Moreover, our own outline of an engaged theory of globalization provided in Chapter 5 highlights the importance transdisciplinarity in both research and teaching. A characterization of these 'globalization studies' as discipline bound simply does not stand up to critical scrutiny. Khondker (2013: 528) makes the same point when he notes that the assertion of an earlier wave of globalization studies lacking interdisciplinarity begs empirical support.

Hence, there appears to be little empirical evidence for the second criticism of the field rooted in the alleged distinction between globalization studies and global studies and its corresponding historical narrative. It is arguably the case, as we documented in Chapter 3, that global studies lacks integrated, developed theories of globalization, but that is a completely different point. Finally, much evidence points to the fact that earlier studies of globalization were every bit as transdisciplinary as research conducted under the subject heading of 'global studies'.

The Third Criticism: Theory–Practice Gap

Scholars levelling the criticism of a theory–practice gap against global studies rely on another difference thesis: namely, the discrepancy between the analytic or programmatic promise of global studies and its empirical manifestation as 'global studies as it actually exists'. Their charge is that global studies is intellectually 'barely developed' and its programmes and conferences resemble a 'scaffolding without a roof' (Pieterse, 2013a: 500). Even some scholars who have been spearheading the collective effort to establish global studies as a new field of enquiry in the academic landscape have argued that this goal has remained elusive, especially with regard to its two core institutional ambitions of creating genuinely trans-disciplinary programmes and escaping the gravitational pull of existing international studies and area studies programmes that remain steeped in methodological nationalism (Appelbaum, 2013: 547–8; Axford, 2013: 779–80; Scholte, 2016).

In light of the evidence offered earlier in this chapter concerning thriving programmes and centres around the world, however, actually existing global studies seems to be in far better condition than these critics would have us believe. Much of the empirical data shows that there are promising pedagogical and research initiatives underway in the field. In particular, landmark programmes like those established at UCSB or RMIT University have successfully incorporated most of the features we associate with the ambitious programmatic promise of global studies.

Unfortunately, however, even a cursory survey of the large bulk of actually existing global studies programmes suggests that closing of the theory–practice gap at flagship institutions like UCSB represents the exception rather than the rule. This means that this third criticism appears to be on target for a large number of programmes that have adopted the 'global studies' label. In many cases, the activities placed under the heading of 'global studies' did not involve the generation of innovative programmes, but amounted to little more than a cosmetic facelift of existing offerings in international studies, comparative studies, regional studies, and development studies. Some universities, like the University of Hawai'i at Mānoa, chose the rather conventional route of creating undergraduate major and minor tracks in global studies within the existing framework of 'interdisciplinary studies' that contains a significant number of other unorthodox programmes. These offerings tend to be supported by academics in traditional departments who volunteer their time or are assigned to teach them on a released time basis. In most cases, such 'interdisciplinary' tracks develop few, if any, courses of their own, as the curriculum consists entirely of pre-existing courses from established departments that are deemed appropriate for a global studies major or minor degree. Other universities, like the University of Illinois at Urbana–Champaign and the London School of Economics, opted for integrating global studies as a subfield within conventional department structures—a strategy designed to increase programme menus without making substantive changes to existing teaching and research frameworks.

But perhaps the most troubling development we have observed in recent years stems from neoliberal dynamics that have been impacting the academy. Global studies appears to be increasingly used as a convenient catchphrase by academic entrepreneurs who follow economic incentives offered by universities to 'cash in' on a label that has proven to be highly popular with students. Turned into an instrumental mechanism for generating revenue, global studies has become an appealing generic brand. Attached to a growing number of conventional area studies curricula, international studies offerings, and diplomacy and foreign affairs programmes, the designation also serves the purpose of boosting the institution's intellectual and instructional appeal without having to make substantive changes to the familiar teaching and research agenda. Rather than signalling a substantive programmatic transformation taking place in the international academic landscape, the proliferation of the designation 'global studies' in many academic units, course titles, textbooks, academic job postings, and extracurricular activities all too often reflects the growing power of the neoliberal imperative in higher education. Unfortunately, these vacuous appropriations have caused considerable damage to substantive global studies programmes at leading institutions. In addition, they have cast an ominous shadow over the future development of the field.

In spite of these obvious failures, however, let us note that the institutional realization of the field's lofty programmatic vision in the current academic landscape is no easy task. Global studies faces the formidable challenge of expanding its foothold in the dominant environment of single-discipline departments while at the same time continuing its work against the prevailing order. To reconcile these seemingly contradictory imperatives, global studies must retain its perilous ambition to project issues of global–local relations across the conventional disciplinary matrix yet accept with equal determination the pragmatic task of finding some accommodation within the very disciplinary structure it seeks to transform. Such exasperating attempts to satisfy these diverging impulses force global studies scholars to play three distinct roles— depending on the concrete institutional opportunities and constraints they encounter in their academic home environment.

First, they might have to assume the role of *intrepid mavericks* willing to establish global studies as a separate discipline—that is, as a first but necessary step towards the more holistic goal of transformation. The collective efforts of scholars located in the previously mentioned landmark institutions represent an impressive model of how such difficult maverick activities can lead to remarkably successful outcomes. However, as Armin Krishnan has pointed out, leaving one's discipline behind does not mean the wholesale abandonment of one's original disciplinary interests: '[P]ractically every new discipline starts off necessarily as an interdisciplinary project that combines elements from some parent discipline(s) with original new elements and insights' (2009: 34).

To be sure, mavericks must possess a bold spirit of adventure that makes it easier for them to leave their original disciplinary setting behind to cover new ground. And being a maverick always carries the considerable risk that they and their new field might fail.

Second, if their academic context demands it, global studies scholars must be prepared to embrace the role of *radical insurgents* seeking to globalize established disciplines from *within*. This means working towards the goal of carving out a global studies dimension for specific disciplines such as political science or sociology. A specific example of such an insurgence would be Peter Dicken's fierce critique of his own discipline—human geography—for failing to engage properly with intellectually and economically significant globalization debates. Dicken (2004: 5) famously challenged his disciplinary colleagues to take up what he considers the 'central task for geographers'—to pay more attention to contemporary global issues and concerns such as the spatial outcomes of globalization that set the framework for crucial social dynamics in the twenty-first century. It is heartening to note that his plea did not fall on deaf ears, for one can find today many human geographers at the cutting-edge frontiers of global studies research.

The final role to be assumed in this long and uncertain quest to bridge the theory–practice gulf is that of *reflexive nomads*. We use the term 'nomads' here in the rich anthropological sense of people moving self-consciously across the intellectual and social landscape—not in the popular culture sense of aimless souls wandering with no fixed address. Such nomadism requires reciprocally constitutive relations with that landscape, not simply the desire for transcendence of boundaries. Thus, neither do we use 'nomadism' in the post-structuralist sense of free, smooth, and unbounded or 'rhizomic' movement as espoused by Gilles Deleuze and Felix Guattari (1987). Reflexive nomadism is embodied in global studies scholars who travel across and beyond several disciplines, critically (and positively) aware of the disciplinary baggage they carry with them, and travelling in order to reconfigure old *and* new knowledge around concrete globalization research questions and projects. Contra dominant contemporary ideologies of freedom and mobility, we note that baggage is not always a bad thing. Reflexivity in our sense means that 'overturning' the old disciplines is not done for the sake of it. It does not involve leaving behind old disciplinary strengths just for the thrill of intellectual travel. The reflexive nomadic role demands that students of the global slow down and explore the vast literatures of other disciplines on pertinent subjects that are usually studied in isolation from each other.

The Fourth Criticism: Postcolonial Scepticism

The final criticism discussed in this chapter emanates from postcolonial thinkers located both within and without the global studies field. As Robert Young explains, postcolonial theory is a related set of perspectives and principles that involves a conceptual reorientation towards perspectives or forms of knowledge developed outside the West—in Asia, Africa, Oceania, and Latin America (2003: 6–7). By seeking to insert alternative insights into the dominant power structures of the West and beyond, postcolonial theorists attempt to change the way people think and behave to produce more just and equitable relationships between the different peoples of the world. Emphasizing the connection between theory and practice, postcolonial intellectuals consider themselves critical thinkers challenging the alleged superiority of Western cultures, racist attitudes, and economic inequality separating the Global North from the Global South. This includes the persistence of 'orientalism'—a discriminatory, Europe-derived mindset so brilliantly dissected by late postcolonial theorist Edward Said (1979). As Young concludes, postcolonialism is a socially engaged form of critical thinking 'about a changing world, a world that has been changed by struggle and which its practitioners intend to change further' (2003: 7).

A significant number of postcolonial and indigenous theorists have examined the connections between globalization and postcolonialism (Krishna, 2009; Soguk, 2010; Singh, 2013). While most have expressed both their appreciation and affinity for much of what global studies stands for, they have also offered incisive critiques of what they see as the field's troubling geographic, ethnic, and epistemic location within the hegemonic Western framework. For example, the noted ethnic studies scholar Ramón Grosfoguel offers an apt summary of such critical postcolonial concerns: 'Globalization studies, with a few exceptions, have not derived the epistemological and theoretical implications of the epistemic critique coming from subaltern locations in the colonial divide and expressed in academia through ethnic studies and women studies. We still continue to produce a knowledge from the Western man's "point zero" god's-eye view' (2005: 284).

Other postcolonial thinkers, like the World Social Forum-connected scholar–activist Boaventura de Sousa Santos, have taken their epistemic criticism beyond the confines of global studies in their indictment of the hegemonic academic framework as failing to recognize the different ways of knowing by which people across the globe provide meaning to their existence. In fact, his charge of 'cognitive injustice' moves far beyond conventional academic approaches and methodologies, deeply penetrating into the supposedly counter-hegemonic territory of most of the critical theories we discussed in this chapter. de Sousa Santos (2014) argues that genuine radicalism seems no longer possible in the Global North because 'Western, Eurocentric critical theory' has lost the capacity to learn from the experiences of the world. Haunted by a 'sense of exhaustion', he charges, the tradition of critical theory has lapsed into irrelevance, inadequacy, impotence, stagnation, and paralysis. Hence, his ideal of 'epistemological justice' contains the radical demand to end what he calls 'epistemicide'; that is, the suppression and marginalization of epistemologies of the South by the dominant critical theories of the North. de Sousa Santos (2014) concludes that if the critical impulse is to survive in the twenty-first century, it is imperative for globalization scholars around the world to distance themselves from the Eurocentric critical tradition that has provided only weak answers to the strong questions confronting us in the global age.

Postcolonial critics like Grosfoguel and de Sousa Santos provide an invaluable service to global studies by highlighting the conceptual parochialism behind its allegedly global theoretical and practical concerns. Indeed, their intervention suggests that global studies thinkers have not paid enough attention to the postcolonial imperative of contesting dominant Western perspectives. They also force all scholars working in the field to confront questions that are often relegated to the margins of their intellectual enquiry. Is global studies sufficiently critical to include the diverse voices of the multitude and to speak to the diverse experiences of disempowered people around the world? What sort of new and innovative ideas have been produced by public intellectuals who do not necessarily travel along the theoretical and geographical paths frequented by Western globalization scholars? Are there pressing issues and promising intellectual approaches that have been neglected in global studies? Some of these questions also point to the central role of the English language in the young field. With English expanding its status as the academic lingua franca, thinkers embedded in Western universities still hold the monopoly on the production of critical theories. Important contributions from the Global South in languages other than English often fall through the cracks or only register in translated form on the radar of the supposedly 'global' academic publishing network years after their original publication.

At the same time, however, it behoves us to acknowledge the progress that has been made in global studies to significantly expand its 'space of tension' by welcoming and incorporating Global South perspectives. As early as 2005, a quarter of the contributions featured in Appelbaum and Robinson's *Critical Globalizations Studies* anthology came from authors located in Africa, Asia, and Latin America. Since then, pertinent criticisms from within that demanded the inclusion of multiple voices and perspectives from around the world have proliferated. Most importantly, Darian-Smith and McCarty's previously discussed delineation of the field has gone a very long way in meeting the postcolonial challenge by showing concrete ways in which to decentre European knowledge and include non-Western epistemologies. As they emphasize, 'There is a pressing need for research dealing with global issues to incorporate knowledge produced outside the Euro-American academy, and to understand this scholarship as a vital source of inspiration and innovation' (Darian-Smith and McCarty, 2017: 8).[6]

Taking postcolonial criticisms seriously also requires global studies scholars to challenge taken-for-granted assumptions on the part of Western scholars to speak for others in the Global South. In this context, we must not forget that it was the Mexican Zapatista movement—mostly composed of indigenous *campesinos* in the region—that confronted neoliberal globalization with a resounding '*Ya basta!*', thus inaugurating what eventually became the global justice movement. In this context, let us also note the glocalization of the West reflected in the fact that academic institutions in the Global North—and the United States in particular—have become a magnet for postcolonial scholars from around the world. As Razmig Keucheyan has emphasized, 'For today's critical theorists, U.S. universities constitute a site of recognition comparable to Paris for writers in the first half of the twentieth century' (2013: 73).

Thus, our response to the postcolonial scepticism displayed towards global studies points to a similarly mixed dynamic to the one we identified in the first criticism. While there has been recent progress in incorporating non-Western perspectives and approaches in a systematic way, there still remains plenty of room for further improvement in the emergent field.

Conclusion

The four major criticisms discussed in this chapter have guided our examination of the grand promise of global studies in linking theoretical concerns to concrete issues in higher education. In addition to their specific insights, these criticisms provide a necessary corrective to the idealized and romanticized accounts that often accompany the rise of a new academic endeavour. In fact, the authors of the present study can probably be found guilty of this charge more than once in the preceding chapters of this work. As we noted, most fledgling academic fields are

[6] See also Comaroff and Comaroff (2012).

prone to displaying a certain kind of youthful arrogance expressed in exaggerated aspirations to 'set things straight' while claiming that they are serving as bastions of intellectual progress. Global studies is no stranger to such boastful behaviour. At times, its invidious airs of superiority displayed towards conventional disciplines have given just cause for consternation, as have some of its hubristic and ultimately unproven claims to novelty and universality. Expressing a necessary spirit of moderation, Habibul Khondker reminds us, '"Global" need not be imperial; it can coexist and build on local, national, and regional studies' (2013: 527–8).

Ultimately, then, our exploration of the current state of global studies in the context of these four major criticisms reveals that the field has only partly delivered on its promise. Significant challenges remain and much work needs to be done to synchronize its programmatic vision with its institutional manifestations. But its existing limitations and shortcomings are hardly surprising in light of only three decades' worth of sustained work on a topic as complex as globalization. Jan Aart Scholte puts it best:

Even if the field of 'global studies' remains underdeveloped, understandings of the human condition have considerably globalised across the academy as well as wider society. Even if methodological nationalism and methodological localism continue to hold substantial sway, they are more frequently and more deeply challenged—and rightly so in the view of current material and discursive circumstances. (2016: 223)[7]

As most of its critics emphasize, one of the greatest tasks of global studies for the next decade is to keep finding practical ways around the disciplinary walls that still divide the academic landscape today. This mission requires the emergent field to attract scholars willing to assume the burden of intellectual leadership. They must develop a clear agenda for transdisciplinarity that can inspire students and readers. Animated by an ethical imperative to critically globalize knowledge, such transdisciplinary efforts may contain the potential to reconfigure our discipline-orientated academic infrastructure around issues of global public responsibility (Kennedy, 2015; Mittelman, 2017). Such integrative endeavours should be undertaken steadily and tirelessly—but also carefully and with the proper understanding that diverse and multiple forms of knowledge are sorely needed to engage with a global public. The necessary appreciation for the interplay between academic specialists and generalists must contain a proper respect for the crucial contributions of the conventional

---

[7] Barrie Axford (2013: 2) comes to a similar assessment: 'For the study of globalization has yet to affect a paradigm change in the social sciences, though it may well constitute a "positive problem shift" in how knowledge about the social is constituted'.

disciplines to our growing understanding of globalization. But the time has come to take the next step in the required reconfiguration of global knowledge production. The rising global imaginary demands nothing less from global studies students hailing from all disciplines and fields of enquiry.

8   Making Sense of the Populist Challenge to Globalization

As we noted in Chapter 1, the early twenty-first century has *not* witnessed the 'total exhaustion' of all alternatives to the ideology of liberalism (cf. Fukuyama, 1989). Rather, intensifying globalization dynamics have culminated in the Great Unsettling of conventional institutional arrangements and social routines. The related contest of worldviews has recently been linked to what some commentators have called the 'retreat of Western liberalism', 'the crisis of liberal-democratic politics', 'the rupture in liberal democracies', and even the outright 'failure of liberalism' (Luce, 2017; Deneen, 2018; Mouffe, 2018; Castells, 2019). While such obituaries to the liberal tradition may yet turn out to be premature, it has nonetheless become obvious that its post–Cold War fantasy of an 'end of history' has been incinerated in the crucible of space–time compression involving both ideas and matter.

Over the last few years, the ongoing ideological confrontation between the market globalism of dominant neoliberal forces, the justice globalism of alterglobalization activists, and the religious globalism of jihadist Islamists has been expanded, as a familiar contender wearing new clothes has re-entered the arena: right-wing national populism.[1] Indeed, its unexpected surge in the current global political landscape—and the crucial role played by the new digital media in this process of ideological revival—has prompted influential commentators to coin apposite phrases such as 'new populist wave', 'populist explosion', 'populist moment', or

---

[1] Some observers like William E. Connolly (2017) argue that the 'populist' designation does not fit current radical right-wing strains such as Trumpism. Rather, he prefers the term 'aspirational fascism'. In our argument, Trump's brand of national populism shows a number of similarities to the ideology of fascism, but the designation 'fascist' requires a careful definition that relates to both its form and content. We understand fascism as a form of nationalist authoritarianism that contains a number of key characteristics: (1) it uses populist appeal (the dominant form of ideological address); (2) it appeals to cultural, political, and economic revival or rebirth (positive ideological content); (3) it blames and reviles 'others'—internal and external—for the disadvantaged plight of the 'multitude' (negative ideological content); and (4) this multitude *chooses* to respond to an externalized set of threats from a 'hostile world' by *actively* letting itself be 'bundled together'—a central symbol of fascism—by an authoritarian leader (the dominant subjective form of followership).

'populist temptation' (Judis, 2016; Taguieff, 2016; Brubaker, 2017; Eichengreen, 2018). Its illiberal and authoritarian leanings stand in stark contrast to the pluralist and inclusive values of liberal democracy. It is a global phenomenon linking Victor Órban's Hungary, Jair Bolsonaro's Brazil, Norbert Hofer's Austria, Marine Le Pen's France, Matteo Salvini's Italy, Jarosław Kaczyński's Poland, Nigel Farage's United Kingdom, Pauline Hanson's Australia, Iván Duque's Colombia, Rodrigo Duterte's Philippines, and, of course, Donald Trump's United States of America. The content of this cluster of movements is economically anti-globalist, but its practice is culturally globalizing, with each of the movements communicating with and learning from each other.

Although populisms of the classical ilk have been a constant feature on the global political map for more than a century—starting with the agrarian populism of the American People's Party and cresting in the long wave of Latin American populisms—the current developments have been writing a remarkable new chapter in the global history of populism. It began with the notable upswing of right-wing national populism in liberal Western democracies in the 1980s and 1990s, and reached its climax in the current populist conjuncture, defined most spectacularly by the stunning triumphs of Trumpism in the United States and Brexit in the United Kingdom, as well as the electoral successes of other European national populist parties (Betz, 1994; Taggert, 1997; Berlet and Lyons, 2000; Camus and Lebourg, 2017; Rovira Kaltwasser and Taggert, 2018; Zito and Todd, 2018; Norris and Inglehart, 2019).

The French philosopher Pierre-André Taguieff (1984) coined the term 'national populism' in reference to the political discourse of Jean-Marie Le Pen and his newly founded French political party, the *Front National* (FN)—renamed in 2018 as the *Rassemblement National* (RN). Soon after the FN's founding in 1984, some of its key politicians openly embraced Taguieff's initially critical term 'with much pride' (Jäger, 2016: 16). Its advocates tend to imagine a mythical national unity, often based on an essentialized identity through permutations of the cultural, including ethnic relations. They claim to defend and protect the common people against the treachery of corrupt elites and parasitical social institutions. Calling for a direct relationship between the leader and the people, national populists tend towards an eccentric combining of right-wing political values, libertarian cultural orientations, and left-of-centre economic policies (Camus and Lebourg, 2017: 13).

A growing number of scholars have followed Taguieff's terminology and adopted 'national populism' as the umbrella term for a range of radical right-wing variants linked to different regions across the world (Wodak et al., 2013). It is important to note, however, that various forms of left-wing populism have been on the march as well—a development that has been accompanied by a steady stream of progressive academic publications that recommend populism as an effective political strategy to revitalize the enervated left (Grattan, 2016; Gerbaudo, 2017; Mouffe, 2018). Moreover, the appeal of nationalist discourses for left-wing populist leaders has been reflected in the strong performance of Senator Bernie Sanders in the 2016 US presidential campaign and the recent landslide victory of the seasoned Andrés Manuel López Obrador in the 2018 Mexican presidential election.[2]

In this chapter, we argue that the new wave of right-wing populism is intricately connected to shifting perceptions of the role of globalization in the world. This observation is not new. In his prescient speech delivered at Harvard University's Weatherhead Center for International Affairs in the wake of the 1997–98 Asian Financial Crisis, then-Secretary General Kofi Annan (1998) observed a 'growing backlash against globalization' manifested in three reactions:

The first, and perhaps most dangerous reaction, has been one of nationalism. ... Globalization is being presented as a foreign invasion that will destroy local cultures, regional tastes, and national traditions ... The second reaction has been to resort to illiberal solutions—the call for the man on the white horse, the strong leader who in time of crisis can act resolutely in the nation's interests. ... The third reaction against the forces of globalization has been a politics of populism. Embattled leaders may begin to propose forms of protectionism as a way to offset losses supposedly incurred by too open an embrace of competition, and too free a system of political change. Their solutions is for a battered nation to turn away and inward, tend to its own at whatever cost, and rejoin the global community only when it can do so from a position of strength. In this reaction, globalization is made a scapegoat for ills which more often have domestic roots of political nature. Globalization, having been employed as political cover by reformers wishing to implement austerity programmes, comes to be seen as a force of evil by those who would return to imagined communities of earlier times.

Hence, for Annan, politics was at the root of globalization's difficulties. This means that an egalitarian politics of multilateralism, pluralism, social justice, and human rights can not only serve as a bulwark against a politics of populism, but also inspire a more inclusive form of globalization that works for all, especially the disadvantaged regions of the Global South.

Annan's early insights thus demonstrate that the perception of the ominous link between neoliberal globalization and populism had already taken shape in the heyday of globalization at the end of the twentieth century. What took most pundits by surprise, however, was the

---

[2] This chapter focuses on right-wing variants of national populism.

magnitude of the backlash against globalization—a reaction that was amplified considerably in the wake of the 2008–09 Global Financial Crisis. Therefore, the trajectory of neoliberal globalization was both a consequence of and contributor to what we are calling the Great Unsettling (Moffitt, 2016; Anselmi, 2018). As Slavoj Žižek has noted, 'The rise of rightist populism is a feature common to all countries caught up in the vortex of globalization' (2010: viii). In short, this new 'anti-globalist' form of national populism is now being *practiced* across the world. Its ubiquity is not only a sign of its global geographical reach and growing political potency, but also exposes two glaring and potentially self-defeating paradoxes.

Firstly, its denunciation of globalization notwithstanding, national populism has itself become part of a multidimensional global process cutting across national borders and cultural lines of demarcation (Moffitt, 2016; Anselmi, 2018; Norris and Inglehart, 2019). Secondly, as Michael Kazin (1995: 283) pointed out more than two decades ago, the most serious problems facing humanity today are global in nature and thus are simply not reducible to national populism's nationally or racially bounded categories of 'the people' and 'the elites'. In other words, by comparison with an emergence of national populism and fascism in the mid-twentieth century, contemporary populism has a deeply ambivalent relation to both the state and global relations. Still, its contradictory tendencies depend upon both for its impact.

What, then, are we to make of this profound right-wing populist challenge to both the idea and the process of globalization? Recent efforts to tackle this question seem to have raised more questions than produced answers. For example, why has right-wing populism's antagonistic rhetoric of 'hard-working people' versus 'globalist elites' found so much resonance, especially among the white working classes and large segments of the middle class in the Global North? What explains its tremendous adaptability to political and cultural contexts as different as France, Hungary, the United States, Brazil, and the Philippines? Why are so many national populist leaders seemingly immune to fact-based criticisms and appear to pay little if any political price for their obvious moral lapses, serious policy blunders, and blunt attacks on traditional pillars of democracy, including an independent judiciary and the free press? From this expanding list of quandaries spawned by this populist conundrum, there is one more question situated at the heart of this book that we need to understand: why and how did neoliberal market globalism come to be so startlingly contested by a relative newcomer that occupies such an orthogonal position in the ideological landscape of the twenty-first century?

Our argument is that a resilient anti-globalist strain of right-wing populism has been born over the past couple of decades, responding to the Great Unsettling. Its ascent confirms the destabilization of once taken-for-granted shibboleths, including the central importance of the unfettered markets. Today's chronic condition of instability brings traditional right-wing populism into a mutually beneficial yet rather odd relationship with the alt-right, anarcho-capitalists, and religious fundamentalists. In the United States, the successful convergence of surging Trumpists and established Tea Partiers compounds the situation. In this chapter, we offer a conceptual approach that can help to explain the populist challenge. We argue that the contemporary form of national populism is one that runs counter to conventional explanations of the phenomenon, for this particular strain of 'anti-globalist populism' has amassed a surprising ideational substance that defies commonplace dismissals of the apparent messiness of its expressed ideas.

Using our four-level subjective approach introduced in Chapters 4 and 5, we move between the analytic levels of ideas, ideologies, imaginaries, and ontologies to investigate anti-globalist populism. At the level of ideas, it might appear as a compilation of superficial sound bites and performed fury. But our analysis suggests that anti-globalist populism is not just a superficial and inconsistent narrative spun by idiots or aspirants. Rather, it has condensed ideologically into a significant configuration with patterns of discourse that have endowed it with an uncanny political potency. This ideational 'thickening' of populism has occurred as political leaders have learned to recast 'globalization' and 'globalism' as pejorative terms and placed them alongside more established populist concepts of 'corrupt elites' and a moral 'people'. This means that the portrayal of populism in the pertinent social science literature as a 'thin-centred' ideology that merely appropriates ideas from established thought systems to fatten its content does not capture the waxing symbolic content patterns of today's rising strain of anti-globalist populism. Hence, the essential contention of this chapter—resonating with the central thesis of the present study—is that both objective and subjective globalization dynamics deeply matter in the formation of the current populist wave.

Secondly, moving from analysis of ideological patterns to the contestation of social imaginaries, our argument is that the rise of the global imaginary—a process typically portrayed in the popular discourse as taking off with the 1991 collapse of the Soviet Union—is a long-term process that has spawned significant contestations across several generations.[3] One significant contestation was embodied in the alter-globalization movements, which were often youth based and drew on similar dynamics in the 1960s. The second challenge—related to the first—occurred a decade later in the wake of the Global Financial Crisis and assumed the form of large anti-capitalist skirmishes spearheaded by the Occupy Wall Street and *Indignados* movements (2011–12) that recall similar movements in the 1930s. Today, the pushback against globalism emanates from an older, alienated stratum of white working-class people who contest the neoliberal claim that 'globalization is good' by means of a national populism dead set against a borderless world and hostile to all forms of cosmopolitanism. For this reason, 'globalism' has become the central derogatory term of this new strain of populism.

The evolving trajectory of these contestations provide strong evidence for our argument that an older and continuing national imaginary is clashing with an emergent global imaginary that has been striving for ideational dominance for some decades now. Ironically, the global is being actively opposed by people who advance the cause of the national in explicitly global terms—even as they criticize globalization processes. As we will show later in the chapter in our analysis of political speeches delivered by Donald Trump and Nigel Farage, it is no coincidence that the key proponents of anti-globalist populism revile the global while at the same time forging global populist alliances that facilitate mutual learning and the transmission of slogans and tropes coined by these populist leaders.

Thirdly, anti-globalist populism must be understood in its larger social context as an unsettling of the ontological comfort associated—at times with nostalgic hindsight—with everyday *modern* life. However shallow that surface of comfort may have been across the twentieth century, it survived serious challenges such as the real possibility of nuclear annihilation and the emerging sense of the ecological fragility of our planet. Expressed at the categorical level of analysis, our argument is that anti-globalist populism both manifests and contributes to a sharpening sense of *ontological insecurity* that now affects all social strata, but most intensely the marginalized, the alienated, the precarious, and the older generation.

---

[3] It is worth remembering that the emergence of a national imaginary occurred across several generations from the late eighteenth century until the early twentieth century. What was in the first decades of the new century experienced as an 'explosion' of the national imaginary actually required two 'world wars' to bring home the sense of national integration to 'peripheral' regions of some Western nations where core constituencies had taken the national for granted for at least two or three generations. See, for example, Eugen Weber's influential study, *Peasants into Frenchmen* (1976).

The concept of ontological security was made famous by Anthony Giddens (1990). Following R. D. Laing (1965), Giddens defined the condition in relatively flat terms as the emotional or psychological sense of security held in place by the routinization and regulation of everyday life. Giddens suggested that this security was supported by what he called 'trust in abstract systems'. However, as he also acknowledged, abstract systems ranging from globalizing financial and commodity systems to medical and pharmaceutical systems are also socially 'disembedding'. As Giddens (1990: 53) suggested, 'These [systems] "lift out" social activity from localised contexts, reorganising social relations across large time–space distances'. His point follows the earlier pioneering work of Geoff Sharp, who argued that processes of material abstraction push social ties 'to be extended in space and in time. It creates a setting whereby the participant is "lifted out" of the relationships of everyday life and where at least subjectively persons experience themselves as the authors of their own creations' (1985: 62). It is important to note that this process of 'lifting out' has been associated with contradictory consequences. While it is experienced, in the first instance, as both liberating and globalizing, it also rattles people's sense of normalcy and shakes up their routines. Thus, it both qualifies and calls into question the taken-for-granted security of earlier ways of knowing and acting. Moreover, Sharp observed that the disembedding process tends to spawn a collective desire for a return to the 'simpler' days of the past 'golden age':

The person, as placed within this more directly universalized cultural setting, is 'lifted out' of particular institutional configurations defining the given round of life of a class. The clear sense of a structured life pattern which this provided, the system of constraints built into every class situation and attendant ideology within classical capitalism, begin to pass into dissolution as the institutional functions are reconstituted and reallocated under the aegis of a new level of constitutive dominance. (1985: 68)[4]

Situated within the analytical framework of our book, Sharp's new emerging 'level of constitutive dominance' is what we refer to as 'the postmodern'. At the same time, however, we must emphasize that the Great Unsettling reverberates through all of the subjective layers of people's contemporary experience: ideas, ideologies, imaginaries, and ontologies. The current intensifying dynamic of ontological insecurity comes to the fore through layers of competing thought systems, the

---

[4] In a similar argument offered in the 1980s, one of the present authors described the 'processes of postmodern relativism' as 'undermining deeply embedded ontological attachments and relationships, creat[ing] the grounds on which responsiveness to the appeal of the new nationalism is based' (James, 1984: 160).

rubbing-against-each-other of social background understandings, and the contradictions between basic existential conditions. With particular reference to the new anti-globalist populism, these destabilizations manifest in fights over the nature of knowledge (e.g., Trump's 'fake news' or 'alternative facts'), the consequences of hotly contested spatial boundaries (e.g., Trump's 'beautiful wall', designed to enhance the security of US citizens threatened by 'Mexican rapists'), and tensions over the meanings of identity (e.g., Trump's tirades against the perceived excesses of 'political correctness' and some leading voices of the #MeToo or #BlackLivesMatter movements).

After a brief opening overview of some influential perspectives on populism, this chapter offers an appraisal of some major criticisms levelled against the ideological paradigm by advocates of competing approaches. It then uses select campaign speeches delivered by Donald Trump and Nigel Farage to illustrate the ideological thickening of anti-globalist populism. Our methodological approach here—morphological discourse analysis (MDA) in the context of engaged theory—also allows us to connect our textual examination with our larger theoretical argument about existing frictions between competing social imaginaries that reach down to the ontological level of social formations.

The Ideological Approach and Its Critics

Like all keywords in the social sciences, populism is an 'essentially contested concept' (Gallie, 1964). Its notorious slipperiness—reflected in sprouting adjectives such as 'chameleonic', 'mercurial', 'episodic', 'culture bound', or 'context dependent'—has been blamed for the many failed attempts to construct a hegemonic meaning (Taggert, 2000; Arter, 2010). As Francisco Panizza (2005: 1) observed some years ago, it has become somewhat of a cliché to preface any major discussion of the subject by lamenting the lack of clarity about the term 'populism' and casting doubts about its usefulness for political analysis. For this reason, some scholars have written off the term altogether as a journalistic stereotype or political epithet that serves more as an instrument to discredit political opponents than a useful lens of social-scientific analysis. Marco d'Eramo (2013: 8), for example, sees the concept's sole academic utility as a 'hermeneutical tool for identifying and characterizing those political parties that accuse their opponents of populism'.

Critics often utilize the findings of quantitative case studies to bolster their assertion that, 'populism quite obviously falls short of the status of ideology' (Hawkins, 2010; Aslanidis, 2016: 89). From their perspective, populism's only option to fatten its ideational substance lies in its chronic need to cannibalize existing thick ideologies such as conservatism or fascism. Without the ingestion of conceptual chunks taken from other thought systems, critics argue, populism's ontic status remains that of an empty signifier, which 'can be filled and made meaningful by whatever is poured into it' (Mény and Surel, 2002: 6; Laclau, 2005: 38–43). Or, as Taguieff puts it, populism is a 'political style capable of being crystalized in various symbolic forms and identified in multiple ideological loci— adopting each time the colours of the receiving locus' (2007: 168).

From such denials of populism's ideological stature, it is only a moderate step to disavow the ideational approach altogether, something we clearly contest. For example, Chantal Mouffe proclaims, with no justification, that populism 'is not an ideology and cannot be attributed to a specific programmatic content' (2018: 11). Similarly, Paris Aslanidis calls for an end to what he characterizes as a 'knee-jerk association of populism with ideology' (2016: 89). Predictably, the article ends with the suggestion to 'replace ideology' with what its author considers to be the 'superior analytical and methodological perspective' of 'discursive frame analysis'—a formal quantitative methodology deemed more capable of addressing the 'cognitive aspects of populist argumentation' without falling prey to 'unscientific' normative implications that are part and parcel of the ideological paradigm (Aslanidis, 2016: 101). This is full-blown modernist theory at its most confident and least successful.

This presupposition of populism's ideological thinness has been generally accepted in the academic literature. It plays directly into the hands of other style-based critics who insist that populism belongs to something that is prior to all ideological content and choice—a 'logic of politics' that remains autonomous from any ideological project and therefore can interact easily with any ideological orientation (Laclau, 2005; Pantazopoulos, 2016). Even more rounded critics, such as Rogers Brubaker (2017), who concede that theoretical investigations of national populism should include attempts to map its ideational fingerprint, insist that what makes it possible to characterize a phenomenon as belonging to the genus 'populism' is not a particular set of related ideas and values, but the 'stylistic repertoire' upon which it draws.

Unfortunately, the main proponents of the ideological approach have failed to push back against their critics. In fact, they unintentionally accelerated the stylistic turn by ceding crucial intellectual terrain all too readily and prematurely. For example, Cas Mudde and Cristóbal Rovira Kaltwasser (2017), two leading advocates of the ideational perspective, have legitimized the 'thin' definition of populism that cements its status as a weak ideational cluster composed of only three core concepts: the people, the elite, and the general will. Similarly, Ben Stanley (2008: 102) has affirmed populism's alleged ideological thinness reflected in four distinct but interrelated core concepts: the people and the elite; the antagonistic relationship between these two homogenously presented entities; popular sovereignty; and the moral valorization of 'the people' that contrasts sharply with the denigration of 'the elite'.

The problem with this claim for populism's conceptual thinness is threefold. It reinforces arguments made by style-orientated critics who cite populism's inherent conceptual 'elasticity' and 'promiscuity' as evidence for its lesser status as a 'political impulse' rather than an 'ideology' (Kazin, 1995). Swapping theoretical disadvantages with political advantages actually strengthens the position of scholars who elevate the populist supply side of 'logic' over the demand side of 'ideas'. If the critics are indeed right in their assumption that all of the action lies in 'modes' of political performance, then it is difficult to see why one should bother studying barren conceptual configurations.

Secondly, by presenting thinness as the defining conceptual condition of populism that applies to all of its subtypes and across time and space, populism is rendered a static entity endowed with an unchanging essence. Moreover, its alleged limited number of core concepts locks populism into the prison of perpetual thinness, thus making a jailbreak an unlikely option. Rather than reducing it to a thing endowed with fixed properties, this chapter projects a more dynamic understanding of populism as a variable and unstable configuration whose ideational content can wax and wane as a result of ideational flows and changing social contexts.

The third problem follows from the previous point. Their ontological commitment to thin-centredness provides the partisans of the ideational approach with very little research incentive to engage periodically in ideological mapping exercises of the latest permutations and subtypes of national populism, such as Trumpism.

Morphological Discourse Analysis

This chapter uses MDA—a powerful methodological approach we integrate into our engaged theory framework—to map and critically evaluate the ideological structure of what we are calling 'anti-globalist populism'. As we described in Chapter 4, ideologies are patterned public clusters of normatively imbued ideas. They are conceptual maps that help people to find simple ways through the complexity of their political universes. Translating deep-seated social imaginaries into concrete political programmes and agendas, ideologies contend for control of political meanings and offer competing plans for public policy. They thus play a key role in consolidating social forces as political groupings and alliances. Indeed, the perpetual struggle over the definition of meaning places ideologies at the heart of all political processes.

MDA shows how discursive formations are critical to how ideologies (mis)represent, legitimate, integrate, and, most importantly, 'decontest' their core values and claims. Here, decontestation (Freeden, 1996) is the variable process of slowing swirling ideas into simpler patterns of common-sense language. Successfully decontested ideas are held as truth by large segments of a given population with such confidence that they no longer appear to be assumptions at all. Thus, the interlinked semantic and political roles of ideology suggest that patterned use of language translates into political power—that is, the power of deciding 'who gets what, when, and how' (Lasswell, 1958).

The key difference between Freeden's analysis of ideology and the morphological method used here is our more open conceptualization of the basic ideological units that carry meanings. Clusters of ideas can usefully be disaggregated into relatively static elements according to levels of decreasing contestation from core and adjacent concepts to peripheral concepts—à la Freeden—but we can also evaluate ideologies on the basis of their ability to arrange concepts of roughly equal significance into meaningful 'decontestation chains' or 'central ideological claims'. While these claims rarely appear verbatim in texts, they nonetheless represent realistic composites of linked concepts in the form of mini-narratives.

Ideological morphologies can thus be pictured as patterned ideas engaged in both (mis)*representing* reality *and* performatively (re)*producing* reality.[5] By bringing together the two principal concerns of discourse analysts and morphological ideology analysts with broader ideational–material analysis, this method facilitates a synthesis of content-based and style-orientated approaches to the study of populism, but in an integrated framework. After all, as Benjamin Krämer (2014: 46) notes, a 'style' is never symbolically neutral, for any mode of political articulation relies on more or less consistent messages being delivered. Similarly, Ruth Wodak emphasizes the importance of analysing right-wing populism as a phenomenon that 'always *combines and integrates form and content*, targets specific audiences and adapts to specific contexts' (2015: 3, emphasis added). The effort to bring together form and content explains our attention to the construction of central decontestation chains. It also

---

[5] Here, the concept of '(mis)representation' is associated with Louis Althusser's social thought (1971), while the concept of '(re)producing' is intended to evoke Pierre Bourdieu's notion of 'reproduction strategies' that generate meanings 'in a system of strategies generated by the *habitus*' (1990: 16).

explains our linking of the rather weak concept of 'style' to questions of *social form*, including contemporary and conflicting ontologies of space, knowing, and performance. In these terms, populist leaders *perform* truth and post-truth with all of the weight of *modern* conviction politics, but using the unsettlement of *postmodern* relativism to say, 'I know: trust me, and be very afraid of those Others who espouse the break-up of older verities'.

What criteria should be used, then, to distinguish rather incoherent clusters of ideas from a mature political ideology? Following Michael Freeden (1996: 485–6), we suggest that the maturity of ideologies should be assessed according to three cardinal criteria: their degree of *distinctiveness*; their context-bound *responsiveness* to a broad range of political issues; and their *effectiveness* in producing conceptual frames of common sense. To this we add a fourth consideration: their capacity for dealing with possible ontological contradictions—in this case, the tension between continuing cosmologies of traditional religious faith, dominant modern ideas of a human-made world, and an emergent postmodern relativism. Thus, the question of whether national populism can be considered a coherent political ideology must be resolved on the basis of its ability to distinguish itself from other ideologies through distinct concepts and claims; to respond to a broad range of political issues; and to present decontested explanations of our world, including its ontological tensions.

This analytic process, then, is conducive to revising old and developing new typologies and classification schemes that serve as preconditions for grasping the ideological thrust of national populisms; that is, how ideas existing in a dialectical relationship with social and historical circumstances affect political and social change. It contributes to a better understanding of the shifting ideological landscape in the twenty-first century and the crucial role that globalization—in both its objective and subjective dimensions—has been playing in this transformative process.

The morphological analysis performed in this chapter draws on a set of empirical data in the form of public speeches made by then-Republican Party candidate Donald J. Trump during the US electoral campaign between March and October 2016, as well as additional public remarks delivered between 2016 and 2018 on American soil by Nigel Farage, the former leader of the United Kingdom Independence Party (UKIP). Farage was the driving force behind Britain's 2016 referendum in favour of the country exiting the European Union.[6]

[6] All of the speeches are listed in Appendix 1.

We understand that a fuller empirical analysis would also map the myriad of mixed popular culture reference points of the populist right and alt-right—including their weaponizing of films such as *The Matrix* and *V for Vendetta*, films that were made with a very different political intent—or the appropriation of pop music symbols by political figures who claim that, for example, 'Taylor Swift Is an Alt-Right Pop Icon' (Yiannopoulos, 2016). With that proviso, we offer the following analysis as a way of establishing the condensation of meaning at the centre of what appears to be a proliferating promiscuity of meanings on the right. All of the speeches were analysed with a view to answering the following three sets of questions:

- What is the ideational significance of 'globalization' and 'globalism' in these texts?
- How are these concepts used to (re)produce meaning?
- Is there evidence for the (re)production of distinct ideological claims or decontestation chains centred on globalization concepts, and, if so, what sorts of (mis)representations do they produce?

Mapping Trumpism: The Significance of Globalization

Appearing prominently in all of Trump's public remarks are the concepts of 'the people' and 'the elites'. This confirms the rare agreement among populism scholars that these keywords sit at the very heart of all explanatory schemes of the phenomenon. The concept of 'the people' is, first and foremost, decontested in *national* terms by means of the adjacent concept 'American'. But this process has two strands that wind around each other without ever becoming a single thread. Along one of these treads, the presidential candidate addresses 'the American people', who he also imagines as a homogenous community 'united in common purposes and dreams' and enjoying the privilege of living in the 'greatest nation on Earth' (Speech 9). Along the other strand, the people are identified as '*common* people'— especially as 'workers', 'working people', and 'middle-class people'. Indeed, these crucial adjacent terms appear frequently in Trump's speeches and are often embedded in nationalist narratives: 'The legacy of Pennsylvania steelworkers lives in the bridges, railways, and skyscrapers that make up our great American landscape' (Speech 5). This involves a (mis)representation of past securities. Trump imbues 'the people' with meanings that are sharpened by additional adjacent terms such as 'sovereignty' and 'independence' (Speeches 5, 7, 9, 11, and 17). The concepts, too, are consistently linked to nationalistic themes such as his celebration of America's unique political system manifested in 'a government of the people, by the people, and for the people' (Speeches 7 and 10).

This confirms the presence of three major populist meanings of 'the people' as sovereign, as common people, and as the nation (Mudde and Rovira Kaltwasser, 2017: 9–11). We also found ample evidence for Jan-Werner Müller's (2016: 38) contention that the populist core concept of 'the people' is imbued with a deeply moralistic hue: Trump's campaign speeches are rife with essentialist depictions of the 'pure' character of the 'American people' in such moralistic superlatives as 'great', 'patriotic', 'loyal', 'hard-working', 'daring', 'brave', 'strong', 'energetic', 'decent', 'selfless', 'devoted', and 'honest'. Consider, for example, one striking (mis)representation highlighting some of the essential qualities of the American people: 'Americans are the people that tamed the West, that dug out the Panama Canal, that sent satellites across the solar system, that build great dams, and so much more' (Speech 4).

Trump continues his decontestation of the core concept 'American people' by making the familiar populist turn to its 'Others': elites, outsiders, and foreign agents. Accordingly, he asserts that the people's proven loyalty to and hard work for the nation has been 'repaid with total betrayal' (Speeches 4, 5, and 17). In this we see the evocation of a deep ontological insecurity. Slandered as 'deplorables' and demeaned by the coercive discourse of 'political correctness', 'American patriots who love our country and want a better future for all of our people' have been robbed of their dignity and respect. However, thanks to their 'common sense'—expressed in their 'clear understanding of how democracy really works'—the American people will debunk this deception and refuse to sit idly by as they are 'being ripped off by everybody in the world' (Speeches 3 and 14).

At this point in his decontestation of 'the American people', Trump begins to draw on the notion of the people's unmediated and incorruptible 'general will', which, though thwarted and ignored, is bound to reassert itself and 'smash the establishment' (Speeches 3 and 11). Roused by true tribunes of the people—such as Donald Trump himself—ordinary Americans are encouraged to 'create a new American future' in which the people will be 'first' again (Speech 17). In a joint campaign appearance with Trump, Nigel Farage offered a powerful affirmation of this activist construction of 'the people' and their 'true aspirations': 'I come to you from the United Kingdom with a message of hope and a message of optimism. It's a message that says if little people, the real people, if ordinary decent people are prepared to stand up and fight for what they believe in, we can overcome the big banks, we can overcome the multinationals ...' (Speech 1). In this passage, we see the drawing of a crimson line across which national and global imaginaries clash (but more of this in a moment).

This antagonistic turn in the construction of 'the people' leads us to the second core concept: the 'guilty' party identified as 'elites', 'the establishment', 'politicians', and 'the leadership class' (Speeches 5, 11, 14, and 16). Undermining the will of the people with the help of the 'corporate media', these economic, political, and cultural insiders are accused of 'rigging' the system of representative democracy—most clearly manifested in the 'Washington swamp'—to the end of advancing their morally corrupt practices of 'selling out the wealth of our nation generated by working people' and filling their own pockets (Speech 17). Confirming Stanley's depiction of populism's conceptual core (2008: 102), our analysis finds that Trump and Farage decontest the meaning of 'the elites' or 'the establishment' in terms of a denigrated 'other' that contrasts sharply with the valorization of 'the people'. Most importantly, Trump links the meaning of 'the elites' to the notion of 'globalist enemies' working against the interests of the country. While some of them are explicitly identified as domestic actors such as 'Wall Street bankers' or 'Washington politicians', many are characterized as 'foreign agents', which include both individuals such as George Soros and other members of the 'international financial elite' or entire countries like China, Mexico, and Japan, which are denounced for the alleged misdeeds of 'subsidizing their goods', 'devaluing their currencies', 'violating their agreements', and 'sending rapists, drug dealers, and other criminals into America' (Speech 3).

Trump consistently showcases 'Hillary' and 'the Clintons' as the 'un-American' epitome of the corrupt globalist elites, thus turning the former Secretary of State and American President into carriers of a global imaginary whom ordinary people cannot trust. This is a politically effective and rhetorically skilled move that allows Trump to collapse the distinction between domestic and global foes by creating a unified enemy image under the sign of 'globalization'. An abbreviated list of Hillary Clinton's 'crimes against the American people' includes proposing mass amnesty for illegal immigrants; advocating for open borders; spreading terrorism; pursuing an aggressive, interventionist foreign policy; making America less secure; robbing workers of their future by sending their jobs abroad; ending American sovereignty by handing power over to the United Nations (UN) and other 'globalist' institutions; abandoning Israel in its national struggle for survival; supporting free-trade agreements inimical to American interests; tilting the economic playing field towards other countries at America's expense; and advancing global special interests.

Most importantly, Trump persistently employs the terms 'global' or 'globalist' as adjacent concepts that flesh out the precise meaning of the elites' betrayal as reflected in the crimes of 'crooked Hillary' and the 'global establishment' she represents. His decontestation of 'the elites' allows us to identify a central ideological claim that associates the decontested meanings of the core concepts of 'the people' and 'the elites' with the adjacent term 'global':

Corrupt elites betray the hard-working people by shoring up a global order that makes them rich and powerful while compromising the sovereignty and security of the homeland and squandering the wealth of the nation.

This powerful decontestation chain helps Trump to present his electoral campaign against Hillary Clinton, the treacherous 'globalist' par excellence, as something much bigger than just a familiar political contest that repeats itself every four years. Rather, he frames the presidential election as a Manichean struggle that pits America against two 'globalist' enemies: a hostile 'world order' and 'a leadership class that worships globalism over Americanism' (Speech 5). At the same time, by linking the global imaginary to the ideas of a 'global establishment', he delegitimizes the still-dominant global imaginary as the fabrication of Others. During his many stump appearances of the 2016 campaigning season, this assertion of an irreconcilable opposition between 'Americanism' and such an imaginary grew into Trumpism's central ideological claim, appearing in almost every speech, including his acceptance speech at the Republican National Convention in Cleveland, Ohio:

Americanism, not globalism, will be our credo.

In this context, it is important to remember that the meaning of 'credo' carries deeply *traditional* religious connotations that signify the very essence of an alter-modernist belief system. The constant repetition of this 'Americanist credo'—and its numerous permutations such as 'Hillary defends globalism, not Americanism' or 'Hillary wants America to surrender to globalism'—indicates the enormous significance of globalization-related concepts in Trump's political discourse (Speeches 5, 6, 8, 9, 10, 11, and 12). Warning his audience not to surrender to 'the false song of globalism', the national populist candidate emphasized that, 'The nation-state remains the true foundation for happiness and harmony' (Speech 2). This is an all-embracing cultural claim. Here, Trump links 'globalization' to both national security *and* ontological security through direct appeals to women as embodied figures of the comprehensiveness of 'ordinary' security: 'Women', he quips in an apparently gratuitous fashion, 'also value security. They want a Commander-in-Chief that will defeat Islamic terrorism, stop the massive inflow of refugees, protect our borders, and who will reduce the rising crime and violence in our cities'

(Speech 16). Here, the figure of 'women' becomes the trope for ontological sensitivity. He is with them.

In political terms, Trump turns 'globalism' into both a set of misguided public policies and a 'hateful foreign ideology' devised by members of 'the global power structure' who plot 'in secret to destroy America' (Speeches 4, 7, 14, and 17). Here, Trump associates the neoliberal conceptual centrepiece of 'globalization' with what he calls the 'complete and total disasters' of immigration, crime, and terrorism that are 'destroying our nation' (Speeches 1 and 16). Immigration in particular receives ample treatment in the form of vigorous denunciations of the establishment's 'globalist policies of open borders' that endanger the 'safety' and 'security' of the American people. Once again, 'Hillary' becomes a convenient signifier in Trump's decontestation of globalization as a nefarious process of border erasure.

For Trump, all globalists serve the larger material process of 'globalization', which he defines as an elite-engineered project of 'abolishing the nation-state' and creating an international system that functions 'to the detriment of the American worker and the American economy' (Speeches 4, 5, and 16). In short, the populist candidate denounces both the economic and political dimensions of 'globalization' by arranging suitable core and adjacent concepts such as 'jobs', 'free trade', 'financial elites', 'open borders', and 'immigration' into potent narratives.

With respect to its economic dimension, Trump accuses globalization of 'wiping out the American middle class and jobs' while making the 'financial elites who donate to politicians very, very, wealthy. I used to be one of them' (Speeches 4 and 5). Almost all of the speeches analysed here contain substantial discussions of the dire economic impacts of globalization as reflected in disadvantageous international trade deals, outsourced American jobs, stagnant wages and salaries, the crumbling of America's manufacturing base, hostile foreign corporate takeovers, and unfair, corrupt economic practices devised by the likes of China and Mexico and aided by treacherous domestic politicians who have 'sold America to the highest bidder' (Speeches 9, 12, 13, 14, and 17).[7] But such lengthy tirades against the nation's 'globalist enemies' are always followed by passionate assurances that America's dire situation could be reversed under the anti-globalist leadership of Donald J. Trump. At times, he delivers this message with surprising policy detail, thus providing clear evidence of Trumpism's responsiveness to concrete political problems (Speech 5).

---

[7] For an insightful discussion of the significance of the anti-free trade narrative in Trump's national-populist discourse, see Skonieczny (2018; 2019).

For Trump, the realization of his campaign slogan 'make America great again' requires the systematic and dichotomous separation of the 'national' from the 'global' in all aspects of social life. Politically, the construction of this binary supports his claim that 'the American people' support a nationalistic leader who is 'not running to be President of the World', but 'to be President of the United States': 'I am for America— and America first' (Speech 16). In other words, the inherent greatness and goodness of the American people must be reactivated in the patriotic struggle against the essential evil of globalization and its domestic hand-maidens. As Trump puts it, 'The central base of world power is here in America, and it is our corrupt political establishment that is the greatest power behind the efforts at radical globalization and the disenfranchise-ment of working people' (Speech 17).

Yet, as is the case with Trump's economic narrative, the decontestation of the negative political consequences of globalization is always combined with assurances of the impending glorious rebirth of the nation. Trump's 'anti-globalist' optimism can thus be articulated in a third central ideological claim:

The defeat of globalism and its treacherous ideologues will usher in a bright future through the glorious rebirth of the nation.

And it is important to note that Donald Trump did not abandon his anti-globalist populist oratory after his 2016 electoral victory. Quite to the contrary, his ultranationalist attacks on 'globalism' became enshrined in most of his major public speeches. Two years into his presidency, Trump delivered a high-profile address at the 73rd session of the UN General Assembly that contained the following ideological centrepiece:

We will never surrender America's sovereignty to an unelected, unaccountable, global bureaucracy. America is governed by Americans. We reject the ideology of globalism, and we embrace the doctrine of patriotism ... To unleash this incred-ible potential in our people, we must defend the foundations that make it all possible. Sovereign and independent nations are the only vehicle where freedom has ever survived, democracy has ever endured, or peace has ever prospered. And so, we must protect our sovereignty and our cherished independence above all.[8]

At a pre-midterm election rally in Texas a month later, Trump una-bashedly referred to himself as a 'nationalist' and urged his audience not to be ashamed to use the word. As he explained, the term 'nationalist' signified the opposite of 'globalist': 'You know what a globalist is, right?

---

[8] See Donald J. Trump, 'Remarks by Donald J. Trump to the United Nations General Assembly: www.whitehouse.gov/briefings-statements/remarks-president-trump-73rd-session-united-nations-general-assembly-new-york-ny.

You know what a globalist is? A globalist is a person that wants the globe to do well, frankly, not caring about our country so much. And you know what? We can't have that'.[9]

Indeed, there seems to be little evidence that the American President embraces anti-globalist populism for *purely* instrumental reasons. Rather than treating it as a mere 'strategy' or 'style', Trump's speeches reveal not only his deep commitment to specific anti-globalist ideas and values, but also the richness of the ideational environment in which they are rooted.[10]

Conclusion

As our analysis of these selected speeches suggests, Trumpism remains locked into a fierce decontestation struggle with market globalism over the meaning of globalization. It attempts to break the ideological hegemony of market globalism's core concepts through relentless attacks on the five central claims of its neoliberal adversary: globalization is about the liberalization and global integration of markets; globalization is inevitable and irreversible; nobody is in charge of globalization; globalization benefits everyone; and globalization furthers the spread of democracy (Steger, 2009). To some extent, then, anti-globalist populism replicates the strategy of justice globalism, amassing ideational gravity by contesting market globalism's central claims and filling them with contrary contents and strong appeals to 'the people'. This approach requires both ideological challengers of neoliberal market globalism to move 'globalization' and 'globalism' to their conceptual core while at the same time shoring up their adjacent and peripheral symbolic environments. Yet, unlike the chief codifiers of justice globalism who attempted to formulate an ideological alternative to market globalism that drew on the rising *global imaginary*, anti-globalist populists like Trump or Farage seek to reinvigorate a *national imaginary* that has come under significant strain from the destabilizing dynamics of globalization.

---

[9] Trump, cited in Peter Baker, '"Use that Word"! Trump Embraces the "Nationalist" Label', *New York Times*, 23 October 2018: www.nytimes.com/2018/10/23/us/politics/n ationalist-president-trump.html. Similarly, Marine Le Pen (2013) argues that the real cleavage in French politics is not between the left and right, but between nationalists and globalists.

[10] Most current national populist leaders share Trump's anti-globalist rhetoric. For example, RN's leader Marine Le Pen identifies 'globalism' as the 'second enemy' next to 'Islamism'. For Le Pen, globalism consists of two principal elements: transnational capitalism and multiculturalism (Galston, 2018: 56). In fact, in a 2017 speech in Lyon that kicked off her presidential campaign, Le Pen went so far as to characterize 'Islamic fundamentalism' as 'another form of globalization' (Vinocur, 2017).

To be sure, contemporary forms of national populism have been building upon a longer history that reaches back to the 1970s and 1980s when European 'neo-populisms' first sought to exploit the emerging legitimation crisis of democratic political systems (Anselmi, 2018: 38). Yet, as we demonstrated in this chapter, these neo-populisms have been reconfigured around the growing significance of the concepts of 'globalization' and 'globalism', with a corresponding thickening of its adjacent and peripheral symbolic environment. Again, the flow of globalist ideas from the periphery to the ideational core of the evolving thought system appears to have been a gradual process that occurred over several decades.[11] By the mid-2010s, this process had led to a sufficient thickening of national populism's morphology, which changed its ideational status from a thin-centred to a mature ideology capable of standing on its own conceptual feet. While our initial MDA findings need to be confirmed and further developed in future qualitative and quantitative analyses of contemporary national populist narratives and images, corroborating empirical evidence of this dynamic has already been confirmed in recently published studies.[12]

For example, in their analysis of dozens of formal speeches made by Donald Trump during the 2016 electoral campaign, Michele Lamont and her coauthors confirm that one of the central features of Trump's discourse is its emphatic description of workers as hard-working Americans who are victims of globalization: 'By focusing on globalization as a source of deindustrialization, Trump repeatedly framed the problems experienced by working-class Americans as structural and removed blame from them' (2017: S165). Similarly, in his recent discussion of structural trends that gradually expanded opportunities for populism, Rogers Brubaker highlights the role of unfettered neoliberal globalization in the negative association of the concept with the lifestyle of culturally and economically mobile, 'rootless cosmopolitans' (2017: 363). These 'others' are severely stigmatized as 'indifferent to the bounded solidarities of the community and nation'.

---

[11] For the ideational continuities between earlier discourses of national populism articulated by Ross Perot, Lou Dobbs, and Patrick Buchanan and European populists in the 1980s and 1990s and Trumpism, see Steger (2009; 2017). Similarly, Mudde and Rovira Kaltwasser (2017: 38) argue that Southeast Asian populism appeared in the wake of the 1997 Asian Economic Crisis, when politicians blending nationalism and populism started to attack neoliberal 'globalization' and the domestic elites who had implemented these 'globalist' policies. Such developments confirm the significance of Federico Finchelstein's (2017) call for historically sensitive studies that chart the evolutionary dynamics of thought systems.

[12] For the importance of the visual dimension in the analysis of political ideologies, see Tommaso Durante (2018).

The changeability and adaptability of national populist ideologies also underscores their responsiveness to material factors such as increasing inequality, growing migration flows, erosion of traditional collective identities, decreasing legitimacy of conventional political institutions, and the segmentation of the digital media environment. All of these circumstances are likely to increase the resonance of anti-globalist populism's ideological claims across a wide range of ecological, economic, political, and cultural changes associated with globalization (Bonikowski, 2017: 202–3; Norris and Inglehart, 2019). Taken together, ideas and material context, economics and culture, and politics and policy work in favour of a 'global systemic shift' that has unsettled the deeply ingrained assumptions and routines associated with the national imaginary (Benedikter, 2013). Hence, a proper attention to shifting social contexts goes hand in hand with a rejection of the false dichotomy between ideas and material forces as rival causal agencies in favour of linking conceptual maps to what happens on the ground, and vice versa (Taylor, 2004: 31). As Rogers Brubaker (2017: 369) emphasizes, explaining the current populist moment requires a multilayered explanatory strategy that includes attention to the structural trends of global social change. Often appearing in the form of 'crises' of ontological security, the systemic shifts linked to globalization have gradually expanded opportunities for populism and thus have served as the superconductors of national populism's ideological claim to protect the 'little people' against domestic and foreign threats to their security.

The political significance of our findings seems obvious. By enhancing their ability to respond to a wide array of political questions, rising ideologies such as national populism also broadened their appeal to ever-larger segments of the population. A number of commentators have argued that we find ourselves at the brink of a 'new phase in the evolution of the global order as well as a new phase of antiglobalism, with contestation of the global neoliberal order rising from both the regions that have established this order and new non-Western contenders to power' (Oldani and Wouters, 2019: 1). Indeed, national populism's thickening ideological status reflects the ability of its anti-globalist strain to transcend the proximate contexts from which it emerged. Far from remaining a short-lived phenomenon of 'protest populism' (Kriesi and Pappas, 2015), the anti-globalist populist variant might actually develop into an enduring ideological stream—just as the originally thin ideational clusters of fascism and communism evolved into thick-centred conceptual constellations as a result of their fierce ideological competition with mature ideologies such as liberalism, conservatism, and socialism.

This leads us to our final point of this chapter. Up to now, there has not been sufficient recognition in the pertinent academic literature of the role of globalization-related concepts in the changing morphology of national populism. This research deficiency can be partly explained by the widespread theoretical commitment to the alleged conceptual thinness of populism, as well as by the general reluctance to bridge the conceptual and methodological divides that separate the main approaches to the subject. We suggest that any attempt to make sense of the current populist challenge requires that questions of ideology be brought back into the current style-centred analyses of contemporary variants of national populism. Indeed, the formidable task of understanding such a complex and multifaceted phenomenon as national populism must begin with the clear recognition that its current anti-globalist strain constitutes a reconfigured ideational cluster that has evolved from previous iterations. Thus, globalization continues to matter in our unsettled times, even—and perhaps especially—when its current populist opponents seek to disavow its relevance and deny its benefits.

Around the world at the summits of the various international organizations, a number of tropes are regularly expressed as the 'truths' about the current trajectories of global cities. Mayors, city officials, academics, and urban practitioners seem to speak with one voice. Whether it be UN-Habitat, Metropolis, United Cities and Local Governments, ICLIE, or C40,[1] and at congresses such as the World Urban Forum, keynote speaker after keynote speaker begin their recitals with what has become a series of stock refrains. The first refrain is that we now live on an urban planet, and global cities are its leading centres. Speakers usually turn to a single statistic: more than 50 per cent of people now live in cities. Although this event occurred in the first years of the twenty-first century, it took some years for this magic number—'50'—to dominate the global urban imaginary.

The second refrain alleges that cities serve now as the engines of global economic growth, which is integral to their economic future. In a related third refrain, cities are proclaimed as *the* basis of a sustainable planetary future. The final sound bite asserts that cities need to be smarter and more technologically savvy. 'Smart cities are the future' is a common chorus trumpeted from the podiums of many urban conferences.

These four refrains presume a global refiguring of the human condition that places cities at both the centre of Anthropocene ecological challenges *and* of continuing global growth economics. Remarkably, the domain of culture is usually left out. At the same time, however, the quiet realization that nation-states still largely set the terms for urban governance means that all of these refrains tend to be linked in a political decontestation

[1] We use the term 'international organizations' here because it still signifies the conventional way of designating such organizations. Of course, these are all global organizations. For example, ICLEI was founded in 1990 as the 'International Council for Local Environmental Initiatives' (note the concept of inter*national*), but now is simply 'ICLEI —Local Governments for Sustainability', the acronym currently just an empty signifier, with that name assuming its global remit. Similarly, C40 describes itself as 'a global network of large cities taking action to address climate change', with its name assuming its reach. Once consisting of 40 cities, it now has 96 members (www.c40.org/history).

chain: cities should be centred in all regimes of global governance. This linking imperative takes various ideological forms. The technocratic and liberal left seeks a political alternative in which 'mayors rule the world' (Barber, 2014). The democratic to socialist left advocates 'the right to the city' as the basis of a global process of community inclusion (Samara, He, and Chen, 2013). And the neoliberal right suggests that the corporate city does best freed of its state-regulative limits (Vazquez-Barquero, 2002). At times overlapping but mostly conflicting, these discourses have one premise in common: globalization matters. Indeed, we are witnessing the globalization of an urban movement that brings together strange bedfellows in common purpose—the centring of cities. At least for the moment, different political lineages find agreement in this global urban imaginary.

Surprisingly, then, the 'global cities' framework seems to escape the impact of the Great Unsettling. Or, at the very least, it does not yet have the intensity of *subjective* impact that we have found in other areas of social life. Objectively, of course, cities *are* places of turmoil, tension, and contradiction. Just as human beings face a comprehensive crisis of social life on this planet, urban settlements face a practical and existential crisis of sustainability. After all, nearly a billion people across the planet live in favelas, shanty towns, and slums. Subjectively, however, cities appear in the pertinent discourse as crucibles of hope. As Onookome Okome writes, 'We live in the age of the city. The city is everything to us—it consumes us, and for that reason we glorify it' (cited in Davis, 2006: 1). It may be true that the city does consume us, but this still begs the question as to the reasons for this disjuncture between objective patterns of practice and subjective projections of the future of cities. It is indicative of this quandary that, while it has become all but impossible to find utopian writings in politics and literature, utopian blueprints for urban living abound in architecture and planning. One stream of urbanists are actively reimagining precincts as ecotopias and are painting cities futuristic green (Marshall, 2016), although previous urban utopias have been criticized as failures. The authoritarian tradition of Corbusian radiant cities, the liberal-socialist tradition of Ebenezer Howard's garden city concept, and the architectural tradition of Frank Lloyd-Wright's broadacre city have all been discredited as being elegant idealisms drawn up without attention to the structural framing of consumerism, suburbanization, and the dominance of privatization. The new urban utopians boldly ignore those critiques.

Like all ideological narratives, these refrains contain strong elements of empirical and interpretative truth. But as with the decontestation chains of populism discussed in Chapter 8, there is much to be done to show how the urban chorus also works to misrepresent the world. For example, let us consider former United Nations (UN) Secretary General Ban Ki-moon's carefully restrained remarks in the preface to UN-Habitat's *World Cities Report*:

As the world has transformed, so have urban areas. Today, cities are home to 54 per cent of the world's population, and by the middle of this century that figure will rise to 66 per cent. While cities face major problems, from poverty to pollution, they are also powerhouses of economic growth and catalysts for inclusion and innovation. With vision, planning and financing, cities can help provide solutions for the world. (UN-Habitat, 2016)

There is nothing in these words that is not well founded in considerable empirical research. Moreover, the paragraph appears to be well balanced. Still, this short passage, too, partakes in a flawed global urban imaginary articulated ideologically in the four refrains. It is necessary to confront these claims in order to become more reflexive about their dominant meanings. Such a critical scrutiny represents the indispensable first step if urban practice is to achieve its practical hopes: namely, the development of global cities that promote flourishing social life-worlds while enhancing the complexity of natural life on this planet. Despite their disarming simplicity, these refrains possess a complex framing that requires us to recognize the partial truth of each of the claims while carefully showing how they (mis)represent the world in ideologically charged ways. Each refrain assumes a global imaginary that naturalizes the nexus between urban development, economic growth, and planetary sustainability. The placing of economics as the dominant domain of action in particular will be a critical focus of our investigation.

Refrain 1: 'We Now Live on an Urban Planet, and Global Cities Are Its Leading Nodes'

As we noted above, in the early part of the twenty-first century, the 50 per cent statistic caught the imagination of urbanists. One of its earliest and most influential invocations was both graphic and dramatic:

Sometime in the next year or two, a woman will give birth in the Lagos slum of Ajegunle, a young man will flee his village in west Java for the bright lights of Jakarta, or a farmer will move his impoverished family into one of Lima's innumerable *pueblos jovenes*. The exact event is unimportant and it will pass entirely unnoticed. Nonetheless it will constitute a watershed in human history, comparable to the Neolithic or Industrial revolutions. For the first time the urban population of the earth will outnumber the rural. Indeed, given the imprecisions of Third World censuses, this epochal transition has probably already occurred. (Davis, 2006: 1)

First and foremost, Marxist geographer Mike Davis used the magical '50' number to introduce his thesis that we were becoming a planet of slums. One-sixth of the world's population, he noted, was now living in informal settlements. However, this darker thesis was quickly lost in what might be called 'the ascendancy of the global city'. Let us be clear here: there is no doubt that the world has become an urban planet and that cities—all contemporary cities—are globalizing. But we are questioning three related things: the claims made about the ascendancy of global cities; the emphasis on global ranking systems for cities; and the reductive understanding of cities in terms of the dominance of economics. In particular, we are concerned that statistics on financial flows and services have become the master measures of cities becoming global.

To track the story of this trend, we need to go back a few decades. The concepts of the 'global city' and the 'urban planet' grew up together in the 1980s. They began life as complementary tropes, but gradually became separate claims, at least in the academic literature. Shifts of meaning and recursions make this a complicated story, and these concepts were challenged at various times by writers suggesting that the new communications technologies would disperse urban development into local–global homesteads (Toffler, 1981). Nevertheless, references to the 'global city' and the 'urban planet' became dominant in the discourse of urbanists across the late twentieth century.

The first reference to the idea of the 'global city' had its origins in the notion of the 'world city'; that is, cities as integrated into what John Friedmann, in a carefully qualified argument, called the 'world capitalist system' (1986). Influential think tanks such as the Globalization and World Cities Research Network were concurrently formed to measure the global (economic) connectedness of cities, defined in terms of the number and significance of global corporate headquarters being hosted by a city. These were sophisticated ventures. However, for all the care with qualifying what was meant by connectivity, the new global indices confirmed the slide into the dominance of economics as the measure of all things. Across the 1990s, the concept of the 'global city' turned in an ideologically charged, economic designation that named cities in terms of their global financial integration and singled out certain cities as more important than others. This had consequences for urban practice. By the first decade of the 2000s, cities were actively competing for higher standing on the various indicator sets designating what it took to be a *global city*. Thus, the concept of the 'global city' often serves as a catalyst of professional careerism. Economic standing has acquired considerable status, and city leaders want it.

The second concept, of the 'urban planet', initially emphasized global processes that went beyond the economic. In the early 1970s, Barbara Ward's study, *An Urban Planet?* (1971), linked economics and ecological questions. And across the 1970s and 1980s, a series of neo-Marxist geographers writing in what we earlier called the neo-classical mode (Chapter 3)—Henri Lefebvre, David Harvey, and the early Manuel Castells—began exploring the relationship between cities and global capitalism. Lefebvre, for example, described a *process* of planetary urbanism, focusing on urbanization as produced by forces much larger than itself. However, because that lineage also focused on global capitalism (the mode of economic production and exchange), planetary urbanism, too, came to be largely reduced to economic processes. Neil Smith's preface to the English-language translation of *La Révolution Urbaine* (Lefebvre, 1971) provides a fascinating example of how the domain of economics becomes the taken-for-granted frame for understanding global cities. At first, he recognizes that Lefebvre is *not* lifting out particular cities for special designation, but he then very quickly writes as an aside: 'The *true* global cities of the twenty-first century may well be those large metropolises that are simultaneously emerging as production motors not of national economies but of the global economy' (Lefebvre, 1971: xx, emphasis added). *True* global cities? It is a giveaway phrase. Here, already, the domain of economics has become an objectified thing against which cities are measured.

All of this was the context for Saskia Sassen's important book, *The Global City: New York, London, Tokyo* (1991). Perhaps it is no wonder that she defined a global city in terms of economic processes. By the 1990s, economics had come to be presented as the oxygen that cities breathe. According to Sassen, global cities are 'sites for (1) the production of specialized services needed by complex organizations for running a spatially dispersed network of factories, offices and service outlets; and (2) the production of financial innovations and the making of markets, both central to the internationalization and expansion of the financial industry' (1991: 11) Supported by the Globalization and World Cities Research Network, of which Sassen was a founder with Peter Taylor and others, three cities—New York, London, and Tokyo—thus became central to all thinking about global cities. These cities, with Paris sometimes added to make a foursome, were said to constitute a new urban regime of global control. This move set the terms for how cities came to imagine themselves.

However, if we shift our attention away from the mode of exchange, particularly financial flows and services, then very different conclusions can be drawn about the hierarchy, spread, and meaning of global cities. Take, for example, the mode of communications we discussed in Chapter 5. If we focus on the intersection of mediatism *and* capitalism, then a very different group of cities is thrown up: Los Angeles, Mumbai, and San Francisco. From the mid-twentieth century, Los Angeles was a pre-eminent globalizing city. There, the dominant media of connectivity moved from analogue celluloid to digital encoding, as Hollywood stretched a particular approach to distributing the moving image across the globe. Los Angeles became the home of the Western movie industry. It is also the home of Snapchat, a communications and social media company with 187 million active users around the globe, as it is to Tinder, the global social search agency and dating app with 3.7 million paying global subscribers. Mumbai is the home of the Hindi-language film industry, colloquially called Bollywood. Linked to the global spread of the Indian diaspora, different statistics suggest that Bollywood sells more movie tickets across the world than Hollywood. The third 'global city' on this list, San Francisco, is the centre of social media in the world, with a number of massively important companies headquartered there. Facebook, with 2.2 billion active users around the world, is based in Menlo Park in the San Francisco Bay Area. Twitter, with 335 million active users, has its headquarters in downtown San Francisco. Instagram began development in San Francisco in 2010. And Reddit, a news aggregation and discussion site, currently ranked the sixth most visited website in the world, is based in San Francisco.

It is a straightforward point that we are making: naming 'global cities' depends firstly on what is being measured. And, just to be clear, we are simply using Los Angeles, Mumbai, and San Francisco as counterexamples, not as additions to an expanding empirical list. Secondly, naming global cities also depends upon what period in history we are focusing on. Surely Rome, Constantinople, Berlin, Vienna, and Madrid as the centres of globalizing empires would be added to the list at different times in world history. And to complicate matters further, why wouldn't cities that experienced the intersection of globalizing empires formed by flows of power not also make the list? It was not just powerful European or North American cities that experienced the push and pull of globalization or found themselves at the crossroads of transcultural interchange. Let us take a city that few of our readers would ever have visited: the capital of Timor Leste, Dili. It was established as an administrative town by the Portuguese in October 1769, a year before the English explorer Captain Cook 'discovered' Australia and two decades before the French

Revolution centred on the City of Paris. It was a crossroads of global relations, formed at the intersection of the English, Dutch, Portuguese, and Chinese empires. The global and the local mingled on the streets of Dili. The extensive writings of visitors such as the naturalist Henry Forbes and the novelist Joseph Conrad in the 1880s confirm the plural origins of the peoples there, including indigenous and other native populations. Nineteenth-century descriptions of Dili suggest that a form of multi-culturalism that was developing there was comparable to the most cosmopolitan of European cities, such as London, Lisbon, and Madrid.

One of the variations on the 'ascendancy of global cities' refrain is that just as the nineteenth century was the century of empires and the twentieth century was the century of nation-states, the twenty-first century will be the century of cities. This also needs substantial quali-fication. Cities have always been important to processes of globaliza-tion, including the development of empires and nation-states. Have we forgotten so quickly that in the middle of the twentieth century Washington and Moscow were the names of the contending political regimes that ruled the global Cold War between nation-states? Earlier still, cities were the loci of globalizing empires, at least going back to the period when the Romans declared that the City of Rome and the Orb of the World were one (as elaborated in Chapter 6). In the sixteenth century, for example, the City of Seville witnessed the return of the sailing vessel *Victoria*, carrying the first humans to circumnavigate the globe. Does not that centring of Seville in the Age of Discovery make it a global city? From the nineteenth to the early twentieth centuries, the City of London was the centre of an empire that colonized more than a quarter of the total land area of the Earth. Does not this make London a global city long before its global dominance in the world of digital financial services? In the nineteenth century, following the Spanish Empire's use of the same epithet, London described itself as the metropole of an empire upon which the sun never set. In short, both the idea of the twenty-first century being the century of cities and the contemporary dominant use of the term 'global cities' as a new regime partake of a dominant imaginary based on the idea that the globalization at its core connects and channels flows of capital based in cities. It is a distorted representation of the complex and interwoven processes of globalization that has come to matter more and more as it contributes to a distorting 'urban entrepreneurialism' (Hollands, 2015).

Proponents of the diverging conception of 'planetary urbanism' took a different tack. Working in what we earlier described as the complexity mode of theorizing (Chapter 3) and taking their lead from Lefebvre (1971), these writers argued that cities needed to be understood as dissolving into planetary urbanism. In Andy Merryfield's words, they are *no longer* material entities, but relativized spaces:

'Planetary' suggests something more alive and growing, something more vivid than the moribund 'global' or 'globalization'. 'Planetary' truly charts the final frontier, the telos of any earthly spatial fix, of an economic, political and cultural logic that has not been powered by globalization but is one of the key constituent ingredients of globalization, of the planetary expansion of the productive forces, of capitalism's penchant to annihilate space by time, and time by space.

The inner boundedness of the traditional city and of our traditional notion of the city form was prised open by the advent of the industrial city, by capitalist industrial production shedding its geographical and temporal fetters, by the development of new modes of transport, by the invention and reinvention of new technologies, products and infrastructure, by sucking people in when business cycles surged, only to spit them out when markets dipped. From once being absolute spaces, cities became relative spaces, spaces relative to one another in what would, in the second half of the twentieth century, become a global hierarchy, dictated by comparative economic advantage. (Merryfield, 2013)

The problem with this important questioning of the singularity of cities and their assumed technical political boundaries is that it firstly misreads processes of disembodied boundary traversing as completely novel and bringing about an epochal metamorphosis. As we described in Chapter 6, these processes were emergent long before the late twentieth century. Secondly, it is overtaken by a post-structuralist relativism that completely dissolves the entity called 'cities' into flows.

Jeb Brugmann (2009), for example, proclaims the existence of an urban revolution that has already transformed the planet into a single City (with a capital 'C'), a single converging, connected urban system. He has taken the urban connectivity of this global imaginary to extend everywhere. His analysis breaks down on almost every level. Obviously, there is uneven connectivity and separation across the globe, with continuing non-hinterland rural zones and many places on the planet that are not comprehensively incorporated into a so-called flat earth (Friedman, 2007). Obviously, new and intense competition has developed between globalizing cities, competition that means that the notion of a single urban system cannot be conflated with a utopia of globalizing social interrelations. Globalization and urbanization are not the same process, even if the orbits of cities have become increasingly globalized. Still, the problems with Brugmann's analysis point to the consolidating dominance of a global imaginary. This explains why, for him and others, the connected urban complex thus becomes the globe. What is accurate in his analysis is that the dual forces of urbanization and globalization (along with many others) are changing the planet. But to understand this compounding change we need a very different kind of methodology.

Refrain 2: 'Cities Are Now *the* Engines of Global Growth'

Cities are certainly *associated* with economic growth, but this has happened through the dominance of a very particular global assemblage characterized by technologically magnifying capitalist production, abstracting financial exchange, space-traversing communications media, and objectifying techno-scientific enquiry. It is not because of urbanization per se. Put figuratively, cities are more like the chassis of economic growth than its engine. Here, an associated development should not be treated as the same as a driving force. In other words, just because cities changed across the period associated with driving capitalism, it does not mean that cities caused economic growth. This kind of *methodological urbanism* is as problematic as the methodological globalism we earlier called into question (Chapter 5). According to UN-Habitat (2016: 310), 'Cities have emerged as economic powerhouses driving the global economy. Cities are engines of economic growth and development. No country has achieved its level of development without urbanizing. Increased productivity due to urbanization has strengthened the weight of urban areas and reduced poverty'. This passage fundamentally confuses correlation and causation.

Writing with passion, Edward Glaeser's bestselling book, *Triumph of the City: How Our Greatest Invention Makes Us Richer, Smarter, Greener, Healthier, and Happier* (2011), argues the same thing in more compelling but equally problematic ways. The situation is much more complex than this associative logic would suggest. There is no direct evidence that cities either reduce poverty or produce wealth in themselves. Certainly, they bring the uneven material benefits of proximity, density, and economies of scale, but they also are home to increasingly inequalities and degrading informality. In the words of the commentator with which we began this chapter, we have *also* become a *planet of slums* (Davis, 2006).

Rather than cities producing growth, across the twentieth century, urban settlements, urban hinterlands, *and* vast swathes of rural land were *all* remade as growth producers by global capitalism, mediatism, and techno-scientism. At the same time, we can also say that cities became the prime places where people came to live during the period that has come to be known as the crisis of the Anthropocene (Gibson, Rose, and Fincher, 2015). This does not mean that this crisis can be *seen* everywhere. For a large, wealthy minority in some parts of the world, life in the city continues to be materially comfortable, once dreary Central

Business Districts have been turned into entertainment zones. Any sense of face-to-face discomfort or community isolation is being recoloured by the relentless imperatives of Facebook and media connectivity. The well-to-do urban Global North continues to export an increasing number of the urban problems associated with crude industrialism to the Global South or to the peripheral zones of their own countries. And while the hardware supporting chic urban lifestyles is being manufactured under Dickensian conditions in places like Shenzhen, China, and Dhaka, Bangladesh, post-industrial cities are dressed in the cosmetic glamour of urban renewal.

Conversely, it should be made very clear that it is not cities per se that caused the problems. Rather, it was the same processes associated with massive economic growth that, in conjunction with the population bomb, have brought us to planetary crisis. As we noted in Chapter 5, abstracting capitalist *production*, financial *exchange*, cyber-*communications*, and techno-scientific *enquiry* are currently both the prime forces of economic growth *and* the source of human vulnerability and ecological precarity. By transferring the prime-mover status to cities—rather than to the dominant forces of production, exchange, communications, enquiry, and so on)—the ideologues of 'urban ascendancy' give the impression that changing the world can be managed through some sensitive urban planning. This is not to diminish the importance of good urban planning, of course, but to suggest that practices and ideas are bigger than the urban locations in which we now tend to live.

Refrain 3: 'Cities Need to Be Smarter'

During the same period in which the writing of political and literary utopianism went into mortal decline, images of urban futures became linked to a new techno-scientific utopianism in architecture and urban planning. The notion of 'urban futures' now conjures up scenarios of techno-scientific urban management, machine-automated systems such as driverless cars, and buildings clothed in green walls. Enter the words 'urban future' into a web search engine and the images that come up are all technological green. Here, again, we are not criticizing the turn towards sustainable cities or the use of technology, but rather their ideological framing that tends to distort questions of what should be done.

The earlier greenfield cities gave us the disasters of the technopolis, the multifunction polis, and the less-than-satisfactory outcomes of Canberra–Brasilia–Dubai. They look best from the air. Canberra was beautifully designed as a garden city, but largely failed to consider transport other than cars, or to achieve cultural vibrancy. Brasilia was designed to look like a butterfly from above, but has been criticized as a half-satisfactory futuristic fantasy. Dubai, the ultimate fantasy, has reclaimed precincts that reach into the ocean designed to look like a palm tree, but it continues to be an ecological disaster.

The current trend towards 'smart cities' is equally problematic. It heralds technology-led urban utopias with their reductive focus on the economics of information and communications technologies. Technology is treated as *the* basis for effecting an urban vision of efficiency, including eco-efficiency, and liveability. Why did the label 'smart city' take over from 'knowledge city' or 'intelligent city' or 'information city'? It was not just the attractive assonance between the words 'smart' and 'city'. It was because of a globalizing vision linked to a series of corporate campaigns by a group of big tech companies: IBM, Cisco, Fujitsu, General Electric, Siemens, and Phillips. Together, this group have been called the 'Urban Intelligence Industrial Complex' (see Hollands, 2015). The leader in this process was IBM's 'Smarter Planet' project, beginning in 2008 and presaging its 'Smarter Cities' campaign in 2009. It was more than just an advertising program: 100 Smarter Planet forums took place around the world in 2009, thus drawing globalization and smart cities into a common 'global urban imaginary'.

The main drivers of urban technologizing were consequential and real. There were increasing pressures on space through intensifying urbanization and density, leading to the need for real-time systematic information feedback loops. There were increasing pressures on time linked to the emphasis on performance and efficiency, particularly around transport and productivity. There were increasing pressures on resources linked to the climate change crisis and the need to use resources more sustainably. These are real problems that need to be addressed, but the problem with the 'smart city' concept is that it was based on a one-dimensional proposition: technology is the answer. The proposition was underpinned by a further pressure: globalizing corporations now lived in the world of what was called the 'shareholder economy'. Increased pressures on profit generation meant that big tech companies were looking for new markets. Estimates of the value of the global 'smart city' market in 2020 range between US$20 and US$40 billion.

Hence, for all the need to harness technologies to respond to real pressures, a number of pertinent ideological strains actually buttress the distorting discourse of 'urban investments' across the world.

Strain 1: The 'Internet of Things' Will Fundamentally Change the Way in Which We Live, Work, and Consume

Rather, it should be said that we are already in a period of intensifying digital transformation that began in the 1970s with the Internet. The future is much more uneven, uncertain, and unsettled than such singular pronouncements suggest. It is equally likely that the IoT, as the Internet of Things is called by the cognoscenti, will only have a marginal impact on how we live and consume. For example, web-connected fridges that automatically order food will probably not fundamentally change how we eat. What is more likely is that the IoT will become increasingly critical to businesses as an interconnected, commodity-chain analytic system. This seems true for a number of compelling reasons: decreasing operating costs; enhancing the possibility of consumer-specific ordering and just-in-time production; and monitoring and assessing consumption patterns. In summary, the IoT is a confirmation of a qualitative shift that began with the late-twentieth-century communications revolution. The IoT remains dependent on a developing digital information network, it still requires a computing device, and it still uses data. What is more reasonable is the less dramatic argument that various platforms of digital communication will become increasingly central to the way in which we live.

Strain 2: We Are Moving from a Materialist World to a Post-materialist World

More accurately, it can be said that we are witnessing, on the one hand, a contradictory and uneven global shift in values associated with ideologies of individual self-actualization and, on the other, an explosion of commodity capitalism, those beliefs about post-materialism belied by actually increasing material and other consumption. The misplaced argument was first made by the World Values Survey, a massive global research project that has been conducted since 1981 and is led by the American political scientist Ron Inglehart. Because the project focused on values, it missed the other reality: namely, that we are consuming more and more things, counted simply as the sheer value of material objects produced in the world. It is equally true—particularly in the wealthy West—that we are becoming increasingly demanding of services and non-material experiences. But this means, in other words, that we are consuming more and more material things *and* immaterial processes. Looking back on the post-materialist argument, Inglehart now suggests that, 'To some extent, Postmaterialism was its own gravedigger. From the start, the emergence of radical cultural changes provoked a reaction among older and less secure strata who felt threatened by the erosion of familiar values' (2018: 175). Here, he is referring to the new wave of national populism we discussed in Chapter 8. But the evidence for this post facto claim specifically relating to post-materialist questions of consumption is thin. It has more bearing on the current culture wars concerning values themselves, and this is much more convincing.

Strain 3: We Are Now Entering the Age of the 'Sharing Economy'

To the contrary, the present is still dominated by corporate variations on the digital exploitation of people's desire for flexibility. The prime global examples usually given to support this claim are Uber and Airbnb, but these companies do not exemplify the 'sharing economy' as such—they are digital platforms (see Refrain 1) that have found a way of exploiting a gap in the current market between embodied, on-the-ground living and digitally enhanced service provision. There is the potential for 'driverless cars' becoming a just-in-time shared service, but what is equally likely is that driverless cars will either be privatized as personal limousines or become driverless private taxis.

Strain 4: Big Data Will Change Everything

Rather than changing everything, big data is just the latest trend in a longer-term process of monitoring and codifying everything, focusing on patterns of consumption and their financial implications. The data will do nothing in itself. Not only does its effect depend upon how the data sets are interpreted, but they also depend upon the nature of privacy laws. The biggest impact again will be on businesses. There seems little doubt that corporations will demand increasing data on consumer activity.

Strain 5: People Are Wowed by the Future Possibilities of Technology

At variance with this claim, the evidence suggests that people have been fed so much hype that they have developed an ambivalent and contradictory response to technology. On the one hand, while they are open to using it, even fetishizing it, they are suspicious of claims that it will change their lives. Western consumers in particular are increasingly cynical about marketing promises. On the other hand, they have high expectations about technologies on offer, and get annoyed very quickly when these do work as the promises suggest.

Refrain 4: 'Cities Provide the Basis for a Sustainable Future'

Rather than the simple point that it appears to be, the claim that cities provide the basis for a sustainable future presents us with a confronting paradox. Cities are both at the heart of the ecological problems facing this planet *and* developing a positive and sustainable mode of urban living is the only way that we will be able to sustain social life as we know it past the end of this century. If only because of the world's current population growth, returning to a predominance of rural living is no longer viable. Sustainably increasing the density of our urban settlements along with increasing energy efficiency and less resource use is the only alternative. But this is not because cities are essentially more sustainable than rural settings. It is rather because building on small, self-contained plots of land can no longer save the planet. If, without changing other social forces, we divided the non-urban world into rural allotments to cope with a burgeoning global population, we would only speed up the crisis. Research by bodies such as the Food and Agriculture Organization estimates that 0.5 hectares of land per person are needed for adequate local self-sufficiency. According to the World Bank, the United States has only 0.49 hectares of arable land per citizen, while China has 0.08 hectares and Vietnam has 0.07 hectares. In short, unless there is a revolution in the way we live, these figures would not allow for local self-sufficiency.[2] This means that our task for the foreseeable future is an urban-orientated one.

The claim that cities provide the basis for a sustainable future also tends to be read as predominantly an ecological proposition. Rather, as we have been consistently arguing as part of our engaged theory, any projects for sustainable change need to bring ecological, economic, political, and cultural questions back into an integrated relation. Moreover, the refrain tends to be read as advocating modernization through smarter technologies, and this, too, demands a more integrated approach across different ontological formations. All contemporary cities, including those in the Global South, tend to be designed around a core modern configuration of asphalt, glass, concrete, technologies, cars, and mobile citizens. Modernization has brought with it an apparently mandatory system of major thoroughfares, often including a freeway cutting through the cityscape from an international airport to a downtown area of concentrated semi-rise corporate buildings. It has ushered in traffic lights, roundabouts, and private-property markets. It has reordered nature, determining the run-off directions of rainwater, the gradients of rising ground, and

---

[2] See http://data.worldbank.org/indicator/AG.LND.ARBL.HA.PC.

the courses of creeks. In summary, for all of the political gestures to social heritage, local nature, and indigenous colour, and whatever the aesthetic content of the ensuing built environment, the dominant design regime is predominantly abstract modern in its form.

This is a large part of the problem. Across the globe, urban design tends to remake nature with the modern neatness and cultural flatness of a computer-generated verge pattern. However sensitive to cultural difference various individual designers may be, urban planning as a regime tends to be technically and economically orientated, increasingly globalized, and ontologically modern. Processes of globalization, now most often enacted through local–national decisions and desires, have systematized the dominant layer of design outcomes, from the whole spatial configuration of the city down to the smallest, most taken-for-granted processes. Across the world, to take the simplest of examples, red–amber–green light sequences and flashing lights are screwed to the top of metal poles to guide vehicle movement. This is not a bad thing, but it is certainly a globalized process associated with the way that car use dominates the urban landscape. Private-property boundaries determine land use. And the capitalist market decides what is important.

One example of a global city is sufficient to illustrate the depth of this point. Until its political overturning, beginning in 1990, the people of Johannesburg lived under apartheid. During this time, modern urban design confirmed the spatial desegregation. Across the 1970s, the city landscape was being modernized in what was then called the International Style. In 1975, for example, Ponte City, a cylindrical skyscraper of 54 storeys, was built in the whites-only area of Hillbrow, making it the highest residential tower in Africa. In the same year, the Western Bypass section of the N1 was completed as a route around the city centre to access Witwatersrand. Construction began in 1975 on the M1 De Villiers Graaff freeway connecting the south, including Soweto, to the city centre and extending to Sandton, the wealthy northern commercial centre of Johannesburg. All of these developments confirmed the apartheid spatial configuration of a poor south of concrete shacks and no work and a wealthy north of commercial buildings, green leafy suburbs, and service jobs—available to those in the south who could bear the two-hour peak travelling times. Now, nearly 30 years after the end of political apartheid, this spatial configuration is still the case, and according to Melissa Tandiwe Myambo (2017), if anything, this division has become starker.

Dismantling the political apparatus of apartheid following 1990 was a remarkable political feat, but spatial questions are proving more intractable. Despite all of the attempts to change the unequal structure of the city by talented and committed planners, racial spatial separation is still palpable. In 2003, Johannesburg began an explicit programme to become a 'global city'. However, the area between Soweto and the downtown area of Johannesburg, linked by a freeway that was massively upgraded, still remains a nether zone of slag heaps and undermined wastelands. It is one of the many legacies of the past division.

Even the new Bus Rapid Transit system called *Rea Vaya*, linking the poor south and the rich north, has not made a significant difference. In 2013, the bus project was called 'Corridors of Freedom', recognizing the complexity of the spatial divide. The *Rea Vaya* bus system still has great potential. However, the images used to promote this shift were of ultra-slim African women with young children strolling along a modern street flanked by banks and health clinics. These were the gentle images of neoliberal gentrification with the emphasis on 'increased freedom of movement as well as economic freedom'. In a city with the highest Gini coefficient in the world, it makes sense to concentrate on overcoming economic inequality, but not necessarily framed in this way. Changing such a cityscape, built in concrete in the 1950s–2000s, will require a slow revolution across all of the domains of social life—not just creating a 'global city' overnight.

As the Circles of Social Life method reflected in Figure 9.1 shows, Johannesburg is a complex city with uneven strengths and weaknesses.[3] In 2013, when the first Circles profile was done in that city, Johannesburg was attempting to use its vigour for political engagement to strengthen the sustainability of its transport system, including the *Rea Vaya*. The current municipal regime, which assumed power in 2016, has firmly returned to the prior modernization programme, and the results can be seen in the comparative 2018 profile (Figure 9.2). They show subtle but important changes *and* many continuities.

In 2013, the weakest subdomain was that of 'Built-Form and Transport', including in the area of public transport. This has been strengthened over the past five years, but without making a significant

[3] Developed by Paul James (2015), Liam Magee, Andy Scerri, and their collaborators, the Circles of Social Life approach develops new indicators that treat each social domain as part of an integrated social whole. In contrast to the usual conceptual put forward in the triplet of economic, social, and environmental activities, economics is not considered an independent master domain outside of social relations. To be sure, economics is important, but when treated as primary, it threatens to downplay cultural and ecological ways of life. Easily applicable to global cities such as Johannesburg, the Circles of Social Life approach can be adapted to measure the urban sustainability across four domains of social practice of equal importance: economics, politics, ecology, and culture (see Figures 9.1 and 9.2). Thus, anchored in very strong analytical foundations, this adapted Circles of Sustainability approach becomes practically useful in the crucial task of measuring the quality of contemporary urban life.

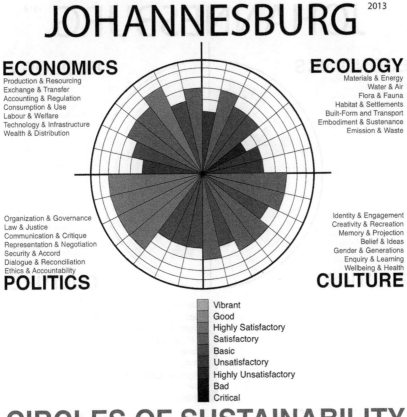

JOHANNESBURG ²⁰¹³

ECONOMICS
Production & Resourcing
Exchange & Transfer
Accounting & Regulation
Consumption & Use
Labour & Welfare
Technology & Infrastructure
Wealth & Distribution

ECOLOGY
Materials & Energy
Water & Air
Flora & Fauna
Habitat & Settlements
Built-Form and Transport
Embodiment & Sustenance
Emission & Waste

POLITICS
Organization & Governance
Law & Justice
Communication & Critique
Representation & Negotiation
Security & Accord
Dialogue & Reconciliation
Ethics & Accountability

CULTURE
Identity & Engagement
Creativity & Recreation
Memory & Projection
Belief & Ideas
Gender & Generations
Enquiry & Learning
Wellbeing & Health

Vibrant
Good
Highly Satisfactory
Satisfactory
Basic
Unsatisfactory
Highly Unsatisfactory
Bad
Critical

CIRCLES OF SUSTAINABILITY

Figure 9.1 Sustainability profile of Johannesburg, 2013

difference to overcoming the legacies of apartheid. The new train system, for example, goes from the international airport to the business district of Sandton, and up to the capital Pretoria. At the same time, wealth inequality has become worse.

Concluding Remarks

Where do we go from here? If our planet is to survive and our cities are to flourish, we need to go back to basics: ecologically, economically, politically, and culturally. Cities express our aspirations and hopes. They are local citadels of the evolving global urban system, built to protect us from

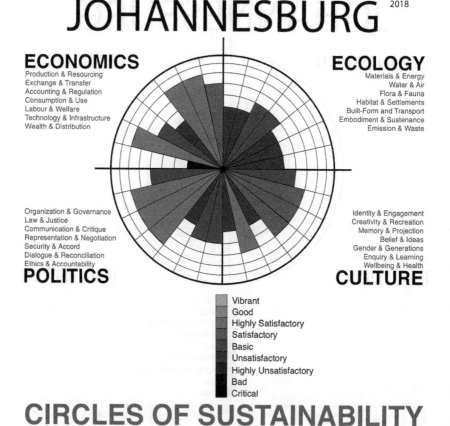

Figure 9.2 Sustainability profile of Johannesburg, 2018

our fears and insecurities. Family by family, person by person, the world's population is gravitating towards the bright lights of urban intensity and high mass consumption. Across the globe, unevenly but inexorably, people have been entering the process that Raymond Williams calls 'mobile privatization' (1974)—making our lives increasingly private, linked more to each other by the mediation of television, the Internet, and social media than by public engagement in the street or in community settings. Individual by individual, the denizens of cities turn on air conditioners to cope with the higher temperatures we all have produced and to meet our private needs for increasing levels of comfort—thus paradoxically increasing the production of the greenhouse gases that lead to higher temperatures. In other words, cities represent the best and worst of us. They are home to the crassest and the very grandest things that we can achieve. Conversely, to save our cities, we need to attend to our own weaknesses.

This is not the place to lay out what needs to be done. It ranges from an ecology of consuming less and an economics of production focused on basic needs, to ontological questions of how to live together and with nature. As a way of concluding, let us finish with cultural questions of engagement, an issue that is usually subsumed by the emphasis on economics. A number of writers from Jane Jacobs (1961) and Richard Sennett (1994) to David Harvey (2013) and Sharon Zukin (2010) have argued that, rather than becoming just spaces of abstract connectivity, contemporary cities need to be built in such a way as to encourage enriching forms of *embodied friction* between different peoples. They argue that social life needs to return to the streets as more than simulated or commodified authenticity. Locals and strangers should rub shoulders —even sometimes perhaps uncomfortably—as they move through in locally defined *places*.

While agreeing with this vision, our argument presented in the present study goes further, stretching the argument across different ways of understanding practice and meaning, from ideas to ontologies. In Chapter 10, we will develop this point in relation to an *engaged cosmopolitanism* that grounds social life in both the local— understood as places crossed by layers of spatiality, temporality, and embodiment—and the global—understood as Planet Earth, limited and grounded, historically the *place* in which we became human. For the moment, we can say that alternative urban practices need to begin by framing arguments for more embodied connectivity in debates over the different ideological refrains that we have used to structure this chapter. For example, understanding the contradictions of the emerging emphasis on post-material values would allow us to confront the new romanticism associated with 'rubbing shoulders' in cities. For all of the social virtues of the post-material cafe society, it can also become an empty aesthetics in which the strangers who drink coffee at adjacent tables become colourful characters in a self-regarding mise en scène.

A deeper alternative in this area requires a reflexive understanding of the ontological framing of 'embodied friction', a creative facilitation of positive and painful intersections of engagement that allows for different ontological orientations to be present in the same place. As Tony Fry (2012) has emphasized, this includes our relationships with nature as well as with fellow human beings. The establishment of modern town squares and the creation of urban commons—Tahrir Square in Egypt, Taksim Square in Turkey, Tiananmen Square in Beijing, Shahbagh Square in Dhaka, or Washington Square in New York—represent necessary yet minimal conditions of positive connectivity. To be sure, we have seen how such urban commons provide the setting for both short-lived political revolutions and quiet, relaxing afternoons in the park with family or friends. But the politics of the town square still tends to remain largely one-dimensional. Neither strangers nor nature are more than a backdrop to the personal. In the context of complex globalization, the urban project must dive much deeper.

Designing creative ontological engagement—rather than just abstracted connectivity—entails building localities in a way that explicitly and reflexively recognizes ontological difference across different social formations, such as between relations of indigenous and customary meaning, cosmological traditionalism, constructivist modernism, and relativizing postmodernism. It entails allowing various ontological frictions to play themselves out across the social–natural continuum. Local public spaces should facilitate people 'rubbing shoulders', but good design and positive engagement should also explicitly consider the different ontological meanings that 'rubbing shoulders' or 'confronting nature' have for different people.

Drawing upon the Principles for Better Cities developed using the Circles framework, this would entail changes, for example, in the cultural subdomain of *identity and difference*: active public recognition during all urban development projects and practices of the complex layers of community-based identities. Here are some basic suggestions:

- By being aware of and/or acting practically upon local needs for diverse language use, from education practises to street signage and public transport announcements;
- By designing public spaces and places to promote comfortable hospitality and intimate conviviality, including across the boundaries of cultural difference; and
- By negotiating openly and positively through inclusive planning processes to include the diverse architectures, spatial configurations, and aural ecologies associated with different kinds of religious and ritual observance, from places of worship and pilgrimage sites to multifaith and secular spaces.[4]

In short, it is not local or globalizing connectivity per se that is either the problem or the answer. Rather, we submit that ideologies of 'connectivity'—tethered to the placing of economics as the dominant domain of

---

[4] See www.circlesofsustainability.org/principles.

action—have come to overwhelm all other ways and modes of living in local places such as global cities. A critical confrontation with the overarching global urban imaginary is the first step in the comprehensive process of developing more holistic and integrating understandings of urban life in a world where globalization still matters greatly.

10   Living in the Unsettled World of the Anthropocene

Humans have globalized their impact upon Planet Earth, and this bearing is being embedded into something as basic as its rock formations. Whether it be spheroidal carbonaceous particles (soot), radioactivity from nuclear bomb testing, or micro-fragments of plastic, the materiality of human activity is now being recorded in the bedrock of our globe. This simple and critically important claim is the basis of the new geological semi-declaration that we are living in the age of the Anthropocene.[1] The concept of the 'Anthropocene' is now everywhere—hailed, contested, and normalized—even before it has been universally adopted.

In one of the earliest non-official announcement stories, *The Economist* in 2011 showed a 'Spaceship Globe' splitting at its seams. 'Welcome to the Anthropocene', said the headline: 'Humans have changed the way the world works. Now they have to change the way they think about it, too'. Thus, a decade on from when—following Paul Crutzen and Eugene Stoermer's (2000) intervention—the term first took off, even a pro-capitalist, pro-globalization business magazine acutely understood the broad consequences of the concept.

It is one of those moments where a scientific realisation, like Copernicus grasping that the Earth goes round the sun, could fundamentally change people's view of things far beyond science. It means more than rewriting some textbooks. It means thinking afresh about the relationship between people and their world and acting accordingly. (*Economist*, 2011)

This call to 'act accordingly', however, like most of the media discussion, has left everything up for grabs. In its simplest definition, the Anthropocene has become the period in which humans have had a discernible geological impact upon the globe. But its practical, engaged meaning has tended to

---

[1] In June 2018, the International Commission on Stratigraphy did actually announce a new division in earth-time, but it was not to confirm what most people assumed already to be a global convention—the Anthropocene. Rather, they officially name a new chapter in Earth's history as a section of the still-current Holocene Epoch—the Meghalayan Age, beginning 4,200 years ago and marked by specific chemical signatures found in stalactites and stalagmites.

remain clothed in arcane scientific debate, detailed documentation, and hear-no-evil deferral of radical change. Even the starkly obvious relationship between the Anthropocene and globalization is left implicit—an omission we intend to rectify in this chapter.

Scientists documenting these massive changes are clear about two things. Firstly, from the period of the Industrial Revolution around 1800, Earth-system changes were initiated by an enormous expansion in the use of fossil fuels. Secondly, with a 15-fold increase in the global economy from the middle of the twentieth century, the planet experienced a 'Great Acceleration' of resource use, population growth, transport use, global tourism, and carbon emissions: 'Human activities have become so pervasive and profound that they rival the great forces of Nature and are pushing the Earth into planetary *terra incognita*' (McNeill and Engelke, 2014; Steffen et al., 2015; Steffen, Crutzen, and McNeill, 2007: 614). *Terra incognita?* Why do they use an old cartography phrase from the first attempts in the second century of the Common Era to map the known globe? The phrase was first used to signify the shadow regions of the globe—those areas of mystery that could not be mapped; places where dragons lived. Now it is being used to suggest that human global impact has reached such proportions that we can no longer do more scientifically than measure the proxy indicators of its compounding ecological consequences. The whole globe seems to have now become a dark zone, a space '*incognita*'.

As big and important as that scientifically documented claim is, our concern is that it remains a critique that works only at the first analytical level of empirical documentation—that is, by carbon accounting or some other 'green' balance sheet. It does not seek to understand *why* we have reached such a situation. As Isabelle Stengers writes, the coming 'barbarism doesn't fear critique. Rather it nourishes itself on the destruction' (2015: 110). It is for this reason that Jason Moore (2017a) has argued that the Anthropocene is better described as the Capitalocene, the era in which a particular driving mode of production/exchange—capitalism—increasingly came to consume nature as an exploitable resource.

We want to go further still. This is bigger than capitalism, and it is certainly bigger than an ecological crisis. Indeed, we are concerned that accentuating a series of accelerating metrics with its singular emphasis on ecological crisis misses the current compounding ecological, economic, political, and cultural ruptures of the human condition. These ruptures taken together add up to what Moore calls a 'metabolic shift' (2017b)—or what we have described in the present study as an ontological remaking of the dominant global formation of humans living on Planet Earth: a Great Unsettling.

As we write this paragraph, a fairly ordinary day in world history, 17 November 2018, events around the world testify to its tensions and contradictions. In London, activists marking Extinction Rebellion day and protesting against the lack of government action on climate change block all the bridges across the Thames. Across the Channel, protestors calling themselves 'Yellow Jackets' take to the streets in a series of French cities seeking cheaper fossil fuel prices—effecting an obverse challenge that depends upon normalizing climate change. One person is killed and dozens are injured in the street riots. In California, 1,011 people are listed as missing as the most destructive wildfire in its history burns largely out of control. As Bruno Latour (2018: 43) observes, terrestrials living in the Anthropocene are no longer dealing with small fluctuations in the climate, but rather with an upheaval that is mobilizing the Earth system itself. And yet, President Trump claims that these events have nothing to do with climate change—a denial that, paradoxically, organizes *all* politics at the present time, even if many ordinary people are not yet aware of it. The problem becomes one of who, speaking with complete *modern* certainty, could proclaim that these fires are caused by the climate crisis? We are thus living in a world in which all certainties are embraced and vigorously contested at the same time.

In this context, the present chapter begins with the concept of 'the Anthropocene', linked particularly to the question of global climate change, and seeks to broaden its ecological emphasis to understand its political and cultural dimensions. Previously, in Chapter 6, we discussed the unsettling of global–local relations in the economic domain through the impact of abstracting and disembodied financial capital. In this chapter, we now turn to the ecological/political/cultural nexus of risk and insecurity in the period of the Great Unsettling. Our opening gambit suggests that despite the long history of humans experiencing risk, the destabilizing subjective sense that anthropogenic risk could be totalizing and species wide (that is, 'global') is surprisingly recent. In a parallel argument, this chapter insists that naming the current period as the Anthropocene only just begins to provide an understanding of the nature of human impact, leaving out the new meta-colonization of the globe as a set of 'ecological services' to be foundationally re-engineered for alternatively saving and exploiting. This theme leads to an extensive treatment of human security and risk. In that section of the chapter, we argue that the global emphasis on security has been accompanied by an unsettling of the very concept of 'security'.

How can we respond to this global complexity? Resisting the currently fashionable notion of 'deglobalization'—the belief that both the process and the concept of globalization have had their day and are exiting the centre stage they have dominated for three decades—we refuse to give up on the global as one of the key organizing principles of politics. Thus, the last part of the chapter turns to outlining a grounded form of cosmopolitanism that affirms the relevance of globalization and a global covenant (Held, 2004), while seeking to avoid getting caught in the institutional requisites of practical cosmopolitanism with its focus on establishing a single global political governance system. At the same time, our vision attempts to dodge the ideological strictures of liberal cosmopolitanism with its emphasis on freedom as the source of all that is good (Sen, 2009).

The Anthropocene, Climate Change, and the Global Imaginary

How could such a difficult and technical term as 'the Anthropocene' enter the global public lexicon with such passion and reach? Answering this genealogical question also entails responding to an apparently orthogonal question: why did the confronting conceptual thinking that lies behind the concept take so long to engender global public debate? The beginnings of an answer to both of these pivotal questions converge on a single condensed locus of explanation. It has taken a globalizing existential crisis for the meaning of planetary human impact to hit home. And then, when it finally did, the force of this realization has engendered every imaginable response from despair to denial, from direct action to deferral—which have subsequently compounded the controversy and hence added to the contested prominence of the concept.

The concept of 'the Anthropocene' has antecedents in the nineteenth century when Antonio Stoppani, an Italian Catholic priest and geologist, coined a cognate term—'the anthropozoic era'. The American philologist George Perkins Marsh quickly took up the concept in his extraordinary book, *The Earth as Modified by Human Action* (1874). He carefully quoted Stoppani's argument that the creation of humankind involved the emergence of 'a new telluric force which in power and universality may be compared to the greater force of the earth' (1874: 39). In short, both writers were beginning to think globally about human impact. It was not a dominant way of thinking, but it was distinctively and powerfully emergent amongst certain groupings of intellectuals. Some writers were then beginning to rethink the human relation to nature, and this rethinking took the form of globalizing nature's enduring potential to destabilize life and our inability as humans to respond adequately.[2] In this context, the now largely archaic term 'telluric' meant terrestrial or earthly—the Earth as a planet, a heliocentric globe. In their terms, God may have created 'man', but humanity had subsequently come to have a profound and global impact on those works of creation.[3]

In the long period since the publication of those two books—just as we documented in the case of the concept of 'globalization' (Chapter 2)—the notion of humanity as a global telluric force emerged episodically along largely isolated branches of knowledge. And, like the shift from the recognition of the global to a public discussion of the forces of globalization, it has taken more than a century for the broad notion of 'the Anthropocene' to go public. The first part of the answer, then, is that before the concept of 'the Anthropocene' could take hold, it required an emergent global imaginary to become a dominant way of framing our understanding of our relations to others and to nature. By the late twentieth century, the idea that humans were having a global ecological impact had become a framing (though admittedly uneven) orientation across the global political sphere—an orientation at that stage still without a name.

Now, nearly two decades on from its first explicit use in 2000, 'the Anthropocene' has shaken the world with an unusual force. This is generally recognized, at least in the many commentaries on the topic. We want to take this common observation further in the context of the larger argument of this book. The next part of our answer to the initial two questions begins to do that. The concept of 'the Anthropocene' found generative ground in a world that was *already* experiencing the seismic liquefaction of previously taken-for-granted verities. Over the past decade, this foreboding sense of planetary complexity has drawn in all but the most hardened economic growth advocates. Now, debates actively

---

[2] The examples here range from Friedrich Nietzsche's (1883) 'last man'—tired and pathetically seeking security—to Mary Shelley's *The Last Man* (1826), an equally tragic figure, but more knowing. In one recent lineage of the 'last man' tradition—the Nietzschean line —Francis Fukuyama's book *The End of History and the Last Man* projected a realized utopia of liberalism. His writing, a symbolic touchpoint of our narrative, was based bizarrely on what he supposed was the 'fundamentally un-warlike character of liberal societies ... evident in the extraordinarily peaceful relations they maintain among one another' (1992: 262).

[3] Stoppani's original Italian read as follows: '*una nuova forza tellurica, che, perla sua potenza e universalità, non avienca in faccia alle maggiori forze del globo*' (1873: 732). Lest there be any doubt of the force of his argument, the first sentence of the book reads: '*La dinamica terrestre ci ha aveleto mano le force che goverano il globo, e tendono a modificarlo continua mente*', translated literally as, 'The Earth's dynamics have been handing us the forces that govern the globe, and those forces tend to modify it continuously' (1873: 3). In this early rendition, the Earth is the agent of conferral, while humans have become the force of change. With the Great Unsettling, we are taking for ourselves elements of that agency of conferral.

resound through the halls of academe and the seminar rooms of international organizations—though less urgently in the world's parliaments and boardrooms—suggesting that climate change may represent a basic human impact upon the Earth: existential in its meaning, potentially disastrous in its consequences. These consequences can be *denied*, but they can no longer be ignored.

According to a recent report by the Intergovernmental Panel on Climate Change (IPCC), the world reached 1°C global warming above pre-industrial levels in 2017, and it is heading towards 1.5°C within a decade or so—the *high confidence range* predicted for this threshold is between 2030 and 2052. With more than 2°C global warming, it has been suggested that the world will head towards global chaos, albeit with more severe impacts in the equatorial regions. To give some sense of the difference between the two thresholds, at 1.5°C, the IPCC estimates that around 80 per cent of coral reefs will be gone; at 2°C, it will be 99 per cent destroyed (Intergovernmental Panel on Climate Change, 2018). Nether scenario is good. In response, most parliamentary and boardroom debates separate out the issues, maintaining a focus on growth capitalism with a changed rhetoric—balancing growth and sustainability—as the dominant decontestation message would have it. But the point remains. The question of the anthropogenic impact on the planet can no longer be ignored completely—as the knee-jerk denials of Trump and company confirm. Thus, it has to be either contested or normalized.

The third part of our answer is that the concept enhances the sense of technical momentousness, however, because the dominant focus on 'green accounting' misses the way in which humans have gone beyond just having a global *impact* upon geo-nature—it simultaneously underplays what the shift means. This is perhaps the most important point, for it implies that debates about the consequences of human-induced ecological change tend to be played out on registers that pass each other like ships in the night. How can disaster metrics counter those who welcome Armageddon as a sign of God's revelation? How can science-based disaster talk reverse the energy use of people who already use mass consumption as a way of seeking meaning in an unsettled world? Since the middle of the twentieth century, something fundamental has changed. Certainly, we are still exploring nature's farthest reaches, redirecting its waterways, open-cutting its resources, and commodifying its animals, including ourselves. However, in a qualitative leap beyond those processes, we are now also *reconstituting* the foundations of that 'nature' (Sharp, 2018). Older ways of living in relation to our environments continue across the planet—from customary embeddedness and cosmological custodianship to modern conservation, extraction, and exploitation. But by the mid-to-late twentieth century, the unsettling was becoming more fundamental. Techno-science had intersected with capitalism to accelerate the task of reconstituting the very building blocks of nature: atoms, cells, genes, and so on. These were once elements that humanity took as the stable basis of 'everything'. Other building blocks that were missing from or only incipiently part of the scientific lexicon in the mid-twentieth century—quarks, the Higgs boson, genes, ripples in space and time, nucleotides, and chromosomes—soon also came to be interrogated for what they could offer human knowledge and material desires.

In short, what came to public consciousness with the first splitting of the atom—the reconstitution of the *nature* of nature—has now, in a globalizing process, extended to everything from nanotechnology, bioengineering, stem-cell therapy, and DNA manipulation to geo-engineering and terraforming. To use Martin Heidegger's concept, we continue to treat the globe as a 'standing reserve' (1977: 17), but at a supercharged level. During this period, bioscience became a dominant global industry, but that is not the most salient point here. Rather, what our narrative is adding once again is consideration of a seismic shift—this time exemplified in the changing dominant *form* of human ecological engagement. Humans are now meta-colonizing the globe, not just colo-nizing it. We humans are thus setting up the global conditions for rapidly deepening our own vulnerability as a species.

Beyond Human Security: Towards Considerations of Human Survival

Is this same process also evident from the perspective of political security? The world has always been a dangerous place, but questions of global–local security, we would suggest, now go to the heart of the human condition. Over the past couple of decades, a number of developments have occurred that pose serious practical and conceptual challenges to conventional policy frameworks and responses. More than that, they challenge the basic conceptions of 'security' and 'risk'. Most obviously, this ties back to the recognition that climate change poses a foundational risk to human social life as we currently know it. But developments such as nuclear weapons and globalizing terrorism also completely destabilize the prior basis of modern military security—namely, the assumption that more military engagement and investment will bring more security.

In the process, the institutions such as the state that once were said to ensure security now carry the genesis of our deepening insecurity. This includes the recognition that the security state has been itself part of the problem, as is the current dominant response to retreat to conventional notions of security by military and state surveillance means. As Paul Battersby and Joseph Siracusa (2009: 206) write: 'Were a singular human security to achieve the mantle of uncontested good, a rush to subvert its logic and rhetorical value for political ends would surely follow. The "securitization" of everything could perversely result in the denial of the very freedoms that human security advocates hold dear'.

Before elaborating on the Great Unsettling of basic security questions, we should first document the more obvious changes to the global landscape. Since the middle of the twentieth century—isolated counterexamples such as the Indian–Pakistani standoff notwithstanding—security challenges have increasingly moved away from interstate military tensions towards complex global processes or unconventional transnational localized violence. They no longer accord with conventional models of state-based military threats of the deployment or use of conventional military force. Rather, they involve non-state or multiple actors, or complex processes such as ecological, political, and economic recursions resulting in ongoing destabilization such as through the mass flight of displaced peoples or the generation of new sources of terrorism. In other words, even in these relatively simple terms, contemporary security questions challenge the relevance and efficacy of conventional, militarized, state-based security responses, especially those conducted as stand-alone actions.

In fact, most if not all of the developments over the last few years that challenge human security occur locally with global consequences. Long after the disastrous international responses that gathered together under the name of the 'Global War on Terror', major terrorist attacks continued to devastate cities as diverse as London, St Petersburg, Stockholm, Berlin, Mogadishu, Aden, and Ankara. Global health crises ranging from diseases such as HIV/AIDS, SARS, Ebola, the Zika virus, and tuberculosis, to the embodied consequences of people coping with zones of localized transnational conflict and social depravation continued with unabated regularity. This local-to-global impact was exemplified in the 'refugee crisis' that hit Europe and the Americas between 2015 and 2018. The proximate origins of each of these streams of displaced persons were immediate and local–regional, but the determinative frame was global and the consequences of each stream reverberated across the planet.

At the global political level, untenable stress has subsequently been placed on the United Nations (UN) system through opposing developments and demands, including discord in the Security Council, disregard of international law, and the creation of security or peace-building crises by member states and increasing demands for UN involvement in peace-keeping, humanitarian relief, and crisis governance. The list goes on and on: we have seen the exacerbation of regional settings of political violence with further problems often also caused by inappropriate global humanitarian intervention: deep insecurity and violence continue in the Congo, Sudan and South Sudan, Afghanistan, and Iraq, with associated problems such as political instability. What at a different time would be considered bounded local activities now have global consequences. The brutal Israeli military responses to the 2018 Gaza border protests and deadly incursions into the Occupied Territories rebound around the world. And to this we can add weapons proliferation, including the intensified security dilemma in Northeast Asia, particularly involving North Korean efforts to develop nuclear weapons.

The common thread linking all of these issues is how, in various ways, they constitute serious threats to the welfare of persons and communities from the local to the global, not just to the security of states. They are truly local–global threats. These threats have arisen in the complex interactions between economic turmoil, crises in governance, identity politics, human rights abuses, ethnic tension, religious and political violence, state policy, and individual beliefs.[4] In this context, it becomes all the more unhelpful that conventional security studies have laid much of the blame for much of the global insecurity on the so-called failed states of the Global South (and then treated the best way forward as intervening from the outside to effect state-building). This is a recurring irony of globalizing insecurity. Nation-states that were once seen as the security providers for the peoples of the world are now, in their fragility, being blamed for a basic shift in the nature of war from interstate to intrastate conflict.

While the use of conventional policy responses has sometimes been appropriate, increasingly the application of conventional policies—financial, diplomatic, and military—has worsened the compounding crises. The dominant reflex to read non-conventional security challenges through the lens of conventional state-based analysis has gravely distorted policy and imposed significant additional costs in human and financial terms.

One alternative to both mainstream security and the line of critical security studies has been developing through attention to the concept of *human security*. It first emerged in mainstream political debate after the

---

[4] A rare book that attempts to link the immediacy of these challenges into a scenarios-based projection of different futures is Heikki Patomäki's *The Political Economy of Global Insecurity: War, Future Crises and Changes in Global Governance* (2008).

UN Development Programme's (UNDP) 1994 *Human Development Report*. Here, *human security* was defined as having two main aspects: safety from chronic threats such as hunger, disease, and repression; and protection from sudden and harmful disruptions in the pattern of daily life. The rationale for the elaboration of the concept of *human security* in the UNDP's report, and a concern that continues to underpin this alternative range of critical approaches to the way security is understood and practiced, was the need to contest conventional approaches to security that seemed to be marginal to the daily threats facing people around the world.

As the UNDP notes, 'Human security is a child who did not die, a disease that did not spread, a job that was not cut, an ethnic tension that did not explode in violence, a dissident who was not silenced. Human security is not a concern with weapons—it is a concern with human life and dignity' (United Nations Development Programme, 1994: 22). Conceiving of security as *human security* importantly widens the domain of what should be considered as security threats and what agents are capable of redressing these threats. However, the profound weakness with this approach is that it tends to work in a paradigm that treats insecurity—from structural violence to food insecurity—only as that which has recognizable effects on the bodies of individuals. It is insecurity that changes our quotidian lives in a way that we can understand directly, concretely, and palpably. How is such an approach to take account of the fact that the new risks and threats have become increasingly disembodied and abstracted in their form? It is to this question that we now turn.

Insecurity and the Globalization of Exterminism

We have documented some unsettling empirical changes, but these only begin to get at the ontological depth of the shift in the meaning and practice of the security/insecurity binary. As we began to discuss earlier, in this time of the Great Unsettling, conventional attempts at enhancing security tend to be counterproductive and even contradictory, too often producing the opposite of their intended outcomes. This has been exacerbated, as Neil Curtis (2009) points out, by a widespread apocalyptic excitement giving rise both to a hypersensitivity about attacks on local and national sovereignty and an anticipatory revelling in the emergent possibilities offered by impending chaos. Threats become treated as personifications of evil. Counter-violence becomes a crusade. This new apocalyptic sensibility—ranging from alt-right and populist versions to religious globalism—brings together a *modern* sense of risk and a (neo-) *traditional* sense of millennial hope—a hope for life after the great battle of

Armageddon—with a *postmodern* relativizing that unsettles both. As a consequence, greater structural insecurity now follows almost every heightened security intervention. The Global War on Terror and the exponential capacity for interconnected cross-border state surveillance are exemplary cases of this process of contradictory recursion. Every response produces counter-responses and every counter-response produces the necessity of new step changes.

Nuclear security/insecurity is perhaps the paradigm marker of this spiralling risk cycle of contradictory outcomes. Politically, the bomb, which was developed as the ultimate weapon for enhancing security, led to an insecurity race that was enumerated in the new concept of 'megadeaths'. In cultural terms, the bomb unsettled centuries-old cross-civilizational tropes about the light as the source of life and enlightenment. The Hiroshima explosion, described as the light of 'a thousand suns',[5] instead brought darkness. Defended as bringing peace, the Hiroshima devastation brought the mass carnage of civilians in an act of state terrorism. 'I have become Death, the shatterer of worlds', said J. Robert Oppenheimer after the first atomic explosion that he helped to make possible (Hinkson, 1982).

We can attempt to mark the levels of risk and insecurity, but their actual meaning is now the purview of experts. *The Bulletin of Atomic Scientists* doomsday clock, marking the potential end of humanity, now hovers at two minutes to midnight (Mecklin, 2018). This compares to the beginning of the Cold War, when we entered the first phase of global exterminism[6] associated with a military nuclear doctrine called mutual assured destruction (MAD). Then, the clock was set at seven minutes to midnight. With the doctrine of MAD, we had arrived at a state where the risk of massive retaliation and the possibility of blowing up the world became the basis of global 'security'. It became clear that we were living in a different kind of world when the quest for global security came to depend upon being prepared to destroy the conditions for human life on Earth.

Since the 1960s, we have added the compounding potentials of nuclear proliferation, nuclear winter, intercontinental ballistic missiles, multiple independently targetable re-entry vehicles, and the missile shield Star Wars, as well as 'limited' nuclear war capabilities and computer-automated nuclear launch systems—one appropriately called 'the Dead Hand'. In this context, contemporary examples of North Korea's nuclear

---

[5] The reference here is to the *Bhagavad Gita*, quoted by J. Robert Oppenheimer.
[6] The reference here is to E. P. Thompson's important essay, 'Notes on Exterminism: The Last Stage of Civilization' (1980).

and missile tests and tensions between Putin's Russia and Trump's United States are only the surface expressions of a contradictory doomsday machine that cannot be understood by just adding up the numbers. Through all of this, perhaps the most perplexing thing here is that the global imaginary of nuclear insecurity is not at breaking point. Rather, the nuclear threat has receded into the generalized unsettlement of our times: lifted into high relief by a newspaper headline one day, dropped into the background the next.

Nevertheless, we are confronted with confounding paradoxes. Because the process is increasingly abstracted from lay understanding and practice, we are now at a point in human history when we need scientists and interpretative experts to tell us about the darkness (and light) of our future. It is not possible to know what is happening, even to the long-term patterns of the weather from just how it feels on our skin or in our hearts. And, ironically, it is dedicated work in these same *fields* of natural and social science by intellectually trained experts acting at the intersection of techno-science, capitalism, and the military–industrial complex that has brought us to this point of crisis. To be sure, those scientists and policymakers have been charged with delivering the desires of ordinary people for more and more of 'whatever'—security, comfort, consumption goods, mobility. But in the process they have brought us to the current conjuncture where self-exterminism is possible, and now by various means: either with a bang or a whimper.

A century ago, apart from images mediated though religion, such as through the apocalyptic projections of the Judaic–Christian *Revelation*, the Hindu *Pralaya*, or the Norse *Ragnarök*, people found it difficult to comprehend the *end of the world* as they knew it. Or, to put it the other way around, eschatology as a focus of 'the end of times' was rife, but very few people could imagine us humans doing it to ourselves. In that period, romantic intellectuals found it meaningful to separate out apocalypse (revealing through destruction) and millenarianism (living again through glorious rebirth). Now that empirical exterminism is actually possible, the new apocalyptic stories shock us momentarily without revealing what alter-global/local pathways might look like.

Popular cultural renditions of the 'end of the world' in film and television similarly rehearse the ontological drama of this change, but with little practical effect. A decade ago, millions of viewers across the globe watched what was then a new phenomenon: speculation on what would happen to the world after the extermination of all humans. Alan Weisman's book, *The World without Us* (2007), was followed by a National Geographic documentary called *Aftermath: Population Zero* and a History Channel series called *Life after People* (2009). The programmes depicted gardens of Eden growing in the absence of humanity, with post-human hope coming out of apocalyptic despair. This process is similar to the nuclear reversal of light and dark: another example of the unsettling of older existential categories.

The many contemporary apocalyptic and post-apocalyptic documentaries and films—*I am Legend* (2007), *Melancholia* (2011), *Goodbye World* (2013), *Extinction* (2015), *A Quiet Place* (2018)—are no longer even what have in the past been called 'critical dystopias', used to reflect on the human condition and to imagine how we might act otherwise. The only counter-practices in these popular culture representations are individual and heroic survivalism—keeping the vampires, zombies, and terrorists at bay at night while working stoically during the day in a laboratory to unlock the secret of individual–planetary survival. It hardly works as a transitional practice prefiguring alternative and more sustainable worlds.

The Transformation of the World

Consumed by this question of a fundamental and qualitative shift occurring on the global level, the German sociologist Ulrich Beck (1944–2015) drafted a major book on the subject during the last years of his life. The 'unfinished book' is particularly relevant here to understanding the meaning of tumultuous change. Beck's life had spanned the period of the Great Unsettling from World War II until the semi-announcement of the Anthropocene, and in these last years he writes with compelling urgency. The preface of *The Metamorphosis of the World* begins with damnation: 'The world is unhinged', he says. 'As many people see it, this is true in both senses of the word: the world is out of joint and it has gone mad. We are wandering aimlessly and confused, arguing for this and against that' (2016: xi). His is a powerful statement, describing an encompassing hermeneutic of the present condition.

Very quickly, however, his argument moves to hyperbole. He writes: 'But a statement on which most people can agree, beyond all antagonisms and across all continents, is "I don't understand the world any more". The aim of this book', he says, 'is to try to understand and explain why we no longer understand the world' (2016: xi). This is quite distinct from our argument that we are entering a world *framed* by uncertainties, relativized both objectively and subjectively, and where the standpoints for understanding the world are ontologically cleaved. From the other side of the equation, Beck's rationale for writing misses the simple fact that in this world there are many people who have returned to older verities and claim to understand it completely. As we noted in Chapter 8, contemporary anti-globalist populists like Victor Órban, Marine Le Pen, Nigel Farage, and Donald Trump actually believe that they understand this unsettled world intimately. The abiding sadness is that an increasing number of people believe their beliefs. Another sadness is that, because the world appears to be too complex to do otherwise, many others have uncritically given over their trust to technocratic experts who have reduced understanding to metrics, statistics, and codified simplifications.

Just as Beck's rhetoric becomes hyperbolic, his method moves between precise overstatement and messy allusion—perhaps all the problems that any unfinished draft would present. His argument in summary is that changes in our contemporary world are so epochally comprehensive, so tumultuous, that the language of social change can no longer capture it. Rather than massive change, transformation, or even revolution or crisis, he contends that we are going through a process of *metamorphosis*: a 'complete transformation into a different type, a different reality, a different mode of being in the world' (2016: 6). This, he says, adds up to *Copernican Turn 2.0*. At the core of this metamorphosis, he insists that we need to understand that instead of the world revolving around nation-states, it is imperative to think of the globe as the star around which nation-states revolve.

Given that the present study also argues for a foundational shift of existential proportions, Beck's *Metamorphosis of the World* provides a way of clarifying what we are not saying. Among many other points of contention, the first difference concerns the nature of social change; the second turns on the relation between the national and global; and the third relates to the spaces of practical action, which Beck says in one of his moments of singular overstatement 'are *inevitably* constituted in a cosmopolitan way' (2016: 8, emphasis added).

The Question of Social Change

If we begin with the first issue on which we part company—social change —one key problem with Beck's pronouncement is that *not* everything has changed. Nor does the present fundamental shift change everything comprehensively. His method offers no satisfactory or systematic way of saying more than one thing at a time, except, that is, through messy or contradictory points of qualification. A basic *transformation*, one so critical that it goes to the heart of the human condition, can be dominant (our position) without involving the *metamorphosis* of everything (Beck's originating position). In fact, by the end of his first chapter, Beck is already qualifying his own position: '[T]his does not mean', he says, 'that I think of *everything* that occurs in society today—in the economy and in politics, the world of work, the education system and the family, etc.—as a metamorphosis' (2016: 19, emphasis in original). What, then, is the nature of this process of metamorphosis that is both all-encompassing and partial?

Reading through Beck's exhortations about how metamorphosis confounds all ways of understanding other than his, it is difficult to get to the bottom of this process. What it comes down to is that metamorphosis is a non-intentional, non-ideological, and almost inexorable process of meta-change that occurs behind our backs: 'It slinks in, as it were, through the backdoor of side-effects' (2016: 48). Here, again, without a way of bringing together analytically different levels of analysis, Beck has to first universalize his claims (metamorphosis occurs behind our backs) and then qualify them. For Beck, we have not willed metamorphosis, but at the very same time, he exhorts, 'Haven't climate scientists set a transformation of capitalism in train that is self-destructive ...?' (2016: 117). He thus misses the intertwined relations between what we have been describing variously as contestations over (ideological) meaning, tensions between national and global imaginaries, and contradictions between ontological formations. He can offer no explanation of social determinants, nor layers of social framing. Metamorphosis is just happening, undetermined and unwilled.

Let us bring in another important contemporary writer as a counterpoint: the French sociologist and philosopher of science, Bruno Latour. Of the same generation as Ulrich Beck, he opens his recent book *Facing Gaia* with apparently very similar concerns:

As we hear one bad piece of news after another, you might expect us to feel that we had shifted from a mere ecological crisis into what should instead be called *a profound mutation in our relation to the world*. And yet this is surely not the case ... A strange situation: we crossed a series of thresholds, we went through total war [with nature], and we hardly noticed a thing! (2017: 8–9, emphasis in original)

Again, we do agree with Latour's suggestion of 'a profound mutation'. But it is not quite true, of course, that we have 'hardly noticed' the shift. Many people have noticed. Many have responded, even if without sufficient effect. Here, we can forgive Latour the hyperbole given the momentousness of the change. The core problem here is rather that, like Beck's middle-range theorizing, Latour's flat method induces him to describe the unsettling in all of its *empirical* (and philosophical) complexity, and then to embrace that unsettling.[7] Latour's method demands a radical empiricism that eschews generalized explanation except through mapping the vast networks of singular acts that gave rise to contingent outcomes. And ironically, in this process, accepting his description of a human war against the Earth becomes his only positive source of change. For Latour, it is through embracing the relativized multiplicity of the world fragmented by the war on Gaia (not the interconnectedness of 'the Globe') that will make it possible for us to choose again to be grounded in the Earth. For Beck, almost to the contrary, it is the inevitable globalization of meaning—cosmopolitanization—combined with what he calls 'emancipatory catastrophism' that will break open 'a sanctimonious national autistic world' (2016: 117). This is to begin to evoke the second set of differences.

The Relation between Globalization and the Nation-State

A further issue on which we part company with Beck comes firstly from his implied treatment of globalization as being in dualistic opposition with the nation-state, and, secondly, his treatment of globalization as *the* carrier of metamorphosis, sweeping all before it, for good and ill. On the first point, as we have argued consistently in the present study, these 'entities' maybe in tension, but they are not commensurable categories that can be put in a dualistic or essentially antagonistic relation. The nation-state is a community polity, while globalization is a process—two very different things. The nation-state is a modern community institution globalized across the nineteenth century to become the dominant container of political power and human imaginings, while globalization names a set of processes extending social relations across world-space that have occurred across much of human history and only gave rise to the emergence of a dominant imagery in the late twentieth century. There is no singular opposition or dualism here, let alone a productive one.

On the second point, according to Beck, metamorphosis is happening as 'a side-effect of what is so casually referred to as "globalization"' (2016: 55). This is to put more weight on processes of globalization than even we would want to do. Certainly, globalization matters immensely, but it is not *the* singular cause of a global shift that is unsettling life as we know it. Here, without any tools to do otherwise, Beck embarks upon the kind of

---

[7] This does not mean, of course, that Latour accepts the givenness of androgenic climate change. It means rather that he accepts the unsettling of the human condition as a positive source of change. For us, the unsettling can only be adequately responded to with a reflexive negotiation of processes in tension. Neither Latour's (ontologically flat) defence of pluralism nor Beck's 'emancipatory catastrophism' seems very compelling.

methodological globalism that we cautioned heavily against in Chapter 5. Here, the comparison between Beck and Latour is stark, but neither writer is helpful in understanding globalization. Beck believes in the global, while Latour thinks that 'the Globe' is exemplary of the problem of abstracting meaning beyond empirical description. For Latour, 'the Globe' needs to be put in capital letters to show how humans reify the processes of globalization. He seeks, in short, to overcome 'the curse of the Globe' (Latour, 2017: 245; 2018). Drawing on Peter Sloterdijk's work on the global that we critically analysed earlier in Chapter 3, Latour goes further to make the figure of the Globe the metaphor for all that is wrong with the world: 'the Globe is not that of which the world is made but, rather, a Platonic obsession *transferred* into Christian theology and then *deposited* in political epistemology to put a face—but an impossible one—on the dream of total and complete knowledge' (2017: 127, emphasis in original). Or, expressed more colloquially: 'The global, when it is not the attentive analysis of a reduced model [the size of an "ordinary pumpkin"], is never anything but a tissue of globabble' (2017: 130). Here, from the opposite perspective to Beck, Latour again seems to make the Globe matter too much.

Much more could be said, but this takes us to the third point of contention in this dialogue with Beck and Latour: the spaces of practical action. We will use this contention to conclude the chapter because it concerns the question of what is to be done in an unsettled world.

Concluding Reflections on Cosmopolitanism and Spaces of Action

This chapter, building upon themes treated previously in this study, has begun the work of developing a reflexive understanding of the complex layers of the contemporary Great Unsettling by focusing upon the intersection of ecological crisis and political insecurity. Seeking to understand what it means to live in the unsettled world of the Anthropocene, our analysis has moved its focus from patterns of empirical change to the sources of ontological disruption. To do so, we selected an approach that can treat the global as larger than a pumpkin (contra Latour), but smaller than that a totalizing source of a cosmopolitism (contra Beck). Moreover, as we suggested previously, ideological contestations over the meaning of the global still have to be fought out in the everyday life of our concrete glocal dwellings.

But in order to make a case for the continued relevance of the global in a context that increasingly is being read through the lens of 'deglobalization', we need to articulate the global imaginary in ways that differ from current dominant understandings. As the literary scholar Claire Colebrook writes:

It is the possibility of extinction or the end of human time that forces us to confront a new sense of the globe: far from being an unfortunate event that accidentally befalls the earth and humanity, the thought of the end of the anthropocene era is both at the heart of all the motifs of ecological ethics and the one idea that cannot be thought as long as the globe is considered in terms of its traditional and anthropocentric metaphors. (2015: 60)

The chapter has acknowledged the dire situation in which we find ourselves. Intensifying modernization overlaid by the confounding postmodernizing of the post–World War II period have globalized new kinds of risk and insecurity. These tend to be more disembodied risks than has been previously known. They are abstracted risks layered across older continuing forms of palpable risk. Rather than just being dangerous events, these new partly visible, mostly invisible, and always entangled complex risks are patterned processes: background radiation, acidification, ozone depletion, global warming, global dimming, local–global terrorism, and nuclear exterminism. Rather than being temporary or short term, these risks are structurally long term and planet changing. They are globalizing rather than simply localized. And they are manufactured by humans in very practical ways, while being defended (or decontested) in distinctively ideological narratives. They are abstract processes in the sense that we cannot necessarily *directly* see or feel them, but they are materially abstract both in themselves and in their effects in that they are constituted in the practices and ideas of people as they seek to reproduce our conditions of existence. In the process, they/we are destroying our planet as we know it.

Although Ulrich Beck and Bruno Latour would describe this world in dire straits from different perspectives, they might agree that we are in need of a response that neither leads to an aesthetic of fear (Nietzsche's pathetic 'last man'), nor to more of the same—apocalyptic pronouncements vacillating with relative complacency or individualized heroism set against a general deferral of the consequences of action. We need to imagine an alternative collective political response that retains hope in the global—even in its tattered, time-worn expression of 'cosmopolitanism'—but goes beyond placing our faith in compelling orators, whether of the uplifting kind such as Tony Blair to Barack Obama or in the angry populist mode such as Donald Trump or Jair Bolsonaro. On this we agree. But let us turn again to Beck and Latour to accentuate some alternative pathways while clarifying our own.

For Beck, it seems that intensifying globalization and the associated cosmopolitan turn will shift us out of the current mess as one of its unintended side effects—without revolution, and even without organized political attention. His alternative is based on social learning formed in this setting of emancipatory catastrophism. Firstly, metamorphosis is turning cities into cosmopolitan risk communities. They are becoming translocal places where 'invisible risks often become visible ... the interplay of collapse and awakening' (2016: 168). Secondly, metamorphosis is already producing a 'global risk' generation of multiple pluralistic differences, a generation that is 'unideological':

It knows what doesn't work any more without knowing what does work ... On the world stage of the generations the roles are clearly distributed: the elderly are clearly the *Neanderthals* and the young global generation are members of *Homo cosmopoliticus*. They are the ones for whom the metamorphosis has become second nature, while the older generation experience it as a threat to their existence. (Beck, 2016: 189)

We contest both of these points on account of overgeneralization. In Beck's terms, we thus remain Neanderthals, while the young *Homo cosmopoliticus* will, in their expectation and a normative horizon of global equality, potentially reset the future on a different pathway. This, to us, seems a vain hope. An ability to live with contradiction could just as easily turn to self-absorption; and as Beck acknowledges, this new generation in the Global North is already engaged in a battle to retain the resource advantages of old.

For Bruno Latour, it certainly is not globalization and the turn towards cosmopolitanism that provide the answer: For him, globalization 'means that *no one knows where to live any longer*' (2017: 278, emphasis added). Rather, positive transformation will come through recognizing our earthbound limits as 'terrestrials' living among other terrestrials in the concreteness of our endangered 'dwelling places' of a miniscule 'critical zone' a few kilometres thick between our planet's atmosphere and its bedrock (Latour, 2018). In other words, living in the unsettled world of the Anthropocene means to give up utopian hopes in both the vanishing Local and the receding Global and instead to find new ways of coming back 'down to earth' as embodied terrestrials (2017: 244; 2018). Latour's emphasis on recognizing earthbound limits appears to be much closer to a concrete 'space of (political) action' akin to what we are arguing than Beck's, but that apparent kinship also quickly proves to be spurious. Evoking Carl Schmitt's famous friend/enemy binary allegedly located at the core of the political, Latour argues that action must begin with the recognition that we, the *earthbound terrestrials* of the Anthropocene, are in a war with the (modern) *Humans*.

Conversely, we want to continue to engage the global by espousing an engaged cosmopolitanism that provides an alternative to Beck's and Latour's respective positions. Its closest resonances are with what some scholars have called 'critical cosmopolitanism' (Mignolo, 2002), 'rooted cosmopolitanism' (Appiah, 2002), 'embedded cosmopolitanism' (Erskine, 2008), or 'vernacular cosmopolitanism' (Diouf, 2002). The term 'engaged' has been chosen here as most apposite not only because it corresponds to our larger theoretical framework of an engaged theory of globalization. We also selected it because it refers to the reflexively *engaged* epistemological status of an abstracting claim: namely, that ethics, however generalizing it might be, needs to be engaged in actual on-the-ground dialogue and deliberative debate between individuals, communities, peoples, philosophers, and agents on behalf of others—dead and alive, still to be born, and other than human. Engaged cosmopolitanism takes grounded social relations, including particularized or embodied social relations with known others, as crucial to qualifying the potentially thin emptiness of abstracted cosmopolitanism. But at the same time, *pace* Latour, it takes the process of analytical abstraction as crucial to qualifying the possible parochialisms and self-limiting interests of particularism.

A number of propositions underlie this position. First, while it is both philosophically possible and necessary to abstract moral agency, ethics is always grounded in the *particular* social contexts of persons connected through layers of different kinds of relationship, from the local, with 'place' as the locale of meaningful social relations, to the global, with the 'Earth' as the ground of human history, even as humans reach beyond it. When seen from this perspective, the global is treated as a special kind of 'particular' social context or habitus. Just as locales, communities, and nations have their own histories, the global has its own long histories of human relations: sodalities of religion, empires of domination, trade routes of silk, movements against slavery, sojourns in emigration—all told from various perspectives. In this argument, cross-cutting histories, including the global history of being human, frame us all. Global history carries what Andrew Linklater (2010) calls 'the ambiguity of human interconnectedness'.

Moreover, our engaged cosmopolitanism argues that persons are unable in practice, even during philosophical moments of working through techniques of abstraction, to completely disengage from this manifold local–global context in order to enter the sphere of neutral moral deliberation. How could they? This is what defines them as human. It suggests that the overriding emphasis on *freedom* by liberal cosmopolitans is a reductive consequence of not reflexively considering their own assumed politics. Even when liberals claim to have stripped their grounding claims of all ideological presumptions, it is salutary to remember that conceptions of freedom, liberty, autonomy, and choice form one of the dominant ideological clusters of our time.

Secondly, while cross-border criticism and solidarity—both of which are requisite to meaningful discussions of local and global justice—are complicated by the particularistic grounding, it is possible to achieve both through reflexive translation, deliberation, and debate across such boundaries. As G. E. R. Lloyd (2012) demonstrates compellingly, this reflexive translation entails the recognition that there are ontologically different ways of being in the world, most of which take the *dominance* of modern abstraction and rational neutrality as anathema to being human.

Thirdly, while ecological, cultural, political, and economic boundaries remain important parts of the human condition, one of the core ethical principles of cosmopolitanism is that spatial boundaries are not lines on a moral map that mark the extent of the ethical domain. Proximate or distant, friend or enemy, insider or outsider, each person and community on the planet needs to be considered as part of and equal in any ethical framework.[8] Part of the reflexivity of a grounded cosmopolitan ethics is that even very localized ethical dialogues need to be conducted openly, bringing into contention the ethical frames of others. Others, whether close or far, need to be considered as ethical equals. That is, themes of belonging and mobility, inclusion and exclusion, freedom and obligation are in a dialectical relationship with one another, and they have been so across global history in different ways across different traditions. Through such an understanding we might begin to feel our way towards new ways of living in these unsettled times of the Anthropocene—together, as a global community of diverse communities.

---

[8] Versions of these propositions are argued at length in Erskine (2008). It should be carefully noted, however, that she handles them quite differently from our rendition here.

11   Concluding Reflections

Beyond fleeting newspaper headlines or passing academic fads heralding 'globalization's failure', this book, first and foremost, has advanced the case for globalization's continued relevance in both theory and practice. At the same time, however, the stark reality of the Great Unsettling looms large in our study as we concede that the world in the early twenty-first century faces significant disintegrative threats. The destabilization of familiar life-worlds is well underway. Deep social volatility is occurring on a scale and at a speed perhaps never before seen in human history. Global economic growth is uneven and plagued by contradictions, resulting in troubling consequences such as the seismic shift from secure long-term employment to precarious short-term work, increasing automation, the dismantling of long-standing social welfare policies, and the rise of inequality within countries and, in some ways, between countries.

The associated climate of insecurity and loss of identity has penetrated people's consciousness down to the ontological layer. As Heikki Patomäki (2018) points out, heightened existential uncertainty and insecurity often function as potent triggers of social-psychological pathologies such as anxiety, resentment, anger, hatred, moral indifference, and antagonistic self–other attitudes, which, in turn, strengthen tendencies towards social disintegration and escalating conflicts. Immigration fear-mongering has only added to this volatile mixture. Amplified by the new digital media, these mutually reinforcing material and ideational dynamics have shaped 'public opinion' in support of the populist reinvigoration of the stressed national imaginary—a phenomenon widely interpreted as a 'globalization backlash' (Bremmer, 2018; Latour, 2018; Crouch, 2019).

But it is precisely the intensity of the current scepticism towards globalization—both the process and the idea—that has animated our engagement with the global in our unsettled times. Our discussion has drawn from and extended the lively globalization debates of the last three decades. Acknowledging the substantial progress made in recent years in the development of explanatory and normative global theory, we nonetheless attempted to stretch the existing body of scholarship on globalization by examining the structural conditions and complex dynamics of global social formation under the contemporary unsettled conditions characterized by heightening ideological tensions, worsening ecological conditions, and growing political instability.

As social constructivists who have long paid special attention to the subjective aspects of globalization, we explored in some detail how specific ideologies, imaginaries, and ontologies of globalization serve as crucial drivers of meaning construction and knowledge production. We summarized positions, analysed claims, and offered theoretical propositions that built on the extant literature as well as further developing crucial arguments we had advanced in our previous published work on the subject. Hence, this study presented us with an especially welcome opportunity to assemble our ideas on the subject succinctly and in one place while at the same time developing them in a more systematic, sustained, and problem-orientated manner.

To this end, we employed an unusually comprehensive approach that cuts across two broad research categories that global studies scholars often tackle in isolation from each other: the study of specific social problems or political issues as they relate to globalization; and the study of the concept and theories of *globalization* itself. At the same time, we brought together objective and subjective dimensions that are usually treated separately. By reflecting on both global problems and the very nature of the process—objectively and subjectively—we pursued lines of enquiry that are of major import to contemporary social change. Our linked theory–practice framework allowed us to show how current moments and events inform the quest for novel knowledge, and vice versa. Thus, we self-consciously drew connections between the mounting theoretical and practical challenges to globalization.

Two propositions in particular underpinned our critical reappraisal of globalization in dark times. Firstly, we acknowledged that both the process and the idea of globalization have only partly delivered on their grand promise. Introducing a first outline of an *engaged theory of globalization*, we argued that current challenges have presented us with an important opportunity to both assess contemporary dynamics of increasing complexity and respond to the main assumptions, perspectives, scope, and methods of extant globalization research for the purpose of deepening our insight into our subject. Serving the goal of developing enhanced forms of reflexivity, our theoretical outline emphasized the cultivation of critical thinking as an indispensable tool to expand our understanding of our own place on an interdependent planet endangered by the consequences of unsustainable practices. Indeed, tackling the glocal problems associated with the Great Unsettling actually requires a *strengthening* of our orientation towards the global and the planetary in innovative ways.[1]

Secondly, we recognized that the thematic of our book inherently entails a tension between offering critical responses to the current moment of globalization-in-crisis—especially the danger of falling into the trap of 'presentism'—and developing new knowledge for the long-term quest to understand the social transformations of our time. But rather than seeking to erase this tension by opting for one objective at the expense of the other, we deliberately made it part of our discussion as we addressed and assessed current theoretical and practical challenges to globalization. For example, President Donald Trump's unadorned scorn for 'globalist' trade and immigration policies was not treated as a novel event in itself, but instead linked to the deeper social context of populist ideas, new social movements, and clashing social imaginaries. Our pursuit of the conflicting goals of engaging the global in the present moment *and* developing pertinent long-term knowledge of globalization highlighted the importance of the theory–practice connection that continues to play a paramount role in all modern critical theory traditions, from Karl Marx to Michel Foucault and beyond.

Ultimately, our preferred way of handling this strain was to link contemporary globalization matters to the investigation of the changing forms of globalization. Indeed, examining globalization and understanding its real-world impacts requires researchers to move across the four levels of analysis we introduced in Chapters 4 and 5. Our analytic approach has the advantage of making it possible to identify and investigate the dominant *and intersecting* forms of globalization in *any* particular historical period. In practice, of course, these forms are entangled in the dominant, enduring, emergent, and residual modalities we described in Chapter 6. This point is crucial to avoiding rigid categories of epochalism. For example, our framework allows us to argue that embodied globalization—a form referring to the movement of peoples across the world and remaining enduringly relevant in the movements of refugees, emigrants, travellers, and tourists—is not the defining form of contemporary globalization, even though it remains ever present and critically important. Similarly, object-extended globalization—a form characterized by the global movement of objects, in particular traded commodities, as well

---

[1] In this sense, despite working with an antithetical method to Bruno Latour's Actor Network Theory, we deeply appreciate his introduction of the term 'terrestrial'—earthbound creatures among other earthbound species—as a key concept intended to bolster his political project of creating ecologically and socially sustainable 'dwelling places' (Latour, 2018).

as early objects of exchange and communication such as coins and notes —should not be seen as the defining form of the present, though it contributes to what we have called the 'blanketing effect' of contemporary globalization.

Indeed, our engaged theory framework enables us to push back much more effectively against the influential assertion that globalization no longer matters in our alleged age of 'deglobalization'. Confined to the level of empirical analysis—the surveying of detailed empirical instances of globalizing processes and activities—such claims typically present embodied and object-extended forms of globalization as though these were the currently dominant manifestations and thus represent the sole standards by which to judge the allegedly diminishing significance of globalization.

To be sure, empirical data seem to confirm the widespread impression that globalization is in decline. For example, the tone of news stories containing the word 'globalization' in leading US and UK newspapers has recently taken a sharply negative swing (Ghemawat, 2017). A major index measuring object-extended and embodied forms of globalization has recorded a downward movement in 2017—the first since 1975—and is expected to flatline or further decrease over the next few years (KOF Globalization Index, 2018). World trade in goods and services has levelled off significantly, buttressing that notion that we have reached 'peak trade' and might be approaching the limits of economic integration. Often associated with globalization, automation is estimated to result in anything from a 20 to 30 per cent fall in global merchandise trade over the next decade. Cross-border financial flows have dipped from 22 per cent of world gross domestic product in 2007 to merely 6 per cent in 2016— about the same level as in 1996. Since the 2008 Global Financial Crisis and its ensuing Great Recession, transnational bank flows and foreign-direct investment have stagnated at lower levels. While the costs of communication have been falling quickly and consistently over the past decades, global transportation costs have been extremely jittery and sluggish, plagued by uncertainty around highly volatile oil prices and shifting consumption patterns (Sharma, 2016; Livesey, 2017).

Turning to cross-border flows of people, the deglobalization claim made on empirical grounds and confined to specific forms of globalization seems to hold up as well. Governments in developed countries have taken drastic measures to further tighten their immigration policies. Like most of the newly elected populist governments in Europe, the Trump administration has been reinforcing national borders, vowing to keep out Mexican migrants, and banning refugees from select Muslim countries. Admittedly, neoliberal globalization in the 1990s and 2000s was translated primarily in terms of increased mobility for goods, firms, and capital, and not for people. Still, immigration policies in advanced economies in the late 2010s—especially with regard to low-skill migrants—are much more restricted today than they were in the nineteenth century or even in the immediate post–World War II period (Peters, 2017: 2). What is new about processes of migration and asylum seeking in the last few decades is the increased diversity and spread of immigrant destinations across the globe and the numbers of internally displaced persons—not the simple fact of the movement of people.

But even if we agreed to confine our investigation to the initial level of empirical analysis, the consideration of additional forms of globalization would significantly weaken the 'deglobalization' argument. While contemporary globalization still entails significant embodied and object-extended dynamics, its dominant integrative/differentiating form today is disembodied globalization and, to a somewhat lesser extent, agency-extended globalization, such as the spread of more than half a million US military personnel in hundreds of locations across the globe. In other words, the defining dominant condition of contemporary globalization is the movement of abstracted capital and culture—including words, images, electronic texts, or encoded capital and cryptocurrencies—through processes of disembodied interchange. Indeed, the latest available data on digital global flows show that disembodied globalization has neither stalled nor declined. Rather, the amount of cross-border bandwidth in 2014 has grown to be 45 times larger than in 2005, suggesting that the world has become more connected than ever. Rather than succumbing to the powerful siren song of deglobalization, commentators attuned to these disembodied dynamics have heralded a 'new era of digital globalization' (McKinsey Global Institute, 2018).

Moreover, while it is empirically important to bring in ominous data pointing to the slowing down of some forms of globalization—and to take these trends seriously—the analytical framework presented in the present study avoids the reduction of globalization to its main *objective* manifestations; that is, to lines of direct (material) connectivity. Such common perspectives neglect not only crucial subjective dynamics such as the globalization of anti-globalist populist narratives, but they also tend to focus on economics as the primary, objective form of globalizing impact. Political and cultural relations also matter. Moreover, our theoretical framework points to the utility of overlaying the conventional domain mode of globalization theory focused on economic, ecological, cultural, and political dimensions with a new classification scheme that distinguishes between four major forms of globalization expressed in terms of different modes of integration and differentiation. Again, these modes range from relations held together *and* separated by the embodied movement of people to more abstract relations where the bodies of people cease to be the defining condition of the particular mode of globalizing relations.

To recognize that the dominant integrative form of globalization today is 'disembodied' also opens up new perspectives on old themes in social theory. For example, it informs the study of 'power' by bringing into sharper focus a form of power derived from controlling or exploiting the disembodied movement of capital and culture: finance capital, global communications, and so on. Emerging across the various modes of practice, disembodied power has an extraordinary capacity to affect generalized change at a distance. However, this does not mean that such power floats across the world and above the fray. The dominant form of contemporary globalization—structured as relations of disembodied power —reverberates with increasing intensity and systematicity upon the bodies of the people across the world. This power takes many forms, such as the capacity to launch a long-term war against ISIS—beginning in 2014 with Coalition airstrikes in Syria and Iraq involving an average daily cost of US$11.9 million (McLaughlin, 2016). Another example would be the consequences of a relatively unregulated global financial system abstracting time and space at one level while lending money to people without the capacity to pay back their mortgages at another. Disembodied power is always in contention in the layered structuring of power in this age of unsettling globalization.

Hence, our approach to globalization matters presented in this study shores up our central contention that globalization still matters a lot; just not in the same way it did 25 years ago. To call the contemporary phase 'deglobalization' is a misnomer because its narrow empirical approach privileges one form of globalization at the expense of the others that have grown in stature.[2] Globalization should not be essentialized, for it is a living, changeable, and complex matrix of processes whose principal forms move at different speeds and at different levels of intensity. While object-extended and embodied forms of globalization have been in trouble since the 2008 Global Financial Crisis and the more recent populist explosion, disembodied and agency-extended forms of globalization have been intensifying.

On an ideological level, however, there is little doubt that the populist attacks on 'globalization' have found a receptive audience, especially

---

[2] As we argued in Chapter 5, such empirical approaches to globalization can be characterized as 'narrow' or reductive for the simple reason that they omit the kinds of issues that can only be handled by moving to the more abstract levels of analysis that we described as conjunctural, integrational, and categorical.

among the working classes in the Global North beset by economic and cultural anxieties. But their ideological 'deglobalization' agenda has resonated much less in a Global South buoyed by the expansion of its middle class as a result of 'globalization'. Paradoxically, then, the anti-globalist backlash has been strongest in those Western liberal democracies that presented themselves as the vanguard of market globalism and its neoliberal ideals of free trade, flexible immigration, and unobstructed capital and information flows. But the paradox goes even deeper. Populist denunciations of globalization notwithstanding, the mounting antiglobalist wave is itself a globalizing phenomenon that is sweeping across all continents. The enduring dynamics of space–time compression, inherent even in anti-globalist populism itself, suggest that globalization continues to provide the overarching conceptual framework and master metanarrative in an age that has increasingly come to doubt its lasting significance. In short, globalization continues to matter, as it serves as a touchstone for intense popular and academic debates on the future of worldwide interconnectivity, including those populist interventions critical of the phenomenon itself.

Ultimately, then, we sought to present a more holistic picture of globalization framed by a broad range of intertwined theoretical perspectives and practical concerns. Attentive to the long historical trajectory of evolving global formations, we explored the conditions and limits of our knowledge of the subject by employing a conceptual framework that helps us understand the momentous social transformations that characterize our global age. As the immense maelstrom of globalization continues to gyrate, it draws its potency from the ongoing interplay of the opposing forces of social integration and fragmentation (Rosenau, 2003). Under heavy fire from a proliferating cast of critics, globalization faces perhaps the toughest test so far regarding its suitability in solving the global problems of its own making. Indeed, the Great Compression of time and space and the Great Unsettling are two sides of the same coin—a global dialectic of 'creative destruction' playing itself out in a myriad of local, national, and regional settings.[3]

By mapping the complexity of globalization as it operates across all spatial scales, we consciously delved into specific instances of creative destruction without abandoning our theoretical task of drawing out broad

---

[3] The Austrian political economist Joseph Schumpeter (1942) coined the term 'creative destruction' to characterize the driving forces of capitalism. Tellingly, the phrase has been adopted in our age of digital globalization as the name of a popular survivalist computer game played in a borderless virtual world. We do not use the term positively as Schumpeter did, but acknowledge that the adjective 'creative' points to the constitutive and life-changing nature of such destructive forces.

patterns of social practice and meaning. We did not shy away from making critical and normative claims about what is and ought to be happening—and why—while at the same time reflecting on the adequacy of our methods for knowing and judging. The dual demands of simultaneously stepping into the world and abstracting from it have guided the chapters of this book as we sought to enrich our understanding of the shifting dynamics of globalization; engage some of the crucial global issues of our time; encourage the formation of transformative political agency; and advance a logic of transdisciplinarity through the production of knowledge of the global that both informs and draws from related themes across the social sciences and humanities.

Appendices

APPENDIX 1
LIST OF SPEECHES, CHAPTER 8, 'MAKING SENSE
OF THE POPULIST CHALLENGE TO
GLOBALIZATION'

Donald Trump

1 Address at the AIPAC Policy Conference in Washington, DC, 21 March 2016.
2 Address on foreign policy at the National Press Club in Washington, DC, 27 April 2016.
3 Address announcing candidacy for president in New York City, 16 June 2015.
4 Address at Trump SoHo in New York City, 22 June 2016.
5 Address on American economic independence in Monessen, Pennsylvania, 28 June 2016.
6 Address introducing Governor Mike Pence as the 2016 Republican Vice Presidential Nominee in New York City, 16 July 2016.
7 Address accepting the presidential nomination at the Republican National Convention in Cleveland, Ohio, 21 July 2016.
8 Address to the Detroit Economic Club, 8 August 2016.
9 Address at a rally in Fredericksburg, Pennsylvania, 20 August 2016.
10 Address at the Luedecke Arena in Austin, Texas, 23 August 2016.
11 Address at the Mississippi Coliseum in Jackson, Mississippi, 24 August 2016.
12 Address to the American Legion in Cincinnati, Ohio, 1 September 2016.
13 Address at the Cleveland Arts and Social Sciences Academy in Cleveland, Ohio, 8 September 2016.
14 Address at a rally in Toledo, Ohio, 21 September 2016.
15 Address at a rally at Sun Center Studios in Chester Township, Pennsylvania, 22 September 2016.
16 Address at a rally at the Berglund Center in Roanoke, Virginia, 24 September 2016.

17 Address at the South Florida Fair Expo Center in West Palm Beach, Florida, 13 October 2016.

Nigel Farage

1 Address at the Mississippi Coliseum in Jackson, Mississippi, 24 August 2016.
2 Address at the Conservative Political Action Conference in Washington, DC, 24 February 2017.
3 Address at the Conservative Political Action Conference in Washington, DC, 23 February 2018.

APPENDIX 2
AN OVERVIEW OF ENGAGED THEORY, EXPRESSED AS LEVELS OF ANALYSIS

Levels of the Social	DOING	ACTING	RELATING	BEING
Levels of Analysis	I. Empirical	II. Conjunctural	III. Integrational	VI. Categorical

Increasing epistemological abstraction of the standpoint of analysis

Objects of Analysis: I Levels of Social MEANING	IDEAS	IDEOLOGIES	IMAGINARIES	ONTOLOGIES
Objects of Analysis: II Levels of Social RELATIONS	Regimes of Social ACTIVITY	Modes of social PRACTICE	Themes of social INTEGRATION	Categories of social BEING
	• Groups • Communities • Networks • Institutions • Fields • Events • Assemblages	• Production • Consumption • Exchange • Communication • Mobility • Organization • Enquiry	• Accumulation-Distribution • Needs-Limits • Identity-Difference • Freedom-Authority • Inclusion-Exclusion • Security-Risk • Wellbeing-Adversity	• Temporality • Spatiality • Embodiment • Epistemology • Performativity • Objectivity • Subjectivity
Objects of Analysis: III Levels of Social FORMATION	Domains of social ACTIVITY	Formations of social PRACTICE	Formations of social INTEGRATION	Formations of social BEING
		E.g.		
	• Ecological • Economic • Political • Cultural	• Techno-scientism • Capitalism • Bureaucratism • Mediatism	• Face-to-face relations • Object-extended relations • Agency-extended relations • Disembodied relations	• Customary • Traditional • Modern • Postmodern

Figure A.1 An overview of engaged theory, expressed as levels of analysis

Bibliography

A

Abu-Lughod, J. L. (1989), *Before European Hegemony: The World-System AD 1250–1350*, New York, Oxford University Press.

Agnew, J. (2009), *Globalization and Sovereignty*, Lanham, Rowman & Littlefield Publishers.

Albrow, M. (1996), *The Global Age: State and Society beyond Modernity*, Cambridge, Polity Press.

(2007), 'A New Decade of the Global Age, 1996–2006', *Globality Studies Journal*, no. 8, pp. 1–17.

Al-Rodhan, N. and Stoudman, G. (2006), 'Definitions of Globalization: A Comprehensive Overview and a Proposed Definition', www.academia.edu /2969717/Definitions_of_Globalization_A_Comprehensive_Overview_and_ a_Proposed_Definition-_The_International_Relations_and_Security_Networ k_ETH_Zurich_June_19_2006. Accessed 11 November 2018.

Altbach, P. (2016), *Global Perspectives on Higher Education*, Baltimore, Johns Hopkins University Press.

Althusser, L. (1971), *Lenin and Philosophy and Other Essays*, New York, Monthly Review Press.

Alvargonzález, D. (2011), 'Multidisciplinarity, Interdisciplinarity, Transdisciplinarity, and the Sciences', *International Studies in the Philosophy of Science*, vol. 25, no. 4, pp. 387–403.

Amar, P. (2013), *The Security Archipelago: Human Security States, Sexuality Politics, and the End of Neoliberalism*, Durham, Duke University Press.

Amin, A. (2004), 'Regulating Economic Globalization', *Transactions of the Institute of British Geographers*, vol. 29, pp. 217–33.

Amin, S. (1990), *Maldevelopment: Anatomy of a Global Failure*, London, Zed Books.

(1997), *Capitalism in the Age of Globalization: The Management of Contemporary Society*, London, Zed Books.

Anders, G. (1972), *Endzeit und Zeitende: Gedanken an die atomare Situation*, Munich, Beck.

Anderson, B. (1983), *Imagined Communities, Reflections on the Origin and Spread of Nationalism*, London, Verso.

(1991), *Imagined Communities*, rev. edn., London, Verso.

Anderson, L. (1982), 'Why Should American Education Be Globalized? It's a Nonsensical Question', *Theory into Practice*, vol. 21, no. 3, pp. 155–61.

Anheier, H. K. and Juergensmeyer, M., eds. (2012), *Encyclopedia of Global Studies*, 4 vols., Thousand Oaks, Sage Publications.

Annan, K. (1998), 'The Politics of Globalization', Address to Harvard University at the Weatherhead Center for International Affairs, 17 September 1998. https://academy.wcfia.harvard.edu/politics-globalization-hon-kofi-annan. Accessed 28 December 2018.

(2001), 'Kofi Annan on Global Futures', *The Globalist*, 6 February. www .theglobalist.com/kofi-annan-on-global-futures. Accessed 28 December 2018.

Anonymous (1959), 'European Communities', *International Organization*, vol. 13, no, 1, pp. 174–8.

Anselmi, M. (2018), *Populism: An Introduction*, New York and London, Routledge.

Appadurai, A. (1990), 'Disjuncture and Difference in the Global Cultural Economy', *Theory, Culture & Society*, vol. 7, no. 2–3, pp. 295–310.

(1996), *Modernity at Large: Cultural Dimensions of Globalization*, Minneapolis, University of Minnesota Press.

Appelbaum, R. (2013), 'Comments on Jan Nederveen's Essay, "What Is Global Studies?"', *Globalizations*, vol. 10, no. 4, pp. 545–50.

Appelbaum, R. P. and Robinson, W. I., eds. (2005), *Critical Globalization Studies*, London and New York, Routledge.

Appiah, K. A. (1997), 'Cosmopolitan Patriots', *Critical Inquiry*, vol. 23, no. 3, pp. 617–39.

(2002), 'The State and the Shaping of Identity', in G. B. Peterson, ed., *The Tanner Lectures on Human Values XXIII*, Salt Lake City, University of Utah Press.

Archer, K. (2013), 'Searching for the Global in Global Studies', *Globalizations*, vol. 10, no. 4, pp. 521–5.

Archibugi, D., Held, D., and Kohler, M., eds. (1998), *Reimagining Political Community: Studies in Cosmopolitan Democracy*, Stanford, Stanford University Press.

Arendt, H. (1958), *The Human Condition*, Chicago, University of Chicago Press.

Arnoldi, J. (2004), 'Derivatives: Virtual Values and Real Risks', *Theory, Culture & Society*, vol. 21, no. 6, pp. 23–42.

Arter, D. (2010), 'The Breakthrough of Another West European Populist Radical Right Party? The Case of the True Fins', *Government and Opposition*, vol. 45, pp. 484–504.

Aslanidis, P. (2016), 'Is Populism an Ideology? A Refutation and a New Perspective', *Political Studies*, vol. 64, no. 1S, pp. 88–104.

Axford, B. (1995), *The Global System: Economics, Politics, and Culture*, Cambridge, Polity Press.

(2002), 'Enacting Globalization: Transnational Networks and the Deterritorialization of Social Relationship in the Global System', in G. Preyer and M. Bos, eds., *Borderlines in a Globalized World: New Perspectives in a Sociology of the World-System*, New York, Springer-Verlag.

(2013), *Theories of Globalization*, Cambridge, Polity Press.

(2016), 'Introduction: Global Scholarship from Within and Without', *Protosociology*, vol. 33, pp. 5–15.

B

Bach, O. (2013), *Die Erfindung der Globalisierung: Entstehung und Wandel eines zeitgeschichtlichen Grundbegriffs*, Frankfurt, Campus Verlag.

Baldwin, R. (2016), *The Great Convergence: Information Technology and the New Globalization*, Cambridge, Harvard University Press.

Barber, B. (2014), *If Mayors Ruled the World: Dysfunctional Nations, Rising Cities*, New Haven, Yale University Press.

(1996), *Jihad vs. McWorld*, New York, Ballantine Books.

Barnet, R. and Cavanagh, J. (1994), *Global Dreams: Imperial Corporations and the New World Order*, New York, Simon & Schuster.

Barnet, R. and Muller, R. E. (1974), *Global Reach: The Power of Multinational Corporations*, New York, Simon & Schuster.

Barrow, C. W. and Keck, M. (2017), 'Globalization Theory and State Theory: The False Antinomy', *Studies in Political Economy*, vol. 98, no. 2, pp. 177–96.

Bartelson, J. (2000), 'Three Concepts of Globalization', *International Sociology*, vol. 15, no. 2, pp. 180–96.

Battersby, P. and Siracusa, J. M. (2009), *Globalization and Human Security*, Lanham, Rowman & Littlefield Publishers.

Bauböck, R. (1995), *Transnational Citizenship: Membership and Rights in International Migration*, London, Edward Elgar.

Bauder, H. (2014), 'The Possibilities of Open and No Borders', *Social Justice*, vol. 39, no. 4, pp. 76–96.

Bauer, P. T. (1981), *Equality, the Third World and Economic Delusion*, London, Weidenfeld and Nicolson.

Bauman, Z. (1998), *Globalization: The Human Consequences*, New York, Columbia University Press.

(2000), *Liquid Modernity*, Cambridge, Polity Press.

(2012), 'Times of Interregnum', *Ethics and Global Politics*, vol. 5, no. 1, pp. 49–56.

Bayart, J.-F. (2008), *Global Subjects: A Political Critique of Globalization*, Cambridge, Polity Press.

Baylis, J. and Smith, S. (2001), *The Globalization of World Politics*, Oxford, Oxford University Press.

Beck, U. (1992), *Risk Society: Towards a New Modernity*, London, Sage Publications.

(1999), *World Risk Society*, Cambridge, Polity Press.

(2000), *What Is Globalization?* Cambridge, Polity Press.

(2007), 'The Cosmopolitan Condition: Why Methodological Nationalism Fails', *Theory, Culture & Society*, vol. 24, no. 7–8, pp. 286–90.

(2016), *The Metamorphosis of the World*, Cambridge: Polity Press.

Beck, U., Giddens, A., and Lash, S. (1994), *Reflexive Modernization: Politics, Tradition, and Aesthetics in the Modern Social Order*, Stanford, Stanford University Press.

Bell, D. (1960), *The End of Ideology: On the Exhaustion of Political Ideas in the 1950s*, Cambridge, Harvard University Press, 1988, edn with 'Afterword'.

Bello, W. (2013), *Capitalism's Last Stand? Deglobalization in the Age of Austerity*, London, Zed Books.

Benedikter, R. (2013), 'Global Systemic Shift: A Multidimensional Approach to Understanding the Present Phase of Globalization', *New Global Studies*, vol. 7, no. 1, pp. 32–46.

Bentley, J. (1993), *Old World Encounters: Cross-Cultural Contacts and Exchanges in Pre-modern Times*, Oxford, Oxford University Press.

Berger, P. and Huntington, S., eds. (2002), *Many Globalizations: Cultural Diversity in the Contemporary World*, Oxford, Oxford University Press.

Bergesen, A. ed. (1980), *Studies of the Modern World-System*, New York, Academic Press.

Berlet, C. and Lyons, M. (2000), *Right-Wing Populism in America: Too Close for Comfort*, New York, Guilford Press.

Betz, H.-G. (1994), *Radical Right-Wing Populism in Western Europe*, New York, St Martin's Press.

Beyer, P. (1994), *Religion and Globalization*, London, Sage Publications.

Bin Laden, O. (2005), *Messages to the World: The Statements of Osama Bin Laden*, Lawrence, B., ed., London, Verso.

(2007), Untitled transcript of the video-taped message (6 September), www .msnbcmedia.msn.com/i/msnbc/sections/news/070907_bin_laden_tran script.pdf.

Bisley, N. (2007), *Rethinking Globalization*, Houndmills, Palgrave Macmillan.

Bhagwati, J. (2000), *The Wind of the Hundred Days: How Washington Mismanaged Globalization*, Cambridge, MA, MIT Press.

(2007), *In Defense of Globalization*, New York, Oxford University Press.

Blaney, D. L. and Inayatullah, N. (2010), *Savage Economics: Wealth, Poverty and the Temporal Walls of Capitalism*, London, Routledge.

Blaut, J. (1993), *The Colonizer's Model of the World: Geographic Diffusionism and Eurocentric History*, Guilford Press, New York.

Bobbio, N. (1996), *Left & Right: The Significance of a Political Distinction*, Cambridge, Polity Press.

Bonikowski, B. (2017), 'Ethno-nationalist Populism and the Mobilization of Collective Resentment', *British Journal of Sociology*, vol. 68, no. S1, pp. 181–213.

Bourbeau, P. (2018), 'A Genealogy of Resilience', *International Political Sociology*, vol. 12, pp. 19–35.

Bourdieu, P. (1990), *The Logic of Practice*, Cambridge, Polity Press.

(1998), *Acts of Resistance: Against the Tyranny of the Market*, New York, New Press.

(2003), *Firing Back: Against the Tyranny of the Market 2*, London, Verso.

Bourguignon, F. (2015), *The Globalization of Inequality*, Princeton, Princeton University Press.

Boyd, W. (1921), *The History of Western Education*, London, Adam & Charles Black.

Boyd, W. and MacKenzie, M. M., eds. (1930), *Towards a New Education*, London, A. Knopf.

Brecher, M. (1963), 'International Relations and Asian Studies: The Subordinate State System of Southern Asia', *World Politics*, vol. 15, no. 2, pp. 213–35.

Brecher, J., Costello, T., and Smith, B. (2000), *Globalization from Below*, Boston, South End Press.

Bremmer, I. (2018), *Us vs. Them: The Failure of Globalism*, New York, Penguin.

Brenner, N. (1999), 'Globalisation as Reterritorialisation: The Re-scaling of Urban Governance in the European Union', *Urban Studies*, vol. 36, no. 3, pp. 431–51.

——— (2017), *Critique of Urbanism: Selected Essays*, Basel, Birkhauser.

Briggs, A. and Burke P. (2002), *A Social History of the Media: From Gutenberg to the Internet*, Cambridge, Polity Press.

Bronner, S. (2011), *Critical Theory: A Very Short Introduction*, Oxford, Oxford University Press.

Brown, W. (2017), *Undoing the Demos: Neoliberalism's Stealth Revolution*, New York, Zone Books.

Browning, G. (2011), *Global Theory from Kant to Hardt and Negri*, Basingstoke, Palgrave.

Brubaker, R. (2017), 'Why Populism?', *Theory and Society*, vol. 46, pp. 357–85.

Brucan, S. (1975), 'The Systemic Power', *Journal of Peace Research*, vol. 12, no. 1, pp. 63–70.

——— (1984), 'The Global Crisis', *International Studies Quarterly*, vol. 28, no. 1, pp. 97–109.

Bruckner, P. (2010), *The Tyranny of Guilt: An Assault on Western Masochism*, Princeton, Princeton University Press.

Brugmann, J. (2009), *Welcome to the Urban Revolution: How Cities Are Changing the World*, London, Bloomsbury.

Brysk, A., ed. (2002), *Globalization and Human Rights*, Berkeley, University of California Press.

Bude, H. (2018), *The Mood of the World*, Cambridge, Polity Press.

Buszynski, L. (1980), 'Vietnam Confronts China', *Asian Survey*, vol. 20, no. 8, pp. 829–43.

Byung-joon, A. (1980), 'South Korea and the Communist Countries', *Asian Survey*, vol. 20, no. 11, pp. 1,098–107.

C

Campbell, P., MacKinnon, A., and Stevens, C. (2010), *An Introduction to Global Studies*, Hoboken, Wiley-Blackwell.

Cameron, A. and Palan, R. (2004), *The Imagined Economies of Globalization*, London, Sage Publications.

Caillé, A. and Dufoix, S. (2013), *Le Tournant Global des Sciences Sociales*, Paris, La Decouverte.

Camus, J.-Y. and Lebourg, N. (2017), *Far-Right Politics in Europe*, Cambridge, MA, Harvard University Press.

Canclini, N. C. (1995), *Hybrid Cultures: Strategies for Entering and Leaving Modernity*, Minneapolis, University of Minnesota Press.

Carpenter, E. and McLuhan, M., eds. (1960), *Explorations in Communications*, Boston, Beacon Press.

Carver, T. (2004), 'Ideology: The Career of a Concept', in T. Ball and R. Dagger, eds., *Ideals and Ideologies: A Reader*, 5th edn., New York, Pearson-Longman.

Castles, S. (2000), *Ethnicity and Globalization*, London, Sage Publications.

Castells, M. (1996–98), *The Rise of the Network Society*, 3 vols., Cambridge, Blackwell Publishers.

(2000), 'Materials for an Exploratory Theory of the Network Society', *British Journal of Sociology*, vol. 51, no. 1, pp. 5–24.

(2009), *Communication Power*, Oxford, Oxford University Press.

(2010), *The Rise of the Network Society. The Information Age: Economy, Society, and Culture*, 2nd edn., 3 vols., Vol. 1, Malden, Wiley-Blackwell.

(2012), *Networks of Outrage and Hope: Social Movements in the Internet Age*, Cambridge, Polity Press.

(2019), *Rupture: The Crisis of Liberal Democracy*, Cambridge, Polity Press.

Castoriadis, C. (1975), *The Imaginary Institution of Society*, Cambridge, Polity Press.

Cerami, C. (1962), 'The US Eyes Greater Europe', *The Spectator*, 5 October, p. 495.

Chanda, N. (2007), *How Traders, Preachers, Adventurers and Warriors Shaped Globalization*, New Haven, Yale University Press.

Chaplin, J. (2012), *Round about the Earth: Circumnavigation from Magellan to Orbit*, New York, Simon & Schuster.

Chase-Dunn, C. (1989), *Global Formation: Structures of the World Economy*, Oxford, Blackwell Publishers.

Chirico, J. (2014), *Globalization: Prospects and Problems*, Thousand Oaks, Sage Publications.

Chomsky, N. (1999), *Profit over People: Neoliberalism and Global Order*, New York, Seven Stories Press.

Christian, D. (1991), 'The Case for "Big History"', *Journal of World History*, vol. 2, no. 2, pp. 223–38.

Christoff, P. and Eckersley, R. (2013), *Globalization and the Environment*, Lanham, Rowman & Littlefield Publishers.

Chumakov, A. N. (2008), предмете и границах глобалистики ('On Globalistics Subject Matter and Limits'), *Vek globalizatsii*, vol. 1, pp. 7–16. www .socionauki.ru/journal/articles/142634. Accessed 15 October 2018.

Clark, I. (1999), *Globalization and International Relations Theory*, Oxford, Oxford University Press.

Claude, I. L. (1965), 'Implications and Questions for the Future', *International Organization*, vol. 19, no. 3, pp. 835–46.

Cohen, R. (1987), *The New Helots: Migrants in the International Division of Labour*, Aldershot, Gower.

Cohen, R. and Kennedy, P. (2000), *Global Sociology*, Basingstoke, Palgrave Macmillan.

Colebrook, C. (2015), *Death of the PostHuman: Essays on Extinction*, London, Open Humanities Press.

Comaroff J. and Comaroff, J. (2012), 'Theory from the South: Or, How Euro-America Is Evolving toward Africa', *Journal of Social Anthropology and Comparative Sociology*, vol. 22, no. 2, pp. 113–31.

Conceição, S. C. O., Samuel, A., and Biniecki, S. M. Y. (2017), 'Using Concept Mapping as a Tool for Conducting Research: An Analysis of Three Approaches', *Cogent Social Sciences*, no. 3, 1404753. Available at https://doi.org/10.1080/23311886.2017.1404753.

Connolly, W. (2017), *Aspirational Fascism: The Struggle for Multifaceted Democracy under Trumpism*, Minneapolis, University of Minnesota Press.

Conrad, S. (2017), *What Is Global History?* Princeton, Princeton University Press.

Cook, D. (1976), 'Book Review of Harish Kapur, *China in World Politics*', *Pacific Affairs*, vol. 49, no. 4, p. 707.

Cooper, C.A. (1999), 'The Chicago Defender: Filling in the Gaps for the Office of Civilian Defense, 1941–1945', *Western Journal of Black Studies*, vol. 23, no. 2, pp. 111–17.

Cosgrove, D. (1994), 'Contested Global Visions: One-World, Whole-Earth, and the Apollo Space Photographs', *Annals of the Association of American Geographers*, vol. 84, no. 2, pp. 270–94.

(2001), *Apollo's Eye: A Geographic Genealogy of the Earth in the Western Imagination*, Baltimore, Johns Hopkins University Press.

(2003), 'Globalism and Tolerance in Early Modern Geography', *Annals of the Association of American Geographers*, vol. 93, no. 4, pp. 852–70.

Cox, R. (1996), *Approaches to World Order*, Cambridge, Cambridge University Press.

Crouch, C. (2011), *The Strange Non-death of Neoliberalism*, Cambridge, Polity Press.

(2019), *The Globalization Backlash*, Cambridge, Polity Press.

Crum, R. (2011), *Globish: How English Became the World's Language*, New York, Norton.

Crutzen, P. J. and Stoermer, E. F. (2000), 'The "Anthropocene"', *Global Change Newsletter*, vol. 41, no. 17, pp. 17–18.

Curtis, N. (2009), 'Restraining Evil: Apocalyptic Narcissism and the War on Terror', *Arena Journal*, no. 32 (new series), pp. 153–75.

D

Darian-Smith, E. (2015), 'Global Studies: The Handmaiden of Neoliberalism?', *Globalizations*, vol. 12, no. 2, pp. 164–8.

Darian-Smith, E. and McCarty, P. (2017), *The Global Turn*, Berkeley, University of California Press.

Davis, M. (2006), *A Planet of Slums*, London, Verso.

Decroly, J. O. (1929), *La Fonction de Globalisation et l'Enseignement*, Brussels, Lamertin.

Delanty, G. (2009), *The Cosmopolitan Imagination*, Cambridge, Cambridge University Press.

Della Porta, D. and Tarrow, S. eds. (2004), *Transnational Protest and Global Activism*, Lanham, Rowman & Littlefield Publishers.

Della Porta, D., Andretta, M., Mosca, L., and Reiter, H., eds. (2006), *Globalization from Below: Transnational Activist and Protest Networks*, Minneapolis, University of Minnesota Press.

De la Torre, C., ed. (2015), *The Promise and Perils of Populism: Global Perspectives*, Lexington, University of Kentucky Press.

Deleuze, G. and Guattari, F. (1987), *Thousand Plateaus: Capitalism and Schizophrenia*, Minneapolis, University of Minnesota Press.

Deneen, P. (2018), *The Failure of Liberalism*, New Haven, Yale University Press.

D'Eramo, M. (2013), 'Populism and the New Oligarchy', *New Left Review*, vol. 82, pp. 5–28.

De Sousa Santos, B. (2014), *Epistemologies of the South: Justice against Epistemicide*, Boulder, Paradigm Publishers.

Diamond, J. (1997), *Guns, Germs, and Steel: The Fates of Human Societies*, London, Vintage.

Dicken, P. (1992), *Global Shift: The Internationalization of Economic Activity*, 2nd edn., New York, Guilford Press.

(2004), 'Geographers and "Globalization": (Yet) Another Missed Boat?', *Transactions of the Institute of British Geographers*, vol. 29, no. 1, pp. 5–26.

(2015), *Global Shift: Mapping the Changing Contours of the World Economy*, 7th edn., London, Sage Publications.

Diouf, M. (2002), 'The Senegalese Murid Trade Diaspora and the Making of a Vernacular Cosmopolitanism', in C. A. Breckenridge, S. Pollock, H. K. Bhabha, and D. Chakrabarty, eds., *Cosmopolitanism*, Durham, Duke University Press.

Douglass, M. (2000), 'Mega-urban Regions and World City Formation: Globalisation, the Economic Crisis, and Urban Policy Issues in Pacific Asia', *Urban Studies*, vol. 37, no. 12, pp. 2,315–35.

Drucker, P. (1969), *The Age of Discontinuity: Guidelines to Our Changing Society*, London, Heinemann.

Dufoix, S. (2012) *La Dispersion: Une Histoire des Usages du Mot Diaspora*, Paris, Éditions Amsterdam.

(2013a), 'Penser la globalisation', Sciences Humaines, www.scienceshumaines.com/penser-la-globalisation_fr_30697.html. Accessed 13 September 2018.

(2013b), 'Between Scylla and Charybdis: French Social Science Faces Globalization', unpublished manuscript.

Durante, T. (2018), 'Visual Ideology and Social Imaginary: A New Approach to the Aesthetics of Globalization', *Spaces and Flows*, vol. 9, no. 1, pp. 15–34.

E

Eagleton, T. (1991), *Ideology: An Introduction*, London, Verso.

Eatwell, R. and Goodwin, M. (2019), *National Populism: The Revolt against Liberal Democracy*, London, Penguin Random House.

Economist (2011), 'Welcome to the Anthropocene', *The Economist*, 26 May, www.economist.com/leaders/2011/05/26/welcome-to-the-anthropocene. Accessed 16 November 2018.

Edelman, M. (1964), *The Symbolic Uses of Politics*, Chicago, University of Illinois Press.

(1988), *Constructing the Political Spectacle*, Chicago, University of Chicago Press.

Eichengreen, B. (2018), *The Populist Temptation: Economic Grievance and Political Reaction in the Modern Era*, New York, Oxford University Press.

Eisenstadt, S. N. (2003), *Comparative Civilizations and Multiple Modernities*, 2 vols., Leiden and Boston, Brill.

Elliott, A. and Lemert, C. (2006), *The New Individualism: The Emotional Costs of Globalization*, London, Routledge.

El-Ojeili, C. and Hayden, P. (2006), *Critical Theories of Globalization*, Basingstoke, Palgrave Macmillan.

Epstein, G. A. (2005), *Financialization and the World Economy*, Cheltenham, Edward Elgar.

Eriksen, T. H. (2014), *Globalization: The Key Concepts*, 2nd edn., London, Bloomsbury.

Erskine, T. (2008), *Embedded Cosmopolitanism: Duties to Strangers and Enemies in a World of 'Dislocated Communities'*, Cambridge, Cambridge University Press.

Etzioni, A. (2004), 'The Emerging Global Normative Synthesis', *Journal of Political Philosophy*, vol. 12, no. 2, pp. 214–44.

F

Falk, R. (1999), *Predatory Globalization: A Critique*, Cambridge, Polity Press.

Farnsworth, C. H. (1981), 'Outlook: Toughening Attitudes on World Trade', *New York Times*, 8 February. www.nytimes.com/1981/02/08/world/outlook-toughening-attitudes-on-world-trade.html. Accessed 4 October 2018.

Featherstone, M., ed. (1990), *Global Culture: Nationalism, Globalization and Modernity*, London, Sage Publications.

Featherstone, M, Lash, S., and Robertson, R., eds. (1996), *Global Modernities*, London, Sage Publications.

Ferguson, N. and Zakaria, F. (2017), *Is This the End of the Liberal International Order?* Toronto, House of Anansi Press.

Finchelstein, F. (2017), *From Fascism to Populism in History*, Berkeley, University of California Press.

Fish, S. (1980), *Is There a Text in This Class? The Authority of Interpretative Communities*, Cambridge, MA, Harvard University Press.

Fisher, M. S. and Downey, G. (2006), *Frontiers of Capital: Ethnographic Reflections on the New Economy*, Durham, Duke University Press.

Forgacs, D. (1984), 'National-Popular: Genealogy of a Concept', in *Formations: Of Nation and People*, London, Routledge.

Foucault, M. (1991a), 'Politics and the Study of Discourse', in G. Burchell, C. Gordon, and P. Miller, eds., *The Foucault Effect: Studies in Governmentality*, Chicago, University of Chicago Press.

Foucault, M. (1991b), 'Governmentality', in G. Burchell, C. Gordon, and P. Miller, eds., *The Foucault Effect: Studies in Governmentality*, Chicago, University of Chicago Press.

(1998), *Aesthetics, Methods, and Epistemology: Essential Works of Foucault, 1954–1984*, New York, New Press.

270   Bibliography

(2010), *The Birth of Biopolitics: Lectures at the College de France, 1978–1979*, New York, Picador.

Frank, A. G. and Gills, B. K., eds. (1993), *The World System: Five Hundred Years of Five Thousand?* London, Routledge.

Frank, T. (2000), *One Market under God*, New York, Anchor.

Freeden, M. (1996), *Ideologies and Political Theory: A Conceptual Approach*, Oxford, Oxford University Press.

(2003), *Ideology: A Very Short Introduction*, Oxford, Oxford University Press.

Freeman, M. (1998), 'Theories of ethnicity, tribalism and nationalism', in K. Christie, ed., *Ethnic Conflict, Tribal Politics: A Global Perspective*, Richmond, Curzon Press.

Friedman, J. (1994), *Cultural Identity and Global Process*, London, Sage Publications.

Friedman, T. (1999), *The Lexus and the Olive Tree: Understanding Globalization*, New York, Farrar, Straus and Giroux.

(2005), *The World Is Flat: A Brief History of the Twenty-First Century*, New York, Farrar, Straus and Giroux.

(2007), *The World Is Flat 3.0: A Brief History of the Twenty-First Century*, New York, Picador.

Friedmann, J. (1986), 'The World City Hypothesis', *Development and Change*, vol. 17, no. 1, pp. 69–83.

Fry, T. (2012), *Becoming Human by Design*, London, Berg.

Fukuyama, F. (1989), 'The End of History?', *The National Interest*, vol. 16, pp. 3–18.

(1992), *The End of History and the Last Man*, New York, Free Press.

(1995), *Trust*, London, Hamish Hamilton.

G

Gallie, W. (1955), 'Essentially Contested Concepts', *Proceedings of the Aristotelian Society*, vol. 56, pp. 167–98.

(1964), *Philosophy and the Historical Understanding*, London, Chatto & Windus.

Gallie, W. (1964), *Philosophy and the Historical Understanding*, New York, Schocken Books.

Galston, W. (2018), *Anti-Pluralism: The Populist Treat to Liberal Democracy*, New Haven, Yale University Press.

Garrett, S. (1976), 'Nixonian Foreign Policy: A New Balance of Power, or a Revived Conflict?' *Polity*, vol. 8, no. 3, pp. 389–421.

Gates, B. (1999), *Business @ the Speed of Thought*, New York, Warner.

Geertz, C. (1964), 'A Study of National Character,' *Economic Development and Cultural change*, vol. 12, no. 2, pp. 205–9.

Gellner, E. (1983), *Nations and Nationalism*, Cambridge, Basil Blackwell.

George, S. (2004), *Another World Is Possible If . . .*, London, Verso.

Gerbaudo, P. (2017), *The Mask and the Flag*, Cambridge, Cambridge University Press.

Ghemawat, P. (2017), *The Laws of Globalization*, Cambridge, Cambridge University Press.

Gibson, K., Rose, D. B., and Fincher, R., eds. (2015), *Manifesto for Living in the Anthropocene*, New York, Punctum Books.

Giddens, A. (1985), *A Contemporary Critique of Historical Materialism, Vol. 2: The Nation-State and Violence*, Cambridge, Polity Press.

(1990), *The Consequences of Modernity*, Cambridge, Polity Press.

(1999; 2002), *Runaway World: How Globalisation Is Reshaping Our Lives*, London, Profile Books.

(2009), *The Politics of Climate Change*, Cambridge, Polity Press.

Gilpin, R. (2000), *The Challenge of Global Capitalism: The World Economy in the 21st Century*, Princeton, Princeton University Press.

Gill, G. 2002. 'Landscape as Symbolic Form: Remembering Thick Place in Deep Time', *Critical Horizons*, vol. 3, no. 2, pp. 177–99.

Gills, B., ed. (2000), *Globalization and the Politics of Resistance*, New York, St Martin's Press.

Glaeser, E. (2011), *Triumph of the City: How Our Greatest Invention Makes Us Richer, Smarter, Greener, Healthier, and Happier*, Harmondsworth, Penguin.

Goodhart, D. (2017), *The Road to Somewhere: The Populist Revolt and the Future of Politics*, London, C. Hurst and Co.

Goody, J. (1986), *The Logic of Writing and the Organization of Society*, Cambridge, Cambridge University Press.

Gordon, D. M. (1988), 'The Global Economy: New Edifice or Crumbling Foundations?', *New Left Review*, vol. 188, pp. 24–68.

Gowan, P. (1999), *The Global Gamble*. London, Verso.

Ghosh, B. (2011), *Global Icons: Apertures to the Popular*, Durham, Duke University Press.

Graber, D. (1976), *Verbal Behaviour and Politics*, Chicago, University of Illinois Press.

Gramsci, A. (1971), *Selections from the Prison Notebooks*, Q. Hoare and G. N. Smith, eds. and trans., New York, International Publishers.

Grattan, L. (2016), *Populism's Power: Radical Grassroots Democracy in America*, New York, Oxford University Press.

Gray, J. (1996), *After Social Democracy: Politics, Capitalism, and the Common Life*, London, Demos.

(1998), *False Dawn: The Delusions of Global Capitalism*, New York, New Press.

Grosfoguel, R. (2005), 'The Implications of Subaltern Epistemologies for Global Capitalism: Transmodernity, Border Thinking, and Global Coloniality,' in R. P. Appelbaum and W. I. Robinson, eds., *Critical Globalization Studies*, New York, Routledge.

Guéhenno, J.-M. (1995), *The End of the Nation-State*, Minneapolis, University of Minnesota Press.

Gunn, G. (2018), *Global Studies: A Historical and Contemporary Reader*, 2nd edn., Dubuque, Kendall Hunt Publishing.

H

Habermas, J. (1971), *Knowledge and Human Interests*, Boston, Beacon Press.

(1990), *The Philosophical Discourse of Modernity: Twelve Lectures*, Cambridge, MA, MIT Press.

Haight, R. (1982), 'Review of Charles McCoy, When Gods Change: Hope for Theology', *Journal of Religion*, vol. 62, no. 4, pp. 435–8.

Hannerz, U. (1992), *Cultural Complexity*. New York, Columbia University Press.

(1996), *Transnational Connection: Culture, People, Places*, London, Routledge.

Haraway, D. J. (1997), *Modest_Witness@Second_Millennium*, Routledge, New York.

Hardt, M. and Negri, A. (2000) *Empire*, Cambridge, MA, Harvard University Press.

(2005), *Multitude*, London, Hamish Hamilton.

Harper, L. C. (1944), 'He Is Rich in the Spirit of Spreading Hatred', *Chicago Defender*, 15 January, pp. 1–4.

Harvey, D. (1989), *The Condition of Postmodernity: An Enquiry into Origins of Cultural Change*, London, Basil Blackwell.

(1995), 'Globalization in Question', *Rethinking Marxism*, vol. 8, no. 4, pp. 1–17.

(2003), *The New Imperialism*, Oxford, Oxford University Press.

(2005), *A Brief History of Neoliberalism*, Oxford, Oxford University Press.

(2013), *Rebel Cities: From the Right to the City to the Urban Revolution*, London, Verso.

Hawkins, K. (2010), *Venezuela's Charismo and Populism in Comparative Perspective*, Cambridge, Cambridge University Press.

Hay, C. and Marsh, D., eds. (2000), *Demystifying Globalization*, Basingstoke, Palgrave.

Healey, D. (1961), 'The Crisis in Europe', *International Affairs*, vol. 38, no. 2, pp. 145–55.

Hedetoft, U. and Hjort, M. (2002), *The Postnational Self: Belonging and Identity*, Minneapolis, University of Minnesota Press.

Heidegger, M. (1977), *The Question Concerning Technology*, New York, Harper & Rowe.

Held, D. (1995), *Democracy and the Global Order: From the Modern State to Cosmopolitan Governance*, Stanford, Stanford University Press.

(2004), *Global Covenant: The Social Democratic Alternative to the Washington Consensus*, Cambridge, Polity Press.

Held, D. and McGrew, A. (2007), *Globalization Theory: Approaches and Controversies*, Cambridge, Polity Press.

Held, D., McGrew, A., Goldblatt, D., and Perraton, J. (1999), *Global Transformations*, Cambridge, Polity Press.

Helleiner, E. (1994), *States and the Reemergence of Global Finance*. Ithaca, Cornell University Press.

Helpman, E. (2018), *Globalization and Inequality*, Cambridge, MA, Harvard University Press.

Herndon, B. P. (1995), *A Methodology for the Parallelization of PDE Solvers: Application to Semiconductor Device Physics*, PhD dissertation, Stanford, Stanford University.

Hersh, J. and Brun, E. (2000) 'Globalisation and the Communist Manifesto', *Economic and Political Weekly*, vol. 35, no. 3, pp. 105–8.

Hiller, H. H. (1979), 'Universality of Science and the Question of National Sociologies', *The American Sociologist*, vol. 14, no. 3, pp. 124–35.

Hilferding, R. (2010), *Das Finanzkapital: Eine Studie zur jüngsten Entwicklung des Kapitalismus*, Vienna, Verlag der Wiener Volksbuchhandlung Ignaz Brand & Co.

Hingley, R. (2005), *Globalizing Roman Culture: Unity, Diversity and Empire*, Abingdon, Routledge.

(2006), 'Projecting Empire: The Mapping of Roman Britain', *Journal of Social Archaeology*, vol. 6, no. 3, pp. 328–53.

Hinkson, J. (1982) 'Beyond Imagination: Responding to Nuclear War', *Arena*, no. 60 (first series), pp. 45–71.

(1993), 'Postmodern Economy: Value, Self-formation and Intellectual Practice', *Arena Journal*, new series no. 1, pp. 23–44.

Hirst, P. and Thompson, G. (1996), *Globalization in Question*, Cambridge, Polity Press.

Hochschild, A. (2017), *Strangers in Their Own Land: Anger and Morning on the American Right*, New York, New Press.

Hollands, R. G. (2015), 'Critical Interventions into the Corporate Smart City', *Cambridge Journal of Regions, Economy and Society*, vol. 8, no. 1, pp. 61–77.

Holton, R. (1998), *Globalization and the Nation-State*, Houndmills, Palgrave Macmillan.

(2008), *Global Networks*, Houndmills, Palgrave Macmillan.

Hoogvelt, A. (2001), *Globalization and the Postcolonial World: The New Political Economy of Development*, Baltimore, Johns Hopkins University Press.

Hopkins, A. G., ed. (2002) *Globalization in World History*, New York, W.W. Norton.

ed. (2006), *Global History: Interactions between the Universal and the Local*, London, Macmillan.

(2018), *American Empire: A Global History*, Princeton, Princeton University Press.

Hurrell, A., and Woods, N., eds. (1999), *Inequality, Globalization, and World Politics*. Oxford, Oxford University Press.

I

Inglehart, R. (2018), *Cultural Evolution: People's Motivations Are Changing and Reshaping the World*, Cambridge, Cambridge University Press.

Inglis, D. and Robertson, R. (2005), 'The Ecumenical Analytic 'Globalization', Reflexivity and the Revolution in Greek Historiography', *European Journal of Social Theory*, vol. 8, no. 2, pp. 99–122.

(2006), 'From Republican Virtue to Global Imaginary: Changing Visions of the Historian Polybius', *History of the Human Sciences*, vol. 19, no. 1, pp. 1–18.

Intergovernmental Panel on Climate Change (2018), *Global Warming of 1.5°C*, www.ipcc.ch/report/sr15. Accessed 18 October 2018.

Iriye, A. (2012), *Global and Transnational History: The Past, Present, and Future*, New York, Palgrave.

J

Jacob, C. (1999), 'Mapping in the Mind: The Earth from Ancient Alexandria', in D. Cosgrove, ed., *Mappings*, London, Reaktion Books.

Jacobs, J. M. (1961), *The Death and Life of Great American Cities*, New York, Random House.

Jäger, A. (2016), 'The Semantic Drift: Images of Populism in Post-war American Historiography and Their Relevance for (European) Political Science', *Populismus Working Papers*, no. 3, pp. 1–25.

James, H. (2001), *The End of Globalisation: Lessons from the Great Depression*, Cambridge, MA, Harvard University Press.

James, P. (1984), 'The Nation and Its Post-modern Critics', *Arena*, no. 69 (first series), pp. 159–74.

   (2006), *Globalism, Nationalism, Tribalism: Bringing Theory Back In*, London, Sage Publications.

   (2010), 'Arguing Globalizations: Propositions towards an Investigation of Global Formation', in M. B. Steger, ed., *Globalization: The Greatest Hits*, Boulder, Paradigm Publishers.

   (2012), 'Globalization, Approaches to', in H. Anheier and M. Juergensmeyer, eds., *Encyclopedia of Global Studies*, 4 vols., Thousand Oaks, Sage Publications.

   (2015), *Urban Sustainability in Theory and Practice: Circles of Sustainability*, London and New York, Routledge.

   (2018), 'What Does It Mean Ontologically to Be Religious?', *Arena Journal*, no 49/50, pp. 56–100.

James, P. and Steger, M. B. (2014), 'A Genealogy of Globalization: The Career of a Concept', *Globalizations*, vol. 11, no. 4, pp. 417–34.

   (2016), 'Globalization and Global Consciousness: Levels of Connectivity', in R. Robertson and D. Buhari, eds., *Global Culture: Consciousness and Connectivity*, Farnham, Ashgate.

James, P. et al., eds. (2006–14), 'Central Currents in Globalization' series, comprising.

   Globalization and Violence, Vol. 1–4, London, Sage Publications, 2006; *Globalization and Economy, Vol. 1–4*, London, Sage Publications, 2007; *Globalization and Culture, Vol. 1–4*, London, Sage Publications, 2010; and *Globalization and Politics, Vol. 1–4*, London, Sage Publications, 2014.

Jameson, F. (1991), *Postmodernism or, the Cultural Logic of Late Capitalism*, London, Verso.

Jameson, F. and Miyoshi, M., eds. (1998), *The Cultures of Globalization*, Durham, Duke University Press.

Jansen, R. (2015), 'Populist Mobilization: A New Theoretical Approach to Populism', in De la Torre, C., ed., *The Promise and Perils of Populism: Global Perspectives*, Lexington, University of Kentucky Press.

Jones, A. (2006), *Dictionary of Globalization*, Cambridge, Polity Press.

   (2010), *Globalization: Key Thinkers*, Cambridge, Polity Press.

Jorgenson A. and Kick, E., eds. (2006), *Globalization and the Environment*, Leiden, Brill.

Judis, J. (2016), *The Populist Explosion: How the Great Recession Transformed American and European Politics*, New York, Columbia Global Reports.

(2018), *The Nationalist Revival: Trade, Immigration, and the Revolt against Globalization*, New York, Columbia Global Reports.

Juergensmeyer, M. (2000), *Terror in the Mind of God: The Global Rise of Religious Violence*, Berkeley, University of California Press.

(2008), *Global Rebellion: Religious Challenges to the Secular State, From Christian Militias to Al Qaeda*, Berkeley, University of California Press.

(2011), 'What Is Global Studies?', *Global-e Journal*, www.21global.ucsb.edu/global-e/may-2011/what-global-studies. Accessed 23 March 2018.

(2013), 'What Is Global Studies?', *Globalizations*, vol. 10, no. 6, pp. 765–9.

ed. (2014), *Thinking Globally: A Global Studies Reader*, Berkeley, University of California Press.

Juergensmeyer, M., Griego, D., and Soboslai, J. (2015), *God in the Tumult of the Global Square: Religion in Global Civil Society*, Berkeley, University of California Press.

Juergensmeyer, M., Steger, M., and Sassen, S., eds. (2019), *The Oxford Handbook of Global Studies*, Oxford, Oxford University Press.

Jones, A. (2006), *Dictionary of Globalization*, Cambridge, Polity Press.

K

Kaldor, M. (2003), *Global Civil Society: An Answer to War*, Cambridge, Polity Press.

Kamola, I. (2014), 'US Universities and the Production of the Global Imaginary', *British Journal of Politics and International Relations*, vol. 16, no. 3, pp. 515–33.

Kaufer, D. S. and Carley, K. (1993), 'Condensation Symbols', *Philosophy and Rhetoric*, vol. 26, no. 3, pp. 201–26.

Kazin, M. (1995), *The Populist Persuasion: An American History*, New York, Basic Books.

Keane, J. (2003), *Global Civil Society?* Cambridge, Cambridge University Press.

Kennedy, M. (2015), *Globalizing Knowledge: Intellectuals, Universities, and Publics in Transformation*, Stanford, Stanford University Press.

Kenway, J. and Fahey, J. (2009), *Globalizing the Research Imagination*, London and New York, Routledge.

Keohane, R. (1984), *After Hegemony*, Princeton, Princeton University Press.

Keohane, R. and Nye, J. (1977; 2000), *Power and Interdependence: World Politics in Transition*, Boston, Little Brown.

Kerr, C. (1979), 'Education for Global Perspectives', *Annals of the American Academy of Political and Social Science*, vol. 442, pp. 109–16.

Kesting, H. (1959), *Geschichtsphilosophie und Weltbürgerkrieg*, Heidelberg, Karl Winter.

Keucheyan, R. (2013), *The Left Hemisphere: Mapping Critical Theory Today*, London, Verso.

Khondker, H. H. (2013), 'Globalization, Glocalization, or Global Studies: What's in a Name?', *Globalizations*, vol. 10, no. 4, pp. 527–31.

Kiewiet, C. W. (1953), 'Let's Globalize Our Universities', *Saturday Review*, 12 September, pp. 13, 70.

King, A. D. (1991), *Global Cities*, London, Routledge.

King. S. (2017), *Grave New World: The End of Globalization and the Return of History*, New Haven, Yale University Press.

KOF Globalization Index (2018), ETH Zürich. www.kof.ethz.ch/en/forecasts-and-indicators/indicators/kof-globalisation-index.html. Accessed 2 January 2019.

Kofman, E. and Youngs, G., eds. (1996), *Globalization: Theory and Practice*, London, Pinter.

Kolodziej, E. (1971), 'Revolt and Revisionism in the Gaullist Global Vision: An Analysis of French Strategic Policy', *Journal of Politics*, vol. 33, no. 2, pp. 448–77.

Koselleck, R. (2002), *The Practice of Conceptual History: Timing History, Spacing Concepts*, Stanford, Stanford University Press.

(2004), *Futures Past: On the Semantics of Historical Time*, New York, Columbia University Press.

Kotz, D. (2015), *The Rise and Fall of Neoliberal Capitalism*, Cambridge, Harvard University Press.

Krämer, B. (2014), 'Media Populism: A Conceptual Clarification and Some Theses on Its Effects', *Communication Theory*, vol. 24, pp. 42–60.

Kriesi, H. and Pappas, T., eds. (2015), *European Populism in the Shadow of the Great Recession*, Colchester, ECPR Press.

Krishna, S. (2009), *Globalization and Postcolonialism: Hegemony and Resistance in the Twenty-First Century*, Lanham, Rowman & Littlefield Publishers.

Krishnan, A. (2009), *What Are Academic Disciplines? Some Observations on the Disciplinarity vs. Interdisciplinarity Debate*, Southampton, University of Southampton National Centre for Research Methods.

Krücken, G. and Drori, G., eds. (2009), *World Society: The Writings of John W. Meyer*, New York, Oxford University Press.

Krugman, P. (2003), *The Great Unravelling: Losing Our Way in the New Century*, New York, W.W. Norton.

Kruse, A. H. (1969), *Souslinoid Analytic Sets in a General Setting*, Providence, American Mathematical Society.

L

Lacan, J. (1949), 'The Mirror Stage as Formative of the Function of the I as Revealed in Psychoanalytic Experience', lecture delivered at the 16th International Congress of Psychoanalysis, Zurich, 17 July.

Laclau, E. (2005), 'Populism: What's in a Name?', in F. Panizza, ed., *Populism and the Mirror of Democracy*, London, Verso.

Laing, R. D. (1965), *The Divided Self: An Existential Study in Sanity and Madness*, London, Penguin.

Lamont, M., Park, B. Y., and Ayala-Hurtado, E. (2017), 'Trump's Electoral Speeches and His Appeal to the American White Working Class', *British Journal of Sociology*, vol. 68, no. S1, pp. S153–80.

Lamy, P. (1976), 'The Globalization of American Sociology: Excellence or Imperialism?', *American Sociologist*, vol. 11, no. 2, pp. 104–14.

Langhorne, R. (2001), *The Coming of Globalization: Its Evolutionary and Contemporary Consequences*, Basingstoke, Palgrave.

Lash, S., and Urry, J. (1987), *The End of Organized Capitalism*, Polity Press, Cambridge.

Lash, S. and Friedman, J., eds. (1992), *Modernity and Identity*, Oxford, Blackwell.

Lasswell, H. (1958), *Politics: Who Gets What, When, How*, New York, Meridian Books.

Latouche, S. (1996), *The Westernization of the World*, Cambridge, Polity Press.

Latour, B. (2010), 'Networks, Societies, Spheres: Reflections of an Actor Network Theorist'. Keynote speech for the International Seminar on Network Theory: Network Multidimensionality in the Digital Age. www.bruno-latour.fr/sites/default/files/121-CASTELLS-GB.pdf. Accessed 9 July 2018.

(2017), *Facing Gaia: Eight Lectures on the New Climatic Regime*, Cambridge, Polity Press.

(2018), *Down to Earth: Politics in the New Climatic Regime*, Cambridge, Polity Press.

Lawrence, B., ed. (2005), 'Introduction', in O. Bin Laden, *Messages to the World: The Statements of Osama Bin Laden*, London, Verso.

Lechner, F., and Boli, J., eds. (2000), *The Globalization Reader*, Oxford, Blackwell.

Lefebvre, H. (1971), *La Révolution Urbaine*, Paris, Editions Gallimard.

Lefort, C. (1986), *The Political Forms of Modern Society*, Cambridge, Polity Press.

Le Pen, M. (2013), cited in 'Dédiabolisation', *The Economist*, 12 October. www.economist.com/europe/2013/10/12/dediabolisation. Accessed 23 June 2018.

Levison, M. (2006), *The Box: How the Shipping Container Made the World Smaller and the World Economy Bigger*, Princeton, Princeton University Press.

Levitt, T. (1983), 'The Globalization of Markets', *Harvard Business Review*, vol. 61, no. 3, pp. 92–102.

Linklater, A. (2010), 'Global Civilizing Processes and the Ambiguity of Human Interconnectedness', *European Journal of International Relations*, vol., 16, no. 2, pp. 155–78.

Lindblom, C. and Zúquete, J. P. (2010), *The Struggle for the World: Liberation Movements for the 21st Century*, Stanford, Stanford University Press.

Livesey, F. (2017), *From Global to Local: The Making of Things and the End of Globalization*, New York, Pantheon.

Lloyd, G. E. R. (2012), *Being, Humanity, and Understanding: Studies in Ancient and Modern Societies*, Oxford University Press, Oxford.

Luce, E. (2017), *The Retreat of Western Liberalism*, New York, Atlantic Monthly Press.

Luttwak, E. (1999), *Turbo-Capitalism*, New York, HarperCollins.

Lynch, K. (2003), *The Forces of Economic Globalization: Challenge to the Regimes of International Commercial Arbitration*, The Hague, Kluwer Law International.

Lyotard, J.-F. (1979), *The Postmodern Condition: A Report on Knowledge*, Minneapolis, University of Minnesota Press.

M

McCarty, P. (2014), 'Globalizing Legal History', *Rechtsgeschichte/Legal History*, vol. 22, pp. 283–91.

McCluhan, M. (1994), *Understanding the Media: The Extensions of Man*, Cambridge, MA, MIT Press.

McCoy, C. S. (1980), *When Gods Change: Hope for Theology*, Nashville, Abingdon Press.

McCrum, R. (2010), *Globish: How the English Language Became the World's Language*, New York, Norton.

McFarlane, R. and Bleyzer, M. (2003), 'Taking Iraq Private', *Wall Street Journal*, 27 March.

McKinsey Global Institute (2018), 'Digital Globalization: The New Era of Global Flows'. www.mckinsey.com/business-functions/digital-mckinsey/our-insights /digital-globalization-the-new-era-of-global-flows. Accessed 2 October 2018.

McLaughlin, E. (2016), 'Two Years of US-Led Airstrikes in ISIS in Syria and Iraq in Numbers', 8 August. https://abcnews.go.com/International/years-us-led-airstrikes-isis-syria-iraq-show/story?id=41206050. Accessed 19 June 2018.

McLuhan, M. (1964), *Understanding the Media*, New York, McGraw-Hill.

McNeill, J. R. and Engelke, P. (2014) *The Great Acceleration: An Environmental History of the Anthropocene since 1945*, Cambridge, MA, Harvard University Press.

McNeill, W. H. (2008), 'Globalization: Long Term Process or New Era in Human Affairs?', *New Global Studies*, vol. 2. no. 1, doi:10.2202/1940-0004.1015.

Mamdani, M. (1996), *Citizen and Subject: Contemporary Africa and the Legacy of Late Colonialism*, Princeton, Princeton University Press.

Mandelbaum, M. (2002), *The Ideas That Conquered the World: Peace, Democracy and Free Markets in the Twenty-First Century*, Washington, DC, PublicAffairs.

Mann, M. (1986), *The Sources of Social Power, Vol. 1: A History of Power from the Beginning to A.D. 1760*, Cambridge, Cambridge University Press.

 (1997), 'Has Globalization Ended the Rise of the Nation-State?', *Review of International Political Economy*, vol. 4, no. 3, pp. 472–96.

Marsh, G. P. (1874), *The Earth as Modified by Human Action*, 2nd edn., New York, Scribner Armstrong and Company.

Marshall, A. (2016), *Ectopia 2121: A Vision for Our Future Green Utopia—In 100 Cities*, New York, Arcade Publishing.

Martell, L. (2007), 'The Third Wave in Globalization Theory', *International Studies Review*, vol. 9, pp. 173–96.

Martens, P., Caselli, M., De Lombaerde, P., Figge, L., and Scholte, J. A. (2015), 'New Directions in Globalization Indices', *Globalizations*, vol. 12, no. 2, pp. 217–28.

Martinelli, A. (2018), 'National Populism and the European Union', *Populism*, vol. 1, pp. 38–58.

Maranhao, T. and Streck, B., eds. (2003), *Translation and Ethnography: The Anthropological Challenge of Intercultural Understanding*, Tucson, University of Arizona Press.

Marx, K. and Engels, F. (1848), *The Communist Manifesto*, London, Lawrence & Wishart, centenary edn., 1948.

Mathisen, T. (1959), *Methodology in the Study of International Relations*, Westport, Greenwood.

Mazlish, B. (2006), *The New Global History*, New York, Routledge.

Mazrui, A. (1977), 'Boxer Muhammad Ali and Soldier Idi Amin as International Political Symbols: The Bioeconomics of Sports and War', *Comparative Studies in Society and History*, vol. 19, no. 2, pp. 189–215.

Meadows, P. (1951), 'Culture and Industrial Analysis', *Annals of the American Academy of Political and Social Science*, vol. 274, pp. 9–16.

Mecklin, J., ed. (2018), 'It Is 2 Minutes to Midnight: The 2018 Doomsday Clock Statement', *Bulletin of the Atomic Scientists*, pp. 3–8.

Mény, Y. and Surel, Y., eds. (2002), *Democracies and the Populist Challenges*, Basingstoke, Palgrave Macmillan.

Merrifield, A. (2013), 'The Urban Question under Planetary Urbanization', *International Journal of Urban and Regional Research*, vol. 37, no. 3, pp. 909–22.

Merton, R. (1949), *Social Theory and Social Structure*, New York, Free Press.

Metzinger, T. (2010), *The Ego Tunnel: The Science of the Mind and the Myth of the Self*, New York, Basic Books.

Meyer, J. (2000), 'Globalization: Sources and Effects on National States and Societies', *International Society*, vol. 15, pp. 235–50.

(2007), 'Globalization: Theory and Trends', *International Journal of Comparative Sociology*, vol. 48, no. 4, pp. 261–73.

Michel, J. B. et al. (2011), 'Quantitative Analysis of Culture Using Millions of Digitized Books', *Science*, vol. 331, no. 6,014, pp. 176–82.

Micklethwait, J. and Woolridge, A. (2000), *A Future Perfect: The Challenge and Promise of Globalization*, New York, Random House.

Mignolo, W. D. (2000), *Local Histories/Global Designs: Coloniality, Subaltern Knowledges and Border Thinking*, Princeton, Princeton University Press.

(2002), 'The Many Faces of Cosmo-polis: Border Thinking and Critical Cosmopolitanism', in C. A. Breckenridge, S. Pollock, H. K. Bhabha, and D. Chakrabarty, eds., *Cosmopolitanism*, Durham, Duke University Press.

Mignolo, W. D. and Schiwy, F. (2003), 'Transculturation and the Colonial Difference: Double Translation', in T. Maranhao, and B. Streck, eds., *Translation and Ethnography: The Anthropological Challenge of Intercultural Understanding*, Tucson, University of Arizona Press, pp. 12–34.

Milanović, B. (1999), *True World Income Distribution, 1988–1993: First Calculations Based on Household Surveys Alone*, Washington, DC, World Bank.

(2013), 'Global Inequality by Numbers: In History and Now: An Overview', The Heyman Center, http://heymancenter.org/files/events/milanovic.pdf. Accessed 23 May 2018.

(2016), *Global Inequality: A New Approach for the Age of Globalization*, Cambridge, MA, Belknap Press.

Mills, C. W. (1956), *The Power Elite*, Oxford, Oxford University Press.

Mittelman, J. H., ed. (1996), *Globalization: Critical Reflections*, Boulder, Lynne Rienner.

(2000), *The Globalization Syndrome*, Princeton, Princeton University Press.

(2004), *Whither Globalization? The Vortex of Knowledge and Ideology*, London, Routledge.

(2017), *Implausible Dream: The World-Class University and Repurposing Higher Education*, Princeton, Princeton University Press.

Mishra, P. (2017), *The Age of Anger: A History of the Present*, London, Penguin.

Moaddel, M. and Talattof, K., eds. (2002), *Modernist and Fundamentalist Debates in Islam*, New York, Palgrave Macmillan.

Modelski, G. (1968), 'Communism and the Globalization of Politics', *International Studies Quarterly*, vol. 12, no. 4, pp. 380–93.

(1972), 'Multinational Business: A Global Perspective', *International Studies Quarterly*, vol. 16, no. 4, pp. 407–32.

Moffitt, B. (2016), *The Global Rise of Populism: Performance, Political Style, and Representation*, Stanford, Stanford University Press.

Moghadam V. (2008), *Globalization and Social Movements: Islamism, Feminism, and the Global Justice Movement*, Lanham, Rowman & Littlefield Publishers.

Mouffe, C. (2018), *For a Left Populism*, London, Verso.

Mooney, A. and Evans, B., eds. (2007), *Globalization: The Key Concepts*, London, Routledge.

Moore, J. W. (2017a) 'The Capitalocene, Part I: On the Nature and Origins of our Ecological Crisis', *Journal of Peasant Studies*, vol. 44, no. 3, pp. 594–630.

(2017b), 'Metabolic Rift or Metabolic Shift? Dialectics, Nature, and the World-Historical Method', *Theory and Society*, vol. 46, pp. 285–318.

Mudde, C. and Rovira Kaltwasser, C. (2017), *Populism: A Very Short Introduction*, Oxford, Oxford University Press.

Müller, J.-W. (2016), *What Is Populism?* Philadelphia, University of Pennsylvania Press.

Munck, R. (2002), *Globalisation and Labour: The New 'Great Transformation'*, Zed Books, London.

(2007), *Globalization and Contestation: The New Great Counter Movement*, London, Routledge.

Myambo, M. T. (2017), 'Africa's Global City: The Hipsterification of Johannesburg', *New Left Review*, no. 108, pp. 75–86.

N

Nairn, T. and James, P. (2005), *The Global Matrix: Nationalism, Globalism, and State Terrorism*, London, Pluto.

Nau, H. (1978), 'The Diplomacy of World Food: Goals, Capabilities, Issues, and Arenas', *International Organization*, vol. 32, no. 3, pp. 775–809.

Nerriere, J. P. and Hon, D. (2009), *Globish the World Over*, New York, International Globish Institute.

Newell, P. (2012), *Globalization and the Environment: Capitalism, Ecology, and Power*, Cambridge, Polity Press.

Nietzsche, F. (1883), 'Thus Spoke Zarathustra (1883)', in *The Portable Nietzsche*, Harmondsworth, Penguin, 1982.

Northrup, D. (2005), 'Globalization and the Great Convergence: Rethinking World History in the Long Term', *Journal of World History* vol. 16, no. 3, pp. 249–67.

Norris, P. and Inglehart, R. (2019), *Cultural Backlash: Trump, Brexit, and Authoritarian Populism*, Cambridge, Cambridge University Press.

O

Offe, C. (1985), *Disorganized Capitalism*, Cambridge, Polity Press.

Ohmae, K. (1990), *The Borderless World: Power and Strategy in the Interlinked World Economy*, New York, Harper Business.

(1995), *The End of the Nation-State: The Rise of Regional Economies*, New York, Free Press.

Oldani, C. and Wouters, J., eds. (2019), *The G7, Anti-globalism, and the Governance of Globalization*, London and New York, Routledge.

Olson, S. (2003), *Mapping Human History: Genes, Race and Our Common Origins*, Boston, Houghton Mifflen.

Osterhammel, J. and Petersson, N. (2005), *Globalization: A Very Short History*, Princeton, Princeton University Press.

Ovid (8 CE), *The Metamorphosis*, Amherst, University of Massachusetts Press, 2001 edn.

P

Paley, M. D. (1993), 'The Last Man: Apocalypse without Millennium', in A. A. Fisch, A. K. Mellor, and E. H. Schor, eds., *The Other Mary Shelley: Beyond Frankenstein*, Oxford, Oxford University Press.

Panizza, F., ed. (2005), *Populism and the Mirror of Democracy*, London, Verso.

Pantazopoulos, A. (2016), 'The National-Populist Illusion and a "Pathology" of Politics: The Greek Case and Beyond', *Telos Online*, www.telospress.com/the-national-populist-illusion-as-a-pathology-of-politics-the-greek-case-and-beyond. Accessed 29 June 2018.

Paris, R. (2003), 'The Globalization of Taxation? Electronic Commerce and the Transformation of the State', *International Studies Quarterly*, vol. 47, pp. 153–82.

Parsons, T. (1951), *The Social System*, New York, Free Press.

Patomäki, H. (2001) *Democratising Globalisation: The Leverage of the Tobin Tax*, London, Zed Books.

(2008), *The Political Economy of Global Insecurity: War, Future Crises and Changes in Global Governance*, London and New York, Routledge.

(2018), *Disintegrative Tendencies in the Global Political Economy: Exits and Conflicts*, London and New York, Routledge.

Peccei, A. (1969), *The Chasm Ahead*, New York, Collier Macmillan.

Peck, J. (2010) *Constructions of Neoliberal Reason*, Oxford, Oxford University Press.

Perroux, F. (1962), 'The Conquest of Space and National Sovereignty', *Diogenes*, vol. 10, no. 1, pp. 1–16.

282   Bibliography

(1964), 'L'Économie Planétaire', *Tiers-Monde*, vol. 20, no. 20, pp. 843–53.
Peters, M. (2017), *Trading Barriers: Immigration and the Remaking of Globalization*, Princeton, Princeton University Press.
Piketty, T. (2014), *Capital in the 21st Century*, Cambridge, Belknap Press.
Pieterse, J. N. (2004), *Globalization or Empire?* New York, Routledge.
  (2012), 'Periodizing Globalization: Histories of Globalization', *New Global Studies*, vol. 6, no. 2, pp. 1–25.
  (2013a), 'What Is Global Studies?', *Globalizations*, vol. 10, no. 4, pp. 499–514.
  (2013b), 'Global 5.0', *Globalizations*, vol. 10, no. 4, pp. 551–6.
  (2015), *Globalization and Culture: The Global Melange*, 3rd edn., Lanham, Rowman & Littlefield Publishers.
Pomeranz, K. (2001), *The Great Divergence: China, Europe, and the Making of the World Economy*, Princeton, Princeton University Press.
Poole, R. (2008), *Earthrise: How Man First Saw the Earth*, New Haven, Yale University Press.

Q

Quartiroli, I. (2011), *The Digitally Divided Self: Relinquishing Our Awareness of the Internet*, Milan, Silens.

R

Reich, R. (1991), *The Work of Nations*, London, Simon & Schuster.
Ricoeur, P. (1984), *Time and Narrative*, Chicago, University of Chicago Press.
Ritzer, G. (1993), *The McDonaldization of Society: An Investigation into the Changing Character of Contemporary Social Life*, Thousand Oaks, Sage Publications.
  (2007), *The Globalization of Nothing*, London, Sage Publications.
Robb, J. (2007), *Brave New War: The Next Stage of Terrorism and the End of Globalization*, Hoboken, John Wiley & Sons.
Robertson, Robbie (2003), *Three Waves of Globalization: A History of a Developing Global Consciousness*, London, Zed Books.
Robertson, Roland (1990), 'Mapping the Global Condition: Globalization as the Central Concept', *Theory, Culture & Society*, vol. 7, no. 2–3, pp. 15–30.
  (1992), *Globalization: Social Theory and Global Culture*, London, Sage Publications.
  (1994), 'Globalisation or Glocalization?', *Journal of International Communication*, vol. 1, no. 1, pp. 33–52.
  (2009), 'Differentiational Reductionism and the Missing Link in Albert's Approach to Globalization Theory', *International Political Sociology*, vol. 3. no. 1, pp. 119–22.
  (2015), 'Beyond the Discourse of Globalization', *Glocalism: A Journal of Culture, Politics and Innovation*, vol. 1, p. 13.

Robertson, Roland and Chirico, J. (1985), 'Humanity, Globalization, and Worldwide Religious Resurgence: A Theoretical Exploration', *Sociological Analysis*, vol. 46, no. 3, pp. 219–42.

Robinson, W. I. (2004) *A Theory of Global Capitalism: Production, Class and State in a Transnational World*, Baltimore, Johns Hopkins University Press.

(2005), 'What Is a Critical Globalization Studies? Intellectual Labor and Global Society', in R. P. Appelbaum and W. I. Robinson, eds., *Critical Globalization Studies*, New York, Routledge.

(2011), 'Global Capitalism Theory and the Emergence of Transnational Elites', *Critical Sociology*, vol. 38, no. 3, pp. 349–63.

(2014), *Global Capitalism and the Crisis of Humanity*, New York, Cambridge University Press.

Rodrik, D. (1997), *Has Globalization Gone Too Far?* Washington, DC, Peterson Institute for International Economics.

(2012), *The Globalization Paradox: Democracy and the Future of the World Economy*, New York, W.W. Norton.

Rolnick, P. A. (1997), 'The Innovating Covenant: Exploring the Work of Charles S. McCoy', *Tradition & Discovery: The Polanyi Society Periodical*, vol. 24, no. 3, pp. 15–28.

Rosenau, J. (1976), 'International Studies in a Transnational World', *Millennium*, vol. 5, no. 1, pp. 1–20.

(1990), *Turbulence in World Politics: A Theory of Change and Continuity*, Princeton, Princeton University Press.

(2003), *Distant Proximities: Dynamics beyond Globalization*, Princeton, Princeton University Press.

Rosenberg, J. (2000), *The Follies of Globalization Theory*, London, Verso.

(2005), 'Globalization Theory: A Post Mortem', *International Politics*, vol. 42, no. 1, pp. 2–74.

Rossiter, N. (2017), *Software, Infrastructure, Labor: A Media Theory of Logistical Nightmares*, New York, Routledge.

Roth, K. (2017), 'The Pushback Against the Populist Challenge', in *Human Rights Watch World Report, 2018*, New York, Human Rights Watch, www .hrw.org/sites/default/files/world_report_download/201801world_report_ web.pdf. Accessed 3 January 2019.

Roudometof, V. (2012), 'Global Studies, Current Academic Approaches to', in H. Anheier and M. Juergensmeyer, eds., *Encyclopedia of Global Studies*, 4 vols., Thousand Oaks, Sage Publications.

(2016), *Glocalization: A Critical Introduction*, London, Routledge.

Rovira Kaltwasser, C. and Taggert, P. (2018), *The Oxford Handbook of Populism*, New York, Oxford University Press.

Roy, O. (2004), *Globalized Islam: The Search for a New Ummah*, New York, Columbia University Press.

Rudolf, W. and Tschohl, P. (1977), *Systematische Anthropologie*, Munich, Fink Verlag.

Runciman, D. (2013), 'Destiny vs. Democracy', *London Review of Books*, vol. 35, no. 8, pp. 13–16.

Rupert, M. (2000), *Ideologies of Globalization: Contending Visions of a New World Order*, New York, Routledge.

Rupert, M. and Solomon, S. (2005), *Globalization and International Political Economy: The Politics of Alternative Futures*, Lanham, Rowman & Littlefield Publishers.

Ruggie, J. G. (1993), *Multinationalism Matters: The Theory and Praxis of an Institutional Form*. New York, Columbia University Press.

Russell, W. (2005), 'No Academic Borders? Transdisciplinarity in University Teaching and Research', *Australian Universities' Review*, vol.48, no. 1, pp. 35-41.

S

Sachs, J. (2005), *The End of Poverty: Economic Possibilities for Our Time*, New York, Penguin.

Sachsenmaier, D. (2011), *Global Perspectives on Global History: Theories and Approaches in a Connected World*, Cambridge, Cambridge University Press.

Said, E. (1979), *Orientalism*, New York, Vintage.

Samara, T. R., He, S., and Chen, G., eds. (2013), *Locating Right to the City in the Global South*, Abingdon, Routledge.

Sartre, J.-P. (2004 [1940]), *The Imaginary*, London, Routledge.

Sassen, S. (1991), *The Global City: London, Paris, New York*, Princeton, Princeton University Press.

(1996), *Losing Control: Sovereignty in the Age of Globalization*, New York, Columbia University Press.

(1999), *Globalization and Its Discontents*, New York, Free Press.

(2000), 'Digital Networks and the State', *Theory, Culture & Society*, vol. 17, no 4, pp. 19–33.

(2001), *The Global City: New York, London, Tokyo*, 2nd edn., Princeton, Princeton University Press.

(2003), 'Globalization of Denationalization?', *Review of International Political Economy*, vol. 10, no. 1, pp. 1–22.

(2006), *Territory, Authority, Rights: From Medieval to Global Assemblages*, Princeton, Princeton University Press.

(2007), *A Sociology of Globalization*, New York, W.W. Norton.

(2010), 'The Global Inside the National: A Research Agenda for Sociology', *Sociopedia.isa*, no. 1, pp. 3–10.

Saul, J. R. (2005), *The Collapse of Globalism: And the Reinvention of the World*, London, Penguin.

Schaeffer, R. (1997), *Understanding Globalization: The Social Consequences of Political, Economic, and Environmental Change*, Lanham, Rowman & Littlefield Publishers.

Schumpeter, J. (1942), *Capitalism, Socialism and Democracy*, New York, Harper and Brothers.

Scholte, J. A. (2000), *Globalization: A Critical Introduction*, Basingstoke, Palgrave Macmillan.

(2005), *Globalization: A Critical Introduction*, 2nd edn., Houndsmills, Palgrave Macmillan.

(2011), *Building Global Democracy? Civil Society and Accountable Global Governance*, Cambridge, Cambridge University Press.

(2016), 'Whither Global Theory?', *Protosociology*, vol. 33, pp. 213–24.

Scott, A., ed. (1997), *The Limits of Globalization: Cases and Arguments*, London, Routledge.

Scott, J. (2017), *Against the Grain: A Deep History of the Earliest States*, New Haven, Yale University Press.

Sen, A. (2009), *The Idea of Justice*, Cambridge, MA, Harvard University Press.

Senghaas, D. (1973), 'Conflict Formations in Contemporary International Society', *Journal of Peace Research*, vol. 10, no. 3, pp. 163–84.

Sennett, R. (1994), *Flesh and Stone: The Body and the City in Western Civilization*, London, Faber and Faber.

Shapiro, M. (2012), *Discourse, Culture, Violence*, London and New York, Routledge.

Sharma, P. (2016), *The Rise and Fall of Nations: Forces of Change in the Post-crisis World*, New York, W.W. Norton.

Sharp, G. (1985), 'Constitutive Abstraction and Social Practice', *Arena*, vol. 70, pp. 48–82.

(1997), 'An Overview for the Next Millennium', *Arena Journal*, new series no. 9, pp. 1–8.

(2018), 'The Natural World and After . . .', *Arena Journal*, new series no. 49/50, pp. 253–351.

Shaw, M. (2000), *Theory of the Global State: Globality as an Unfinished Revolution*, Cambridge, Cambridge University Press.

Shelley, M. (1826; 1996) *The Last Man*, in A. McWhir, ed., *The Last Man: Mary Wollstonecraft Shelley*, Ontario, Broadview Books.

Singh, S. (2013), *Globalization and Money: A Global South Perspective*, Lanham, Rowman & Littlefield Publishers.

Silk, L. (1972), 'The New Globalists', *The York Times*, 25 October.

Sklair, L. (2002), *Globalization: Capitalism and Its Alternatives*, 3rd edn., Oxford, Oxford University Press.

Skonieczny, A. (2018), 'Trading with the Enemy: Narrative, Identity, and US Trade Politics', *Review of International Political Economy*, vol. 25, no. 3, pp. 1–22.

(2019), 'Populism and Trade: The 2016 US Presidential Election and the Death of the Trans-Pacific Partnership', in D. Nabers, R. Pateman, and F. Stengel, eds., *Populism and World Politics*, Houndmills, Palgrave Macmillan.

Slater, J. (1976), 'Is United States Foreign Policy "Imperialist" or "Imperial"?', *Political Science Quarterly*, vol. 91, no. 1, pp. 63–87.

Slobodian, Q. (2018), *The End of Empire and the Birth of Neoliberalism*, Cambridge, MA, Harvard University Press.

Sloterdijk, P. (2011), *Spheres, Vol. 1: Bubbles*, Los Angeles, Semiotext(e).

(2013), *In the World Interior of Capital: For a Philosophical Theory of Globalization*, Cambridge, Polity Press.

(2014), *Spheres, Vol. 2: Globes*, Los Angeles, Semiotext(e).

(2016), *Spheres, Vol. 3: Foams*, Los Angeles, Semiotext(e).

Smallman, S. and Brown, K. (2015), *Introduction to International and Global Studies*, 2nd edn., Chapel Hill, University of North Carolina Press.

Smith, A. (1991), *The Ethnic Origin of Nations*, London, Wiley-Blackwell.

Smith, J. (2008), *Social Movements for Global Democracy*, Baltimore, Johns Hopkins University Press.

Soros, G. (2002), *On Globalization*, New York, Public Affairs.

Sparke, M. (2013), *Introducing Globalization: Ties, Tensions, and Uneven Integration*, Hoboken, Wiley-Blackwell.

Spencer, J. H. (2014), *Globalization and Urbanization: The Global Urban Ecosystem*, Lanham, Rowman & Littlefield Publishers.

Soguk, N. (2010), *Globalization and Islamism: Beyond Fundamentalism*, Lanham, Rowman & Littlefield Publishers.

Spybey, T. (1996), *Globalization and World Society*, Cambridge, Polity Press.

Srnicek, N. (2017), *Platform Capitalism*, Cambridge, Polity Press.

Stanley, B. (2008), 'The Thin Ideology of Populism', *Journal of Political Ideologies*, vol. 13, no. 1, pp. 95–110.

Stearns, P. N. (2010), *Globalization in World History*, Abingdon, Routledge.

Steffen, W., Broadgate, W., Deutsch, L., Gaffney, O., and Ludwig, C. (2015), 'The Trajectory of the Anthropocene: The Great Acceleration', *The Anthropocene Review*, vol. 2, no. 1, pp. 81–98.

Steffen, W., Crutzen, P., and McNeill, J. (2007), 'The Anthropocene: Are Humans Now Overwhelming the Great Forces of Nature?', *Ambio*, vol. 36, no. 8, pp. 614–21.

Steger, M. B. (2002), *Globalism: The New Market Ideology*, 1st edn., Lanham, Rowman & Littlefield Publishers.

(2005), *Globalism: Market Ideology Meets Terrorism*, 2nd edn., Lanham, Rowman & Littlefield Publishers.

(2008), *The Rise of the Global Imaginary: Political Ideologies from the French Revolution to the Global War on Terror*, Oxford, Oxford University Press.

(2009), *Globalisms: The Great Ideological Struggle of the 21st Century*, 3rd edn., Lanham, Rowman & Littlefield Publishers.

ed. (2011), *Globalization and Culture*, 2 vols., Cheltenham, Edward Elgar Publishing.

ed. (2014), *The Global Studies Reader*, Oxford, Oxford University Press.

(2017a), *Globalization: A Very Short Introduction*, 4th edn., Oxford, Oxford University Press.

(2017b), 'Reflections on "Critical Thinking" in Global Studies', *Protosociology*, vol. 33, pp. 19–40.

(2018), 'Globalization versus the State: False Antimony of Logical Fallacy? A Response to Clyde W. Barrow and Michelle Keck', *Studies in Political Economy*, vol. 99, no. 1, pp. 97–105.

Steger. M. B., Battersby, P., and Siracusa, J. (2014) *The Sage Handbook of Globalization*, 2 vols., London, Sage Publications.

Steger, M. B, Goodman, J., and Wilson, E. K. (2013), *Justice Globalism: Ideology, Crises, Policies*, London, Sage Publications.

Steger, M. B. and James, P. (2013), 'Levels of Subjective Globalization: Ideologies, Imaginaries, Ontologies', *Perspectives on Global Development and Technology*, vol. 12, no. 1–2, pp. 17–40.

eds. (2015), *Globalization: The Career of a Concept*, London and New York, Routledge.

Steger, M. B. and Roy, R. (2010), *Neoliberalism: A Very Short Introduction*, Oxford and New York, Oxford University Press.

Steger, M. B. and Wahlrab, A. (2017), *What Is Global Studies? Theory and Practice*, London, Routledge.

Stengers, I. (2015), *In Catastrophic Times: Resisting the Coming Barbarism*, London, Open Humanities Press.

Stiglitz, J. (2002), *Globalization and Its Discontents*, New York, W.W. Norton.

(2006), *Making Globalization Work: The Next Steps to Global Justice*, London, Allen Lane.

(2018), *Globalization and Its Discontents Revisited: Anti-globalization in the Era of Trump*, New York, W.W. Norton.

Stoppani, A. (1873), *Corso di Geologia: Volume 2, Gelologia Stratigraphica*, Milano, G. Bernardoni, E. G. Brigola.

Strange, S. (1986), *Casino Capitalism*, Manchester, Manchester University Press.

(1996), *The Retreat of the State: The Diffusion of Power in the World Economy*, Cambridge, Cambridge University Press.

Ström, T. E. (2017), Mapping Google Maps: Critiquing an Ideological Vision of the World, Doctorate of Philosophy, Penrith, Western Sydney University.

T

Tabb, W. (2001), *The Amoral Elephant: Globalization and the Struggle for Social Justice in the Twenty-First Century*, New York, Monthly Review Press.

Taggert, P. (1997), *The New Populism and the New Politics: The Protest Parties in Sweden in a Comparative Perspective*, Basingstoke, Palgrave Macmillan.

(2000), *Populism*, Buckingham, Open University Press.

Taguieff, P.-A. (1984), 'La rhétoric du national-populisme', *Mots: Les Languages du politique*, vol. 9, pp. 113–39.

(2007), *L'Illusion Populiste: Essai sur les démagogies de l'âge démocratique*, Paris, Champs/Flammarion.

(2016), 'The Revolt against the Elites, or the New Populist Wave: An Interview', *TelosScope*, 25 June.

Tarrow, S. (2005), *The New Transnational Activism*, Cambridge, Cambridge University Press.

Taylor, C. (2004), *Modern Social Imaginaries*, Durham, Duke University Press.

(2007), *A Secular Age*, Cambridge, Belknap Press.

Taylor, P. (2016), 'Geohistory of Globalizations', *Protosociology*, vol. 33, pp. 131–48.

Thacker, E. (2005), *The Global Genome: Biotechnology, Politics, and Culture*, Cambridge, MA, MIT Press.

Thompson, E. P. (1980), 'Notes on Exterminism: The Last Stage of Civilization', *New Left Review*, vol. 121 (first series), pp. 3–31.

Thompson, J. S. (2005), *Books in the Digital Age*, Cambridge, Polity Press.

Timberg, S. (1952), 'The Corporation as a Technique of International Administration', *University of Chicago Law Review*, vol. 19, no. 4, pp. 739–58.

Tiryakian, E. (1982), 'Puritan America in the Modern World', *Sociological Analysis*, vol. 43, no. 4, pp. 351–67.

Toffler, A. (1981), *The Third Wave*, London, Pan Books.

Tomlinson, J. (1999), *Globalization and Culture*, Cambridge, Polity Press.

Turner, B. S. (1994), *Orientalism, Postmodernism and Globalism*, London, Routledge.

(2010), *The Routledge International Handbook of Globalization Studies*, London and New York, Routledge.

Turner, B. S. and Khondker, H. H. (2010), *Globalization East and West*, London, Sage Publications.

U

United Nations Development Programme (1994), *Human Development Report*, New York, UNDP.

UN-Habitat (2016), *World Cities Report: Urbanization and Development— Emerging Futures*, Nairobi, United Nations Human Settlements Programme.

Urry, J. (2003), *Global Complexity*, Cambridge, Polity Press.

V

Van de Ven, H. (2002), 'The Onrush of Modern Globalisation in China,' in A. G. Hopkins, ed., *Globalization in World History*, London, Pimlico Random House.

Van Dijk, J., and Poell, T. (2013). 'Understanding Social Media Logic', *Media and Communication*, vol. 1, no. 1, pp. 2–14.

Vajpeyi, D. and Oberoi, R., eds. (2018), *Globalization Reappraised: Oracle or a Talisman*, Lanham, Lexington Books.

Vattimo, G. (1992), *The Transparent Society*, Cambridge, Polity Press.

Vazquez-Barquero, A. (2002), *Endogenous Development: Networking, Innovation, Institutions and Cities*, London, Routledge.

Vinocur, N. (2017), 'Marie Le Pen makes globalization the enemy', *Politico*, 6 February, www.politico.eu/article/marine-le-pen-globalization-campaign-launch-french-politics-news-lyon-islam. Accessed 31 December 2018.

W

Walker, R. B. J. (1993), *Inside/Outside: International Relations as Political Theory*, Cambridge, Cambridge University Press.

Wallerstein, I. (1974), *The Modern World-System: Capitalist Agriculture and the Origins of European World-Economy in the Sixteenth Century*, New York, Academic Press.

(2000), 'Globalization or the Age of Transition? A Long-Term View of the Trajectory of the World-System', *International Sociology*, vol. 15, no. 2, pp. 249–65.

(2011), *The Modern World-System, Vol. IV: Centrist Liberalism Triumphant, 1789–1914*, Berkeley, University of California Press.

Walli, R. (1976), 'US Foreign Policy of Interventionism', *Social Scientist*, vol. 4, no. 6, pp. 41–8.

Waltz, K. (1999), 'Globalization and Governance', *PS: Political Science & Politics*, vol. 32, no. 4, pp. 693–700.

Ward, B. (1971), *An Urban Planet?* Philadelphia, Girard Bank.

Waters, M. (2001), *Globalization*, 2nd edn. London, Routledge.

Weber, E. (1976), *Peasants into Frenchmen: The Modernization of Rural France, 1870–1914*, Stanford, Stanford University Press.

Weisman, A. (2007), *The World without Us*, New York, Thomas Dunne Books.

Weiss, L. (1998), *The Myth of the Powerless State: Governing the Economy in a Global Era*, Ithaca, Cornell University Press.

Wenger, E. (1998), *Communities of Practice: Learning Meaning and Identity*, Cambridge, Cambridge University Press.

Weston, C. (2017). *The Darkness of Globalism*, New York, Create Space Independent Publishing.

Wildavsky, B. (2012), *The Great Brain Race: How Universities Are Reshaping the World*, Princeton, Princeton University Press.

William, J. (2017), *White Working Class: Overcoming Class Cluelessness in America*, Cambridge, MA, Harvard Business Review Press.

Williams, R. (1958), *Culture and Society 1780–1950*, London, Chatto and Windus.

(1974), *Television: Technology and Cultural Form*, London, Fontana.

(1983), *Keywords: A Vocabulary of Culture and Society*, rev. edn., New York, Oxford University Press.

(2005), *Culture and Materialism, London*, 2nd edn., London, Verso.

Wilson, E. K. and Steger, M. B. (2013), 'Religious Globalisms in the Post-secular Age', *Globalizations*, vol. 10, no. 3, pp. 481–95.

Wilson, R. and DIssanayake, W., eds. (1996), *Global/Local: Cultural Production and the Transnational Imaginary*, Durham, Duke University Press.

Wodak, R. (2015), *The Politics of Fear: What Right-Wing Populist Discourses Mean*, London, Sage Publications.

Wodak, R., Khosravinik, M., and Mral, B., eds. (2013), *Right-Wing Populisms in Europe*, London, Bloomsbury.

Y

Yergin, D. and Stanislaw, J. (1998), *The Commanding Heights: The Battle between Government and the Marketplace That Is Remaking the Modern World*, New York, Simon & Schuster.

Yiannopoulos, M. (2016), 'Taylor Swift Is an Alt-Right Pop Icon', Breitbart blog, www.breitbart.com/milo/2016/05/11/taylor-swift-alt-right-pop-icon. Accessed 18 September 2018.

Yudice, G. (2003), *The Expediency of Culture: Uses of Culture in the Global Era*, Durham and London, Duke University Press.

Young, R. (2003), *Postcolonialism: A Very Short Introduction*, Oxford, Oxford University Press.

Z

Zernatto, G. (1944), 'Nation: The History of a Word', *Review of Politics*, vol. 6, pp. 351–66.
Zito, S. and Todd, B. (2018), *The Great Revolt: Inside the Populist Coalition Reshaping American Politics*, New York, Crown Forum.
Žižek, S. (2010), *Living in End Times*, London, Verso.
Zukin, S. (2010), *Naked City: The Death and Life of Authentic Urban Places*, Oxford, Oxford University Press.

Index

Index